THE
LAST
SURE THING

THE LAST SURE THING

THE LIFE & TIMES OF BOBBY RIGGS

BY TOM LECOMPTE

SKUNKWORKS PUBLISHING
EASTHAMPTON, MA

FIRST EDITION

ISBN 0-9711213-0-7

LCCN 2002096085

www.bobbyriggs.com

Cover Design by Stacey Davis, Blend-In, Venice, CA

To My Father:

"Straight and true"

Contents

Contents

Publicity photo of Bobby taken around 1940.

Foreword

Asked once what he'd like his epitaph to be, Bobby Riggs joked: "He Put Women on the Map." Doubtless, he will forever be remembered as the motor-mouthed antagonist to Billie Jean King in their "Battle of the Sexes" challenge in 1973, a match that became a watershed event in women's sports and made tennis history as the most-watched match ever, with more than 30,000 inside the Houston Astrodome and another 90 million worldwide watching on television.

But Bobby Riggs was more than that.

Showman, hustler, huckster, Bobby Riggs was one of the great characters in modern sports—a hardscrabble kid in a highbrow, "sissy" game; the son of a fundamentalist minister; a compulsive gambler; a self-proclaimed male chauvinist whose only mentors in the game were women; a short, wispy-haired fellow with a squeaky voice, a bad haircut, and horned-rimmed glasses who became, somehow, a sex symbol.

Stories about Bobby are legion—stories that manage to grow a bit funnier, a bit more preposterous with each retelling. How he won his first racquet in a game of marbles. How on his first and only trip to Wimbledon in 1939, he won a small fortune on a longshot bet that he'd win the men's singles, men's doubles, and mixed doubles titles. Or how, as an over-the-hill, 55-year-old player, he hustled games by playing around an obstacle course of chairs scattered on his side of the court. Or while wearing an overcoat and snowshoes. Or leashed to a lion cub.

Bobby's contests were not limited to tennis. In 1984, he challenged professional golfer Marilynn Smith to a game in which he was allowed to throw the ball at the green 18 times during the match. In 1975, Bobby ran a 50-mile race across Death Valley against long-distance runner Bill Emmerton, a race in which Emmerton gave Bobby a 25-mile head start. In 1974, Bobby bet daredevil Evel Knievel $25,000 that he could ride a motorcycle from Las Vegas to Twin Falls, Idaho, where Knievel was to attempt his ill-fated jump across the Snake River Canyon (Bobby arrived in time to see Knievel's rocket-powered motorcycle sink beneath the canyon rim, and said, "Oh, my god! Evel is gone and my $25,000 with him!"). In 1983, Bobby played a game of tennis strip tease against six women from the Washington, D.C. Board of Realtors—a piece of clothing per point.

The stories themselves became commodities. For a price, you could have your own Bobby Riggs story. At a hundred dollars a shot, Bobby would take on all comers in these goofy handicap matches. After taking their money, he would hand back an "I Was Hustled by Bobby Riggs" button. It was a badge of honor, like being able to claim you had struck out against Roger Clemens. If you didn't have the time, energy, or inclination to actually play tennis, you could send Bobby the $100 and he'd send you back a button. By the time of his match against Billie Jean King, the stories had become the man, each one adding to the myth, the enterprise that was Bobby.

"If I can't play for big money, I play for a little money. And if I can't play for a little money, I stay in bed that day," Bobby told *60 Minutes'* Mike Wallace in 1973.

Bobby was the "Bad Boy of Tennis" long before players such as John McEnroe and Jimmy Connors inherited the mantle—a nickname slapped on him by the press in the Thirties because of his brashness, his penchant for dice and cards, and his feuds with the tennis establishment. The game was a sport for amateurs then, and those who ran it expected the players to be modest and wholesome. There was no prize money. A system of under-the-table payments evolved that allowed the players to make ends meet, while perpetuating the power of the amateur authorities.

Bobby, however, was too brash and too blatant about taking the covert payments. At one point, he was nearly banned from the game—not for his gambling, which today would have gotten him ousted from sports faster than you can say, "Pete Rose," but for "professionalism."

After a stint in the Navy during World War II, Bobby turned professional. Along with Jack Kramer, Pancho Segura, Pancho Gonzalez, and a handful of other players, he barnstormed across the nation playing tennis in a series of one-night stands in auditoriums, hockey rinks, high-school gymnasiums, any place they could fit their portable canvas court. The success of these tours in the Forties and Fifties laid the foundation for the rest of the game to turn professional in 1968.

Bobby officially retired from tennis in 1952. He married a rich girl and got a regular job. His days as a top player behind him, he should have faded into obscurity. He likely would have had it not been for his intense competitive drive, his knack for showmanship and self-promotion, and a little luck. Following the end of a turbulent 20-year marriage, his "comeback" in the early 1970s launched a whole new tennis career for him—one short on athleticism, but long on bravado.

As sport, the Bobby Riggs-Billie Jean King match meant absolutely nothing. This was about spectacle, not tennis.

Nevertheless, for the fledgling women's tennis tour and the larger women's movement, it was a watershed event. It was both a social and political statement, a declaration of presence. And for a nation weary of the Vietnam War and the ordeal of Watergate being played out each day on television, it provided a much-needed distraction.

Afterwards, Bobby discovered he could make a good living just being himself: playing tennis exhibitions, doing his wacky challenges, traveling the country, hustling at whatever and with whomever came his way. So what if most people considered him a wise-guy, an aging buffoon? He was having the time of his life, and attracting more attention than he ever had when he was at the top of his game.

Had it not been for that one spectacular loss to King, he might also have been remembered as a gifted athlete, a sportsman, and a genuine champion. Though scrappy and brash, he dominated the game in both the amateur and pro ranks. He also had a knack for being in the right place at the right time, with a career that traces the evolution of the modern game.

Bobby died Oct. 25, 1995, from prostate cancer. He was 77. Though no one would call him a beloved sports figure, he was in his way lovable—a genial rogue, a perpetual adolescent who was able to both aggravate and endear. He was a character, a man addicted to competition and the challenge of a contest—any contest. It was this love, this addiction that propelled him to the top of the tennis world and later made him an international celebrity and a social icon.

Writing his own best epitaph, Bobby once said, "The best thing in life is to win. The second best thing in life is to lose… at least you're in the game." In Bobby's case, he usually won, but he made sure he was always in the game.

After letting the whole thing get so big, Bobby suddenly realized that his life from then on would be about losing to Billie Jean King.

1

A Pig Lost in the Astrodome

Everyone's gone: the pretty girls, the reporters, the wheeler-dealers, the groupies, the deadbeats, and the hangers-on. All gone. In an oversized suite at the Astroworld Hotel in Houston it's just Bobby Riggs, alone with the sound of his own breathing and the steady drip of water into the tub. In the silence, he tries to soothe his aching limbs and contemplate how everything had gone so wrong.

Just a couple of hours earlier, he was the toast of the town, the center of attention. What began as his little con, his male-chauvinist pig rant, had snowballed into a nationwide obsession. For weeks, everywhere he went he was surrounded. People wanted to shake his hand, to wish him well, to get him to say something funny, or to tell him to drop dead. Some just wanted to bask in the reflected glow of his dervish charm.

Now, all his plans lay in ruins. Like a grand illusion constructed by a master magician, it had suddenly disappeared in a flash of light and smoke.

With the screams of thousands still ringing in his ears, he replayed points in his head like they were a bad dream. He saw himself running for a ball—a ball he had run for a million times before. He knew just what to do. The point was his. But suddenly the ball's past him. He was nowhere near it. Point, Billie Jean King.

Point after point after point.

It was as if he were having an out-of-body experience. Disbelievingly, he recalled the missed groundstrokes, the blown volleys, and the double faults. *Double faults!* There was a time he went months without double-faulting. His whole game was based on not making mistakes. He even had a name for it: *Airtight Tennis.* Don't waste energy. Don't waste a shot. Don't waste a point. Don't give anything away. Let the other guy make all the mistakes.

Not tonight. Not this match. This time, it was he who made all the mistakes.

Here was Bobby Riggs, the best pressure player in the world playing in the biggest match of his life. What does he do? He blows it. It wasn't even close. Billie Jean won in straight sets, 6-4, 6-3, 6-3. All she had to do was show up. Unbelievable.

Sitting there, he felt tired. He felt sore. He felt angry. But most of all, he felt... *old.*

It had all started as a provocation, a taunt. The women on the tour had been agitating for years for a more equitable share of the prize money from professional tennis. Tennis officials and tournament promoters took the position that the women didn't deserve it, that they played an inferior game to the men. Bobby agreed, and decided to prove it. He threw out a challenge that he, Bobby Riggs, an over-the-hill, 55-year-old player with one foot in the grave, could beat the world's best female player.

He did.

Four months earlier, on May 13, 1973, he defeated—no, destroyed—top woman pro Margaret Court in less than an hour, 6-2, 6-1. The press dubbed it the "Mother's Day Massacre." In winning, Bobby struck a blow for middle-aged men everywhere and, with his sexist prattle, a raw nerve among women. Suddenly, he became a cultural icon, the center of a national debate that pitted men against women, young against old, husbands against wives, bosses against secretaries, fathers against daughters.

Bobby Riggs, however, was no ordinary tennis hacker fumbling through a mid-life crisis. Twenty-five years earlier, he had been the best player in the world. He won at Wimbledon, twice at Forest Hills (now the U.S. Open), and was a three-time U.S. professional champion. Known for his exquisite touch and movement, Bobby Riggs was a tenacious competitor and a strategist who made a career outsmarting bigger, stronger opponents.

People had been selling him short ever since he was a boy: "The kid's too small," "The kid's too weak," "The kid's too loud," "The kid will get what's coming to him." What they didn't know, what none of them knew, was that he was programmed to be a champion. Growing up the son of a fundamentalist minister, tutored by his sports-crazed older brothers, competition had been a way of life for young Bobby. His brothers taught him how to hit, how to catch, and how to run. Bobby's earliest memory was of running a race against an older boy in the neighborhood, a race arranged by his brothers in which Bobby's opponent got a head start. As he grew older, the fierce desire to win became a life force in him.

Then there was his nerve. Bobby thrived under pressure. Indeed, he depended on it. Over the years, he proved time and again that he could never be counted out of a match, no matter how overmatched or how far down.

And, of course, there was his gambling. After all, what is gambling but competition in its most refined form? Who has the ability? Who has the nerve? Who can lay it all on the line and rise to the occasion? Bobby's competitiveness and his compulsion to bet became inextricably intertwined. Betting became fuel for Bobby's competitive engine. If the magnitude of the moment couldn't keep his interest, a good bet always did the trick. To prove it, Bobby once said he never played a tennis match in which he didn't have a bet riding on the outcome. Though certainly an exaggeration, there were enough bets on enough matches that it could have been true.

So what did Bobby know about women's liberation? Nothing, really. What did he care? They were just good lines, a handy gimmick when his second marriage blew up and he was looking for something to do. He had been out of circulation for 20 years. He had quit tennis, slicked back his hair, put on a suit and tie, and got a "real" job. He had raised a family and lived in the suburbs. He had gone straight and played the other guy's game.

But he never lost his competitiveness and his love of the spotlight. Once on his own, he had something to prove. He knew he could still make things happen, earn a million, be a star. They may not have remembered him for winning Wimbledon, or his great battles against legends such as Don Budge and Jack Kramer, but they were going to remember him now.

Sure, after crushing Court he liked to joke that he was the Women's World Champion. But this was huge. This was no nickel 'n' dime hustle. This was big time, bigger than Wimbledon or Forest Hills, bigger than winning the pro tour, bigger than all of them put together. For him, it was a second chance at life, a reincarnation. But it wasn't about tennis. No, this was show biz. And for an old ham like Bobby, it was a natural. If he had to play the villain to pull it off, so be it. He had played the villain before and come out on top.

And if imitation is the sincerest form of flattery, there was a nation of Bobby Riggs wannabes out there. After the Court match, retired professional golfer Jimmy Demaret challenged women's professional tour leader Kathy Whitworth to a winner-take-all match. At Madison Square Garden during a track meet, a 250-pound shot-putter ran a 60-yard dash against a girl sprinter—and beat her. At Princeton University, the women's varsity tennis team's star player, Marjory Gengler, challenged men's junior varsity team player Jeff Oakes to a match. And in Chicago, a group of woman bowlers challenged the men in their academy to a team match. The term "Battle of the Sexes" had been established in the American mindset.

It was a phenomenon Bobby could not quite understand or control, but he relished every moment. The weeks leading up to his big match against Billie Jean King had been a non-stop parade of reporters, photographers, lawyers, business managers, producers, and advertising agencies. Between the interviews, the television talk-shows, and the guest appearances, there was a flood of endorsement deals to weigh, telephone calls to answer, and decisions to put off. And always, always the autographs.

It was the perfect match against the perfect opponent. Bobby had been bugging King for three years to play him. After all, she was the outspoken champion for women's rights. She led the drive for better treatment and larger purses on the women's tour. Not only that, she was a scrappy fighter whose feisty personality and outspokenness made her a natural target for Bobby's chauvinist barbs. For three years, she had turned him down. The way she figured it, she and the women's tour had more to lose than to gain in dealing with this loudmouth—particularly if she lost.

But after Court choked, Billie Jean knew she could not refuse. She accepted Bobby's challenge, then she went into hiding. She avoided the press and worked on the one thing she knew she had to do to win: play tennis. She was not going to be duped like Court, who thought her match against Bobby would be a small exhibition, an easy way to pick up some extra cash. Court had arrived for her match against Bobby and been overwhelmed by the crowds, the press, and the scrutiny. She froze, and went down in flames.

After finally getting the match he had so long desired, Bobby took off like an unguided missile. He reveled in the circus-like atmosphere. He roamed Houston like a puckish P.T. Barnum in horned-rim glasses and tennis shorts, accompanied by his "Bosom Buddies," big-breasted women paid to accompany him around town. Bobby put on tennis exhibitions in parking lots, bank lobbies, and street corners, mugging it up and basking in the attention.

He had intended to practice before the match. But in the swirl of activity, it seemed he'd never quite start, or once he started, something inevitably would interrupt him. There was so much to do: the book-signings, the autograph sessions, the luncheons with civic groups, the television appearances, the newspaper interviews… it was nonstop. At night, Bobby would host lavish dinners (claiming each was his "last supper") followed by sessions in which he'd hold court until 2:00 or 3:00 in the morning, telling anyone who'd listen why he'd win.

Then there were the pills. Mountains of pills. Bobby made a deal with Hollywood nutritionist Rheo Blair, who promised Bobby that if he adhered to his program and imbibed a regimen of 415 vitamin pills, it could make him look and feel years younger. It took three hours to swallow them all. Bobby would show off to reporters as he stuffed fistfuls of the things into his mouth, then duck into the bathroom afterwards to throw them right back up.

Despite all this, Bobby liked his odds. After all, Court had been a better player than Billie Jean. She was, in fact, the number one player in the world. In 1973, she won the Australian, French, and U.S. Opens. She won 18 of 25 tournaments she entered. What's more, she had a winning record over Billie Jean. Yet Court could only get three games off Bobby. Because of this, Bobby liked to say that Billie Jean had two chances: "slim and none. And slim just left town." Victory seemed so easy, so certain, that Bobby promised to jump off a bridge if he lost.

What Bobby failed to enter into his calculations was that Billie Jean was a different player than Court. She was quicker, more aggressive, and had a better volley. Moreover, she thrived under pressure. Like Bobby, she was a player who loved the glare of the spotlight and who time and again rose to the occasion. Unlike Court, Billie Jean would not choke.

Sitting in his post-match tub, Bobby came to understand he had broken the cardinal rule of hustling: he had underestimated his opponent and overestimated himself. He kept telling himself over and over what a terrible thing he had done. He allowed himself to get caught up in the moment, the overnight celebrity and the self-indulgence. He became his own worst enemy. The match was lost before he ever stepped on the court.

To lose was no big deal. But to be unprepared with the world looking on, to let that opportunity slip—that was unforgivable. It was a disaster, a huge, personal disaster.

Bobby felt sick, sick of himself. He felt like drowning in that tub. After such a buildup, he suddenly realized his life from then on would be about losing to Billie Jean King.

Later, at a post-match party in promoter Jerry Perenchio's suite at the hotel, a party meant to be Bobby's coronation as the supreme male chauvinist pig, Bobby was back to form, a drink in each hand and surrounded by his girls. While one rubbed his back, another slid up for a kiss.

"Do you think anybody will want to talk to me now I'm a loser?" Bobby joked.

"I still love you, Bobby," one of his Buddies cooed.

"I can't get over how quick Billie Jean was," Bobby said. "I hit balls past her, but she'd flick them back with unbelievable half-volleys."

Sure, Bobby. She just hit a streak, played out of her head, that's all it was.

"I wasn't at my best," he admitted. "But no alibis... she made the action... she pushed me."

A specially minted medallion was produced for the occasion in anticipation of Bobby's victory. On one side of the coin was an engraved profile of "Emperor" Bobby Riggs; on the other, a cartoonish "Male Chauvinist" swine. Perhaps in 30 years the coins would be worth something. At the moment, they were worth only the cost of the metal used to make them.

Sitting in the corner, a tall, young man held a piglet, a gag gift Billie Jean had presented to Bobby during the televised introductions. The pig, which Billie Jean dubbed Robert Larimore Hustle, got lost during the match, running off in the middle of all the excitement. It wasn't found until after everyone had left, curled up in a corner of the domed stadium. Now the pig was comfortable, nuzzled in the man's arms, munching on a bowl of fried shrimp.

"What is the pig called?" someone asked.

"Pig... just pig," the man answered.

People dribble in to collect on their bets. Dick Butera, a friend and business associate of Billie Jean's, showed off a $10,000 check with Bobby's signature on it. Bobby grimaced every time he thought about the money, but it could have been worse. Butera turned down Bobby's offer to lay another $5,000 on the line midway through the match. He figured Bobby was setting him up, playing possum by throwing the first set as he had so many times in the past. He figured it was a sucker's bet, and turned Bobby down.

In retrospect, Bobby said, "That was the best thing that happened to me that night."

But a part of Bobby could not help but wonder: *What if Butera had accepted the wager?* Might it have been the incentive Bobby needed to turn the match around and win? He would never know.

Also there to collect was the *Ms.* magazine crowd, including writer Nora Ephron and journalist Grace Lichtenstein. The two put together $1,300 in bets between themselves and some friends.

"What about a rematch?" someone asked.

"Sure, I'd like a rematch," Bobby said.

But Billie Jean had said she wouldn't have it. She said so at the post-match press conference and again when she stopped in briefly at the party earlier. "No," she said. "I proved what I had to prove. We women did enough for Bobby Riggs." There will be no rematch, and "no amount of money" could change her mind.

Grandstanding, thought Bobby. She couldn't mean it.

Across the room, Jackie Barnett, a show-biz type who had promoted the Margaret Court match, announced to the crowd, "Listen, there's a rematch clause." Sounding like a fight promoter, he continued, "Oh, Bobby can have a rematch... it's in the contract. It wouldn't be as big next time, but you could do it in Madison Square Garden."

Taking down notes, *Boston Globe* reporter Bud Collins thought to himself, "Barnett is fantasizing."

Deal with it tomorrow, Bobby thought. *It's late and I'm tired. Life goes on. Besides, there is a full schedule of appearances for the next few weeks.*

As Bobby got up to leave, still surrounded by his girls, people came up to console him. "Nice try, Bobby."

"You made the show... you built it... it was your night as much as hers."

Ever gracious, Bobby shook his head in appreciation. *Thanks. Thanks a lot.*

Then, flashing his irrepressible grin, he said with a wave, "I gotta go." He had a bridge to jump off.

Riggs family photograph circa 1919. From left: John, Luke, Gideon, Sanders, Bobby, Frank, Agnes, Mary Lee and David.

2

"Strangers to the things that disturb us."

At first, the two men couldn't look more different. In one photograph, a century old and faded at the edges, is Gideon Wright Riggs Jr., taken just prior to his graduation from Bible college in 1902. Almost 35 years old, he looks young and handsome, neatly dressed in a jacket and bow tie, his fine hair carefully oiled and brushed back. Like all yearbook photos, the pose is rather stiff. The young man's face is turned away from the camera, his eyes focused on something in the distance, as if he is gazing upon his future.

The other photograph shows a young Bobby Riggs, Gideon's son, in a publicity shot taken on a tennis court circa 1940. In the photo, Bobby is about to hit a forehand. The racquet is drawn back with his right hand, his left hand extended forward. His upper body is balanced and controlled. His feet are about a racquet length apart, knees slightly bent, with his weight on his back foot. His sinewy leg muscles are tense as he prepares to swing the racquet and, in the same motion, shift his weight forward, powering the shot. His hair brushed back, Bobby's face is turned away from the camera, his eyes focused on something in the distance—the ball.

Still, the family resemblance is clear: the fine hair, the soft features, the determined eyes; and, if you look hard enough, perhaps the hint of a smirk.

Shortly after the yearbook shot was taken, Gideon left his native Tennessee for Southern California. Moving to Los Angeles, the low-key, fundamentalist minister took what started as a single, struggling congregation housed in a revival tent and grew it into a prominent church with dozens of congregations across the state.

Those who remember Gideon describe a master salesman, able to talk for hours on end, convincing people of the implausible, convincing them that risk and sacrifice in the present would make them far richer in the end. Gideon offered visions of glory and abundance—not of the earthly variety, but of the everlasting.

Friends of Bobby describe a buoyant and gregarious person, a man who could look in your eyes and make you feel like the only person in the world who mattered. Like his father, Bobby could talk for hours on end. And, like his father, he was a master salesman, able to convince people of the implausible and that risk and sacrifice in the present would make them far richer in the end. But unlike Gideon, Bobby's visions of glory and abundance were more temporal than spiritual—they spoke of dollars and cents.

Born and raised in Los Angeles, Bobby came to embrace all that the city represented—the energy, the newness, the opportunity, the narcissism; the chance to obliterate one's past and create—or recreate—oneself anew.

Although he lived most of his 84 years in Los Angeles, Gideon never really left his boyhood home of Tennessee. A farmboy at heart, he belonged to a different place and time.

Gideon's roots trace back to an inconspicuous junction at the intersection of U.S. Highway 31 and Flat Creek Road in Williamson County, Tennessee. Called Riggs Cross Roads for as long as anyone can remember, it has been home to generations of Riggses. Nestled among the rolling hills and small farms characteristic of that part of the state, the Cross Roads lies about 30 miles south of the city of Nashville—and a universe away from the manicured lawns of Wimbledon. Its reputation was of a rural, tight-knit, and deeply religious place.

The Riggs family got its start in America when Edward Riggs stepped off a boat in Boston in 1633. More than a century-and-a-half later, in 1810, David Riggs, the fifth generation of Riggses born in America, settled on the land that would become Riggs Cross Roads. At the time, the area was largely a wilderness of hardwood trees and marshy canebrake, a place hunted by the Creeks, Shawnees, and Chickasaws. David bought the 555-acre tract after selling land in North Carolina.

He chose well. The land had an abundant supply of water provided by several springs and a stream, and was situated at the intersection of the region's major east-west and north-south thoroughfares. David and his sons gradually added to the property. Through hard work and some savvy deals, the Cross Roads grew to about a thousand acres of land, with a comfortable brick house and several log houses used by family members, farm tenants, and slaves. In addition to the major crops of wheat, hay, and tobacco, the farm had a small herd of cattle and a few horses.

Riggs was a prominent name in the area and the Cross Roads became a community center, with a post office, a blacksmith shop, and its own cemetery. It also became a way station for stagecoach lines running from Nashville south to Huntsville, Alabama.

The Civil War, however, changed everything. Like the rest of the South, Tennessee paid a heavy price for its allegiance to the Confederacy. Union soldiers marching through the Cross Roads burned all the fences, stole the livestock, and looted valuables. The collapse of farm prices in the post-war recession meant that farmers already struggling under the harsh policies of Reconstruction could get only a fraction of what they expected for their harvest, if they could sell it at all.

Into this world came Gideon Wright Riggs Jr., born March 18, 1867. While struggling to get the farm back on its feet, the Riggs family endured another calamity when young Gideon's father, Gideon Wright Riggs, a former cavalryman in the Confederate army, died in 1879 at the age of 34, possibly from the lingering effects of wounds received in the war. With Gideon Wright's widow left to raise a family of seven children and manage a rundown farm, 12-year-old Gideon, the eldest child, was forced to grow up quickly.

Despite these hardships, young Gideon found refuge in a small, newly built church that got its start in 1871 when a man arrived at the Cross Roads and started to preach. "There was no meeting house available for preaching," Gideon recalled in a memoir dictated to his daughter-in-law not long before his death in 1952, "so Grandfather gave the preacher permission to preach in a beautiful beech grove." Gideon's grandfather, though not a churchgoer, then donated land and money needed to build a small meeting hall for the church.

"It was fortunate for me the Church was started or I might not have learned about the Church of Christ at all," Gideon said.

The Church of Christ was one of a number of new denominations emerging from the fundamentalist restoration movement then sweeping America's religious landscape. The restorationists sought a return to a religious life guided by biblical writings. To them, all the rules to faith could be found in the Bible, and all the subsequent church hierarchy and traditions that had evolved over the centuries were both unscriptural and elitist, a system designed to create a religious aristocracy.

In its spirit, the movement coincided with the country's growing populist sentiment, a festering resentment by ordinary folks, mostly farmers, over the concentration of wealth and power. Not surprisingly, the restoration movement found fertile ground in the South. As a result, a generation of "farmer-preachers" emerged, spreading the word across the countryside, conducting days-long meetings in tents or temporary meeting houses, or as in the case at the Cross Roads, beech groves.

For the faithful, these were stimulating times, full of rancor and debate. As young Gideon grew up, he became increasingly drawn to it. Later, he recalled discussions with farm hands over the meaning of certain scriptural passages. When a teacher of Gideon's asked her students to write down what they wanted to be, Gideon wrote of his calling: "I had rather be a preacher of the gospel than to possess the wealth of the Rothchild [sic] family... I thought if I could be instrumental in the salvation of one soul I would accomplish more good in the sight of God than if I became a millionaire."

Determined to turn this dream into a reality, in 1897 Gideon enrolled in the Nashville Bible School (now Lipscomb University), a school affiliated with the Church of Christ. Then 30 years old,

Gideon spent five years at the school. His internship included preaching nearly every Sunday before congregations in the Nashville area.

It was at one such Sunday sermons that Gideon likely met Agnes Jones, a teenager 15 years his junior from Antioch, a small hamlet near Nashville. Like Gideon, she had been raised on a farm. And like Gideon, she had a deep religious conviction. Unlike many of his fundamentalist brethren, Gideon was not a fire-breathing pulpit-pounder. Cool and low-key, Gideon stood before the congregation and engaged them with his easygoing manner, his knowledge, and his absolute conviction in the truth of his words. He connected with them because he was, after all, one of them. To Agnes, he must have been like no other preacher she had heard. Perhaps she felt he was not speaking to the group, but directly to her. Here was a man who knew who he was and what he wanted. How could she not be drawn to his confidence and maturity? Add to that the fact he was handsome, with an athletic build and dark, thoughtful eyes. Though neither Gideon nor Agnes left a record describing their courtship, whatever drew Agnes to Gideon was enough to make her trust him to take her away from the only home she had ever known. Away to a strange place thousands of miles away, never to return.

In 1900, with two years of school left, Gideon met Michael Sanders, a Church of Christ member and successful businessman living in Phoenix. After visiting relatives in Boston and Philadelphia Sanders stopped to visit the school on his return to Arizona. He hoped to recruit a few of the faithful to help plant "the Cause in the great West." Gideon was intrigued. For two years, he corresponded with Sanders. Upon graduation in 1902, Gideon immediately packed up and headed west.

Why move to such a strange and far-flung place? He could have stayed at the Cross Roads. A small Church of Christ was already there, built by the man who had inspired Gideon. But even preachers have their ambitions, and while life at the Cross Roads rarely strayed from status quo, the rest of the nation was undergoing vast change. Advances in science and technology were creating a new world. Railroads crisscrossed the nation, telephones replaced telegraphs, and the electric light bulb would make the day stretch into the night. Soon Wilbur and Orville Wright would make the first successful flight of a powered airplane, and Henry Ford would invent the Model T. It was the age of the factory and the corporation, of robber barons and the assembly line, and the country was being transformed from a society of small towns and independent farmers to one of cities and wage earners.

For a minister, confronting these changes might have been irresistible. If science and reason could show the path to the discovery of natural law, then faith and reason could reveal the primal truth in divine law. If Gideon's ambition was anything like the magnitude of the task he faced, it was huge. California was 2,000 miles away, not to mention sprawling, wild, and diverse. By comparison, Gideon's mission to spread the word and establish new churches was so daunting and his success so uncertain.

Gideon first went to Phoenix, where he and another graduate preached for several months inside a large tent obtained by Sanders. Gideon then took the tent to Los Angeles, a bustling city of more than 100,000 people. At the time, it must have seemed equal parts dusty cow town, farming community, Mexican enclave, and industrial upstart. In 1902, most of the city's streets were still dirt. Soon, however, the automobile and the construction of an aqueduct to bring water to the parched Los Angeles basin would kick-start the city's future. In the decade after Gideon's arrival, the city's population more than tripled to 320,000.

After a few months of preaching inside the tent, Gideon found a temporary meeting house on Manitou Avenue in a residential section of the city not far from downtown. Once settled in, Gideon returned to Tennessee. On Aug. 11, 1903, he and Agnes were married.

The Church of Christ was among the most conservative of the restoration sects, demanding a biblical precedent for all church practices. In addition to barring the usual vices such as smoking, drinking, and gambling, the church frowned upon dancing, music, and other forms of entertainment—even movies. Women were not supposed to wear makeup, jewelry, or flamboyant or suggestive clothing. The Church of Christ was also distinguished by an almost total lack of central organization. Each church operated independently, run by evangelists working with little or no outside support.

Gideon, however, was lucky. He had a generous benefactor in Michael Sanders. In 1910, Sanders provided the money to build a permanent home for the church—the first Church of Christ in the state of California—on Sichel Street, not far from the Manitou Avenue meeting house. Sanders also took care of Gideon financially. "I had no agreement with Brother Sanders about money matters as to how much I would receive for my efforts but he treated me as a son and when he died he remembered me in his will," Gideon wrote. With Sanders' help, Gideon bought a house next to the church, a two-story wooden frame house, shingled, with four bedrooms, a large front porch, and a finished attic that Gideon converted into his office. Gideon also owned a four-family apartment house a block away that he rented out to supplement his income. Thus free to pursue his mission, Gideon went on to help establish nearly 50 churches across California, making the Church of Christ a formidable presence in the state.

Gideon may have escaped his Tennessee farmboy roots when he left the Cross Roads, but in many ways he brought them with him to Los Angeles. After all, the Church of Christ had been founded in Tennessee, and its fundamentalist tenets resonated with those of the South. In addition to finding converts to the faith, Gideon served a growing number of transplants to Los Angeles from "back East," a steady stream of people that constituted one of the great migrations in American history. From every corner of the country they came: disaffected Midwesterners, dustbowl Okies, embittered Southerners, opportunists and the down-and-out—all looking for a second chance or a fresh start in life. Gideon also offered his house as a temporary refuge to those newly arrived in the area, people who might need a place to stay, a warm meal, someone to talk to, or just a slice of home.

Had Agnes known what life held in store for her, perhaps she would have reconsidered marrying Gideon. If she expected an idyllic life as the wife of a small, community church preacher, she was certainly disappointed. Los Angeles was a far cry from the pastoral farmlands of Tennessee. Not only that, but Gideon's work was all-consuming, with a routine more like that of a district sales manager than a community pastor. Much of time, he was away from home—preaching, meeting with church members, and helping start other congregations. When he was home, Gideon might as well have been away, as he busily tended to the needs of his own congregation.

"My father," Bobby said, "was a very warm sort of a guy, a good handshaker, as preachers must be. He sometimes got out and played catch and ran some races with us, but mostly he was concerned with the church, mostly up on Cloud Nine preparing his sermons for the next week."

A year after moving to Los Angeles, on August 11, 1904, the date of her and Gideon's first wedding anniversary, Agnes gave birth to their first child, Gideon Sanders Riggs, named after Gideon's friend and benefactor. After Gideon Sanders came David Gillespie (1905), Mary Lee (1908), John Newton (1910), Luke Fulton (1911), and Frank Oliver (1916). The youngest, Robert Larimore Riggs, was born February 25, 1918—the sixth child, the fifth boy, and nearly a generation younger than his oldest sibling.

Gideon lived frugally but took care of his large family. "We were raised poor, but I didn't realize I was poor," his daughter Mary Lee said. With its sprawling front porch, the Riggs house was a hub of activity. Sometimes, when he was not working or away from home, Gideon sat outside on the porch and handed out pennies to the children so that they could buy candy.

Given the size of her family and Gideon's demanding schedule, Agnes had little time for personal pursuits. Indeed, she transplanted to bustling Los Angeles a way of life better suited to an isolated, rural farm. Like her mother, she followed a traditional routine of housework ("Monday – wash day, Tuesday – ironing, Wednesday – baking," as the old hymn goes). She raised her children. She went to church and, when she had time, read a book, usually history or Shakespeare. Quiet and demure, she was a simple woman who didn't pretend to knowledge—or a desire for knowledge—of the wide world. She rarely socialized, had no outside interests to speak of, and only occasionally left the house.

"My mother," recalled Bobby, "was just a plain-looking farm girl from Tennessee… down-to-earth… very hard working, very busy every day taking care of the house and having children and fixing dinner and washing clothes." Other than church services, she and Gideon did little together, and as the years passed and their children moved on they seemed to have less and less in common.

Today a woman in Agnes' place would be considered trapped and intensely unhappy. Like Gideon, however, she belonged to a different time and place. From her gentle demeanor to her staid ankle-length dresses, she was an old-fashioned lady. "A true Southerner," as her family remembered. She loved her children, was deeply religious, and found personal fulfillment in the simple virtues of faith and devotion: faith in God and devotion to family. By that measure, her life may have been complete. No one, least of all her children, ever heard her complain.

Over the years, Gideon occasionally returned to Tennessee to visit friends and relatives, and to preach in the little church at the Cross Roads. Because of his work and his success in a faraway city, Gideon was much admired and respected in his hometown. His visits were events. Friends and family would gather from all over to visit, pick blackberries, swim in the creek, and consume huge feasts of ham, fried chicken, home-grown vegetables, and home-baked pies.

"I thought the country looked better than I had ever seen it before and that it was the prettiest country I had every seen," said Gideon after one visit. But he had no regrets about his decision to move west. After visiting another community near the Cross Roads to preach in 1916, Gideon noted with a mixture of fondness and contempt, "It is a little town without moving picture shows, pool rooms, dance halls, and not even a baseball team. Where such conditions prevail, people go to church because they have no other place to go." Like a war veteran returning with insights beyond the grasp of those who stayed behind, Gideon wrote, "They are strangers to the things that disturb us in the West."

Years later, when Bobby stopped in Nashville to play tennis, family members still living near the Cross Roads came out to see him. Of course, they watched his ability with awe and a pride that one of their own had gained worldwide fame and fortune. But it was pride mixed with disdain. Pride for what he had achieved, but disdain at the way he had achieved it. After all, these people saw humility, hard work, and reverence as fundamental virtues. Bobby was a man who earned his living playing a game. He was a man whose brashness, carefree living, well-publicized gambling, and complete irreverence were anathema to all that they believed. Bobby may have been from the Cross Roads by way of Gideon. But he was definitely not *of* the Cross Roads.

The star on an otherwise pitiable team, Bobby is dwarfed by his teammates in this 1935 photo of the Franklin High School Panthers.

3
Tennis: Game of Kings and Sissies
1918-1932

Bobby was not tall, handsome, and glamorous. Short, cocky, disheveled, with a silly-looking gait often compared to a duck's, he never cut the figure of a world-class athlete. As one friend put it, "If you were in a restaurant and someone pointed over to Bobby and said, 'See him? He's the number one tennis player in the world,' you'd say, 'Sure. Have another drink.'"

Bobby admitted as much. "People have said to me that I must have been a million-to-one shot to become a world champion." Though he may not have been a born athlete, Bobby said he was "programmed to be an athlete of some kind." That it wound up being tennis was incidental. It could as easily have been baseball, track, football, or basketball.

With his mother busy cooking, cleaning, and washing, and his father preoccupied with the church, much of Bobby's upbringing fell to his older brothers. "They handled some of the authority," Bobby said, "but what they mostly handled was my whole athletic program."

The house was off limits to noisy youngsters. The family's social activities revolved around the church, so athletics became the boys' primary outlet. A converted garage behind the house became their clubhouse, with a basketball hoop outside and a Ping-Pong table inside. In the plentiful California sunshine, sporting overalls and bare feet, the Riggs boys spent nearly every waking moment engaged in contests of one kind or another: foot races, table tennis, boxing contests, shooting baskets. The constant activity also made it a headquarters for children in the neighborhood.

Bobby's brothers, particularly Luke and John, seven and eight years older than Bobby, respectively, taught him how to punch and jab, how to run and jump and to shoot tops and marbles, how to go out, cut left, cut right, come back, and catch a pass, and how to swing a baseball bat. Though small for his age, Bobby had a natural gift for speed, agility, strength, and coordination. Bobby's earliest memory was of running a race set up by his brothers against a neighborhood boy a year older than him.

Things changed for Bobby in 1924, when his eight-year-old brother, Frank, died in a freak playground accident. As Bobby recalled, Frank was halfway up a slide when the class bell rang. Frank ran to the top of the slide, toppled off, and hit his head. John, then nine years old, was called out of class by the school principal, who told him about the accident. Frank was conscious and seemed okay, but the principal wanted John to walk him the few blocks home, just in case. About halfway home, Frank passed out and John carried his younger brother the rest of the way.

Agnes put Frank to bed and called the doctor, who did not insist on seeing the boy immediately.

"Why can't Frankie come out and play?" young Bobby asked after school, wondering why Frank was in bed so early. Overnight, a blood clot formed in his Frank's brain and the youth never regained consciousness. Frank, tall and strong, had been expected to be the star of the family, John said. With his death, attention eventually turned to young Bobby.

Bobby was spoiled as a result of the tragedy. "I guess because of Frank they gave me more attention and love and affection than they normally would have," he said. Being the baby of the family also meant Bobby inherited everything the others outgrew, from clothes to athletic equipment.

But if Bobby felt spoiled it wasn't necessarily by his parents. Frank's death meant the attention given him by his older brothers now turned to Bobby. Though he credited his father for his moral foundation, Bobby's brothers exerted the most profound influence on his life. In the clubhouse, Bobby received his true education. His brothers taught him how to compete—how to be faster, tougher, smarter, and more athletic than his peers. They'd test his ability, offering incentives—say, a piece of candy or a ticket to a baseball game—and then pit him against older, stronger kids. They might give his opponents a handicap, allowing them a few yards' head start in a footrace. "Never give up," they told Bobby. "It's all right if a better man beats you, but it isn't all right if you quit."

As Bobby's reward, his brothers might sneak him into University of Southern California football games, where John and Luke ran a hot dog stand. They would hide tiny Bobby inside a cardboard box, telling the ushers it contained extra supplies.

Sports came easily to Bobby and he enjoyed them. His brothers spurred his competitive instincts by arranging contests and betting on the outcome. To Bobby, the deal was always the same. "Win, and you'll get to go to the movies with us. Lose, and you'll get a kick in the ass." With that kind of motivation, Bobby soon learned to find ways within him to win.

Despite such cut-and-dried consequences, Bobby relished the attention he received, and actually enjoyed his brothers' gladiatorial challenges. He was a whirlwind of energy, always in motion, always looking for something to do, something to play. He was also a non-stop chatterbox, a natural ham who loved being the center of attention. Even a case of childhood diphtheria, which might have easily killed the boy, failed to slow Bobby down (although he said the disease damaged his vocal chords, giving his voice its distinctive rasp). The fierce desire to win that his brothers instilled in Bobby became a life force for the young boy. Competition drove him to develop an intensity few could match. No matter what the sport or contest, Bobby would master the basics of a game as well as the subtleties and strategy required to win. When he wasn't competing, he'd practice by himself, honing his technique or figuring out different ways to win—even devising entirely new games he might play. Each year he'd add to his repertoire, learning new games, perfecting old ones. One year, his brother John taught him how to toss cards into a hat. Bobby spent hours perfecting it, to the point where he could sink 20 out of 20.

Soon after Gideon installed the Ping-Pong table in the garage, Bobby took up the game with unrivaled zeal. Coached by his brother John, he played every chance he got, figuring out tactics and dissecting each opponent's weaknesses. After a month, he was the neighborhood champion. The lessons ended when Bobby defeated John, who in turn angrily threw his paddle at his younger brother.

Under his brothers' tutelage, Bobby learned baseball and basketball, and took up track and boxing. He was also tough. One rainy day at Los Angeles' Franklin High School, the coaches figured they'd teach the loudmouthed kid a lesson. Bobby's brother, John, recalled: "They had Bobby box this kid who was quite a bit heavier and taller. In very short order, Bobby floored him. That was the end of that."

Bobby loved games, any games—marbles, dominoes, pool, backgammon, cards. All were part of his dominion—but it was athletics that absorbed him.

Through the practice of punishment and reward, it's not surprising that Bobby also picked up a penchant for gambling, beginning with pitching coins to a line and playing penny-ante poker with his brothers in the shack.

"Every once in a while, Dad would catch us with the cards and would tear them up and give us another lecture on the evils of gambling," Bobby wrote. "But I'm afraid the lesson was lost on me." No one was getting hurt or being forced to play against his will. As Bobby saw it, the stakes were small and it was all in good fun.

The worst days, of course, were Sundays, when Gideon insisted his children attend Sunday school and remain quiet.

At Hillside Elementary School, Bobby played for the school baseball team. He also played basketball, football and ran track-and-field, taking home blue ribbons in the 50-yard-dash and 75-yard-dash. Though he later boasted he could have been a top athlete in any number of sports, his small stature would have proved a disadvantage in many.

When Bobby was 11, John tried out for the Franklin High School tennis team. One day, Bobby tagged along to watch John practice with a friend on some courts in nearby Downey Park. As his brother hit, Bobby became fascinated with the game, and begged John to let him try. Running on the court in his overalls and bare feet ("I hardly had a pair of shoes 'til I was twelve, and then only because you had to have them to go to high school," Bobby later said.), Bobby took a few wild swings at the ball. John pulled Bobby aside. He patiently showed him how to hold and swing the racquet. "You can't just swing any old way," he insisted.

As John tried to give Bobby his first lesson in tennis, a young woman playing on another court stopped to watch. It was none other than Dr. Esther Bartosh, an anatomy instructor at nearby University of Southern California and the third-ranked female player in Los Angeles. She saw something in the awkward-looking boy scampering around the court chasing balls.

"How old is your brother?" she asked John.

"Eleven," John said.

"You know, that's the perfect age to learn the game. If he'd like, I'll be glad to try to teach him how to play."

John knew very well who Bartosh was, and he quickly accepted on Bobby's behalf.

Turning to Bobby, Bartosh said, "You come down here every afternoon after school and we'll see what we can do for you. Do you think you would like tennis that much?"

Bobby answered eagerly, "I'll be here."

As the two boys walked home, John made sure Bobby understood his good fortune. "Mrs. Bartosh is a wonderful player," he told Bobby. "She'll be able to teach you a lot. You're a lucky kid."

Bobby didn't have a racquet, however. He could not expect to borrow John's because he needed it himself. Bobby got another lucky break the next day when he followed John to nearby Sycamore Grove Park to watch him practice tennis. There, one of Bobby's old schoolteachers was using an old tennis racquet to play fetch with his dog. On one throw, Bobby beat the dog to the racquet. He cheerfully approached the man and pleaded, "I can use the racquet better than the dog can, if you'll give it to me." Tickled, the man let Bobby keep it.

It was, Bobby recalled, an old Spalding Top Flite with a small head and a bare wood handle, a piece of which had been sliced off the bottom. "Some of the strings were pretty frayed, so I fastened them down with adhesive tape and took it off to play." The racquet worked well at first, but the dog had chewed up the racquet's wooden throat so badly that it broke after two weeks.

Bobby's next move was vintage Riggs. It was, in fact, his first recorded hustle, and went on to become part of Riggs lore.

Bobby knew a boy on the block who had inherited a racquet from his older sister but never used it because he considered tennis a "sissy" sport. The boy agreed to give up the racquet in exchange for a hundred marbles and two shooters. Bobby quickly accepted. "That accomplished," wrote journalist Jon Bradshaw, "Bobby got down on his knees, not, as his father might have preferred, to give thanksgiving, but to win back the hundred marbles and the two aggies"—which, of course, he did.

B obby's introduction to tennis came at a time when the sport was enjoying its first real boom in this country. The roots of the sport can be traced back to medieval times, but the modern game took shape not long after English gentleman Major Walter Wingfield applied for a patent in 1874 for his portable game "Sphairistike." Wingfield's kit, a game he described as a "New and Improved Court for Playing the Ancient Game of Tennis," sold for five guineas and included balls, four racquets, net, and instruction booklet. The game was an immediate hit, and British enthusiasts began to spread it around the world. The name "Sphairistike" was soon dropped for the simpler "lawn tennis."

As the number of players increased, so did the level of competition. By the time the All England Croquet and Lawn Tennis Club decided to hold the first Wimbledon Championships in 1877, what had been a mishmash of court layouts and rules was standardized—the equipment, the dimensions of the court, the height of the net, the scoring system. Equipment was refined and tactics evolved, and in 1881, the year of the first national championships in the United States, the United States Lawn Tennis Association was founded to help oversee the game and to sanction tournament play.

Until the 1920s, most tennis courts lay behind the gates of private clubs, which had adopted the game as a vigorous alternative to croquet. The tournaments of Wimbledon, the U.S. Championships, and a number of other prestigious events remained rather cliquish affairs for the well-to-do, hosted at exclusive country clubs in which the primary spectators were members and their guests. The game lacked broad appeal, mainly because it was primarily reserved for the leisure class.

The game's stuffy reputation was perpetuated by a strict code of manners and etiquette handed down from the sport's Victorian roots, and was particularly evident in the court attire. Early fashion dictates required men and women to wear white (the better to hide unsightly sweat) and to show as little exposed skin as possible. For men, this meant white-flannel trousers and long-sleeved collared shirts, the same as those worn by cricket players. For women, corsets and full-sleeved, ground-length dresses were the rule. As a result, early tournaments resembled garden parties, with well-dressed club members mingling with elegant looking young men in clean, pressed white pants.*

In the United States, three developments impacted this situation. First was the construction of thousands of municipal courts across the nation. Turn-of-the-century industrialization and urbanization had changed American work habits. With cities and

---

* It would take time and the consternation of the tennis establishment before more comfortable and practical apparel became the norm. Until then, the clothing itself was a handicap for the players. In *The Encyclopedia of Tennis*, published in 1974, fashion designer Ted Tinling recounted the observation of Elizabeth Ryan, then the all-time record holder of Wimbledon titles. At the time, she said, ladies dressing rooms customarily had a rail above the fireplace on which the players' corsets were hung to dry. "It was not a pretty sight," she said, "as many of them were blood-stained from the wounds they had inflicted." For the men, during the course of a long match, their white flannel trousers would become drenched with sweat. Said player Sidney Wood in an interview with the author in June 2001: "We once took Frank Shields, who sweated the heaviest of anybody in the game then, and weighed him before and after a match—and we figured those pants held eight pounds of water."

factories came wage earners, and with them leisure time and the concept of recreational exercise. This necessitated the construction of parks for the cities' sweltering citizens. Concrete tennis courts offered rigorous exercise for people of all ages and both sexes (hence the sport's reputation as a "girl's game"). They also didn't take up much space, were relatively inexpensive to build, and needed very little maintenance. And it didn't hurt to have a tennis-playing president in the White House at the time. Theodore Roosevelt helped give the game a national boost with his famous "tennis cabinet," a regular game kept by the robust commander-in-chief that included administrators and foreign diplomats.

Second, in 1900 a rich Harvard kid named Dwight Davis donated a silver cup to support an international team tennis competition between the United States and Britain. Now known as the Davis Cup, the more compelling team format turned tennis into a true spectator sport.

Third, tennis saw the emergence of its first true stars, Suzanne Lenglen of France and "Big Bill" Tilden of the United States, two players whose flair for drama and sense of showmanship matched their success on the court.

Lenglen, born in Paris in 1899, shocked the staid crowd at Wimbledon in 1919 when she took to Centre Court for the final wearing short sleeves and a revealing calf-length dress. A player who openly wept and pouted during matches, and who sipped brandy between sets, Lenglen defied the game's conventions, but her magnetic personality, grace, and unrivaled skill made her the game's dominant player and top draw, male or female. She won 21 major titles over the course of her career, which included an incredible four-year streak in which she did not lose a single match. Following her retirement from the amateur game in 1926, she accepted an offer by promoter C.C. ("Cash and Carry") Pyle to tour with a troupe of other players in a series of one-night stands across North America, the first such tour of its kind, marking the beginning of professional competitive tennis.

In the men's game, no name looms as large as that of Philadelphia native William T. "Big Bill" Tilden. Born in 1893, he is to tennis what Babe Ruth is to baseball—a player who forever changed the game and against whom all others are compared. From 1920 to 1926, Tilden dominated tennis as no player before or since. He won 10 major singles titles, including seven U.S. singles (six straight from 1920 to 1925) and three Wimbledon championships. He also led the United States during a seven-year reign as Davis Cup champion with 13 successive singles victories. He amassed a 907-62 match record during his amateur career (with 28 of those losses coming in finals) and compiled an amazing .936 winning average. A player with a magnificent array of shots and an even more magnificent ego, Tilden was the consummate showman. He would talk to umpires, interpret rules for the linesmen, and discuss the progress of the tournament with the spectators. He might lose a few games or a set to heighten the drama and prolong the match, anything to keep all eyes on William T. In 1931, he followed Lenglen's lead and signed on for a professional tour, going on to become a staple of the circuit as it grew in the Thirties and Forties. He remained an attraction even as he approached the age of 50. His fortunes collapsed following his conviction and imprisonment on a morals charge in 1947. Though his legend remained, he died of a heart attack, alone and nearly penniless, in 1953.

When asked once where he would rank Tilden among the greatest players of all time, Bobby answered, "I would rank Tilden alone. He is B.C. The others are A.D. You don't rank him. Damn, it's B.C. and A.D. In the Tilden era who was there? Only Tilden. Only Tilden."

Lenglen and Tilden were the game's first marquee players. Their mastery and charisma made them attractions in themselves. They helped usher tennis into a new era, taking it out of the stuffy confines of country clubs and into the popular venues of arenas and stadiums. They also introduced the possibility of competitive tennis as a professional career—a trend taking hold in other sports—and their success attracted a new generation of players. With conservative gusto, many kids across the country put down their baseball bats and basketballs and picked up tennis racquets.

Jack Kramer was 13 years old—a basketball, baseball, and track-and-field nut—when he decided tennis was the sport for him. He remembered going to watch Ellsworth Vines and Tilden play a tennis exhibition in Pomona, California. "I cannot begin to explain to you how majestic they appeared," Kramer said. In their tennis whites, they looked to him like matinee idols: "Here is Ellsworth Vines, six-feet-two-and-a-half-inches tall, 155 pounds, dressed like Fred Astaire and hitting shots like Babe Ruth. From that moment on I never again considered concentrating on any sport but tennis."

Although both Tilden and Lenglen learned to play the game in private clubs, the next generation of great players would, like Bobby, get its start on public courts. Still, because of its haughty roots, arcane rules, and rigid etiquette, the game retained its off-putting image as a sissy sport for rich kids. Like the boy who gave Bobby the racquet in exchange for the marbles, the rest of the neighborhood boys considered tennis a girl's game, and let Bobby know it when he started to play. "It got so bad after a while that I had to steal out the back door of the house so I could get to the courts without passing any of my old pals," Bobby wrote in his book, *Tennis is My Racket*.

B obby didn't care. He didn't have any particular heroes. Games were games, and he just loved to play. With tennis, he found he "got a bigger kick out of standing alone on the court, handling every shot myself, than I ever got from any of the team games I had played."

An eager student, Bobby threw all of his 56 pounds into tennis, reporting faithfully to Bartosh each afternoon after school. Though sometimes brusque, Bartosh was a patient and exacting coach. Having caught Bobby before he had a chance to develop any bad habits, she painstakingly drilled into him the proper way to hold a racquet, how to swing, how to approach the ball, and where to place his shots. Modeling his game on her own style of soft shots and steady back court play, she made sure nothing Bobby did on court was haphazard. It wasn't enough that he simply return the ball. He had to learn to control it. Every shot had to have a purpose and every stroke a meaning. Soon, Bobby lost all interest in other sports, and was spending all of his spare time playing, practicing, or thinking about tennis.

Like Bobby, Bartosh was the child of a minister. She and her husband, Dr. Gerald Bartosh, took up tennis in medical school; each became a noted player in the area. They had no children of their own, and Bobby became something of a surrogate son, eating meals and spending weekends—even holidays— at the Bartosh home. Some of Bobby's friends grew up believing Bobby's parents had given Bobby to Bartosh to raise as her own. John Van Ryn, a former top player who sparred with Bobby, told an interviewer in 1984 that Bartosh "took this little ragamuffin, whose mother was anxious to get rid of him, and went to his mother and asked if Bobby could move in with her... and it seemed like a good idea."

Esther Bartosh, 1936

Bartosh was a tough and critical coach, but Bobby never complained. "I was so anxious to please her that I wouldn't think of arguing with her." Under Bartosh's constant encouragement, Bobby quickly improved. For his twelfth birthday in February 1930, she gave Bobby his first brand-new racquet. Soon afterwards, just a few months after he started playing, she entered Bobby into his first tournament at the Midwick Country Club in Los Angeles. Bobby got all the way to the final, where he ran into top-seeded Robert Underwood, a wealthy and well-coached boy that many viewed as a top prospect.

Bobby lost that match. But the next month Bartosh entered him into another tournament, in which, to everybody's surprise, the scrawny Bobby defeated the highly touted Underwood in the final. Afterwards, Underwood's mother complained to officials that her son couldn't concentrate because of the noise made by a gang from Bobby's block that had come to cheer their friend on.

This began a two-year streak in which Bobby didn't lose a single match. As Bobby rose to become the top player in the 13-and-under division in Southern California, Bartosh continued to push the boy to improve. She refined his strokes, and used his natural ability to chase down balls and his unique feel for the ball to turn him into a first-rate defensive player.

"The important thing is not to miss the ball," she told him. "Tennis matches are won on mistakes. Let the other fellow hit the ball too hard. Let the other fellow hit the ball into the net. Let the other fellow make the mistakes." Like a mantra, she instructed her pupil, "It's not how hard you hit the ball but *where* you hit it."

His brother John, having quickly been surpassed by his younger brother, became Bobby's biggest supporter. He escorted him to practices and tournaments, gave him advice, and shouted encouragement from the sidelines.

Bobby's success in the boys' ranks in Southern California made Bartosh realize what a unique talent she had discovered. To further his progress, she got him a junior membership at the city's oldest private tennis club, the Los Angeles Tennis Club, where she was also a member.

The club was founded in 1922 by a group of friends and players from the city, among them Bill Tilden and May Sutton, the first American to win at Wimbledon. The state, and particularly Southern California, had become a hotbed for the game, largely because the mild weather allowed for year-round play. The group decided to start a tennis club where they could hang out and that would cultivate the talents of the burgeoning number of talented young players coming into the game. While the sport traced its early American roots to exclusive clubs in the East, most of the great players called California home. What evolved was one of the most remarkable institutions in American sports.

The Los Angeles Tennis Club quickly became a tennis mecca. Over the years, it attracted and nurtured more champions than any other place in the history of the game. The list of those who honed their skills there reads like a Who's Who of tennis—Tilden, Ellsworth Vines, Pauline Betz, Don Budge, Alice Marble, Jack

Kramer, Pancho Gonzalez, Stan Smith, Arthur Ashe, Billie Jean King. In fact, of the players enshrined in the International Hall of Fame in Newport, Rhode Island, most cut their teeth at the L.A. Tennis Club. For more than half a century, it was the hub of American tennis, a place that made Southern California synonymous with tennis dominance. Bobby called it "the pipeline."

The $25 membership and $25 in dues each year that Bartosh gave Bobby got him access to training that players today can only dream about. Furthermore, it was done without coaches or psychiatrists, and without the physical therapists or personal entourages that now dominate juniors programs and tennis academies. Bobby learned simply by playing and competing against the world's best players.

A natural order developed at the club: Older players played against junior members, helping them develop their technique and learn what it took to win big matches. The juniors went on to make a name for themselves, creating a succession of talent—from Tilden and Vines to Don Budge and Gene Mako, from Bobby Riggs and Alice Marble to Jack Kramer, Ted Schroeder and Pancho Gonzalez, and on it went.

Set in a pleasant residential area of well-kept bungalows and ranch-style houses, the tennis landmark is surrounded by an unpretentious stucco wall that shelters the facility's 17 hard courts. The club, largely unchanged since Bobby was a boy, is easy to miss if you aren't looking for it. The low-key Spanish-style clubhouse announces none of the club's rich history. The furnishings are comfortable, but not elegant—testimony to the purposefulness of the place. Its exclusivity extends only to its devotion to the sport.

As serious as the tennis instruction was, however, the club was a far cry from the tennis boot camps that characterize today's tennis academies. "This was always a fun club," Mako recalled. In addition to great players, celebrities such as Errol Flynn, Douglas Fairbanks Jr., Humphrey Bogart, Claudette Colbert, Gary Cooper, and Charlie Chaplin hung out—either playing, watching, or occasionally joining the masters for exhibitions, charity events, or just plain fun. Tennis was the "in" sport among the Hollywood set. Flynn, Mako recalled, could hold his own with the best of them. The players and stars would be invited to studio executive Jack Warner's Hollywood estate for all-day tennis parties.

To be surrounded by such an intoxicating atmosphere of glamour, money, and celebrity must have been exhilarating for a young boy, particularly one from such modest means. But if Bobby was star-struck, he never let on. Champion athletes, movie stars, and millionaires all went with the scenery in the Los Angeles tennis scene of the Thirties. Besides, Bobby was there for a purpose.

In charge of the juniors' program at the club was Perry T. Jones, a well-to-do former lumber executive and tennis enthusiast who once won the city's doubles championship. Jones managed the club for more than a quarter century. He was also secretary of the Southern California Tennis Association, two-time Davis Cup captain, and director of the Pacific Southwest Championships, held at the club from 1927 to 1974, and the most important tournament in the United States behind the national championships at Forest Hills. Jones had a knack for singling out promising juniors, and when it came to junior tennis in Southern California, there was no doubt he was the man in charge.

"Mister Jones," as he expected the juniors in his program to address him, was not a ruddy-faced drill sergeant in the mold of well-known tennis coaches Harry Hopman or Nick Bollettieri. Short, stocky, with thinning hair and wire-framed glasses, Jones looked like a crotchety tax attorney, more comfortable in a three-piece suit and suspenders than tennis whites. Prim and proper, he was unfailingly polite, but he could also be gruff and dictatorial, and he ran the juniors' program with an iron fist.

"Just look, act and play like champions," was Mr. Jones' mandate, recalled Schroeder. "If you didn't, you were out of there."

A stickler for "gentlemanly" conduct, Jones insisted on spotless all-white court clothes and impeccable court manners. "I'm more interested in how they live than in how they play," Jones said of his charges. His juniors had to play well and look immaculate. No on-court antics, no arguing over line calls.

During his first trip to Los Angeles to play in a tournament, Oakland native Don Budge recalled being called over by Jones after a particularly impressive win. Expecting to be paid a compliment,

Budge instead saw a frowning Jones. "Budge, those are the dirtiest tennis shoes I ever saw in my life. Don't you ever—don't you *ever*—show up again on any court anywhere at any time wearing shoes like that." Another time, years later, Billie Jean King recalled when, as a young girl, Jones refused to allow her to stand for a photograph with the other junior girls because she was not wearing a tennis skirt.

Those willing to abide by his rules, however, benefited from the club and the association. Jones made sure that "his" juniors got plenty of practice and instruction, were invited to the important tournaments, and got free equipment and travel money.

Bobby was a friendly and vivacious youngster, a funny kid who was easy to get along with. He could be cocky, and he certainly lived by his own set of rules, but Bobby wasn't a phony, he wasn't judgmental, and he didn't bear grudges. He really wanted everybody to like him, and in return he treated everyone the same.

Despite this, and despite Bobby's success on the court, he got little encouragement at the club. Jones was then one of the leading proponents of what was being touted as the California game or the "big game," an attacking style of play in which the player follows his or her serve to the net, ending the point with a sharply angled volley. It was a style of play ideally suited to hard courts, which prevailed in California and the parks where most youngsters started learning the game. As such, Jones preferred his players to be tall and rangy, immaculately groomed, and with powerful serves and flashy games—boys like Gene Mako and Jack Kramer, the archetypes of serve-and-volley tennis. Little Bobby, meanwhile, hit the ball so softly it couldn't break a pane of glass. Content to merely put the ball into play, Bobby rarely came inside the service line, preferring to hang behind the baseline and return the ball until his opponent made a mistake.

Jones told Bartosh, "Riggs is too small. He doesn't have good strokes, and he doesn't hit the ball hard enough. He isn't tall enough to develop a powerful service, and it doesn't look as though he'll ever be big enough to play a good net game."

"They're crazy," Bartosh reassured Bobby, pressing on with the boy's instruction. And Bobby continued to win, beating those players Jones and others considered future contenders.

But Bobby's problems with Jones extended beyond Bobby's small size and defensive style of play. Quite simply, Jones personally disliked Bobby. The director expected his youngsters to be neat, courteous, and respectful. Bobby perpetually showed up looking like he spent the night in a clothes dryer, with rumpled outfits, tousled hair, and scuffed-up sneakers. And his cocky attitude and occasional sass rubbed Jones the wrong way.

There was also the matter of Bobby's gambling.

Junior members, including Jack Kramer, a favorite of Jones and a native of Las Vegas who knew a thing or two about the odds and gambling, enjoyed a friendly bet. So did Ted Schroeder and Bob Falkenburg, both future Wimbledon champions. While waiting for a court, it was common to pitch coins to a line for sodas or play penny-ante blackjack. When it rained, the action went inside, where they played table tennis. Besides, it was the Depression, and nobody had any money. For young players, new balls were always hard to come by so the boys often played for them.

Recalled Ben Press, who grew up in San Diego during the 1930s and played at UCLA before joining the amateur circuit, "Because we were playing for the balls there was no foolin' around. You played a match and you were trying to win, and win as badly as you could." If the balls weren't too worn, he said, you could use them in the next match or trade them in for Cokes.

Among the adult club members, gambling came second only to tennis as a club activity. Big money was constantly changing hands in all-night card games or on-court challenge matches. Wealthier members also bet on the junior matches, rewarding the young players if they won for them.

So it wasn't just that Bobby gambled, it was that he was so flagrant, so obsessive about it. Playing discretely for balls was one thing, but to go around betting $50 or $100 a match—as Bobby was known to do—was quite another.

Bartosh knew about Bobby's gambling, and like many others scolded him and tried to steer him along the straight and narrow.

But as much as Bobby respected Bartosh and admired her as a teacher and as a friend, and as much as he strove to please her, on this matter he would not listen. For Bobby, winning was about more than simple bragging rights. To him, it was an affirmation of personal worth, a statement of his standing among his peers and a source of his sense of well being. But to effectively compete, it had to "mean something." And for that to happen, something had to be at stake. Betting simply provided the personal incentive Bobby needed to win.

Press, who went on to become the head teaching pro at the famous Hotel Del Coronado in San Diego, joked that when he was at the top of his game, "I was just good enough to be beaten by every great player of my era." Against Bobby, the only time Press ever won was when they didn't bet on the match. Without a bet, Press said, Bobby simply could not muster enough interest to win.

Bobby also understood that in competition, having a bet on the outcome intensified matters. The more money, the more pressure. And where most people crumbled under such pressure, Bobby thrived on it. The bigger the bet, the better he played. Yes, Bobby was addicted to gambling, but more to the point, he was addicted to competition and winning.

At the L.A. Tennis Club, practice matches with Bobby invariably involved a wager. Bobby said he typically played for between five and ten dollars a set. Don Budge, an Oakland native who was three years older than Bobby and who frequently practiced at the club, had a different philosophy. "He wanted to play for five dollars," recalled Budge. "But I never liked to bet. He would try and scare you into betting, but I didn't like to do that, so I wouldn't play him." As a result, though the two players frequently socialized at the club and Budge would sometimes stay overnight at the Riggs' home during his trips to Los Angeles, they never played against each other until the first round of the California State Men's Championship in 1933.

Only by waiting around long enough might you get in some straight practice with Bobby. Late in the evenings, recalled Jack Kramer, he and Bobby played four or five games in the fading light before going in to shower.

When not at the club, Bobby hung out at the public courts looking for "practice" matches against adult players or older kids. While his size worked against him with Perry Jones, it was a distinct advantage when wagering. To the gullible, the skinny kid looked like an easy mark, a clumsy pushover, and Bobby did nothing to dissuade them of this notion.

As a result, Bobby picked his opponents carefully. He became an astute observer of human character, learning to study people for their idiosyncrasies and weaknesses.

Exactly what bothered Perry Jones about Bobby—whether it was the boy's style of play, his gambling habits, or simply his personality—ignored the fact that Bobby's success on court should have earned him the support of the club and the association.

Despite Jones' dismissal of his prospects, Bobby knew exactly what he wanted and was driven to achieve it. In 1932, 14-year-old Bobby again went the year without losing a match, putting him in a position to compete in his first state championship. With only three years experience, he was within grasp of being the boys' division champion for the entire state. It was a huge moment for him.

Bartosh was supposed to drive Bobby the 450 miles to the tournament site in Berkeley, but fell sick at the last minute and couldn't go. Bobby's 22-year-old brother John suggested the two of them hitchhike to the tournament. He had five dollars to cover the trip, so the two cleared it with their parents. Gideon arranged for the boys to stay the week at the home of a family friend in Berkeley, another Church of Christ minister.

As a ploy to help get a ride, John had Bobby dress in his tennis whites and carry his racquets under his arm. So there was Bobby, racquets in one arm while he thumbed it with the other, barely five feet tall, dressed in pressed white-flannel pants, short-sleeved white shirt, and matching sweater, looking for all the world like an itinerant choir boy.

The strategy worked, and the success carried over to the tournament. Over the course of six days, Bobby marched through the draw to the final. On Thursday, June 23, 1932, Bobby defeated Harold Goldman of San Francisco in the final of the boys' division, 6-1, 4-6, 6-3.

It was Bobby's first big championship and a watershed moment for him, the fulfillment of his hard work and the ambitions of his brothers and coach, as well as an indication that greater things lie in store. But years later, as Bobby recounted the most significant moments of his career, Harold Goldman's name disappeared. This was unusual, particularly considering Bobby's ability to recall in detail all his other important matches—everything from his opponent, the event, the round of the tournament, right down to set scores, key points, court conditions, and even his meal before the match. Generally, Bobby's memory was so keen he could remember other players' matches better than they could. (He once won a $1,000 bet with Jack Kramer over the number of times Jack's serve had been broken in his 1948 victory over Don Budge in the professional championships at Forest Hills.)

What would make Bobby forget? The only explanation is that something more important occurred to him that week, something more significant than winning his first statewide championship.

After the victory, Bobby asked his host in Berkeley to baptize him in a rite before the entire congregation—a surprising move given that Bobby never showed much interest in church or matters of the spirit, a move made even more surprising because not only was he baptized in a church other than his father's, but he would do so without first consulting his father.

Bobby may have loved his parents, but it is difficult to fathom how he could have felt close to them. Gideon and Agnes showed little interest in their son's achievements. While other parents shuttled their children to and from practice and attended each and every match, Bobby hitched a ride or relied on public transportation to and from practices. If anything, Bobby's parents grew increasingly troubled at how tennis final were making Bobby miss Sunday services, a family obligation. Of course, Bobby was glad to have any excuse to miss church, but he knew his father "took a dim view of the situation." Exactly how much tension this raised in the Riggs household, Bobby didn't say. Still, they never ordered him to quit playing.

Perhaps Bobby's parents considered tennis a childish diversion from life's more serious endeavors. Or perhaps they felt it was just a passing phase—like acne. Having grown up in rural Tennessee, Gideon and Agnes likely had little exposure to recreational and organized sports. The idea that their son might pursue a career in tennis was inconceivable. At the time, except for prize fighting and baseball, organized sports were all strictly amateur. As far as spectator sports went, collegiate games held much more public interest than the provincial club or nascent professional leagues. For Gideon and others who had grown up on farms, the only physical exertion they counted on was a good day's work.

Things were also different around the Riggs household by the time Bobby was born. Gideon was 51. Within a few years cataracts would rob him of vision in one eye and increasingly compromise sight in the other. By the time Bobby was a boy, three of the children—Sanders, David, and Mary Lee—were already out on their own. Time and age had likely softened Gideon's rigid demands and expectations. As for Agnes, after raising seven children she probably welcomed the assistance her sons lent in bringing up Bobby.

It was Bobby's brothers, then, who seem to have really molded the boy. Other than Budge, not one of the players who grew up with Bobby at the club could recall ever meeting Bobby's parents. In fact, when Bobby told his peers he was a minister's son, some thought he was joking.

Bobby recalled at least one occasion when his father attended a match. He remembered Gideon, almost completely blind, sitting on the sideline listening to the ball being struck back and forth and the umpire calling the score. Afterwards, the old man stood beside his son and shook the hands of those who came up to offer their congratulations—much like he would stand atop the church steps after a sermon to shake the hands of his parishioners. Meanwhile, the only time Agnes ever saw Bobby play was at a Los Angeles Tennis Club tournament in 1942, years after he had become an established star. She lacked even the most rudimentary understanding of the game. According to family members, when Bobby came off the court to see how his mother had enjoyed the match, she scowled at him. "Bobby," she said, "that isn't the way to play. You're supposed to hit the ball *to* your opponent." She thought it rude of her son to make the other player run back and forth across the court. Bobby would tell his wife Kay that another time, after he started playing at the club, he asked his mother to buy him a set of tennis whites. What she bought him was a sailor suit.

Although Bobby's parents may not have given him much support or attention, they did give him freedom. For this Bobby must have been grateful, for it allowed him to pursue his dreams without interference or distractions. Perhaps then his baptism offered him the chance to share the importance of his victory in a way his parents might understand. It was a gift, a gesture of his love and appreciation. What did his parents think? Bobby didn't say, perhaps because they didn't respond in the way he would have preferred or expected. But it was one of his last attempts to be part of the Church of Christ and the world of his parents, a world he was quickly leaving behind.

Wrote Bobby without a trace of bitterness years later, "I've never regretted this step. I only regret that I haven't been a better church member and a better Christian through the years." By this, it's hard to think Bobby meant anything other than he wished he could have been closer to his folks, as he showed little interest in organized religion or matters of the spirit during the course of his life. But while he may have meant to use his baptism as a way of showing his appreciation to his parents, it was at the same time a declaration.

Bobby was on his own.

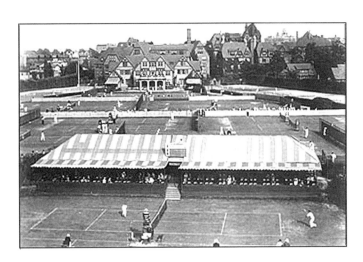

California may have produced more top players, but the East was where a player had to go to make his reputation. The summer grass-court circuit, a series of seven tournaments from Boston to New Jersey ending with the national championships at the West Side Tennis Club in Forest Hills (pictured), were the preeminent tournaments in the country.

4

A Man's Game

1933-1936

On the soft grass in the early afternoon sunshine, Bobby stood on Centre Court at Wimbledon, playing in the gentlemen's singles final before a packed gallery of 16,000 people, including the king and queen, who watched from the Royal Box. Across the net was Bobby's opponent—the legendary "Big Bill" Tilden, or perhaps Don Budge. In the final game, Bobby saw himself moving to his right, hitting a looping forehand on a full run, the ball sprouting a puff of white chalk as it caught the edge of the sideline. A winner. Then, on match point, Bobby hit a deep lob that landed just inside the baseline. After jumping over the net to shake hands with the man he had conquered, Bobby bowed to accept the applause of the crowd and an ovation from the king and queen. He was champion of the world.

It was only a dream. Bobby had never seen a grass court, much less played on one, and what he knew about Wimbledon came from newspapers and the accounts told by those he knew who had played and won there, men like Ellsworth Vines or Tilden himself.

But it was no ordinary dream. This vision had staying power, haunting Bobby and, as only dreams can do, giving him a powerful sense of destiny. "I decided I was going to devote myself completely to the game and become the world's best player," he later wrote. "I knew, deep down, that some day I'd make it come true."

But without hard work, it would remain that, just a dream. "Nobody gets to the top in tennis," Bobby later said, "who hasn't played at least ten years, three hundred days a year, six hours a day. It's a rule of thumb." The bulk of that work, he recalled, occurred between the ages of 11 and 17. Every afternoon after school, Bobby walked and took a combination of trolleys from his home to the L.A. Tennis Club, a commute of an hour and 10 minutes each way.

Under his brothers' tutelage, Bobby had already developed the basic tools of his game. He was quick on his feet, and had terrific anticipation, steely-eyed concentration, and an unwavering confidence. Still, at heart he was a "retriever." His instinct was to hang back, run down every shot, put every ball back into play, and, through sheer physical and mental tenacity, outlast his opponent. In the boys' division, this technique served him well. Bobby could ease the ball over the net, bide his time, and wait for his opponent to make a mistake. But against older, stronger players he could be overpowered. They would ram his puffballs back down his throat for easy winners. He needed to develop a more varied and deeper game in order to counter a steady, stronger attack.

Having won the California state boys' championships, 14-year-old Bobby earned the grudging support of L.A. Tennis Club czar Perry T. Jones, along with some expense money, to travel to the national boys' championships in Culver, Indiana. The tournament was held each summer on the tennis courts of the Culver Military Academy.

Bobby's coach, Esther Bartosh, made the long and dusty trip to Indiana, and watched her protégé survive three rounds of play to reach the semifinal. There Bobby ran into a tall and rangy kid named Don Leavens who, rather than be tempted into hitting winners off Bobby's floaters, matched Bobby pat-ball for pat-ball. He beat Bobby at his own game.

For Bobby, losing was a new experience. Bartosh found him hiding in a corner, choking back tears. Instead of trying to console her pupil, Bartosh blew up. "The first lesson you've got to learn is to be a good loser as well as a good winner," she scolded. "When you lose, you've got to smile and congratulate the boy who beat you. That's just good manners." Take line calls as they come, she said, the good with the bad. Never argue with a linesman or umpire, and always, always, behave like a gentleman. To emphasize her point, Bartosh threatened to quit as his teacher.

Bobby was shocked. He had never heard Bartosh speak this way. She was angry, and dead serious. Had it been anyone else— Perry Jones, for instance—Bobby might have ignored it. But in Bartosh, Bobby had a valuable mentor and a true friend. She stood by him when others—Perry Jones, the tennis establishment, even his parents—ignored him or dismissed his abilities. She saw in him a talent only his brothers understood. Moreover, she knew how to take that talent and mold it into a champion.

Her tactic worked. From that point on, Bobby never pouted after losing a match. He became known as a player who maintained his cool under the most trying circumstances, and one as gracious in defeat as he was in victory. A good thing, because his career would be marked as much by its losses as by its wins.

The next season, 15-year-old Bobby again ruled boys' tennis in Southern California, duplicating most of his victories of the previous year. In July 1933, he sailed into the state boys' championships at Berkeley, confident nobody could beat him. But in the final he ran into a hard-hitting Berkeley native named Bobby Harmon and lost in straight sets.

While there, Bobby also entered the men's championships. In a first round match, he faced a strapping redhead from Northern California, a player known for his powerful play and all-around ability. Seventeen-year-old Don Budge was already considered a top prospect by experts. Budge had refused to play against Bobby at the L.A. Tennis Club because he did not want to play for money, but Bobby knew exactly what to expect from the future great. Although Bobby managed to extend the match to three sets, the older, stronger Budge prevailed, winning 7-5 in the deciding set.

At the nationals in Culver, Bobby reached the final, where he again faced Harmon. Harmon had lost only eight games in the tournament up to that point. Bobby took the first set, 6-4, but lost the final two, 6-0, 6-2.

When he turned 16, Bobby entered the "big leagues" of junior tennis, which included boys ages 16 to 18. This meant Bobby would be going up against players who were often considerably more mature. In preparation, Bartosh coached Bobby to work even harder at improving his game. She focused on getting him to think more strategically, and on boosting his fitness and endurance. She arranged matches against older, better players. She knew Bobby wasn't going to win at this level simply by pushing the ball back, so together they worked on building more depth and variety into his game. Unable to overpower his opponents, Bobby developed a game that relied on touch and guile. Depending on his natural feel for the game, he learned to control the spin, pace, and placement of the ball. With Bartosh's help, he came to approach each match as a chess game, learning an opponent's strengths, probing his weaknesses, moving him around the court, luring him into errors, and, whenever necessary, going on the attack.

In 1934, 18-year-old Gene Mako was the top-ranked junior in Southern California and a player destined to do great things. He was big and strong, with a powerful serve and an aggressive net game. Bobby's situation within the men's tennis game could be precisely gauged in his match against Mako in the final of the Southern California Junior Championships that spring at the Midwick Country Club in Los Angeles. Though Bobby lost in straight sets, 8-6, 6-2, 6-3, the match was declared "the best match of the entire meeting," by *American Lawn Tennis*. "Riggs—16 years old, steady from the baseline and without a doubt the most improved player in Southern California."

In July, on his third trip to Culver, Bobby lost in the quarterfinal to Gil Hunt, a player from Washington, D.C. who had a reputation as a bit of an oddball. Midway through the match, with the score tied at a set apiece and 2-2 in the deciding set, Hunt walked up to the net and said, "The hell with it. It's too hot. I'm defaulting."

Shocked, Bobby said, "Gee, Gil, that won't make these people very happy. You know, they can be awful stuffy. This set won't take much longer. Let's play it out."

Reluctantly, Hunt returned to the court and started slapping wildly at balls. Bobby let up, figuring Hunt was just going to roll over. To his surprise, however, Hunt's shots started falling in, and soon Bobby found himself struggling to stay in the match. Hunt reeled off the final three games to win 6-4, 5-7, 6-3, leaving Bobby to wonder why he hadn't let Hunt go stick his head under an early shower in the first place. Whether intentionally or not, Hunt had gotten the best of Bobby. It should have been a great lesson, but it would not be the last time Bobby would find himself on the losing end of a hustle—even one of his own making.

Hunt went on to the final, where he lost to Mako. At the end of the year, Bobby was the fifth-ranked junior in the nation and the second-ranked in Southern California, behind Mako.

For Bobby, his inaugural year in the juniors' division was a letdown. Progress was measured in victories. The highlight for the year was his upset win over Frank Shields at the Los Angeles County Championships at the West Side Tennis Club. Shields was then the third-ranked player in the United States, a dashing performer with a huge serve and a swashbuckling playing style.

While devoting most of his energy and concentration to tennis, Bobby attended Franklin High School, where he was a resourceful, if less than outstanding student. To maintain his academic standing, Bobby made a deal for a classmate to do his homework for him, a fact he cheekily confessed to 60 years later in a letter to the fellow's daughter. He had to, he explained to the young woman, "otherwise, I never would have graduated. He was much smarter than I."

Through his freshman and sophomore years, Bobby competed in basketball and track-and-field. By his junior year, he concentrated all his energies on tennis. He was the Panther's No. 1 tennis player, the lone bright spot on an otherwise pitiable team. Recalled Bert Brown, a childhood friend of Bobby's and former rival at nearby Belmont High School, most opposing teams simply put their worst player up against Bobby in an effort to win all the other matches.

During four years of play, Bobby went undefeated. Along the way, he won the California Interscholastic Championships at Ojai

Valley three years in a row, a feat no one else had matched. As is tradition, this hat trick allowed Bobby to "retire" the trophy, giving him permanent possession of a beautiful cup dating back to 1896. But Bobby surprised everybody by giving the cup back. He didn't explain why. Perhaps he felt he didn't need the cup to prove to himself what he had achieved, or perhaps, as friend Jack Kramer speculated, he didn't think it was right for him to own something that had such symbolic value.

By 1935, Mako had graduated to the adult circuit, leaving 17-year-old Bobby the dominant junior player in Southern California. At the time, Bobby's closest rival was Joe Hunt, who was a year younger and another product of the L.A. Tennis Club. Over the course of the year, the two met 17 times in finals. Bobby won each time. The crowning confrontation came in the final of the national junior championships in Culver. Down two sets to one, Bobby came back to defeat Hunt in a five-set thriller that the magazine *American Lawn Tennis* characterized as "the sort of tennis that left the gallery's palms slightly callused from applauding the valiant efforts." Relatively unknown to the tennis world until then, Bobby was suddenly heralded as "a boy with the tennis headwork of a veteran and with a bag of strokes, clever tactics, and excellent retrieving ability."

Bobby's play during the tournament so impressed one wealthy tennis fan from San Diego that the fellow offered to pay Bobby's expenses to the national championships at Forest Hills later that summer. "I'm sure you'd enjoy the trip," the man said, "and it would be a wonderful experience for you." But when Bobby sought the unidentified patron out after his victory, the man had bad news, explaining that Perry Jones and the association had ordered him to withdraw the offer. "I don't like to argue with those boys," he explained.

Crushed, Bobby couldn't help but take the association's action personally. He felt that if the offer had been made to anyone else, there would not have been a problem. Angry and hurt, Bobby heard the words "Riggs is too small" echo in his head. He knew then that he was on his own. And, as if he needed more motivation, he had an added incentive to prove Jones and the rest of the association wrong.

Returning to California, Bobby skipped Jones' Pacific Southwest Championships and entered the men's draw at the Pacific Coast Championships in Berkeley. He surprised everyone by reaching the final, where he again faced the powerful Budge. For Bobby, this was a big match, a chance to really prove himself against an up-and-coming star. At first, Bobby seemed uncharacteristically nervous. Budge did pretty much as he pleased, winning the first two sets of the three-out-of-five-set showdown, 6-0, 6-2. But in the third set Bobby settled down, staving off a match point at 4-5 to fight back and win the set, 9-7. He then managed to hold even with Budge through the fourth set until Budge broke through to win the set and match, 6-0, 6-2, 7-9, 6-4. It was a solid showing, and proved to Bobby he could hold his own against the very best.

Having dominated the junior ranks, the new national junior champion decided it was time to pit himself against the men. Although California may have produced more top players, the east was where a player had to go to make his reputation. The summer grass-court circuit, a series of seven tournaments from Boston to New Jersey ending with the national championships at the West Side Tennis Club in Forest Hills, were the preeminent events in the country. Players were required to play the tournaments in order to receive a national ranking, so all the top players tended to make a showing. So in 1936, 18 years old and fresh out of high school, Bobby told Perry Jones he intended to skip his last year as a junior and travel east.

Jones was not convinced. "You're only eighteen, Bobby. You're not ready for the Eastern circuit. You wouldn't do well. What you should do is stay around here and play in more junior tournaments, then go to Culver and defend your junior championship."

But Bobby remained unconvinced. "It isn't going to prove anything for me to win it again. That's not progress." Besides, he had already proven he could play against the men, having defeated Shields and reached the final of the Pacific Coast Championships, where he extended Budge to four sets. "I'd like to have you people sponsor me, but if you won't I guess I'll have to do it alone."

"You're only kidding yourself," Jones told Bobby. "You haven't got a chance of making the first ten... If you go, you'll be strictly on your own. You won't be considered a representative of this association in any way!"

"Okay," Bobby said. "If that's the way you want it, that's the way we'll have it."

Infuriated, Jones shot off letters to tournament officials in the East in advance of Bobby's trip, telling them that Bobby was a fresh, unmanageable player who should not be considered a representative of his association and should receive no special consideration despite his status as national junior champion. The unusual dispute caught the eye of the gossip-hungry press. *Liberty* magazine labeled Bobby the "Bad Boy of Tennis," 40 years before Ilie Nastase and John McEnroe would inherit the mantle.

Bobby carried on undaunted. The previous summer, he had struck up a friendship with Wayne Sabin, a leading West Coast player from Portland with whom he partnered in several doubles events. Sabin, too, was eager to travel east and take his chances against the men. The two decided to go together. With Bartosh's help, the two collected $650 worth of cash and equipment for the cause, much of it donated by Eleanor Tennant, a friend of Bartosh's and another Los Angeles-based tennis coach.

At the L.A. Tennis Club, an older member learned of the boys' plans and offered to not only sponsor them, but drive them there himself. Jack Del Valle, recalled Bobby, was a colorful guy and a bit of a "hero worshipper." He played tennis occasionally, a wild and unorthodox game, but mainly he simply hung around the players to bask in their aura. He drove a big, white, Cord convertible, had more money and time than he knew what to do with, and shared two common interests with Bobby and Sabin: tennis and gambling.

To most club members, Del Valle was a mystery. Foppish in his fancy clothes and flamboyant attitude, he stuck out in a place used to having movie stars walk through the dining room. Del Valle made a point of being conspicuous. He "was a strange guy," recalled Kramer. "He was a shriveled up little guy and wasn't very attractive at all… All the nice people around the club couldn't understand how he got in." No one knew anything about him, his family, or where he got his money. ("He probably had another name and just picked that one," speculated Kramer.) He liked to hang out with the young players, but he really didn't play tennis. "I always thought there was something wrong with him, some way or another," Kramer said. "But Bobby liked him."

Del Valle also fancied himself a bit of a wheeler-dealer. He told the boys that he had spent a lot of his time, as well as his cash, managing prizefighters. "Now," he announced, "I'll manage you two." Bobby didn't worry about Del Valle's background or motivations. He took people at their word. Besides, he saw an opportunity in the man. So in the spring of 1936, the three piled into Del Valle's car and headed east.

Their first stop was in Kansas City and the "Heart of America" tournament at the Rock Hill Tennis Club. The reigning national junior champion came in as a dark horse, but with comparative ease Bobby disposed of the entire draw, defeating the No. 1 seed and the nation's ninth-ranked player, Wilmer Hines, in straight sets, 6-3, 6-2, 6-1. Bobby and Sabin also took the doubles title in straight sets.

In the amateur days, most cities had their own championships, usually hosted by a major tennis club. Places such as Seattle, Salt Lake City, Denver, Houston, Jacksonville, and Hartford all held events, attracting many of the top players from around the country.

This was possible because tennis was an amateur sport at the time. The players cost nothing, or next to nothing; their amateur status held them to receiving only "expenses" (and that to only the biggest star players). Volunteers did the officiating, with players occasionally pressed into service to call lines. Gate receipts were used to pay off a tournament's expenses or to promote the sport. Without the costs of a million-dollar purse and the building of huge stadium complexes, not to mention security, transportation and hotels, amateur events could be put together on a shoestring budget.

After winning in Kansas City, the trio continued eastward, hitting a few other small tournaments along the way. In Cincinnati, Bobby won the Tri-State Championships with a straight-set victory over Charles Harris, the eighth-ranked player in the nation. Del Valle's role as "manager" had since evolved into bookmaker. He'd wander the courts, promoting "his boys," negotiating the odds, and collecting the winnings.

By early July, when the threesome reached Chicago, home to the National Clay Court Championships, Bobby's success had created a buzz. "Everybody was saying how good he was," recalled player Gardnar Mulloy, five years older than Bobby and a veteran of the circuit. Not only that, but no one had ever heard of a player who needed a "manager" before, particularly one like Del Valle.

The National Clay Courts was a major title, attracting the very best players. Winning it would put a very big feather in Bobby's cap. Given the strength of the field, few gave Bobby a chance. Nonetheless, "Del Valle was going around betting for Bobby that he'd win the tournament." Like everybody else, Mulloy said he told himself, "Well, that's impossible."

Curious, Mulloy decided to do a little scouting. "I got smart," said Mulloy. " Bobby was playing a first-round match down on court number 10 or something, so I snuck down there to watch him."

At first, Mulloy may have thought he had the wrong court. Indeed, it would be easy to mistake the skinny youth with the well-greased black hair for one of the ball boys. Not only that, but what Mulloy saw in terms of playing left him even more convinced Del Valle didn't know what he was talking about. The scrawny kid he watched had no power to speak of, rarely got inside the service line, and constantly appeared be struggling. "He was playing this nobody," Mulloy said, "and the guy was giving him a big run—Bobby's running all over the place." At times, Mulloy recalled, Bobby seemed completely uninterested in what he was doing, hamming it up for the crowd, talking to the girls, letting games or whole sets slip by.

After watching for a while, Mulloy "ran back, got a hold of Del Valle, and bet $36—all the money I had."

By the time Bobby reached the final, Mulloy was completely confused. "Bobby kept winning and kept winning and kept winning," Mulloy said. "I couldn't understand it. I'd seen him play this other guy and he wasn't impressive at all."

In each match, Bobby did just enough to win, seemingly snatching victory by the thinnest of margins. But as the matches got tougher, so did his game. As he advanced through the draw, he displayed an uncanny ability to control the pace of a match. He'd switch from stolid defense to forcing offense, mixing soft shots and steady play from the back court with hard drives and aggressive forays to the net.

"Even the most skeptical were forced to admit that Riggs was something more than a 'ball-pusher'," stated *American Lawn Tennis*. Bobby faced the defending titleholder, Frank Parker, dubbed the "boy wonder of American tennis" the year before after winning the tournament at 16. Del Valle bet against overwhelming odds that Bobby would win.

Despite this, and despite the 1,500 spectators who plainly expected Parker to repeat as champion, Bobby was cool and confident as he walked onto the court that Sunday. He had never played Parker before, but he knew Parker played best against an orthodox game, feeding off the pace of an opposing player's ball and answering with pinpoint placements and dazzling passing shots. To counter this, Bobby set out to dismantle Parker by hitting soft slices, refusing to give him anything solid to hit. The tactic worked. Bobby won in straight sets with relative ease, 6-1, 6-4, 6-4.

The win astounded everybody, and made Bobby a hot commodity. Tournament directors across the country suddenly sent Bobby invitations to play in their events. Flush with cash and victory, Bobby and Sabin decided to flaunt their success by designing a pair of matching, monogrammed sport jackets to wear onto the court and around the clubhouse. At each stop, the flashy trio aroused the interest of players and fans as they arrived in Del Valle's fancy car and strutted around in their uniforms.

As he continued eastward, Bobby also learned how the expenses racket worked. For years, the amateur officials who ran the game staunchly opposed all efforts by the players or other outsiders to "open" the game to both amateur and professional players. They perpetuated the myth that athletes who devoted their lives to the sport did so purely for the love of the game and the honor of competition. Naturally, the players loved the game, but few had the means to live up to this ideal, and honor did little to pay for gas, food, and lodging. Instead, an elaborate and inequitable system of under-the-table payoffs evolved to allow players to receive "expenses" for playing. The system, "shamateurism," as it came to be known, was "a thoroughly rotten arrangement," wrote Jack Kramer in his memoir, *The Game*, "rotten except for the few amateur officials who perpetuated it for their own amusement."

Although many other sports were beginning to turn professional at the time, tennis steadfastly resisted. Invented as a lawn party diversion, it was a sport steeped in the traditions of amateur athleticism, a tradition reinforced by the game's country club roots, arcane rules, and rigid code of etiquette. Even a hundred years after its introduction, most of the major tournaments were still played at exclusive clubs. No wonder it would not be until 1968 that the sport opened itself to professionals.

Under USLTA rules, a player could accept only expenses that were "proper, reasonable and moderate and that are not in excess of $10 per day." The rules, however, were never uniformly enforced. Under-the-table payments were an open secret. The tournaments, all of which were sanctioned and overseen by USLTA officials, depended on their ability to attract top players. While the USLTA and its regional sanctioning bodies could obligate a player under its jurisdiction to play an event under threat of suspension, the tournament directors, who also worked under the auspices of the USLTA, had to offer "expenses" along with their invitations to attract other players. And naturally, a better player's expenses were greater than those of an ordinary player. Over time, tournament directors devised increasingly creative ways to skirt the rules, sometimes getting into bidding wars over a player's services. At one tournament, for example, a tournament director "bet" Bobby $100 he couldn't jump over the net two or three times in a row.

In general, the rule of thumb was the farther a tournament was from Forest Hills, literally or figuratively, the more it had to pay top players. A player might earn $400 a week in Florida, $750 in Texas, and $800 in California. The cynical leader in under-the-table payoffs was Perry Jones' Pacific Southwest Championships, which in the late 1940s, according to Jack Kramer, would pay a top player as much as $1,200 to enter.

Stars such as Bobby did well at exploiting the system, but many lesser players struggled to stay on the circuit, either borrowing money or working jobs in the off-season. The label "tennis bum" was very real, as most players were forced either to mooch off one another or rely on the generosity of patrons for basics such as a place to stay, food, and rides between tournaments. Often, players were put up in the homes of a hosting club's members. Otherwise, they were put two-to-a-room in cheap hotels or left to fend for themselves.

"The officials and a handful of the stars enjoyed luxury accommodations," Kramer wrote, "but most players had to settle for old hotels—the Puritan in Boston, the Peninsula in Seabright— or dormitories. At Southampton the lesser players had to bunk in the squash courts. The instant you were eliminated from competition, you had to clear out and fend for yourself. A player would come back from a defeat and find his luggage out on the lawn. As a consequence we wasted a lot of valuable time playing mixed doubles to keep room and board for another day or two."

In light of such hardships, many players gave up the game. Who knows, Kramer wrote, "how many other kids stayed away from tennis because they could see the rotten system for themselves or were advised to take their talents into another sport?"

But if you could stay on the circuit, it was a grand time—a life of genteel poverty, of hanging around country clubs and money, of playing cards and chasing girls. Players not only competed against each other, they were also friends off the court, living together, travelling together, and socializing with one another.

The highlight of every season was the eastern grass court circuit, the series of seven tournaments each summer, leading up to the national championships at Forest Hills. These events were hosted by some of the oldest, most exclusive country clubs in the country. Starting at the Longwood Cricket Club outside Boston in July, the circuit moved to the wealthy enclaves of Seabright on the New Jersey coast, then to the Meadow Club in Southampton, Long Island. This was followed by Rye at the Westchester Country Club outside New York City, the Newport Casino in Rhode Island, and then back to Longwood for the national doubles championships before finishing at the West Side Country Club at Forest Hills in Queens. Because of their prestige and the fact they carried the prospect of a national ranking, these events did not have to offer expenses to attract players.

At the Nassau Country Club in Glen Cove, New York, in late July 1936, Bobby played on his first grass court. Amid an expanse of immaculately cut grass maintained like the surface of a giant putting green, banks of rectangles drawn out in chalk formed the tennis courts. Though few players had access to grass courts, nearly all the major championships except the French and Pacific Southwest Championships were played on grass. Expensive to install, difficult to maintain, and limited in the amount of play they could sustain without damage to the surface, grass courts were always a luxury. As such, only the wealthiest and most exclusive clubs could afford them.

The surface, too, tends to favor big servers who rush the net. Because of the low, irregular bounces, the ball sometimes squirts off the surface like a pinched watermelon seed. Many grass court players prefer to pick the ball off in the air before it hits the ground. Even players who normally prefer to stay back find themselves forced to move to the net or severely adjust their playing style in order to succeed on grass. Compounding the challenge is the fact that variable weather and wear and tear can greatly affect a grass court's playability.

Despite the disadvantage of never having played on grass, Bobby won the tournament, surprising everybody, perhaps even himself. Though he grew up playing on concrete, Bobby felt right at home on grass. The dead bounce of the ball on grass made his drop shots devastatingly effective, and the fact that his opponents generally charged straight into the net opened up opportunities for his penetrating lob. As stated in *American Lawn Tennis*, Bobby put on "a great exhibition… of cool confidence and ability to rise to the occasion."

Bobby was now being compared to the very best. "Riggs may become even better than Don Budge," wrote Stephen Wallis Merrihew, editor of *American Lawn Tennis*, "but he has some things to learn and unlearn before this comes about. On the other hand the newcomer has some shots in his bag that Don does not possess, and he is decidedly more sensational and startling than the man from Northern California."

Crowds started to form around Bobby wherever he played. Sometimes, however, what fans saw came as a bit of a shock. Not only did Bobby's game contradict the common wisdom of how winning tennis was played, his on-court appearance and behavior seemed less than impeccable by eastern standards. In his ill-fitting duck shorts and blue sneakers, he resembled anything but a champion. At the same time, he was bombastic and demonstrative, with a jaunty, cocksure manner. Often after losing a point, he tossed his racquet high in the air, catching it like a majorette ("I never miss," he bragged to one writer). His slicked-back hair was long and unruly. Frequently it fell across his eyes, and when this happened he would stop mid-match, withdraw a comb from a pocket and carefully smooth the errant locks back into place. Often, as he bounced the ball preparing to serve, it would hit his shoe and roll into the court, whereupon Bobby would slowly, methodically walk over, pick it up, walk back, and start the whole ritual over again. His shoelaces, like a small boy's, forever came untied. Deliberately and painstakingly, he would stop play to knot them.

On the changeovers, he would swig water under the umpire's chair and then pour it over his head, or gargle loudly and spit the liquid violently and noisily with a hissing sound for all to see and hear, sometimes sending it in the direction of his opponent. Or he would chat with his opponent, flattering him with praise. Recalled John Nogrady, "I remember I played him once at Longwood. I had won the first set and was leading in the second and he comes over to me and says, 'You know, John, you haven't missed a forehand all day.' Sure enough, the next forehand I dumped into the net. I couldn't hit the damn thing. He was clever that way. If he couldn't beat you, he'd talk you out of it." Eventually, Nogrady said, it got to the point that when he played Bobby, "I'd always go over to the other side because I didn't want him to talk me out of it."

To audiences and writers who expected stoic nobility, Bobby's behavior was boorish. To many players, his behavior was gamesmanship, a ploy to psych them out. Though within the rules, such tactics were not considered sportsmanlike.

Nevertheless, many fans considered the newcomer a refreshing change from the parade of tennis robots favored by the tennis establishment.

Going into the Eastern Grass Court Championships at the Westchester Country Club at Rye, New York in August, Bobby's game was reaching peak form. He got to the final, where he again faced Don Budge. The two hadn't played since the final of the Pacific Coast Championships the year before, when Budge had dispatched Bobby in four sets. Though much improved, Bobby had no realistic hope of beating Budge, now the dominant player in the American game and one of the top players in the world.

Fighting back from a 1-4 deficit in the first set, Bobby managed to win it 8-6. But after this, Budge had his way, running out the final three sets and the match, 6-2, 6-4, 6-3. "The power of Budge's game—service, driving, overhead and at the net—was too much for Riggs," wrote one observer for *American Lawn Tennis*. Still, Bobby's play so impressed the writer that he said of his game, "when he was 'on' in this match he was distinctly a Davis Cup possibility."

During this trip, Bobby also found time to work on his second-favorite pastime. At tournaments, players spent more time waiting around than actually playing, so it was never hard to find a card game in a locker room or in the clubhouse. Generally, it was about the action more than the stakes, a way to kill time between matches or to wait out a rain delay—a two-bit ante for seven-card stud. Every so often, however, some of the wealthy club members got involved and the stakes could get high. The stately Meadow Club at Southampton, Long Island, the Seabright Lawn Tennis and Country Club in New Jersey, or the Westchester-Biltmore at Rye outside New York City were famous for this, and Bobby always arrived prepared, bankroll in hand. So while the eastern grass-court tournaments didn't offer much in the way of expenses, for Bobby there was another fringe benefit in playing them.

At a crap game at Rye in 1936, Bobby first met Champ Reese, an incorrigible gambler and travelling companion to Bryan "Bitsy" Grant, a journeyman top-ten player who shared a similar penchant for gambling. Reese did for Bitsy what Del Valle was doing for Bobby: rounding up bets and negotiating the odds for his player. The night before Bobby's semifinal at Rye against Bitsy, Reese came up to Bobby and said, "A friend of mine would like to bet two hundred dollars that Grant licks you. How about it?"

"Sure. You're on," answered Bobby, who proceeded to beat Grant, 6-3, 1-6, 8-6, 6-1.

The next week at the Newport Casino (now home to the International Tennis Hall of Fame), the final tune-up before Forest Hills, Bobby won his first big grass court title, defeating Parker in a five set marathon, 8-6, 6-4, 8-10, 3-6, 6-1. In doing so, he became the youngest player ever to win the trophy.

The national championships was to be the culmination of Bobby's inaugural campaign, the first of his giant kills. In addition to being the biggest title in the United States, Forest Hills was also the most media-saturated. Bobby, the fifth seed, was suddenly surrounded by reporters, who found him good copy because of his running feud with the tennis brass and his already well-known betting habits. Rising to the occasion, Bobby took the opportunity to announce his "five-year plan."

"Amateur tennis is a stepping-stone," he said. "This year I'll crack the first ten. Next year I'll move up; maybe make the Davis Cup team. Make it in '38, and maybe win the national championship. Win it in '39, maybe the world's championship after that. And then…"

Pro tennis?

"Perhaps," he answered.

It was an audacious statement, coming as it did from someone so young and unproven. The kid had won a couple of tournaments and was already putting himself in the same category as some of the all-time greats. As for the pros, who's to say there would even be a pro tour? Only a handful of players had ever toured professionally, playing a series of one-night stands in arenas and auditoriums in cities across the county. It was a grueling, physically exhausting existence, and a financially risky one, as only a handful of tours had proven successful.

Nevertheless, his confidence brimming, Bobby defeated his doubles partner, Sabin, in the first round, then sailed into the third round, where he faced John Van Ryn, a veteran player 13 years his senior who was primarily a doubles specialist. Liking his odds, Bobby didn't consider Van Ryn much of a threat, to the point, in fact, that the night before the match he became absorbed in an all-night crap game at the Waldorf Towers in New York.

"It was my first experience with really big action," recalled Bobby. "Every high roller in New York was there and I didn't get back to my hotel 'til eight the next morning." That afternoon, the journeyman thrashed Bobby in four sets. "Such return of service and such volleying and smashing by the old master I have rarely seen," reported one writer. It was a humbling loss for Bobby, one that should have warned him on the perils of overconfidence. But as time would tell, the lesson did little to temper Bobby's certainty in himself.

At the end of the year, Bobby was ranked fourth in the country, just behind Budge, Parker, and Grant. On winning percentage alone, Bobby's 42-7 win-loss record (86%) was second only to Budge, who went 30-3 for an incredible 90% winning record. For Bobby, it must have been tough not to gloat when he recalled Perry Jones' words: "You haven't got a chance of making the first ten."

Still, Bobby was in no hurry to get home, perhaps because of his tenuous relationship with Jones and the Southern California Tennis Association, but more likely because he knew his brothers would consider a late-night crap game a poor excuse for his loss to Van Ryn. Instead, he took up an offer by Gardnar Mulloy and headed south.

Mulloy was in charge of the University of Miami's tennis program. He originally went to the school on a football scholarship. After finding himself constantly beaten up on the field, he went to school president Dr. Bowman F. Ashe and proposed forming a tennis team in 1932. Ashe agreed, changing Mulloy's scholarship to tennis and putting him in charge of recruiting a team.

"The weather's wonderful down there," Mulloy told Bobby. "You'll like it, and you'll be able to get in a lot of tennis practice."

A contemporary of Budge's, Mulloy became a fixture of the amateur game for nearly eight decades, with his best years in the late Forties and early Fifties. He was a member of seven Davis Cup teams and a four-time U.S. doubles champion. He continued to play competitively well into his eighties on the seniors' circuit. A lifelong resident of Miami and a graduate of the University of Miami Law School, he was tall, handsome, and amiable. Some players called him "Jughead" because of his lanky build and squared-off crewcut. Most friends simply called him "Gar."

In 1936, the university enrolled only about 600 undergraduates. For dormitories, the school had bought two bankrupt hotels and covered them with cardboard paneling. "We called it Cardboard College after that," recalled Mulloy.

Bobby didn't care so much for school, but if he could swing a deal to get some good practice in, get his expenses paid, and get a college degree in the bargain, why not? Not that he really needed a college education. His single-minded goal was to be a tennis champion. But his parents had made sure that each of their children had the opportunity to go to college, and with such a premium on education, he might have factored pleasing his folks into the equation.

Of course, the concept of getting a college degree was far different from the reality, especially for a kid who scraped his way through high school by having a classmate do his homework. Upon arriving, Bobby found himself housed in the football dorm, where being small, brash, and a tennis player did nothing to endear him to his new bunkmates. The football players, Mulloy said, "called him a sissy and kicked him around a bit." Worse, the school administrators actually expected Bobby to attend classes.

Bobby took comic books to class. That is, when he attended class. When confronted by his professors about his absences, Bobby would reply, "What do I want to go to class for? That's not going to help me win Wimbledon."

Three months into the term, he had to go before the academic dean to explain why he had skipped so many classes and why he should be allowed to stay in school. One of the school's star athletes, Bobby then found himself in the office of Dr. Ashe, who offered him another chance if he made up the lost work and promised not to cut any more classes. Undaunted, Bobby answered to the effect, "Look Doc, I have a proposition. Why don't I go around the country playing tournaments, publicizing the University of Miami, and at the end of four years you give me my diploma—fair enough?"

This was too much, even for the compromising Dr. Ashe. He threw Bobby out of his office. Barely a month after enrolling, Bobby packed up. Before leaving, he met up with Harris Everett, another promising young player convinced by Mulloy to enroll and play for the team. Bobby might have kept his mouth shut, but Everett had a car.

"It's a bum school," Bobby warned Everett. You'll hate it, "and it's so hot here you'll never feel like playing tennis. Let's drive your car back to California."

Everett didn't need to hear any more. He and Bobby packed up his car and headed westward, scheduling a few exhibitions along the way to help raise much-needed cash.

In his one and only tournament as a representative of the University of Miami, Bobby defeated "Coach" Mulloy in the final of the Dade County Championships. Mulloy and Bobby remained friends, but Bobby had a dream to follow. And now, considering his five-year plan, a schedule to keep.

Don Budge (foreground) moves to cut off a passing shot by Bobby during a match at Forest Hills. By 1938, Bobby realized that Budge would be the one player against whom he would measure his progress toward becoming the world's top player.

5

Playing by Their Rules
1936-1938

"**M**aybe we underestimated you, Bobby."

Perry Jones chose his words carefully. In the fall of 1936, after Bobby returned home from Florida, the button-down and fastidious czar of Southern California tennis had sent for him. Bobby's success on the men's circuit the season before had proven Jones' rejection of his talents wrong. But if Bobby had expected Jones to be conciliatory, he was bound to be disappointed. Despite his success, Bobby needed Jones' help more than Jones needed his, and they both knew it. Bobby wanted to reach the next level—to play Davis Cup or get sponsored to Wimbledon. To do this, he would have to make peace with Jones. In the insular world of amateur tennis, Jones was a very powerful figure. Not only did he run the Southern California Tennis Association, he also held sway over the national big wigs and the Davis Cup Committee.

Seated behind his desk in his office at the L.A. Tennis Club, Jones continued. "Anyway, I wish you'd stick around home for a while and play in our tournaments. Give us a hand with our program, and we'll see what we can do to help you." To drive home his point, Jones added, "It would be just as well for you to get back in the good graces of the association. After all, the Davis Cup team will be chosen in the spring."

Never far from Bobby's mind, Davis Cup was second only to Wimbledon, and the pinnacle of many players' careers. To play for one's country was an honor and responsibility that no individual tournament, even Wimbledon, conveyed. There was nothing Bobby wanted more than to play on the Cup team. So he listened politely.

"Okay," answered Bobby cheerfully after Jones finished. "I'll stay here and do my best to be helpful." The two shook hands. For now, a truce existed.

What else may have been said will never be known. Bobby's reputation, however, as a "bad boy," his gambling on matches, and his exploits with Jack Del Valle were well-known. To the starchy Jones, who considered it his duty to maintain the "purity" of the sport, such behavior would reflect badly not just on Bobby, but on the association and tennis as a whole. If Bobby expected the support of Jones and the association, he would have to clean up his act. Jones may not have needed to tell Bobby all this. They may simply have been understood as an unwritten part of the ground rules for the association's support.

Given his ambitions, Bobby was sincere in his effort to toe the line with Jones. As for whether he could control his compulsion to bet on himself, or at least conceal it from Jones and the other tennis watchdogs, only time would tell. But Bobby was game to try.

At the same time, Bobby resolved to further improve his game. With the courts of the L.A. Tennis Club now at his disposal, he went right to work on a daily practice schedule. In addition to working with Esther Bartosh, Bobby renewed an acquaintance with coach Eleanor "Teach" Tennant. At the time, Tennant's prize pupil was Alice Marble, the top-ranked female player in the nation and one of the few female players with a serve-and-volley game. Bobby first met Tennant at the L.A. Tennis Club, where she had Marble practice against male players. Tennant was friends with Bartosh, and had given Bobby advice and financial support for his trip east the year before.

An instructor at the posh Beverly Hills Hotel and the Bishop School in La Jolla, she was also friend and coach to many of Hollywood's biggest movie stars. A vivacious and fiercely independent woman, Tennant promoted an aggressive brand of tennis.

Bobby was not looking for Tennant to turn him into the next Don Budge. The basics of his game were firmly established—the result of Bartosh's patient and demanding preparation. Rather, he turned to Tennant for her deep knowledge of tactics and strategy. Too often, Bobby would rely on his athletic ability and innate touch to maneuver his opponent around the court and run down every ball. Tennant helped him become more analytical, taught him how to adjust his game to his opponent, how to adapt to changing conditions and to use his shots to construct a point.

Each afternoon, the two would meet at the Beverly Hills Tennis Club or on the court at the house Carole Lombard and Clark Gable shared. One of Tennant's celebrity students, Lombard was also a tennis fan, and was happy to share her court. Under Tennant's watchful eye, Bobby and Marble would hit. Using a variety of techniques to bring out the competitiveness in both—precursors to Bobby's future handicapping schemes—Tennant pitted the two players against one another. Marble recalled Bobby was the perfect hitting partner for her "because he hit the ball softer than most men." In other words, he played more like a woman. Still, she said, "how I hated those matches against Riggs! Not because he could beat me, but because I was running my legs off against a human backboard. Painful though it was, Bobby gave me some of the most valuable practice I ever had."

Although arrogant, rowdy, and an incorrigible rascal, "the bane of my existence," Marble joked, Bobby was also "the most lovable player I knew." She was appalled when he took a Thanksgiving gift Lombard had given him and sold it on the way home, but nevertheless described him as sweet, unaffected, funny, and often very generous.

To help Bobby with the commute between his house, the club, and Lombard's house, Bartosh convinced one of the club's wealthy members to advance Bobby the money to buy a car. Though Bobby may have been out of favor with Perry Jones and the majority of the Southern California tennis establishment, his success had won him a circle of supporters. For Bobby and other future stars, such patrons became crucial to their ability to continue playing competitively.

Bobby worked hard at his game, but he also worked hard at playing teacher's pet for Jones, knowing that his Davis Cup hopes hung in the balance. When tournament promoters from the winter tournament circuit in the southern states sent Bobby invitations to play in early 1937, Bobby declined, instead letting Jones decide what events Bobby should play.

The Mid-Winter Championships at the La Cienega courts in Beverly Hills gave Bobby his first chance to measure his progress. But in the final against Don Budge, Bobby played nervously. Budge's sustained attack pushed Bobby all over the court, giving him no chance to get into a rhythm. Budge won, 6-4, 6-4.

Bobby was not playing competitively enough. Practice was no preparation for the pressures of tournament play. In the spring, when he received invitations to play events in Atlanta and Houston, Jones agreed that Bobby needed to start playing more tournaments and arranged for him to make the trip, accompanied by fellow club member Joe Hunt. But Bobby's slump continued. In Atlanta, he lost in the semifinals to his old friend and doubles partner, Wayne Sabin. In Houston, Bobby was tossed in the third round by G. Walter Senior, a journeyman player who never cracked the top ten in the United States.

To fail so miserably on the road was bad enough. When Bobby got home, Jones informed him he had been dropped from consideration for the Davis Cup squad. He accused Bobby of breaking training during his trip, that he'd received word that Bobby and Hunt had "raised hell." Bobby adamantly denied the accusation, saying that he was on his best behavior the entire time. To make matters worse, Hunt retained his position with the team, joining Budge, Frank Parker, Bitsy Grant, Gene Mako, and Wayne Sabin— all players, with the exception of Budge, who Bobby had proven he could beat.

Despite the setback, a group of well-wishers from the L.A. Tennis Club had started a fund to send Bobby to Wimbledon, knowing that no one who wasn't on the Davis Cup team would get the USLTA's help for such a trip.

About 10 days before Bobby was to leave for England, Jones got a telegram from Davis Cup captain Walter L. Pate, asking that Bobby join the team at the West Side Tennis Club in New York as they prepared for the match against Australia. In it, Pate asked Jones' opinion of Bobby's ability, to which Jones replied that he wouldn't recommend Bobby one way or another. When Bobby learned of this, he could only wonder if Jones truly wanted to help him, or just keep him under his thumb.

Nevertheless, Bobby was excited. He returned the money his supporters had raised and headed east. Upon reporting to Pate, Bobby was told to suit up. "You're playing Parker this afternoon," Pate said.

After defeating Parker in two sets, Bobby felt pretty good about himself. The next day, he played Grant, losing in two close sets, and after the match Pate approached him. "It's nice to have you back here," Pate said. "It will be good experience for you to play with men like Parker and Grant, and you'll be able to give them some good practice."

"Practice?" Bobby asked. "What do you mean? I should think I'd have a good chance of winning that second singles spot. After all, I'm ranked No. 4 in the country, and I think I'm a lot better than I was last year."

Pate shook his head. "I'm sorry, Bobby, but you're just here to play practice matches with the Cup team. You won't be considered for the squad."

Bobby couldn't believe it. He had beaten Parker and come close to beating Grant. With the exception of Budge, Bobby knew he could play and beat all the other players on the squad. Furious, he dogged his way through his remaining "practice" matches, losing badly to both Parker and Grant. He thought about the trip to Wimbledon he had surrendered, and for what? He asked Pate about the possibility of going to Wimbledon with the team as an alternate. No, Pate said, "we're not going to take any alternates." As a final insult, the Davis Cup committee changed its mind at the last minute. They would take an alternate, just not Bobby Riggs. Wayne Sabin, a player not even ranked in the top ten, got to go.

For Bobby, that was the last straw.

To hell with Pate, to hell with Jones and all the other brass hats at the USLTA. Bobby resolved to do what he did best: play, win, have fun, and make as much money as possible. While the U.S. team swept Australia with the team of Budge, Mako, and Grant, Bobby wrote his brother John, asking him to drive his car to New York and join him on the summer circuit. John would play the role Del Valle played the summer before, doing the driving, arranging accommodations, and, most important, rustling up betting action.

John and Bobby developed a system. Before a match, John would roam the stands, trying to put down bets on Bobby to win: $5 here, $10 there, as much as he could round up. Before play began, Bobby would look up at John. If John shook his head, it meant there was no bet. Bobby would then start badly, losing the first few games. He'd look up again. If John shook his head, Bobby might lose the first set. He might in fact push the match to the very brink, leaving bewildered fans to wonder what exactly they were watching. Only until he got the nod from his brother, indicating the bet was on, would Bobby dig in and play to win.

"It's a risky way to play," explained Bob Falkenburg, a lifelong friend of Bobby's and the 1948 Wimbledon champion, who saw Bobby employ this tactic. "But Bobby just had a tremendous amount of confidence in himself." And given that Bobby hardly ever blew anyone off the court, it drew little scrutiny. Indeed, after enough come-from-behind victories, it seemed as if Bobby was more comfortable playing that way. Having been brought up by his brothers to compete under pressure, Bobby learned that nothing concentrated his focus like playing on the edge of defeat. Likewise, if the magnitude of the moment couldn't get Bobby interested in winning, a good bet could always do the trick; the bigger the bet, the more the incentive. In this context, money took on a whole different meaning. It was fuel for Bobby's competitive engine.

"If Bobby had any drawback, it was his complete faith in his ability to win in the end," said Jack Kramer. In fact, "Bobby had trouble even conceiving of defeat." It is one reason Bobby habitually dug himself into holes during matches, particularly during a tournament's early rounds. He would play lackadaisically, experiment with trick shots, joke to the crowd, let games or whole sets slip by, and turn what should have been a routine win over a lesser player into a nail-biter.

"Against someone whom he could obviously whip," recalled Budge, "his whole game was suddenly cat-and-mouse. He'd drop-shot, lob, lose interest (and a few games), slice, and spin—but always, always make it very obvious to all that he could win when he really wanted to… until he finally decided, mercifully, to put the poor fellow out of his misery."

The cocky and self-assured youth thrived—indeed depended—on pressure, and if an opponent couldn't provide sufficient pressure, Bobby would find a way to supply it himself. One oft-repeated story, likely embellished over the years, tells of a small tournament in New Jersey in which Bobby had a first-round match against a run-of-the-mill player who would be lucky to get more than a couple of games. After about an hour, a friend of Bobby's went down to the court to see how close Bobby was to finishing off his hapless opponent. To his surprise, the second set had just gotten under way, and it took well over two hours for the match to end. More surprising was the score: Bobby won 6-0, 6-0, 6-0. When asked what had happened, Bobby explained that he had made a bet with himself, "that I could beat the bum by never coming inside the service line."

Only as a tournament progressed would Bobby gradually shed his carefree attitude and knuckle down to business. He later explained that in a tournament's early rounds he didn't want to extend himself. He assumed he could not lose. He did not want to try as hard as he could in every match because he might burn himself out. So he coasted, saving his energy and concentration for a tougher opponent. He could do this because he had an uncanny ability to raise his level of play at will, and thus could never be counted out of a match, no matter how far down. Or, as one writer put it, "Being in the lead against Riggs must carry with it a feeling of futility, knowing that it can't last."

Ironically, for someone so fixated on the accumulation of money, Bobby seemed to have little use for it beyond the freedom it allowed him to live the way he wanted. His needs were few and modest by most standards. Even long after reaching the point where money was no longer a real concern in his life, Bobby preferred to live as if he were one paycheck from the street. Despite occasional indulgences for himself or his family, Bobby never surrounded himself with luxuries: no boats, airplanes, horses, lavish parties, or extravagant clothes—no "high overheads," as he liked to say. Perhaps this was because he grew up in the Depression, or perhaps because he was the youngest of seven children in a minister's family, a family that, though not poor, had little money. Bobby hated spending money when he did not have to. He was unapologetically cheap, even neurotically so, and it would be a source of humor and tension between him and his friends and family for years.

Thrift went to the core of Bobby's soul, permeating everything he did, including his philosophy of how to play his best tennis. Do not give anything away; do not waste anything; do not squander shots; do not surrender points; do not waste energy. Bobby even gave it a name: *Airtight Tennis*. "Airtight Tennis is tennis without holes, tennis without errors. It's defensive tennis. It's keeping the ball everlastingly in play. It's letting the opponent make all the errors. It's Riggs-type tennis," Bobby wrote. Dr. Esther Bartosh may have instructed Bobby in this style of play, but in the pursuit of its perfection he raised it to an art form, making it wholly his own. As an example, Bobby once claimed he went six months in competition without double-faulting.

As a result, Bobby often was not flashy or exciting to watch, but he was devastatingly effective, which allowed him to take the risks he did in toying with lesser opponents. "Ninety-five percent of the matches are won by the defensive player," he said. Many players "want to look good. They'd rather miss five shots, hit as hard as possible, than make one sure shot, hit softly."

Although financial security may have been a longtime concern of Bobby's, he was not greedy in the conventional sense. He was not afraid of money, and not afraid to lose it. In fact, his one and only real indulgence was the money he spent on gambling. But in this context, money was just a way to keep score.

While John was certainly entitled to a cut of Bobby's winnings, that was not his primary motivation. He simply wanted to help Bobby win, and was willing to do whatever it took to make that happen.

As Bobby rose to be the top seed and favorite to win at many of these tournaments, finding suckers to bet against him became increasingly difficult—no matter how far down he was in a match. Because of this, most of Bobby's betting was in doubles play. That or the action moved off-court: to card games, dice, or billiards. While groups of players could often be found in a locker room engrossed in a game of cards, sometimes the wealthy members of the clubs hosting the tournaments would invite the players to join them in a game of cards or dice. In many cases, these were rich and powerful men, men with big egos and fat wallets, men who felt there was no way a scrappy punk like Bobby could beat them at a game that relied on wits and nerve. For someone looking for action, the clubs were fertile ground. Some games stretched late into the night. Bobby learned to get by on just a few hours' sleep, sometimes stepping onto the court only a couple of hours after a big card game.

"All I needed was a facial massage in the local barber shop to revive me and I could play the next morning without sleep," he bragged.

Not only could he play on scant sleep, he could win. And with each victory, Bobby raised his value as a gate attraction. His reputation as a "bad boy" also helped, as fans flocked to see the unruly upstart. Soon tournament directors flooded Bobby with fatter expense offers. Hugh Strange, director of the tournament in tiny Neenah, Wisconsin, offered Bobby $500 for the week plus food and accommodations, a rich sum in those days. When the Utah State Championships in Salt Lake City came in with an extravagant offer for Bobby to play on a week in which he had already committed to an event in Columbia, S.C., Bobby skipped the South Carolina event. The tournament chairman in Columbia threatened to file a complaint against Bobby with the USLTA, but never followed up on the threat, perhaps because to do so would only expose the tournament to sanctions.

By the time Bobby hit the summer grass court circuit, he had suffered only one loss, to Joe Hunt in a five-set battle in the Utah final, a rare win for Hunt over Bobby. Meanwhile, in Europe the team of Budge, Mako, and Frank Parker first defeated Germany, then defending champion Britain, 4-1, to win the Davis Cup for the United States. The team returned with the trophy to a ticker-tape parade in New York.

Still bitter over his rejection, Bobby set his sights on defeating those players picked over him for the Davis Cup squad. At Seabright, Southampton, and Rye, Bobby was unstoppable, winning all three and along the way exacting his revenge on both Frank Parker and Bitsy Grant. Going into the nationals at Forest Hills, his only loss on grass was to Budge in the final at Newport—a surprise to nobody, least of all Bobby. Budge remained too strong a player. Bobby was happy just to extend the match to four sets. He tried to adjust his game, hitting harder and more aggressively than usual, but Budge still dictated play. The big man rushed forward at every chance, making himself an impenetrable wall at the net, winning in four sets, 6-4, 6-8, 6-1, 6-2.

Afterwards, Bobby talked to the press. "The one ambition that I have in life at this moment is to represent the United States on the Davis Cup team and, if possible, to improve my game to such a degree that I will be able to rank as the number one player in America."

At the national championships at Forest Hills, Bobby set out to prove all those who doubted him wrong. Out of more than 70 matches played during the preceding season, he had only two losses: one to Budge in the Newport final and the other to Joe Hunt in Utah.

When he looked at the draw, he must have delighted to see that his second-round opponent would be Gene Mako, another player chosen over him by the Davis Cup committee. Most of those sitting in the gallery surely would have picked the better-known Mako to defeat the higher-ranked Bobby. For one thing, Mako looked like a champion. Elegant in his pristine and crisply pressed white flannel pants, he was tall and strong. Bobby, meanwhile, made his typically scruffy court appearance, wearing ill-fitting shorts with blue sneakers.

Bobby reinforced these expectations by losing the first set, 6-2. But his placid manner and unruffled demeanor was puzzling, all the more so after Mako jumped to a quick lead in the second set.

All of a sudden, Bobby's shots began to find the baseline, and soon he owned it with tantalizing accuracy. He then started irritating Mako with sharply angled shots into the service courts, winning the second and third sets, 6-3, 6-4. Mako tried to blunt the onslaught by taking over the net, only to be caught flat-footed by passing shots. He waved his racquet helplessly as Bobby's shots whistled by, some bringing up a puff of white chalk in the hot air as they nicked the line. An increasingly frustrated Mako leaned back and shook his racquet at the sky, imploring the heavens for help. After finding himself sprawled face down on the turf after a futile lunge for a drop shot, Mako lay still. He beat the turf with his clenched fist, then slowly climbed to his feet to reluctantly face defeat, losing in the fourth set, 7-5.

The spectators meanwhile had switched their allegiance to Bobby, won over by his calm and by his canny tactics. It was the first time in a big tournament that Bobby felt the warming cheers of a friendly gallery. Wrote one observer: "The spectators forgot their manners and the admonishing warnings from the umpire's chair, and were unrestrainedly whistling and slapping one another on the back."

Bobby ran his winning streak to the semifinals, where he met Baron Gottfried von Cramm, the second-ranked player in the world. The elegant German, perhaps the best tennis player never to have won Wimbledon or Forest Hills, was a fan favorite. His stylish play and dashing good looks made him popular wherever he went. He was an athlete of such technical perfection, beauty, and dignity that one spectator said of him, "He plays just like God would play."

The month before, he and Budge played what many considered the greatest match of all time. On Centre Court at Wimbledon on July 30, 1937, in the fifth and deciding match of a Davis Cup contest to decide which country would face defending champion Great Britain, Budge fought back in spectacular fashion. Before a packed gallery, the combatants and close friends—the top two players in the world—traded winners for more than two-and-a-half hours. From two-sets-to-love down and then 4-1 down in the fifth set, Budge clawed his way back. On his sixth match point, leading 7-6 in the fifth set after a crucial break of von Cramm's service, Budge raced down a crosscourt drive. Barely getting to the ball in time, he took a desperate swing before falling to the court, driving the ball down the line and past von Cramm, who had followed the shot to the net. The ball landed perfectly in the corner, a shot Budge could not have placed better if he had walked over and spotted it by hand. Game, set, and match to Budge, 6-8, 5-7, 6-4, 6-2, 8-6. A few weeks later, in an anti-climactic Challenge round, the United States defeated Great Britain to reclaim the Cup after it had spent a decade in Europe.*

Against von Cramm at Forest Hills, Bobby got off to a fast start. Running all over the place and chasing down von Cramm's powerful drives, Bobby outsteadied the German and won the first two sets, 6-0, 8-6, but his races to the corners of the court had left him exhausted by the start of the third set. Von Cramm, a player known for his superior conditioning, had energy to spare. He ran through the final three sets relatively easily, 6-3, 6-2, 6-3.

"Oh," sang the German in open flattery to the press about Bobby's game after the match, "to play tennis like that when you are but nineteen!" Bobby, he said, "is definitely your second-best player. Certainly nobody but Budge can beat him here; and if he goes to the net more often, develops a stronger volley, who knows? He may beat anybody."

In the final, Budge defeated von Cramm in another five-set battle to win his first Forest Hills singles championship. The match, though well played, could not match the drama of the pair's contest a few weeks before, but secured Budge's place as the world's top-ranked amateur player.

A few weeks later, Bobby again snubbed Perry Jones, skipping his Pacific Southwest Championships at the L.A. Tennis Club.

---

* The Davis Cup was then organized into two zones, American and European. The winners of the preliminary zonal competitions would then play each other in the Interzone final, with the winner of that match taking on the reigning champion in the deciding Challenge Round match. The system was changed in 1972 so that all teams played through elimination rounds.

Jones left word at the gate that if Bobby showed up, he would have to pay his way in. Bobby bought a ticket.

In the semifinals of the Pacific Coast Championships in Berkeley in October, Bobby got the chance to vindicate his loss to von Cramm. Remembering the lessons he'd learned a few weeks earlier, Bobby played flawlessly. This time, von Cramm did all the running. Bobby became "touch personified," in the words of one writer. "His deft dipping cross-court backhands, dropping just over the net, either passing the German, or dropping at his feet at almost impossible volleying positions for aggressive returns, were masterpieces." Von Cramm fell in straight sets, 6-4, 6-4, 6-2.

Against Budge in the final, Bobby started hot, winning the first set, 6-4. But he still had no answer for Budge's powerful drives, which had him running all over the court. Exhausted, Bobby found it impossible to keep up with Budge, who ran out the final sets in routine fashion, 6-3, 6-2, 6-4. Despite the loss, Bobby considered the tournament quite a success. By defeating Von Cramm and taking a set off Budge, he felt he had proved himself. Bobby said jokingly of his loss to Budge, "I didn't want to be a hog about it."

At the close of 1937, Bobby was ranked second in the country behind Budge and No. 4 in the world behind Budge, von Cramm, and Wimbledon finalist Henry "Bunny" Austin of Great Britain. Returning home that fall, he celebrated by spending some of the bankroll he had built up aboard one of four floating casinos anchored three miles off the coast of Los Angeles.

Bobby's fortunes had finally turned. While playing at Southampton that summer, he was introduced to tennis fan and financier Edmund C. Lynch, founder of Merrill Lynch. Invited to stay on Lynch's personal yacht while playing in Newport, Bobby told Lynch about his troubles with Jones and the Southern California Tennis Association. Lynch, a tennis fanatic who traveled with his own teaching pro, became convinced Bobby was destined to be world champion, and decided to help Bobby financially in order to give him greater independence. He put Bobby on his personal payroll to the tune of $50 a week: Checks came to Bobby regularly until Lynch's death in 1938.

At the nationals in 1937, Bobby also had the opportunity to meet Lawrence Blaine Icely, president of Wilson Sporting Goods in Chicago. Icely, known to everybody as L.B., was also aware of Bobby's problems with the tennis brass. A tennis booster in his hometown, Icely came up with a deal he thought would help Bobby and elevate the prestige of the Western Tennis Association, Chicago's jurisdiction. If Bobby agreed to move to Chicago and play under the auspices of the WTA, Icely arranged to put him on the payroll of the United States Advertising Corporation for $200 per week, a job he promised would give Bobby all the time he needed to play tennis. It was an easy sell. Bobby packed up for Chicago.

Bobby's arrangement with Icely was not unusual. Jack Kramer was also an employee of Wilson, earning $75 a week from a meat-packing subsidiary of the company in Los Angeles. Playing both ends of the amateur system, the equipment firms not only worked with the associations to attract and develop new players, but quietly helped top players subvert the system, arranging no-show jobs or offering other inducements that allowed them to continue playing under the cloak of "amateur." All this laid the foundation for more profitable endorsement deals once the players turned professional. Of course, the players had no say in the system.

Between his tournament expenses, then averaging between $300 and $500 per tournament, his two "jobs" and his gambling winnings, Bobby was able to support himself quite nicely, particularly by amateur tennis standards. Although frugal by nature, he no longer had to stay at people's homes, bunking with the rest of the "tennis bums" in cheap hotels, scrimping for food, and hitching rides from tournament to tournament. He could afford his own hotel rooms and used a good chunk of his money to buy a sleek Cord automobile, the same kind of car in which Del Valle had driven him around two years before. Bobby wanted to show off.

After arriving "home" in Chicago in October 1937, Bobby was assigned to work the Red Heart Dog Food account for the U.S. Advertising Corp. His assignment was to travel around the city, surveying stores on how a particular product was received. Bobby didn't mind the work so much, but he quickly learned that winter hits hard and early in the Windy City, and for a kid who grew up in balmy Southern California this was a tough adjustment.

After a month, Bobby made plans to travel to Florida to play the winter tournament circuit. As promised by Icely, his employer let Bobby take all the time he needed to play tennis.

Bobby's campaign began at the Sugar Bowl tournament in New Orleans in December 1938, which he won, defeating Joe Hunt in straight sets in the final, 8-6, 6-1, 6-2.

During the early rounds at the Sugar Bowl, Gardnar Mulloy and the other players were standing around, waiting for their matches to begin when they noticed a crowd had formed around Bobby and another fellow. The two were betting on the flips of a coin.

"Bobby'd flip it in the air, go 'Call it,' and then drop it onto the back of his hand," Mulloy said. "Bobby was winning two out of three, and we couldn't figure out what the hell was wrong with it."

Suddenly, Mulloy said, the guy got mad. He said, "I'm tired of this. Let's make one big bet. I'll bet my Cadillac against your Cord."

"We all gasped," Mulloy said. "Bobby goes, 'Okay, okay.' "

"We'll flip it once," the man said.

"Okay," Bobby said. "Whose gonna flip it?"

"It doesn't matter," the man said. "But we'll flip to see who flips it."

"I got a better idea," Bobby said. "I got my hands behind my back. Odd or even?"

"Okay."

Bobby puts his hands back. "Of course," Mulloy said, "Bobby won that, too. And although I couldn't see his hands, it wouldn't surprise me if he changed them to win it."

Before Bobby threw the final flip, the guy put his hand on Bobby's hand and said firmly, "Okay, one time. And this time let it hit the ground. I'll call it in the air."

Bobby went crazy.

"No. No. No. You can't do that," Bobby yelped, his voice rising in falsetto octaves. "That isn't the way we've been playing. You can't change the rules at the last minute."

"Let it hit the ground, Bobby," echoed the crowd.

"No. No. No," Bobby insisted, his voice getting squeakier and more frantic. "You can't change the rules."

"Let it hit the ground, Bobby" the man said threateningly. "Go ahead, flip it. I'll call it in the air."

But Bobby, panic in his eyes, refused, continuing to try to talk his way out of an ever-deepening hole. The man, fed up with Bobby's string of excuses and explanations, grew angry and suddenly lunged at Bobby, certain that he was being cheated. Bobby ran off, hiding somewhere until the situation cooled and the man gave up. Mulloy said he and the others could only laugh and wonder exactly how Bobby might have rigged the throws.*

"You had to watch him," Falkenburg said of Bobby. "He was the kind of guy if he could cheat you out of money, he felt it was okay and he would do it." From golf to poker, it was nothing for Bobby to break the rules or take a peak at your cards.

Where winning was measured in dollars and cents, Bobby was absolutely cold-blooded. Whether the stakes were a dollar or $10,000, he fought for every penny as if very his life depended on it. Bobby did whatever it took, even if it meant bending, or breaking, a few rules along the way.

And like any accomplished hustler, Bobby became a student of the gaff, the scheme, the ruse, and the sham. He learned old tricks, developed new ones, and analyzed a contest from every angle to see how he might get an edge for himself. When he lost or got caught, he immediately dropped it from his repertoire.

Where winning was everything, cheating was just part of the game. He felt there was nothing malicious about it. "If he could trick his way into winning," Falkenburg said, "that was even better. I came to the conclusion that he got his kicks by outsmarting the other guy."

---

* Luck, of course, had nothing to do with it. The odds against Bobby's winning two out of three in a long series of tosses runs into the thousands. Since the other fellow had the option of calling either "heads" or "tails," a two-headed coin would not have worked. A more likely explanation is that Bobby used his thumb to feel the coin after he caught it, enabling him to know without looking which side was heads and which side was tails. After much practice, he could then use sleight of hand to turn the coin over to the desired side before slapping it down on the back of his hand. This would also explain why he refused to let the coin hit the ground. A complete description of this technique can be found in *Scarne's New Complete Guide to Gambling*, by John Scarne, Simon & Schuster.

This also made it difficult for Bobby to trust others under the same circumstances. For example, Mulloy recalled that the week before Rye in 1941, Bobby and a group of other players became involved in a late-night dice game at the Meadow Club in Southampton. There was a violent lightning storm going on when suddenly the lights went out. When they came back on, there was Bobby, lying on top of the pot, face down with his arms around the money. Looking up at a crowd of disbelieving faces, Bobby bounced up and explained, "I don't trust anybody."

"Well, you bugger," answered Mulloy for the group, "we don't trust you, either."

"But the funny thing is," added Falkenburg, "I never saw him do anything wrong in tennis." Though not above ploys to delay a point to catch his breath or distract his opponent, Bobby always played within the rules. He never cheated on line calls, argued over the score, or made excuses after losing. "Anything else he would take advantage," Falkenburg said. "But tennis was above everything else. It was sacred."

After escaping New Orleans, Bobby then went to Florida, where he played a series of tournaments in the Miami area. Now a recognized star, Bobby attracted a crowd at every tournament. Fans were eager to see who this character was. Unfortunately, Bobby also attracted the attention of the watchdogs at the USLTA, who wondered how he could afford to travel in such high style. When it came to playing the expenses racket, as long as the transactions were done discreetly, everyone looked the other way. Bobby, however, did nothing discreetly.

Knowing that he was under scrutiny by the USLTA, Bobby came up with a plan before leaving Chicago. He decided to pay his own way on the circuit with the money he got each week from the advertising agency and Lynch. He then arranged for an official he befriended from the Southern Tennis Association, a division of the USLTA, to collect all his expense checks, telling the tournament committees to mail the checks to the official.

Bobby lost but one match, to Bitsy Grant in the final at the Miami Biltmore. The marathon five-set encounter (3-6, 6-2, 7-9, 8-6, 6-3) was played in sweltering heat, and after shaking hands,

Bobby was carried off the court due to cramping. Like Bobby, Grant was a "retriever," a player who hung back on the baseline and returned every ball until his opponent made an error. In this match, Grant relentlessly soft-balled Bobby into exhaustion, and several times Bobby stopped to have his legs massaged.

Still, with the thought of all those expense checks piling up to keep him warm at night, Bobby returned to Chicago in a buoyant mood. That is, until he tried to contact his Southern Tennis Association friend. "He had disappeared like the last frost," Bobby wrote. "I hardly need mention that my money had taken wings, too."

Making matters worse, he was summoned to appear before the Rules Committee of the USLTA. The committee, led by the venerable Holcombe Ward, president of the USLTA, considered suspending Bobby for "professionalism." The "boys at 120 Broadway," as Bobby called them, referring to the headquarters' address, asked him about the expense money he received on the trip, implying that the amounts paid were far in excess of "normal" expenses.

The questions all seemed inane to Bobby. After all, the money was offered and paid out by other USLTA officials. Why not summon them to a hearing or threaten them with sanctions? But Bobby kept his opinion to himself. Instead, he told the truth: that the money paid to him had been taken by an official of the Southern Tennis Association.

After learning that one of its own had stolen Bobby's money, the committee became more defensive. It suddenly dropped the discussion of sanctions against Bobby. The hypocrisy of the whole thing infuriated Bobby.

"First they pay you money, fighting among themselves to see who can pay most, then they scream that you shouldn't have taken it," Bobby wrote. Even more ironic was that fact that these guardians of the sanctity of the game never asked Bobby—then or ever—about his betting on matches.

On his way out of the USLTA's offices, Bobby asked to use the phone, saying he needed to make a long-distance call.

You'll have to pay for it first, he was told.

Explaining that as an "amateur" he simply didn't have enough money on him, the irrepressible Bobby added, "I tell you what I'll do. I'll flip you for it."

Seemingly invincible, Don Budge overwhelmed opponents with a battering serve, pointed volleying, and blistering overhead. But it was his backhand that became his trademark, a shot he used to end points. "He was so powerful that everybody was afraid of him," Bobby said.

6

"Who's going to feed the Fire Dragon today?"
1938

Don Budge—six-foot-one and 160 pounds—was affable, easygoing, and slightly conceited. Not in a boastful way, but just enough to make it clear to everyone around him that he knew he was special, that he possessed something no one else had or even fully understood. As a child in Oakland, his first loves were baseball, basketball, and football. Tennis came along almost as an afterthought. Although he batted left-handed, he considered himself ambidextrous, a trait he later credited for the development of his devastating backhand, a shot considered by many as the finest the game had ever seen.

When Don was 13, his older brother, Lloyd, dragged him out on the court to be his hitting partner. Don enjoyed the game, but didn't take it up seriously until two years later. Three years after that, in 1933, Don Budge was the national junior champion, and a year later he was named to the Davis Cup team. All before he had even turned 20.

With a game patterned after that of Bill Tilden and Ellsworth Vines—players who bludgeoned opponents from the backcourt—Budge developed into an all-court player, with a battering serve, pointed volleying, and a blistering overhead. But his trademark was his thundering backhand. He would take the ball on the rise, lean in, and swing freely from his hip. The backhand is, for most players, the weaker side, a shot relied on simply to stay in a point. Budge, however, used the shot to end points. And no one—not Tilden, not Vines—could match Budge in his sustained intensity of play. Budge barely gave opponents a chance to breathe, and rolled over them with mechanical ferocity. By 1937, Budge had won both Wimbledon and Forest Hills, and from January 1937 to September 1938 he racked up an incredible 92-match, 14-tournament win streak. The other players took to calling him the "Fire Dragon" because of his shock of red hair and crushing game. At the start of a tournament, they'd gather around the draw sheets as soon as they were posted, eager to see "who's going to feed the Fire Dragon today." For most, it spelled the end of the tournament before they had struck the first ball.

"He was so powerful that everybody was afraid of him," Bobby said.

In view of this, Bobby's quest to become the world's top player would clearly begin and end with Don Budge, five-year plan or no.

After two years playing the circuit, Bobby had risen to No. 2 in the country, posting an impressive string of victories against the world's best players on all surfaces. Still, it was a distant second to Budge. For all his confidence and cockiness, Bobby was the first to admit that he could not overtake Budge.

Budge later explained that his own game relied on fear, the fear he instilled in opponents by his brute power, but also his own fear that his game could fall apart in an instant. Bobby, on the other hand, relied on cunning and guile. Where Budge typically overwhelmed opponents, defeating them by wide margins, Bobby did just enough to win, confident that victory was always his for the taking.

By the end of 1937, however, Budge was ready to abdicate his crown. With his wins at Wimbledon and Forest Hills, he was the game's biggest name, and the opportunity to go professional came up. He saw the success of the professional tour that year between Vines and British champion Fred Perry, which opened before a record-setting crowd of 17,630 at Madison Square Garden and brought in a staggering $58,120 for the night. What better way to cash in on his celebrity and grab a piece of the action? Besides, it offered a chance for him to earn a legitimate living from his talents rather than simply accepting the scraps from the amateur circuit's expenses system. Or as Budge would later say, "Believe me, as sure as nobody ever got rich running amateur tennis, nobody got rich playing it either."

Tennis purists and the amateur authorities had long stigmatized the professional game, saying that it cheapened the sport and turned the players into circus showmen. A few warned Budge that if he turned professional he'd never again be able to walk into a country club through the front door. To this, Budge replied, "I can assure you that however much self-respect one feels going through a front door, he feels a great deal more pride in being able to pay his way whichever door he may go through."

With a $50,000 guarantee dangled before him, Budge was all set to turn pro when Davis Cup Captain Walter Pate approached him and asked him to hold off in order to help defend the Davis Cup. Appealing to Budge's sense of patriotism, Pate promised to support Budge in any way he could to make it pay off for the star in the end. The loyal and appreciative Budge agreed, thus putting Bobby's hopes on hold.

But in order to fulfill his promise to Pate, Budge would have to wait nearly a year. Davis Cup competition was then organized so that the defending champion did not play through the preliminary matches, instead waiting for a challenger to emerge from the elimination rounds to the final Challenge Round. Eager not to simply repeat his accomplishments of the previous year, Budge scouted around for a new challenge, something that would keep him motivated and sharp, something that might truly mark his place in history. What he came up with he whimsically described as "my favorite invention." To the rest of the world and tennis history, it would be dubbed the "Grand Slam."

By this time, tennis was a truly international sport. From two countries in 1900, the Davis Cup had grown to include 27 nations by 1938 (that number would grow to 142 nations by 2003). What better to way to amplify the individual achievement of being the world's No. 1 player than to win the national championships of the four countries that up until then had won the Davis Cup?

This would mean winning the Australian, French, Wimbledon, and United States championships in the same year.

Australian champion Jack Crawford had nearly managed the feat five years earlier in 1933, winning all but Forest Hills, but no one before Budge had thought of actually lumping the four titles into a single accomplishment.

For one thing, the task was simply too daunting. In those prewar days of primitive air travel, few players would consider venturing to compete in each of the four tournaments. By boat it took 21 days to get to Melbourne from the United States. As a consequence, the Australian championships nearly always ended up being a showcase for native talent. The French championships, too, were regularly skipped by many top players, falling as they did so close to Wimbledon and played on clay, a surface that did nothing to help a player prepare for the slick grass at the revered All England Club.

Budge decided to go after the four titles, but to reduce the pressure on himself he told only his doubles partner, Gene Mako, of his plans. The Grand Slam would be his creation, a landmark accomplishment that would redefine the game as no one had since Tilden.

While Budge set sail from San Francisco that winter on the first leg of his quest, Bobby returned to Chicago and his job at the advertising agency working the dog food account. He was the second-best player in the country, but he felt he might as well have been the 102nd best. To most fans, there was Budge and then everyone else. Success, it seemed, had gotten Bobby nowhere. Spurned by the Davis Cup committee and scorned by Perry Jones and the other tennis pooh-bahs in Los Angeles, he was a tennis refugee, biding his time in Chicago and wondering what it would take for him to gain the respect he considered rightfully his.

As soon as the first winter chill set in, Bobby once again made plans to escape Chicago and travel south, accepting invitations to play events in Miami, in the Sugar Bowl tournament in New Orleans, at River Oaks in Houston, and in Atlanta and Chattanooga. This campaign would take him through the spring of 1938, when events in the Midwest were held, then into the summer and the eastern grass-court tournaments leading up to Forest Hills. He would prove himself in the only way he knew how: by winning.

Playing straight through to July, he won 11 singles titles and reached the finals of 13 tournaments. Between singles, doubles, and mixed doubles events, he played nearly 100 tennis matches—this before the eastern grass court circuit had even begun. At Neenah, Wisconsin, Bobby repeated as champion. At the National Clay Courts in Chicago, Bobby won for the third straight year, coming from behind to defeat Gardnar Mulloy. Bobby's victory gave him permanent possession of the nearly 30-year-old trophy. And in Cincinnati at the Tri-State Championships, Bobby also won for the third straight year, sweeping through the field without dropping a set, defeating Frank Parker in the final and retiring that tournament's trophy, the Wilfred M. Tyler Bowl.

With eight weeks left before the United States Davis Cup defense, Bobby's play, wrote one observer, was "heartening to Americans who want the Cup defended successfully."

But the big shots at the USLTA saw it differently. First, Bobby was refused a trip to Wimbledon customarily granted the top two players in the nation. He was told only defending champions would go. Thus it was Budge for singles and Mako for doubles. He then mistakenly assumed his No. 2 national ranking would make him a lock for the second singles slot on the Davis Cup team behind Budge. Wrong again. "Riggs, you'll have to fight it out with all the others," he was told.

"The powers that be were always ready to take care of me. With a brand new excuse," Bobby sneered.

Disappointed but hardly surprised, Bobby resolved to win his spot. Between June 13 and August 13, Bobby played 10 tournaments, winning them all. With the sole exception of Budge, who was out of the country on the third leg of his Grand Slam quest, Bobby played and beat the best players in the country. He won on the grass at Longwood, and for the second straight year took the titles at Seabright, Southampton, and Rye. Opponents expecting to see Bobby sit on the baseline and grind it out were surprised when he "served, drove and volleyed like one to the manner born."

It was a popular misconception that Bobby was a retriever, a "pusher" who merely kept the ball in play. Though not a power-player—and yes, if given a choice of surfaces, Bobby probably would choose a slower surface such as clay—he was also a fine player on faster surfaces such as grass or indoor carpet. His serve, while not as powerful as that of many players, was deadly accurate, and he could place it well enough or put enough spin on the ball to befuddle an opponent. He was fast on his feet and had superb anticipation. He found ways to control bigger, more powerful opponents. He could pin a player back by hitting long, deep shots down the line, run them ragged with short, angled chips and drop shots, or pass them at the net at will.

"He had the most beautiful, graceful, flowing strokes," recalled player George Gondolman. "He had a wonderful serve that he could pinpoint any place on the court. He always kept you off balance. You thought he was going to the forehand, it went to the backhand. You thought you were going to get a twist serve and you get a cut serve. He was fast and light on his feet. He could do everything. He had great courage when he played. Nothing bothered him. He had nerves of steel."

More than any man, said longtime friend and former professional champion Pancho Segura, Bobby could "make the ball talk." He was able to win points outright with his drop shot, which would just clear the net before bouncing sharply to the side. On occasion he could even put enough spin on the ball to make it hit the court, then bounce backward over the net before his opponent could touch it. His lob undoubtedly ranked among the best ever, nearly always landing just inches inside the baseline. Not only that, he could hit it on the run. He volleyed extremely well off both sides and his overhead, though not powerful, was always on target.

The way Bobby assembled these shots strategically was the key to his dominance. "He was always two shots ahead of you," recalled Segura, "setting up the next shot and the next. For example, he would know if you were going to hit down the line and he'd be there waiting for you. Bobby never overpowered you, but he never beat himself. He played within himself... He played just enough to beat you, [and] he had such nerve. If he thought he could beat you, he would bet the house."

If there was one glaring fault in Bobby's game, it was his habit of toying with lesser players. Rather than hit an outright winner, he'd delight in tormenting. He might draw his opponent to the net with a drop shot, then lob craftily to force his opponent to run back for a return, only to be drawn back to net by another drop shot. The series would continue—lob, drop shot, lob, drop shot—until his opponent either missed or gave up, utterly exhausted. Although not a malicious person, Bobby admitted, "I used to get diabolical pleasure, a roguish-type thing, to keep an opponent out on the court, to tease him, to prolong the game and make the score very close." Antics such as these, Jack Kramer said, "rubbed a lot of people in the game the wrong way, and so he never got his due from within."

By the end of his 1938 campaign, Bobby had clinched his spot on the Davis Cup team, though he still believed his inclusion was less a matter of acceptance by the committee than an acceptance of popular pressure. He then skipped the championships in Newport in August, in part to take a "well-deserved rest," but also to avoid getting in trouble over the USLTA's "Eight-Weeks Rule," which forbade players from taking expense money for more than eight tournaments a year under threat of suspension. The rule, which Kramer derisively described as designed "to keep outsiders from whispering about 'tennis bums,' " was routinely flouted by players and used only by the association as a cudgel to keep players in line. Few top players were ever sanctioned, because to do so would threaten a tournament's gate receipts. Still, already on shaky ground with the USLTA, Bobby decided to lay low. Besides, he truly did need a rest. The previous weeks had taken a toll even on the indefatigable Bobby. In January, at the end of a long five-set match against Bitsy Grant under Florida's blistering sun, he had to be carried off the court due to exhaustion and cramping in his legs.

Bobby arrived fresh and ready at the Germantown Cricket Club in Philadelphia in late August to work out with the Cup squad on grass courts as it prepared for its match against Australia.

But when he reported for duty, Bobby found himself "about as important as the batting-practice pitcher on a baseball team. Nobody cared whether I was there or not." It was widely assumed that Budge, back from Europe after winning the third leg of his Grand Slam at Wimbledon, would win his two singles matches, and that he and Mako would win the doubles. Whatever Bobby might accomplish would be inconsequential.

Australian captain Harry C. Hopman skippered a two-man squad consisting of Davis Cup veteran Adrian Quist, a short, scrappy right-hander with an aggressive all-court game, and John Bromwich, a tenacious competitor who was playing his second year of Cup competition. Five years Quist's junior, Bromwich was also one of the most unusual stylists in the game. A natural left-hander who served right-handed, and stroked with two hands on the right side and one on the left, Bromwich had excellent touch and pinpoint placements. By themselves, Bromwich and Quist were formidable singles opponents, though no match for Budge. But together, they had quickly gelled to become one of the world's top doubles teams. It was in them that Australia's hopes really rested.

When the names of Riggs and Quist were drawn for the opening match, "the visitors, from captain Harry C. Hopman down the line, made no effort to conceal their joy." Davis Cup play was a supreme test of nerves, and in Hopman's mind the untested Riggs would be no match for the more experienced Quist. A victory by Quist would place added pressure on the Americans. This, at least, was the thinking.

Bobby, of course, had more riding on the match than just national pride. His career, his ongoing battle against the tennis aristocracy, his whole struggle for legitimacy hinged on how well he rose to this occasion. Despite his long odds, Bobby didn't lay a bet on himself. There was no need. It was self-imposed pressure at its most intense. Bobby responded beautifully, playing one of the finest matches of his career.

Quist won the opening set. But Bobby took over the match from there, employing a clever assortment of drives and slices, lobs and smashes, drop-shots and floaters to keep Quist constantly off balance. Bobby won, 4-6, 6-0, 8-6, 6-1, a victory that shocked everybody and seemed to seal the Australians' fate, particularly after Budge defeated Bromwich in four sets.

Down 2-0, Australian hopes briefly rose after Quist and Bromwich beat a faltering Budge and Mako in the doubles match. Two days later, Budge secured the Cup with a straight-set win over Quist, giving the United States an unbeatable 3-1 lead. The anti-climatic finale pitted Bobby against Bromwich. But Bobby suddenly was AWOL. A search by Davis Cup officials and teammates found Bobby in the country club's basement, pool cue in hand, immersed in a game of billiards. After sinking his shot in the side pocket, Budge recalled, Bobby gathered his racquets and went on-court. With nothing at stake, however, Bobby could not muster his best game, and lost in four sets. Nonetheless, his victory over Quist provided the winning margin, and solidified his reputation as a world-class player, the heir apparent to Budge. Gloated Bobby afterwards, "I feel reasonably sure that much as they wanted to keep the Davis Cup, the USLTA chiefs were anything but overjoyed that it was necessary for me to contribute the winning point."

Brimming with confidence, Bobby arrived at the national championships at Forest Hills. The second American seed (the championships then had two sets of seedings: one for American competitors; another for foreign players), Bobby appeared to have a clear path to the semifinals against Bromwich and a showdown against Budge, who then was looking to complete the final leg of his Grand Slam run. No matter what the outcome, it would be a fitting passing of the torch from the reigning American champion to the next.

The tournament would have a storybook ending, as it turned out, just not the one Bobby envisioned.

From the outset, Bobby struggled to find his game. Upon reaching the quarterfinals, he faced the mercurial Gil Hunt, a potential Top-10 player whose on-again, off-again streakiness left him with a checkered record that mixed "impressive wins with unaccountable losses," according to one commentator. Bobby knew as much, having been beaten by the moody Hunt at the junior nationals three years earlier after talking Hunt out of defaulting midway through a match Bobby assumed was his.

The lesson of that loss, however, had apparently failed to sink in. Bobby entered the concrete, horseshoe-shaped stadium court confident of victory. Hunt caught Bobby off guard and tore through the first set, 6-2.

Explained Hunt: "I had decided before the match that he was a lot better at running and staying in the points." To conserve energy, Hunt decided to rely on winning points and games when they counted most heavily, bearing down during his own service games but only occasionally trying to break Bobby's serve. After being broken early in the second set to give Bobby a 3-0 lead, Gil threw away the set, 0-6.

"Everything he hit was either a winner or a loser—nothing in between," Bobby complained. "I found it hard to get in my rhythm."

The third set proved crucial, as both players fought dearly for possession. Trailing 6-7 in the set, Hunt suddenly seemed so tired that to one observer "it was doubtful whether he had another good shot left in his top-heavy racquet." But whether his exhausted state was a ruse or simply freed him to play with a kind of mindless abandon, Hunt suddenly came to life. Just as he had three years earlier, he started ripping balls all over the court. At 7-7 and behind 15-40 on Bobby's serve, Hunt, "looking as though he was hardly trying," hit four clean winners on service returns to go up 8-7. He then rushed the net to take his own serve and the set, 9-7.

After the third set, the players were given a 10-minute break to shower and change clothes. Bobby, however, stayed on the court and waited for Hunt. As he later recalled, "I was fuming, frustrated, not the least bit tired and, to top it all off, he returned fifteen to twenty minutes later."

The fourth set was a repeat of the second. Hunt got down a break to go 0-3 to Bobby and then decided to throw away the set, 6-0. "He did the same thing, literally giving me another 'bagel job,' " Bobby said. "Again, I won 6-0 but nothing had changed."

Hunt's tactics kept Bobby continually off-balance. In the deciding fifth set, a "whipped" Hunt again pulled out of a hole. From 0-1 and 0-40 down he gained the lead 3-1, only to let Bobby break back for 3-all. Hunt then broke Bobby and held out to win the match, 6-4.

"For the second time, Gil 'psychologized' me," Bobby later groused. "I could only wait 'til next year."

That was to be one of Hunt's last big upsets. In the semifinals, he faced Mako, who had removed Bromwich, the top foreign seed, in a straight-set upset. Mako swept aside Hunt in four sets, 6-0 in the final set.

For Hunt, tennis had never been a priority. He had other ambitions. In high school, he filled his summers with college-level mathematics courses at Boston College. He graduated from the Massachusetts Institute of Technology and went on to become a distinguished mathematician, a part of Albert Einstein's roundtable at Princeton University.

Mako's victory over Hunt in the semifinals made him the first unseeded player to reach the finals of the championships in the tournament's history and set up a final against his good friend and doubles partner, Don Budge. Before 12,000 fans, Budge then rode the wave to the first Grand Slam, defeating Mako in four sets. "Here, truly, is one of the great competitors of sport and one of the most genuine sportsmen to grace the game," wrote *New York Times* reporter Allison Danzig.

On December 20, 1938, in an unprecedented ceremony in Walter Pate's New York office, Budge signed a contract for $75,000 plus a percentage of the gate receipts to turn professional. He would play a series of one-night stands against reigning pro Ellsworth Vines, who defeated Fred Perry that year in a series of head-to-head matches, 48-35. The logistics of touring made it impossible to host full-fledged professional tournaments. The venues were too small and the cost of traveling too great. As a result, the tours evolved into head-to-head contests between the reigning professional champion and the top amateur challenger. After the tour, to infuse new blood and maintain public interest, the next top amateur player would be enticed to sign on for the next year, with the previous year's losing professional dropping out. In this case, Budge, the top amateur, would take on the professional champion, Vines.

Giving Budge his blessing, Pate thanked him for "the good he had done for the amateur game, and the further good he could do the cause of lawn tennis in his new role."

On January 2, 1939, Budge and Vines opened their tour in Madison Square Garden before a standing-room-only crowd of 16,275. Tickets were scaled as high as $7.50, a fantastic price to pay in those days, and the total gate was $47,120. By the time the whirlwind tour ended three months later, Budge edged Vines 22-17, playing before a total attendance of 168,384. The tour was successful, drawing good crowds, but when it ended Vines was burned out. He soon quit tennis to start a new career as a professional golfer. Budge and Fred Perry then toured briefly with much more modest success. Budge dominated, 28-8, making him the undisputed champion of the world. For once, interest in tennis seemed to focus on the professional game rather than the amateur—in large part due to Budge.

Budge's abdication of his amateur crown made Bobby the country's top amateur player by default. It was perhaps a less-than-satisfying route to the top, but Bobby was never one to look a gift horse in the mouth. His 58-7 record stood on its own merits. Besides, he had other things on his mind. He was in love.

The previous July, Bobby had played the Illinois State Championships on the campus of Northwestern University in nearby Evanston. While playing a match on one of the outer courts, he caught the eye of a pretty blond sitting on the roof of a car looking over the fence. Between points, Bobby chatted with the girl.

Her name was Catherine Ann Fischer, a Chicago native and a student at Manhattanville College in New York. She had grown up a rich girl. Her father, Anthony, started his own construction company and made a fortune during the early 1900s designing the scaffolding and construction techniques needed to work on a new type of building being pioneered in the Windy City: the skyscraper. As a result, Catherine—or Kay, as she was known—was a pampered princess among Chicago's elite—complete with a fancy house, private schools, and limousines. The Crash of 1929 bankrupted the business, however, and in the years that followed, the family's finances steadily dwindled.

But on this warm July afternoon none of that mattered. Kay had been dragged to the match by her younger brother, "Bud," who had become a diehard Bobby Riggs fan since the player had moved to Chicago. Bud even kept a scrapbook on Bobby, and when he learned that he was to play nearby he insisted his big sister take him. Knowing nothing about tennis, Kay agreed to go just to make Bud happy. Once there, Bud quickly tracked down Bobby, and upon pointing out his hero, Kay said to herself, "You know, he's pretty cute." Her interest in tennis instantly rose a few notches.

For Bobby, of course, girls were just one of the perks of being a top player. At every tournament, they would gather around, hoping to get the players' attention, to hear about their travels and adventures, to go out to a restaurant or to a dance, and, who knows, perhaps something more. In some cases, the families hosting the players in their homes would throw parties or arrange for their daughters to go out on dates with them.

"When it first happened," groused a local boy at one tournament, "the younger members of the club, at least those unmarried, did not like those people coming here, because all our girlfriends would date these visiting tennis players and we were kind of put on the second level until they all got out of town."

Having grown up around older brothers, Bobby developed an awareness of and interest in sex as a young boy. He said his first experience was when he was seven. He was on a church outing and he and another little girl, a minister's daughter, shared a "show me yours and I'll show you mine" experience. It was a "dry run," confessed Bobby, and it sparked his curiosity, but as a youngster he never had much success with girls, though not for lack of effort. "I was trying all the time," Bobby said, "but I just didn't seem to have the know-how, the knack as far as girls were concerned. I was the type that felt the straightest line was the best, but as you know the direct approach isn't very good. Girls want to be romanced a little bit; they want somebody to spend a little time with them and so forth, and I just never had any feel for that."

The next time Bobby "scored" with a girl was when he was 17 and playing the Pacific Coast Championships in Berkeley. On the amateur circuit, Bobby explained, the basic idea was "to see if you could fuck some waitress in some restaurant in some town where we happened to be playing." Bobby was never much of a ladies' man. "I just came on too fast. All I wanted to do was get laid, and it was pretty obvious. I tried to fuck them all—nice girls, bad girls, whatever."

Sex for Bobby was a conquest, another form of competition. And when it came to girls Bobby typically looked for an edge. According to Kramer, "he was never content to just hand out a good line when he could 'get engaged,' so Bobby got engaged in a lot of towns." The ploy nearly got Bobby in trouble the year before. While playing in Nashville in 1938, Bobby met a "nice Southern girl" and took her out over the course of the tournament. A few tournaments later, while in Cincinnati, the girl showed up, ready to be married. After Bobby broke the news that he wasn't quite ready to "tie the knot," the girl's father came to the rescue, flying up in an airplane to take her home.

At other times, Kramer wrote, "if the girl he was chasing looked like she might be interested in another player, Riggs would tell her (sadly and in the strictest confidence) that the poor fellow was gay." But the last thing Bobby desired or anticipated at this stage of his life was a long-term relationship. Women, he said, "were always strictly incidental, strictly the extras and strictly for the fun." There just was not a lot of room in his life for females. Besides, whatever his adolescent urges, Bobby never lost sight of his main goal: to become the world's best tennis player.

Kay, however, "attracted me more than any girl I'd ever seen," Bobby later wrote. He hoped she would return for the next day's matches and watched for her. After seeing her come in with a group, he got a player friend of his to introduce him to her, and asked if he could drive her home after the matches. She accepted.

Bobby became completely infatuated. They went out on dates, perhaps to dinner or a movie. She would watch as Bobby, then on a high-protein diet, would devour big steaks for breakfast, guzzle milkshakes with raw eggs in them, and gobble vitamins. During one meal, Bobby noticed Kay picking around her vegetables. Since childhood, she explained, they had never appealed to her, but she was forced to eat them "because they're good for you." Bobby reached into his pocket and pulled out a pill. Take this, he said, and you won't have to eat them. Years later, Bobby would sustain himself on an oddball diet that required him to swallow hundreds of vitamin pills a day.

For Kay, Bobby was probably not the kind of boy she had envisioned for herself. He was short, and though not unattractive, he certainly wasn't the most handsome man she had ever seen; he wasn't even the most handsome tennis player. With that broken-toothed grin of his, he bore a surprising resemblance to Dennis the Menace. He was also rough around the edges. His appearance was unkempt—though that could be fixed—he was brash, and he had more bad habits than the devil himself. And then there was that voice: raspy, almost whiney—perhaps she could get used to it.

But he also sweet, funny, courteous, and genuinely nice. There was a generosity about him, and when he talked, he made her feel that she was the only person in the world who mattered. And despite everything else, it was these qualities she felt were the most worthwhile.

Bobby won the tournament, defeating Northwestern undergraduate Seymour Greenberg, and left the trophy with Kay, telling her he would return at the end of the summer to collect it. For several months, it had a prominent place for viewing in the Fischer house.

Becoming the first man to win the singles, doubles, and mixed doubles crowns on his first attempt at Wimbledon, Bobby had, at the age of 21, fulfilled his dream. The reality of that dream, however, was slightly skewed.

7

"I felt I had really arrived."

1939

"Time," Bobby said, "is a strange phenomenon." Life's disappointments tend to soften, small victories become more grandiose, big victories become the stuff of legend, and things that once seemed meaningless blossom in importance. Time, however, also makes it difficult to distinguish between what really happened and what might have happened or what one wished had happened.

Fifty-six years old at the time he made the observation in 1974, Bobby might have been in a position to know. Though history had dutifully recorded wins and losses over the course of his career, when Bobby looked back at a year he fondly recalled as one of his most triumphant, the details had all become a bit sketchy.

In the world of sports in 1939, tennis ranked very low in the public interest. In the sports pages, tennis fans looking for the latest scores had to turn past baseball, boxing, college football, basketball, and usually golf, horse racing, yachting, and rowing… that is, if the scores were there at all. When his editors at the *New York Times* informed him he was assigned to the tennis beat, young Allison Danzig was distraught. To Danzig, who went on to become one of the games' foremost writers, being assigned to the tennis beat seemed a dead end for an aspiring reporter, an indication that you might start looking for work elsewhere.

When Don Budge turned professional, whatever prominence tennis had achieved was lost. In the wake of his Grand Slam achievement, no player could adequately fill the void left by his departure. "Tennis is not the same," lamented one columnist. "Something in it has died. Something that no steam shovel can find disappeared when Budge went out." Fans, too, mourned the loss of Budge, and wondered who might step up to take his place.

But outside events were also about to intrude on the game, and one man in particular would change the face of sports and tennis, as well as the careers of an entire generation of players: Adolf Hitler.

In Europe, tensions with Germany had been building for some time. British Prime Minister Neville Chamberlain's policy of appeasement had failed to stem Hitler's expansionist ambitions, leading to the occupation of Austria, threats against Poland and growing tensions throughout the continent. Across the Pacific, clashes between Japan and China had developed into full-blown war, with the capture of Peking, Shanghai, and other major cities. The United States, though officially neutral, seemed to be girding for the inevitable. President Franklin D. Roosevelt had asked Congress to approve $552 million for defense.

Of course, none of this really mattered to Bobby, who was singularly focused on his goal of becoming a world champion. His ascent to become the nation's No. 1 player had taken a serious load off his mind, even if his achievement was by default. And at long last, the USLTA was obliged to send him to Wimbledon. No excuses.

The pressure off, Bobby decided to stick around Chicago a while, not because of the climate or even his job, but because it afforded him a chance to court Kay Fischer, with whom he had become uncontrollably infatuated. In order to spend more time with her, he skipped the winter tournaments in New Orleans, Houston, and Florida. From October to March, he worked hard at his advertising job ("Don't laugh. I did," Bobby wrote), but he also worked hard at getting to know Kay better, taking her out to dinner and to movies, or simply spending time with her and her family.

A strict Catholic, Kay was not about to have sex with him, but she enjoyed his company (Bobby later joked that the only reason he married Kay was that he "finally had to cave in and get married in order to get it."). By the end of February, he realized he needed to get serious about his game. After winning tournaments in Bermuda, Chattanooga, and Hot Springs, Virginia, Bobby received word from Davis Cup Captain Walter Pate that the USLTA would be sending him to Europe. Scheduled to depart in late May, Bobby was eager to swing back to Chicago to pack his bags and to see Kay.

Upon arriving home, he called up a friend who ran a restaurant to arrange something special. He invited Kay out to dinner. It was Good Friday and Kay was in the middle of a novena, a period reserved for prayer. Bobby took the liberty of ordering for her a large steak. Kay tried to explain that she was only supposed to eat fish. "Don't worry," Bobby assured her, "I've got a special dispensation from the pope." ("I was so dumb I believed him," Kay later said.) While not exactly on bended knee, Bobby made it clear to Kay that should he return from Wimbledon with the trophy, it would be a victory they would share together. As for the novena? As Kay would recall a half-century later, "that was the end of that… I discontinued it immediately."

On May 24, Bobby sailed from New York aboard the *President Roosevelt* bound for Le Havre, France. Bobby's old friend and rival, Joe Hunt, then a midshipman at the Naval Academy in Annapolis, was supposed to join him on the trip to Wimbledon, but his military obligation prevented that. Elwood Cooke, the seventh-ranked player in the country, was selected to take his place. Joining Bobby and Cooke were Helen Jacobs, Sarah Palfrey, and Alice Marble, who was accompanied by her coach and Bobby's former coach, Eleanor "Teach" Tennant. By Bobby's standards, it was a dull trip. Cooke and Palfrey were madly in love, and Marble, though she had long known Bobby and had been his mixed doubles partner, had little to do with him off-court.

From Le Havre, the group took a train to Paris for the French championships. Unlike the spartan accommodations common in the U.S., the French treated the players like visiting royalty. Porters met them at the station and took their luggage to the luxurious Hotel Lancaster, where Bobby and Cooke shared a huge suite. As soon as they were settled in, the hotel chef paid a visit and asked them what they would like to eat and how they would like it prepared. The hotel then tossed a reception for the players, inviting several hundred French tennis enthusiasts and setting out a lavish, champagne-filled banquet. Bobby also enjoyed the nightlife, taking in the famous *Folies Bergere* and some of the City of Light's more exotic venues.

The red clay, or *terre batu*, at Roland Garos Stadium was ideally suited to Bobby's defensive game. The gritty surface blunted the power of big hitters, giving Bobby more time to get to the ball. The stadium's single court also had loads of room on either side in which to run.

Though it was one of the four tournaments making up Budge's Grand Slam, the French championships, like the Australian championships at the time, were not on par with the championships at Wimbledon or Forest Hills. Many of the world's top players skipped the event altogether, deciding to concentrate on grass court play in preparation for Wimbledon, which started two weeks after the clay court event. In 1939, the top Australians skipped all the European events, including Wimbledon, in order to prepare for the Davis Cup; many other players were forced to stay home because of the deteriorating situation with Germany. By all accounts, it was Bobby's tournament to win.

During the championships, Bobby suffered from what he described as "a bad patch of racquet trouble." Although as a beneficiary of Wilson Sporting Goods he had unlimited access to racquets, Bobby explained, "I just couldn't find a racquet with the right kind of feel." Instead, he borrowed one from a different player every day. He still reached the final, playing his typical nonchalant, lackadaisical style and doing just enough to win. To galleries used to seeing big boomers like Don Budge and Ellsworth Vines represent the United States, Bobby's chips, chops, drops, and lobs were a little disconcerting—and a bit of mystery. This was the best the country had to offer?

Meanwhile, on the other side of the draw, another American, Don McNeill, an unknown, hard-hitting Oklahoman from Kenyon College, was working his way through the tournament and impressing audiences with slashing, serve-and-volley tennis—the kind of game fans expected from an American. McNeill arrived in Paris on the tail end of a world tour with the Kenyon tennis team, having traveled to the Far East, India, Egypt, and Europe for exhibitions and tournaments. While honing his game, McNeill defeated some of the world's best players, including India's Ghaus Mohammed, Japanese star Jiro Yamagishi, and the great German, Baron Gottfried von Cramm.

Bobby and McNeill had faced each other more than 10 times going into the finals at Roland Garos stadium, but Bobby had not lost a single set to McNeill, much less a match. At first, there was nothing to indicate this streak would change. Bobby jumped out to a 5-3 lead in the first set, playing with a borrowed racquet, "a monster of a racket, with a five-inch handle."

At that point, however, things unraveled for Bobby. McNeill laid into every ball, following it straight into the net and finishing off points with punishing volleys. His play won him 13 straight games and a two-sets-to-love lead, 7-5, 6-0, with a 3-0 lead in the third. Bobby tried to counter McNeill's attack with a succession of lobs and looping groundstrokes, but in the words of one commentator, "He was lazy and unenterprising and seemed to think that even so he would win." Bobby managed to bring things to a 3-3 tie in the third set, but it was too late. McNeill was simply overpowering, and went on to win the set and the title, 6-3.

Afterwards, McNeill confessed that he never played better in his life. Though typically not given to excuses following a big loss, Bobby admitted that perhaps he had overdone the Paris nightlife.

Bobby's search for a suitable racquet continued after crossing the English Channel. On the grass at Queen's Club, the final tune-up before Wimbledon, Bobby walked on court with 12 different racquets under his arm. His opponent for the championship that day was von Cramm. The two players had swapped victories the previous year, so everything pointed to a tight, competitive match. On this day, however, Bobby was never in the fight. On a rain-soaked grass court, von Cramm dispatched Bobby in less than 20 minutes, winning 6-0, 6-1. Bobby later wrote that after each game he went over to the sideline and picked up another racquet. After using 11 racquets and down 0-6, 0-5, he finally won his first game, to which he jokingly said out loud, "Thank you, Gottfried." To himself he said, "This is the racket I'm going to use at Wimbledon." After the match, he had six made for him. A day later, a headline in the *London Daily Mail* announced, "Ten-racket Riggs wins one game."

Years later, players and historians speculated that perhaps Bobby deliberately threw the match against von Cramm in an effort to boost the odds against him at Wimbledon. Pressed on the matter, Bobby coyly answered that he simply did not play to win. "I was not too keen to win a tournament just before the big one. I was afraid it would be the kiss of death for me."

As for von Cramm, his best and last chance to win the singles title at Wimbledon would be denied to him. He was then living in self-imposed exile in Egypt after spending five months in a German prison. Though a German patriot and stalwart Davis Cup participant, he opposed Hitler's demagoguery and refused to speak for Nazism during his travels. This refusal infuriated his superiors. In 1938, he was convicted on a trumped-up charge of sodomy with a male youth, a charge personally engineered by Gestapo chief Heinrich Himmler. The All England Club refused his entry because of his criminal record (he was only allowed to play Queen's after a heated debate by that club's tournament committee). Returning to Germany, he later was sent to the Russian front, where he won the Iron Cross for bravery, but his steadfast refusal to join any Nazi political or para-military organizations cast him under a cloud of suspicion by his Nazi superiors.

With von Cramm out of the tournament, Bobby was the second seed behind the previous year's finalist to Budge, Britain's Henry "Bunny" Austin. But as Bobby walked the hallowed grounds of the All England Club, surveying the courts separated by hedges and green canvas fences, taking in the scent of fresh-cut grass and roses, he must have had a sense of destiny. This was the culmination of all his hard work; the realization of his youthful dream of five years earlier.

One can only imagine how Bobby felt stepping from the clubhouse into the famed Centre Court stadium, the ivy-covered walls, the court bathed in light with the stands hidden in shadow by the building's open roof, and the fans as quiet as a church congregation. The court's immaculately maintained lawn—cut precisely to 3/16 of an inch using special 10-bladed hand mowers, then rolled hard and flat with a 2,500-pound barrel-shaped roller— resembled, in the words of player Vic Seixas, not so much grass as "cement with fuzz on it."

Bobby might have felt oddly at home, like he had already been there. In a sense, he had. Recalling his years-long dream, he knew this was his moment.

B efore the start of the tournament Bobby walked into one of London's legal bookmaking parlors. An American magazine writer several years later wrote, "This particular bookmaker was confronted a day before the tournament began by a customer with an outrageous notion in his head." As excerpted here from the June 1950 issue of *Sport* magazine, the exchange went like this:

"In America," he said, "we like to make parlay bets. You know, if you win on the first one, all the money goes on the second one, and if you win on the second one, the whole pile rides on the third one—and so on. You know what I mean? Ever hear of it?"

The Englishman nodded his head gravely.

"Well, I want to get down a parlay on this tennis tournament. We've got some pretty good American players in it, you know."

"So I have heard," agreed the proprietor. "Of course, Wimbledon is a world championship tournament." A note of national pride crept into his voice. "There are many fine players here this year, in addition to yours."

"There won't be any of them in the final, I'll bet," said the customer with a grin.

"That," said the bookmaker, who was beginning to get a trifle annoyed, "remains to be seen."

"What I want," the U.S. booster announced, "is to make a bet that this fellow Riggs will win the men's singles, the men's doubles, and the mixed doubles. How about it? What odds will you give on that?"

The bookmaker simply looked pained. Unquestionably, he was beginning to believe everything he had ever read about the crazy Americans. "I can't consider it," he said, frostily. "It's out of the question."

"Why?"

"It's ridiculous. No one man is going to win all those championships. My conscience would not allow me to accept such a wager."

"For cryin' out loud, what's your conscience got to do with it? Don't you want to take my money?"

By now, the Englishman was plainly out of patience. "I shall be pleased to accommodate you if you wish to back Mr. Riggs to win the gentleman's singles," he said, stiffly.

So the bet was made, 10 pounds at 3-1 on Riggs to win the singles, no parlay.

Bobby left the shop, tucking the bookmaker's receipt into his wallet: "Mr. Riggs to win the gentlemen's singles."

On paper, Bobby's performance during the fortnight was spectacular. He advanced to the final with the loss of just two sets, posting impressive straight-set victories over India's Ghaus Mohammed in the quarterfinals and World No. 8 Franjo Puncec of Yugoslavia in the semifinals. On the other side of the draw, Elwood Cooke, Bobby's good friend and doubles partner, played some of the finest tennis of his career, eliminating, among others, top-seeded Austin in straight sets. With the Queen Mother sitting in the royal box, the two Americans took to the court on a beautiful July afternoon. The audience, though surely apprehensive at the sight of two newcomers facing off for the world's preeminent title, remained excited, assured in the knowledge that the magnitude of

Wimbledon and the depth of the field it attracted always produced true champions.

The overwhelming favorite to win, Bobby had played Cooke a dozen times and had never lost. Like Bobby, Cooke preferred to stay on the baseline, keeping the ball in play, driving shots deep into the corners, and occasionally luring his prey into the net, where he could then win the point on a crisp passing shot.

Bobby, however, had many more weapons at his disposal. He could stay back and match Cooke shot for shot. He could charge into the net and end the point with a sharply angled volley. He could lure Cooke in with a deft drop shot, then send him scurrying back with his deadly accurate lob. Bobby could direct his serve all over the service box, sending his opponent lunging in an effort to return the ball. Bobby had the ability to always keep Cooke guessing.

But Cooke's odds looked good. He roared through the first set, winning it 6-2, and was up 5-3 in the second. After all, perhaps no one knew Bobby's vulnerabilities better than his best friend and doubles partner, and Cooke took full advantage.

As he had so many times before, Bobby dug in his heels, adjusted his game, and fought back to go up 6-5. Thinking the set was his, Bobby let up, allowing Cooke to recover his momentum and even the set at 6-6. Again, Bobby adjusted his game, winning his serve and breaking Cooke to take the second set, 8-6.

In their previous matches, Cooke had shown a tendency to fall victim to his own nerves. He missed easy shots, blew big leads, and basically handed the victory to Bobby. Today, however, playing in the biggest match of his life, Cooke remained calm. He breathed deeply, regained his composure and focus, and went out and dominated Bobby in the third set, 6-3. But if Bobby was nervous, he didn't show it. Cooke may have been winning more points than Bobby, but he was paying a high price. Bobby kept the ball endlessly in play, making Cooke hit 15 or 20 shots and keeping his friend on the run. The tactic worked; by the fourth set Cooke was clearly tired, and the mistakes started to add up. Bobby simply outlasted Cooke, winning the final two sets, 6-3, 6-2. Jumping over the net to congratulate his defeated friend, Bobby was now champion of the world. On a beautiful summer's day, in a hard-fought five-setter, Bobby's dream had come true.

But like many an attained dream, the reality was slightly skewed. The fans at Centre Court that day pined for the energy and power of a Budge, Vines, or Fred Perry, particularly since two of the top contenders, Austin and McNeill, were retired early in the tournament. Cooke, though an accomplished player, was hardly a household name and never in the same league as Bobby. Though this was Wimbledon and anything could happen, the match never engaged the interest of the fans.

"Much of the tennis was academically perfect," wrote one London writer, "but from a box-office point of view the men's single final hit a new low." Called one of the strangest as well as one of the dullest Wimbledon final ever, most of the time the two players never seemed in sync, either running off long streaks of games that alternately made their opponent look like "the veriest second-rater" or exchanging long, metronomic cross-court rallies that to fans looked more like practice drills than a Wimbledon final.

Wrote a columnist for the *London Daily Mirror:* "The unfathomable Riggs deliberately finished off his man by slow torture, and if it all was of absorbing interest to students of strokes and strategy, those who like a dash of blood and sawdust with their lawn tennis went out to tea."

And out to tea they went.

Though the entire match lasted only slightly more than two hours, by the middle of the second set many spectators had seen enough. Dubbed the "colossal Wimbledon walk-out" by one newspaper, hundreds of fed-up fans started streaming from Centre Court, clambering noisily over the benches to depart while play was in progress, leaving the two finalists to play to a half-empty house.

However humiliating and unnerving such a spectacle must have been, Bobby came off smiling. He had won the grandest tournament of them all. After his victory, he enjoyed a traditional visit for tea with the Queen Mother—a scene that seems almost comical in retrospect. (King George VI, though a terrific fan and an able player who competed in the men's doubles championship at Wimbledon in 1926, was on a State visit to Canada and the United States with his wife, Lady Elizabeth Bowes-Lyon.) After tea, Bobby returned to the bookmaker's parlor to collect on his 10-pound wager.

The next day, after Bobby and Cooke defeated the British team of Charlie Hare and Frank Wilde, 6-3, 3-6, 6-3, 9-7, to win the gentlemen's doubles trophy, the bookmaker became curious about this Riggs fellow. "He began to wonder if he had done that wild-eyed bettor a favor, after all," the American reporter later wrote. When Bobby and partner Alice Marble reached the final of the mixed doubles championship, the bookmaker became truly concerned. Could he have been wrong? He went to the final to see for himself.

What he saw—the flashing net play, accurate serving, and deadly driving of the Americans—gave him something to think about. The black-haired, short-legged man and the tall, graceful girl rarely missed. It was an impressive demonstration of aggressive tennis technique. Riggs and Marble won hands down.

And then, as he looked closely at the winning team, his eyes widened in astonishment. For there was something oddly familiar about the little man in the white shorts, standing at the net to receive his third championship trophy of the week. The bookmaker could not believe his eyes—the triple-winner was none other than the same "crazy American" who tried so vigorously to get down a parlay bet on one player to win all three titles!

In his first memoir, *Tennis Is My Racket*, written in 1949, Bobby confirmed this version of events. "So I wound up betting ten pounds on myself to win the singles," Bobby wrote. "I got back forty pounds for the ten I invested in myself. I still have the bookmaker's receipt for that bet on 'Mr. Riggs to win the gentleman's singles.'" Years later, a significantly different version of the tale emerged, one in which the reluctant bookmaker consented to Bobby's farfetched bet. In his 1973 autobiography, *Court Hustler*, Bobby rewrote the story to read that the bookie gave him 3-to-1 odds on Riggs winning the singles, 6-to-1 on the doubles, and 12-to-1 on the mixed doubles titles. In this version, the amount bet also metamorphosed, from the original 10-pound wager to 100 pounds. Bobby wrote that after the tournament, "I was at the bookmaker's shop first thing Monday morning to collect on my parlay. It added up to £21,600, the equivalent of $108,000," a small fortune. As this version came to be repeated over the years, the story took on the weight of legend, becoming the cornerstone of what Bobby called "Riggs mythology."

Bobby's first wife, Kay, knew that many of the stories about Bobby's gambling were "way overblown." She said that if Bobby had won that much money at Wimbledon, she would have known about it (Bobby claimed he later blew it all on a gambling binge.). Similarly, his doubles partner, Elwood Cooke, said, "I don't think he bet on himself in London like he says. I would have known. That was just Bobby. He had his fantasies. It was all fun to him." Even Bobby's brother, John, who was privy to everything Bobby did, confided years later to one of Bobby's sons that the big bet was a publicity stunt.

There is some evidence to suggest Bobby might have succeeded in placing the parlay. John Olliff, a British player in 1939 and later a respected tennis writer, wrote in his 1949 book, *The Romance of Wimbledon,* that Bobby "backed himself heavily with a well-known firm of London bookmakers to win all three events." Alice Marble, in her posthumous 1991 memoir, *Courting Danger,* wrote that Bobby said after winning the mixed doubles event, "*everything* depended on our winning" the mixed doubles championship.

Time, however, has covered all footprints of the exact truth. When asked, even Bobby was forced to admit that "over the years in which I've acquired so much notoriety I've found it difficult to separate fact from fiction." Not that he needed such stories to bolster his image. His penchant for gambling was well known, even in 1939. It just made a good story better. Besides, it was not for lack of trying. He had *tried* to place the bet. As far as he was concerned, it may not have happened exactly as he wanted everyone to believe, but it might as well have.

Most important, he won. And he did it on his own terms. He took 18 straight matches—seven in singles, five in doubles, and six in mixed doubles—winning a total 51 of 60 sets played. In winning all three titles, he became one of three men to win the coveted "Triple Crown" (the others were Budge in 1937 and 1938, and Frank Sedgeman in 1952), and the only man to do so on his first attempt.

Returning to the States in July 1939, there was no ticker-tape parade to greet Bobby. Still, given the lashing his play received from the London press, he was probably glad to be back. Even at home, however, tennis writers were calling his game "monotonous" and "uninspiring." The editor of *American Lawn Tennis*, Stephen Wallis Merrihew, called Bobby's victory at Wimbledon a "mediocre" win over a field that was "unrepresentative of the world's best amateur talent." Another doubted his ability to lead the Davis Cup team in its defense the following month, and implored him to "play more aggressively, hit harder, do more forcing and finishing, and thus brighten up the game and make it more attractive." A writer for the *Los Angeles Times* caught up with the pros then on tour and asked them how good the top amateur was. The great Bill Tilden bluntly said he could name a half dozen players who could beat Bobby. Fred Perry, when asked whether Bobby was a great player, answered, "Frankly, I don't know." Ellsworth Vines, meanwhile, told the reporter, "Riggs is one of the few 'dink' shot players I've ever seen to win the title. Show me a truly great tennis player and I'll prove to you that he murdered the ball."

Bobby never said as much, but it is impossible to imagine that such words were not hurtful, particularly coming from players he knew and admired. (Vines later revised his statement, if only slightly, saying that while "I always have been for him and always will, because I like him personally… [but] Bobby is very lackadaisical… [and] isn't particularly colorful to watch.")

In all the derogatory comparisons of his game to Budge's, Bobby might have felt the Great One's presence looming over his career in absence as it had when the two competed against each other. But what else could Bobby do but play his own game? But above all, he was winning. Why be concerned with changing a thing? And in any case, it was not Bobby's style to wage war in the press. He would prove himself the only way he knew how: on the court.

Bobby stumbled at Seabright, his first tournament back home, losing to unheralded Frank Guernsey in his second match. He bounced back, however, winning at Southampton and Rye, with victories in the finals over Sidney Wood and Frank Parker, respectively. The wins allowed Bobby to retire the elegant trophies etched with the names of the heroes tennis fans mourned for—Bill Tilden, Budge, Perry, and Vines—players who themselves never duplicated the feat Bobby accomplished.

In the quarterfinals at Rye, Bobby performed a telling bit of gamesmanship against Bitsy Grant, an old nemesis who had worked Bobby so hard in their previous match that Bobby had to be carried off the court due to cramping and exhaustion.

With the match deadlocked at 3-3 in the final set, Grant suddenly called for a doctor, claiming he had a bug in his eye. Both players had been working hard and Grant was clearly getting tired. Bobby figured Grant was stalling to catch his breath. By the time the delay was over, not only had eight minutes passed, but Bobby's timing had deserted him. Grant proceeded to break Bobby's serve to go ahead 4-3, and it looked like there was no stopping him. "I was fuming," Bobby recalled.

Not to be outfoxed, Bobby started pawing the ground with his foot, recalled Ted Schroeder, who was watching the match. Bobby turned to chair umpire Ben Dwight and asked if he could put on spikes. "Ben, the court is very wet," Bobby explained.

Players were required to ask permission to don spiked shoes, which was given only if the court was damp or the conditions particularly slippery as the shoes damaged the court surface. Dwight looked up and said, "But Bobby, it hasn't rained in days." Nevertheless, to be fair, Dwight climbed down from the chair and started going over the baseline, checking for wet spots.

While Grant cooled his heels, his travelling companion, Champ Reese, was going "bananas." As always, Reese had a big bet riding on Grant, and was furious at Bobby's stall tactics.

After about five minutes, Dwight climbed back up in the chair and announced, "The court is dry. Play shall continue."

The ploy worked. The spark had gone out of Grant's game, and Bobby ran out three successive games for the win, 6-3, 4-6, 6-4. Upon seeing his boy lose, an infuriated Champ Reese "almost punched Bobby in the nose after that match," Schroeder said.

Bobby went on to the final, where he defeated Frank Parker in four sets, 1-6, 6-4, 6-4, 7-5. Though a relatively close match on paper, one official complained that the 2,500 fans who paid to watch were "bored stiff" by the players' interminable backcourt exchanges.

Less prominent, but of greater long-term significance to the game, was a small stand set up behind and above the grandstand court where Bobby and Parker slugged it out. Every afternoon toward the end of the tournament, NBC cameramen and announcers could be seen sending out pictures and a running commentary on the play. Bobby's victory over Parker became the first televised final of a tennis match in the United States. At the time, there were only a few hundred sets operating in the entire country, so the broadcast was less entertainment than experiment. In New York, about 50 people crowded around a boxy set on display in a showroom window to watch the matches on a 12-inch screen. But, according to *American Lawn Tennis,* the experiment was not a smashing success: "When the entire court was shown, the figures of the players were so small and far away looking that only general movements could be followed; the ball was seldom discernible." It would be several decades before television became a mass medium, the creation of which, when married to advertising, would spawn the vast industry of sport we know today. Moreover, no one could have predicted that Bobby would be the center of the greatest televised tennis spectacle in history—a match in many respects created for television.

With the defense of the Davis Cup approaching, Bobby was on a roll. Once again, the United States would play against the

Australian squad of John Bromwich and Adrian Quist. In singles, Bobby and Frank Parker would play No. 1 and No. 2 singles, respectively. But the departure of Budge had left a huge hole. American captain Walter Pate struggled to put together a doubles team the week before the competition at the Merion Cricket Club in Philadelphia. After tinkering with various combinations that included Bobby, Gene Mako, Joe Hunt, Welby Van Horn, and Jack Kramer, Pate settled on the team of Hunt and Kramer, which would then make 18-year-old Kramer the youngest player in Davis Cup history to play a Cup match.

International politics, however, not tennis, overshadowed the event. On Sept. 1, 1939, the day of the draw to determine the order of play for the following day, Hitler began his *blitzkrieg* into Poland. The announcement cast a gloom over the entire affair. People huddled around radios for the latest newsflashes and grabbed newspaper extras. Australian team captain Harry Hopman and Quist, who both had enlisted in the 6th Battalion Machine Gun Corps of Melbourne earlier in the year, believed they would be required to return home immediately to begin military service if war was declared.

Despite the news, the Davis Cup continued. The two No. 1 players, Bobby and Bromwich, would play each other in the first match, followed by Parker and Quist. The assumption was that Bobby would win both his matches, while Parker would defeat Quist, the lesser Aussie, and the US would retain the Cup.

Against the two-fisted Bromwich in the opening match, Bobby put aside all the pressure on him, the doubts of so-called experts, the insults following his Wimbledon victory, and the depressing news from Europe. He played with as much focus and determination as ever, never letting Bromwich in the match. Down two sets to love, Bromwich briefly surged to go up 4-0 in the third, but Bobby shut the door on him, coming back to win the set and match, 6-4, 6-0, 7-5. "Riggs was deadly serious from start to finish, his strategy and tactics were perfect," wrote one observer. "He employed the lob and the drop-shot with success, playing coolly and with great confidence."

Parker then edged Quist, 6-3, 2-6, 6-4, 1-6, 7-5, giving the United States a seemingly insurmountable 2-0 lead. No nation had ever recovered from a two-match deficit to win a Challenge Round.

The following day, with the doubles match scheduled, Great Britain and France declared war on Germany. The Australians were given the solemn news before taking the court. Nonetheless, they held out for a four-set victory over the young Americans, Kramer and Hunt, 5-7, 6-2, 7-5, 6-2. During the match, newsboys outside the stadium shouted, "Extra! Extra!" and during the changeovers, many fans ran out to buy newspapers.

Though it would have been nice for the Americans to win in three straight matches, the result was not unexpected. Most predicted that Bobby's match against Quist would secure the Cup. Bobby had played and beaten Quist the year before and was a much-improved player since then. Even Bromwich took notice. "He was definitely a better player than in 1938," he told the *Sydney Morning Herald*. Bobby, Bromwich said, was "more complete in his methods. Riggs has become something of an all-court player. From being a purely defensive backcourt exponent last year, he has developed a good attacking game, and takes the net position freely. Frankly, I was not prepared for this change when I played Riggs on the first day."

Before Quist took the court that morning, Bromwich gave his teammate a pep talk. "Look here, this tie isn't over yet. If you beat Riggs, I reckon I can win the last one." The two then agreed that the only way for Quist to win was to charge the net at every opportunity.

The plan worked, helped by the fact that Bobby, in his own words, "came out flat... I wasn't loose. I was tensed up. I was afraid to play. All I could do was hit the ball back. Quist would come to the net, and I was afraid to pass him."

A frustrated Bobby struggled to find his volleying touch. His lobs fell short and he mistakenly attacked the forehand of Quist, who repeatedly fired shots past him. Down two sets to love, Bobby resorted to the only sure thing in his repertoire: running. For two sets he outran Quist, and Bobby won them, 6-3, 6-3.

But Quist played smartly. Rather than chase every passing shot and every lob, Quist conceded some points in order to save his energy for the fifth set. The strategy worked. By the fifth and final set, Bobby was nearly too exhausted to continue. He managed to fight off a match point after Quist took a 5-2 lead, bringing the score to 5-4, but Quist recovered his form and served out the victory, 6-4.

In the final match, Bromwich crushed Parker, 6-0, 6-3, 6-1, and the Australians took the cup home, where it would stay for seven years. Though Bobby's loss was only one element in the losing effort, he always blamed himself for the team's defeat, saying he played "scared" that day. He might also have been a bit overconfident, having defeated Quist the year before. Whatever the case, there's no question that a determined Quist played the match of his life to pull out the victory.

The following week at Forest Hills gave Bobby a chance to redeem himself and complete what he hoped would be the final jewel of his amateur crown. As the top seed, it was his for the taking, too. At first, Bobby roared through his half of the draw, dropping two sets en route to the final, his toughest match coming in the semifinals against his old friend and adversary, Joe Hunt, 6-1, 6-2, 4-6, 6-1.

On the other end, a hot newcomer had emerged over the summer: Welby Van Horn. The youth's thundering serve and powerful volleys were drawing inevitable comparisons to Vines and Budge. Van Horn slugged his way through his half of the draw, with three five-set matches and a four-setter, including tough matches against Elwood Cooke in the fourth round, Wayne Sabin in the fifth, and a comeback against John Bromwich in the semifinal, recovering from two sets down to win, 2-6, 4-6, 6-2, 6-4, 8-6.

Despite fans' hopes for a new young gun to take the place of Budge, Bobby's game responded splendidly to Van Horn's power. Van Horn's cannonball serves seemed to come back harder than they were delivered. When Van Horn rushed the net, Bobby passed him, and when Van Horn hung back Bobby came in on the attack. Nothing Van Horn did seemed to work, and Bobby was "able to control the match at will," winning 6-4, 6-2, 6-4.

"I had a good year and beat a lot of good players to get there," Van Horn recalled. "But he was just too good. I wasn't ready... I wasn't ready to get to the final, much less beat him."

On hand to witness Bobby's achievement was Kay. After the tournament, before returning to Chicago, the couple, along with Kay's brother Bud, toured the 1939 World's Fair at Flushing Meadows in Queens, the site that in 1978 became home to the U.S. Open.

It should have been a triumphant victory for Bobby, capping a truly great year. But, with attendance off because of the fair and growing worries over the war, Bobby's first singles title at Forest Hills went virtually unnoticed. Sadly, wrote Allison Danzig, this "was probably the last big national tournament of international representatives until the roar of cannon shell no longer drowned out the ping of racquets in the Old World."

In October, Nazi bombs crashed down on Wimbledon, blowing a hole through the Centre Court roof and taking out a section of seats. During the war, the courts lay untended, the parking lots tilled and planted into victory gardens. For a time, the concrete Stade Roland Garos in Paris was used by the occupying Nazis as a concentration camp for Jews being shipped to camps in the East. In Australia, the Davis Cup was stored in a bank vault, not to be seen again for six years.

Bobby might later joke that he was the world's longest reigning Wimbledon champion, but truly the timing could not have been worse. In tennis, baseball, boxing, and all sports, the careers of an entire generation of players were cut short by the war.

Bobby finished the year playing in the Pacific Southwest tournament, his first time in the event hosted at the L.A. Tennis Club, the courts he used to call home. He lost in the final to Bromwich, 6-4, 6-4, 0-6, 6-3. A week later, he won the Pacific Coast Championships in Berkeley, where he beat another young up-and-comer, a Bay Area native named Frank Kovacs, whose game, like Van Horn's, earned him the title of "the second coming of Don Budge."

Despite all the criticism and ridicule of his game, Bobby was now the No. 1 amateur player in the world, earned legitimately through hard work and determination. He was 21 and had been training since he was 11. He had achieved everything he set out to do in his original "five-year plan." In fact, he had achieved it a year ahead of schedule. "I felt I had really arrived." It was time to celebrate.

On Dec. 9, 1939, Bobby and Kay married in Chicago in a small ceremony at Kay's home. Best man for the event was Frank Froehling, Bobby's doubles partner at the time. Bobby loved Kay. She was someone willing to completely dedicate herself to him and his goals. Whatever goals Kay may have had were subordinated. As with Bobby's brothers, his friend Jack Del Valle, and a host of other people who helped manage Bobby at different stages, she became her husband's best friend, personal assistant, and all-around Girl Friday. But it was a price she was willing to pay.

The next day, she learned exactly what it meant to be married to Bobby. After a night in the Palmer House, Bobby was back on court, competing in the Chicago Indoor City Championships. Bobby played a total of 15 sets in singles, doubles, and mixed doubles. First came a five-set singles marathon against a kid, Jimmy Evert, who later gained fame as the father of champion Chris Evert. Then came a five-set doubles final with partner Froehling. Finally, he played two mixed-doubles matches, a two-set semifinal followed by three-set final. Outside, it was bitterly cold. Inside, it wasn't much warmer. Kay sat huddled in a fur coat inside a freezing 108th Engineer's Armory, watching her new husband.

It was, admitted Bobby, "quite an introduction to married life with a tennis player."

Newly wed and world champion, the only place Bobby could go was down. Here, the new Mrs. Riggs (far left) poses with other tennis wives at Seabright, N.J., in 1941. From left: Kay Riggs, Seva (Mrs. Wayne) Sabin, Miriam (Mrs. George) Toley, and Madeleine (Mrs. Gardnar) Mulloy.

8

*'Never did a champion
lose his crown more gracefully.'*
1940.

L ove.

  Exactly how the word found its way into the tennis lexicon
is a mystery. Before Major Walter Wingfield's invention in 1874,
there was but one game called "tennis." This was the ancient game
known originally to the French as *Jeu de Paume*, or Real Tennis, as
it is called in Britain, or Court Tennis in the United States. In any
case, the game was played indoors on a hard floor of flagstone or
concrete. Wingfield's game of Lawn Tennis retained many of the
basic features and rules of its predecessor, including a ball struck
back and forth over a net by means of a racquet; allowing the ball
one bounce before being struck; allowing two serves to put the
ball in play; and an arcane scoring system in which points are
assigned values of 15, 30, 40, Game. In fact, Wingfield's biggest
innovation was the development of a rubber ball that bounced
on grass. Before this, tennis balls were hard, made from tightly-
bound pieces of cloth and covered with flannel—fine for bouncing
on a stone or concrete surface, but useless on grass.

  The term "love," meaning zero, was part of the strange scoring
system. Its origins, however, are more obscure, leading to some
more imaginative interpretations. The most popular is that it is
derived from the French *l'oeuf*, or egg, perhaps a frenchified version

of the cricket term "duck's egg," when a batter goes scoreless, or simply the old goose egg, a score of zero in a contest.

Love, as in romance, however, has no place in competitive tennis, or so the superstition goes. It's an age-old notion, something to do with the requirements of being a top athlete—or a top anything, for that matter. Love forces one to look beyond oneself. It interferes with that self-absorbed dedication needed to become the best. It is a distraction that saps an athlete's focus; a diversion that drains one's energy and concentration, but also one's sense of purpose. Simply put, it forces a top athlete to lose his or her edge.

No wonder so many athletes refuse to marry until the end of their careers. Those who do often concoct routines designed to insulate themselves from love's pernicious effects.

Bobby, in addition to watching his diet and giving up drinking in preparation for a big event, said he would abstain from sex for a month before playing (but not, ironically, all-night poker games). Other players refused to let their wives travel with them, afraid it might put the hex on their game. Henry Prusoff, the "Russian Bear," as he was called by fellow players because of his beard and long hair, the tenth-ranked player in the country in 1940, traveled with his wife, Dottie, but refused to let her watch him play, even though she was a player herself. To follow her husband's progress, she hid behind a fence or stood beneath the bleachers, watching the match through a sea of legs.

Tennis players may not be more superstitious than other people, but like all athletes they develop their own idiosyncratic rituals. Jack Kramer said he sometimes insisted on using the same ball that won the previous point, keeping the ball boys busy scurrying around trying to find it. Art Larsen, the 1950 U.S. singles champion, was called Tappy because he went around tapping everything with his racquet for good luck. In a series of sequences only he would understand, Larsen would tap the net, the net post, the service line, his doubles partner, and even his opponent. Some players, if they were on a winning streak, insisted on wearing the same outfit day after day (phew!), putting everything back on in the same order they had the day before. Gardnar Mulloy, Prusoff's doubles partner, said he made a point of not stepping on the lines during changeovers.

Don Budge, on the other hand, willfully refused to submit to such superstitions. After winning a match one day, "I had just about put the same shirt I had worn the day before over my head in the same manner I had put it on then, when I stopped myself. Now this, I said to myself, is ridiculous. The shirt didn't win and the shoes didn't win, and I am just not going to get involved with superstition." Determined not to get caught in that trap, Budge said he "developed so many habits to prevent me from becoming superstitious that I developed something of a reverse superstition. Only I think I called it discipline and let it pass proudly." For example, if he came off the court with a blister on his right foot, he would self-consciously take off his left shoe first. For Budge, it was all part of the psychology he built around his game: he not only had to convince his opponents he was invincible, he had to convince himself.

Compared to other players, Bobby was probably less superstitious than most, but he still relied upon behavioral devices to keep his confidence and motivation high. A good bet, of course, always did the trick. Being down a set and three or four games could also force Bobby to dig a little deeper. Fighting for a sense of vindication also proved effective, as his battles with Perry Jones and the other tennis powers-that-be had shown. Over the years, he had grown used to playing the villain. Indeed, the most dangerous circumstance for Bobby was complacency—as he would prove by some of the most significant losses of his career. Without a prize or a world to conquer, Bobby was lost. Happiness and good tennis just didn't mix. He needed that tension.

Marriage, he would learn, would test this premise.

Now a newlywed, Bobby decided to treat his bride to a nice honeymoon. Having forced Kay to spend the first day of their marriage bundled up inside a freezing Chicago armory watching him play four consecutive matches in the Chicago Indoor City Championships, Bobby decided after the holidays in 1939 to travel to Florida. This way, Kay could watch him play tennis under the hot sun.

The first stop on the winter circuit was New Orleans and the annual Sugar Bowl tournament. In late December 1939, Bobby lost in the final to Don McNeill, a man who suddenly seemed to have his number. McNeill defeated Bobby in straight sets. From there, Bobby and Kay traveled to Tampa for the Dixie Championships the first week of January 1940, where Bitsy Grant gave Bobby a beating in the final. Moving to Orlando and the Florida State Championships later that month, Bobby went down in flames again, this time to Prusoff, a player who had never before beaten Bobby. At one point, Bobby said, Prusoff came to the net and said earnestly, "Bobby, I shouldn't be beating you. I'll default." Despite how badly things were going, Bobby refused, explaining, "I wasn't that desperate. Yet."

Kay, however, became convinced she was the problem. She offered, like Prusoff's wife, to stay away from Bobby's matches. Bobby couldn't see how that would help. In fact, he said he felt he played better and tried harder when he knew Kay was watching. But the point became moot after Kay got a message from her family that her mother was very sick and she needed to return home. Bobby subsequently won the South Florida Championships at the end of February in West Palm Beach, defeating Prusoff in straight sets. From there he won events in Daytona, Pensacola, New York, Miami, and Houston, including a five-set victory over McNeill indoors in the National Indoor Championships in New York. Bobby wasn't about to make any connection between Kay's absence and his winning, but Kay said, "I don't know, Riggs, it looks bad."

Superstition, however, had less to do with Bobby's sometimes uninspired performance than the real reason he was playing that winter: money. Now that he was the No. 1 player in the world, it was time to cash in on his standing as the leading gate attraction. Following his wins at Wimbledon and Forest Hills, he played more tournaments and exhibitions than nearly any other top player. Like any athlete, Bobby tried to prime himself for the big events. By playing too much he risked burning out or getting injured. The winter circuit simply offered a good opportunity to pick up some extra cash, and no player was more adept at exploiting the expenses system and wringing money from tournament directors—in many cases setting the standard for other top players to follow.

In fact, for Bobby it was a point of personal pride. If another player managed to extort a given sum from a tournament director, Bobby made sure he got at least the same deal. Gardnar Mulloy recalled one tournament in Florida in which Bobby sat at the gate collecting the money from the ticket-seller every time an admission was sold.

After a few short weeks in the Sunbelt, Bobby built up a respectable bankroll. Having achieved everything he set out to do in his original "five-year plan," his goal now was to turn professional. The best players were in the professional ranks—Don Budge, Ellsworth Vines, and Fred Perry—and Bobby wanted a shot at them. With Wimbledon, the Davis Cup, and many other major international events suspended because of the war, Bobby figured all he had to do was successfully defend his title at Forest Hills to gain an invitation to join the pros.

By the start of the grass court season, Kay was back by his side, and Bobby's form was coming around. Having traded in his fancy Cord, Bobby and Kay traveled around in a roomier Buick Roadmaster. The couple went to 15 tournaments, with Bobby winning nine. Going into Seabright, however, the defending champion and top seed had to be considered an underdog. The hottest player that year was Don McNeill, the hard-charging collegian from Oklahoma. Since his upset of Bobby in the final of the French championships the year before, it was all coming together for McNeill. He and Bobby had played against each other four times that season, with each man winning twice.

Also beginning to make a name for himself was Frank Kovacs from Northern California. Tall and handsome, Kovacs had literally grown up in the shadow of Don Budge. The two lived on the same street in Oakland, a couple of blocks away from each other. Four years younger than Budge, Kovacs was the son of an upholstery worker, Frank Sr., who had emigrated from Hungary in 1910. The tall youth started playing paddle tennis at 12, switching to tennis after several months and getting a few pointers from Budge's older brother, Lloyd, also an accomplished player. After five months of pleading, he convinced his father to buy him his first racquet. It was "a thing of rare beauty, at $3.98," recalled Kovacs. At 14, he scraped up enough money to buy some lessons, and he began to emulate his neighbor, Don Budge.

In many ways his game reminded people of Budge's in its sustained power, with a big serve, picture-perfect groundstrokes, and a punishing return of service. And like Budge, his best shot was his backhand, a shot he liked to hit hard and low over the net at a sharp angle crosscourt. When he played well, Kovacs seemed unbeatable, capable of putting on dazzling displays of talent. He was considered for the Davis Cup team in 1938, but was dropped after his coach and mentor, George Hudson, got into a dispute with the USLTA when it banned him from acting as Kovacs' manager. In response, Hudson threatened to sue.

As brilliant as Kovacs was, he was also wildly unpredictable. A bit of a screwball, he often seemed more interested in hamming it up for the galleries than playing serious tennis. He would joke around, resort to trick shots, and tease his opponent. In the San Francisco City Championships one year, he threw up three balls on his service, striking the middle one for a clean ace. Another time, in the semifinal of a tournament in Glen Cove, N.Y., Kovacs raced down a ball that pulled him far wide of the court, sent up a high lob, and while everyone else watched the ball, he proceeded to sit down in the grandstand and applaud his opponent's smash into an empty court, leaving a bewildered opponent, chair umpire, and many in the audience to wonder where he had disappeared to.

His antics made him popular with fans. Young girls swooned over him, begging for autographs. But many players considered Kovacs' behavior a deliberate attempt to disrupt play and antagonize them. At the same time, Kovacs could also be his own worst enemy. Just as often his behavior would sabotage his own game, as it did in the third round of the national championships at Forest Hills in 1938 against Gene Mako.

As Mako recalled, "First of all, he's 35 or 40 minutes late at Forest Hills, the national championship. The officials come over to me and they say, 'Now look, if you want to you can have him defaulted.' But I don't want a default, so I say let's wait a while.

" 'Well, how long do you want to wait?'

" 'I don't care. Let's wait.'

"About fifteen to twenty minutes later, he comes in with 17 racquets under his arm, sauntering. And he says 'Call it,' [to spin the racquet to decide who serves] and I said whatever I said and he drops all 17 racquets. You see, that's supposed to be funny. In the meantime, by the way, I asked Budge to warm up with me. We always would warm each other up for ten, fifteen, twenty, thirty-minutes before we'd play. Well, I was warm and ready to go, *real* ready. So when I see this chickenshit guy doing this stuff, I say to myself all I have to do is hang in with this guy and I will win. I have no way to lose if I hang in. That's the first thing you have think of when you play with a guy who's chickenshit.

"It was on Court 6 or something, one of the back courts where there aren't bleachers, but people can stand around and watch. And there are maybe 200 people standing around, and they're all tittering and laughing a little bit. He has on sort of a half-assed topcoat or something. It was an overcast day, but it wasn't cold. So we walk out on the court to warm up, and the first ball I hit to him, he hits a backhand on the forehand side. The second ball he hits between his legs, which gets everybody laughing. And then the third one he hits behind his back. Then he says, 'Are you ready?'—like it's a joke. Yes, I am. The guy in the chair goes, 'Linesmen ready? Players ready? Play.'

"He starts serving, and I won the first game and we change sides and he takes a big sweater off. Then I hold serve and break him the second time he serves. He takes another sweater off. He's still got a couple more under there, which I didn't know. Now it's 3-love. Now, I hold serve and break him again. It's 5-love. He takes another sweater off. In the meantime, everybody is laughing. And while they're laughing it's 6-love, 2-love in the second set. I won the first eight games while he was jacking off before he won a game. He's giving me a set plus two games, literally. I won that set 6-2, and then the third set he played like a son-of-a-bitch and I beat him 8-6. So in the most important tournament of the year he loses 6-0, 6-2, 8-6 in the third round because he's an asshole." Mako went on to the final, where he lost to his best friend and doubles partner, Budge, capping Budge's history-making Grand Slam.

Said Budge in 1941 of growing up with Kovacs, "When Kovacs forgot his horseplay, I very often could get only two or three games a set from him… There's nobody he can't beat."

To this Kovacs answered, "Budge is all wrong. Me get serious? Honestly, when I get grim on the court I dump the ball into the net or drive it over the fence. I can't stand the strain of being tense. It makes me want to scream, and sometimes I do. I've got to have laughs to play good tennis." Off court, Kovacs was equally eccentric—funny, often outrageous, and a downright cad. He strung along girlfriends in cities wherever he went, mooching money, meals, and places to stay before unceremoniously dumping them.

Arm trouble sidelined Kovacs for much of 1939, but in the year-end Pacific Coast Championships in his hometown of Berkeley, Kovacs pushed Bobby to the limit, losing 6-3, 2-6, 6-4, 2-6, 7-5, in the final. He spent the winter of 1940 on a tour of the Pacific, returning to the States in late spring. At the National Clay Court Championships in June, the unpredictable Kovacs showed up one day with hair almost down to his shoulders; the next day he arrived completely bald. Asked by a reporter why he shaved his head, Kovacs boasted, "To keep the pretty girls away."

On a blistering hot afternoon at Seabright in 1940, however, Kovacs put aside his clowning. In a three-and-a-half-hour match that Bobby later described as one of his best ever, he and Kovacs met to decide the championship. Before the match, a sister of Edmund Lynch, Bobby's benefactor, offered odds of 10-1 that Bobby would beat Kovacs, who had since let his hair grow back. "For just two bucks they figured to win twenty if Kovacs beat me," Bobby said. "I didn't blame them for betting. At those odds I'd bet on any underdog player to beat the highest-ranking favorite. How much can you lose?"

Kovacs played exceptionally well, hitting with such depth and pace that Bobby—considered the fastest man in the game—could not run down many of his shots. Kovacs was especially successful hitting a sharp angle to one side of the court, followed by a ripping reply to the opposite corner. Bobby could only watch as the shots streaked by. Unable to counter the onslaught, Bobby lost the first two sets quickly, 6-2, 6-0. Those holding 10-1 bets could almost smell the money.

Baffled, exasperated, and tired from running around, Bobby requested a chair at the next changeover. He needed to collect his thoughts. With Davis Cup Captain Walter Pate, USLTA President Holcombe Ward, and Kay looking on, the national champion was downright embarrassed. But when the chair arrived, Kovacs cheekily sat in it and calmly began to comb his hair. A shocked Bobby "fumed, fretted, expostulated—and wound up reclining on the ground." He looked up to chair umpire Ben Dwight and asked if he could put on spiked shoes, hoping to gain some extra speed to chase down Kovacs' lightning bolts.

After consulting with tournament referee Ward, Dwight answered: "No. The courts are dry. Spikes aren't necessary."

In an attempt to throw Kovacs off his game, Bobby started adjusting the length and pace of his shots. The tactic worked, as Bobby started to benefit from Kovacs' errors. Bobby won the third set, 6-3.

During the intermission between the third and fourth sets, Bobby again asked for spikes, and again was refused. But he had begun to turn things around. He started to serve more effectively, at one point pulling off three clean aces in a row. He also started to come to the net behind it, serving out wide and then volleying into the open court. But whenever Kovacs got his racquet on the ball, Bobby likely as not saw it whiz past him. The two traded service breaks for much of the set. Serving at 5-6, 15-40, Bobby saved two match points. First, Kovacs sent a passing shot wide. Bobby then made a beautiful volley off the top of his shoes, allowing him to hold his serve and bring the set to six games all.

Serving again at 8-9 in the fourth set, Bobby ran off 11 straight points to put the set within reach. Serving at 9-10, love-40, Kovacs saved two set points, but Bobby won the third to finally take the set, 11-9.

Early in the fifth set, Kovacs charged out to a 3-1, 40-love lead. Things again looked bad for Bobby, but he managed to break back to even things up. At 5-6 on his own serve, Bobby saved a third match point with another low volley. Deuce. A missed passing shot by Bobby gave Kovacs a fourth match point. Ad-out. After missing his first serve, Bobby hit a careful twist serve to spin the ball into the service box. Kovacs pounded the return, pulling Bobby far out of court. Bobby managed to get to the ball, just barely, but his attempted crosscourt pass was weak, an easy put-away for Kovacs, who stood poised at the net for an obvious kill. Instead of smashing the ball, however, Kovacs, ever the showman, struck a dramatic pose and laid a softly caressed drop volley into Bobby's court.

Before Kovacs had even struck the ball, Bobby started running, having anticipated Kovacs' play. Appearing from nowhere, he got to the ball an instant before it reached the ground, sending it back across and nearly parallel to the net before sliding under the umpire's chair. Meanwhile, Kovacs figured the point was won and the match over. He had taken his racquet and stuck it between his legs, ready to shake hands with his vanquished opponent. Instead, all he could do was helplessly watch as the ball floated past. Point lost. An awestruck Kovacs bowed to Bobby in admiration. Kovacs managed to hold out a few games longer, but the fire had been extinguished from his game. At 7-8, Bobby was finally allowed to change to spikes, and succeeded in winning the final three games and the match, 2-6, 0-6, 6-3, 11-9, 10-8. This was Bobby's third victory at Seabright, allowing him to retire the elegant Seabright Bowl. It also saved Lynch's sister a lot of money.

Asked about the lost match point afterwards, Kovacs said, "Any dub could have made the first match point the easy way. But wouldn't that stop volley have wowed 'em if it worked?"

After the singles final, a thoroughly drained Bobby then had to go on court for the doubles final, where he and Welby Van Horn were to play the team of Ted Schroeder and Jack Kramer. Bobby and Van Horn had beaten the young team in two previous tournaments and were well on their way to doing it again, up two sets to love, 5-0 in the third, when Bobby suddenly seemed to quit trying, missing easy shots and joking around. Van Horn and Bobby ended up losing, 7-9, 8-10, 7-5, 6-3, 6-3.

At first, an infuriated Van Horn thought his partner threw the match, wondering if Bobby had bet big against himself. Actually, recalled Kramer, Bobby bet him and Schroeder $100 each that he would win the match. The truth was Bobby was exhausted from his singles marathon against Kovacs, so he simply went through the motions for the final three sets. "He didn't throw it," Van Horn said years later, "but he was less motivated."

A couple of weeks later, before the national doubles championships in Boston, Bobby sought out Kramer. He wanted to ask him if he would play doubles with him, thinking he could make a little extra money on the side. "He figured that I was still pretty unknown," Kramer recalled, "and he could get a better price playing with the kid." Bobby offered him $1,000 to dump Schroeder and play with him at the national doubles championships at Longwood. Kramer politely refused, but nonetheless took the offer as a compliment, saying later it was the first time he really believed himself a top-notch doubles player. Kramer and Schroeder went on to win the national championships, the youngest team yet to do so.

Going into Forest Hills, the general consensus was that the title belonged either to Bobby, McNeill, or Kovacs. The three had been swapping victories in the events leading up to the nationals. The seeding committee placed the defending champion in the No. 1 position, followed by McNeill and Kovacs. Also lurking in the wings were Frank Parker, Joe Hunt, and Welby Van Horn, the previous year's finalist.

Bobby had an extra incentive to do well at Forest Hills. Jack Harris, promoter of the pro tour with Budge, Vines, and Perry, made it clear to Bobby that waiting for him was a $25,000 guarantee, a percentage of the gate, and a chance to take on Budge.

When the draw for the tournament put Riggs and Kovacs in one half, and McNeill in the other, most tennis experts immediately forecast a McNeill-Kovacs final. True to form, Bobby and McNeill marched through their halves of the draw to the semi-finals. Kramer and Schroeder, both 19, surprised everybody by reaching the semi-finals and quarterfinals, respectively. The biggest news of the tournament, however, was not the ascendancy of Kramer and

Schroeder, the rivalry of McNeill and Bobby, or the utter collapse of the previous year's finalist, Van Horn, who lost in the second round. It was the exit of Kovacs, who lost in straight sets to Joe Hunt in the fourth round. Though Kovacs had proven capable of losing to anybody, the news was the style in which he lost it.

Before the tournament, USLTA head Holcombe Ward sent a letter to Kovacs: "My dear boy, your deplorable clowning on the court, which has marred the current lawn-tennis season, will not be tolerated at Forest Hills. We strongly urge you to be serious." To which Kovacs replied, "My dear Mr. Ward, I will try very hard to be serious on the court during the coming tournament. But something tells me I shall not succeed."

If only Ward knew how grandly Kovacs would fail.

The honchos at Forest Hills tried to isolate Kovacs, or at least deprive him of his audience, by scheduling his early round matches on secluded outer courts. It didn't work, as Kovacs was enormously popular with the crowds, who pushed to get a glimpse of their hero while the cavernous cement stadium remained relatively empty. What the starchy officials of the game did not understand, and would not understand until the game went open, is that tennis players are also entertainers, and that fans would pay as much to watch a character like Kovacs as a perfectionist like Budge. By Kovacs' fourth round match against Joe Hunt, the organizers reluctantly scheduled the match in the main stadium.

Though Kovacs was expected to wallop Hunt, 10,000 fans crowded into the horseshoe-shaped arena, anxious to see what kind of show Kovacs would put on. They didn't have to wait long. Kovacs hadn't been on court five minutes warming up for the match before he had the gallery rippling with laughter. "While the photographers fired away, the strident stringbean chattered to the sidelines, struck Napoleonic poses at the net, pulled off trick shots, and ignored Hunt completely."

The antics continued even after play had begun, and Hunt grew increasingly angry. At 1-all, 15-30 in the third set, a scowling Hunt was fed up. He sat down on the baseline, telling the chair umpire that he refused to continue until Kovacs stopped goofing off. Seeing this, a beaming Kovacs sat down on his baseline. He then playfully pretended to knit as 10,000 startled fans and officials looked on in astonishment.

While Hunt sulked and outraged officials huffed and puffed, Kovacs waved to the spectators, then stretched out on the turf and pretended to snore. After much conferring and pleading with the players, the officials convinced Kovacs to continue playing. The umpire announced, "Players ready? Play." But even after Kovacs stood up and resumed serving, Hunt still sat, fuming, his back turned to Kovacs. He let a few balls fly past him before getting up, then finished off Kovacs rather handily to win in three straight sets, 6-4, 6-1, 6-4.

Naturally, the next day's papers led with the first-ever sit-down strike on center court. A still happy Kovacs said, "What of it, boys? Don't take it so hard. Tennis is only a game." Then, using a line Bobby would borrow later in his matches against Kramer and Billie Jean King, Kovacs added, "Besides, I can beat Hunt every day of the week and twice on Sunday."

Joe Hunt played Bobby in the semifinal, a replay of the year before. This time, however, Bobby had to go all out to beat Hunt, winning after five long, hard-fought sets, 4-6, 6-3, 5-7, 6-3, 6-4. But it had taken nearly everything out of him. Earlier in the week, Bobby had come down with a chest cold, and as the tournament progressed it had gotten worse. After the match with Hunt, he felt bad enough to seek out a doctor. He had a big test before him in the form of McNeil, who had defeated Kramer to reach the final. Was there anything Bobby could do to make himself feel better? he asked. Yes, the doctor answered. Don't play.

That, however, was not an option. The night before the final, Bobby seemed to be running a fever and felt lousy, Kay recalled. She put Bobby to bed early and opened a window in their hotel room to let in a breeze. Overnight, it started to rain and became very cool. When Bobby awoke the next morning, he felt even worse. So bad, in fact, that he told Kay he didn't think he could play. But this was the final and there would be no default.

At the West Side Tennis Club, a decidedly pro-McNeill crowd was on hand, eager to see the rangy Oklahoman beat the puckish Bobby, whom one reporter characterized as "a two-fisted dead-end kid from the wrong side of the Los Angeles railroad track." It was windy, and the rain from the night before made the court slick and slow. The conditions would make it more difficult for both players.

Minus his usual cheerful demeanor, the defending champion gravely took the court. He had defeated McNeill just a couple of weeks earlier at Rye, also on grass, and earlier that spring at the national indoor championships on fast carpet. Both had been long, hard-fought battles; if anything, Bobby figured the wins gave him an edge.

McNeill started off cold. He had trouble getting to the net, and when he did his volleys tended to miss. Meanwhile, Bobby may have surprised himself at how well he played this day, or rather, how well he felt. Instead of trying to rush to the net to end the points quickly, he succeeded in playing his usual game, hanging back, letting McNeill bring the game to him. Bobby won the first set, 6-4.

The gallery was boisterously in McNeill's corner, clapping loudly every time he hit a winner while offering only polite applause each time Bobby hit a nice shot. "I knew Kay was clapping for me, though, and I kept trying," Bobby said. "I always keep trying."

After trading service breaks early in the second set, the two players fought fiercely for control. Given his flu, Bobby wanted to end the match as quickly as possible. If he could take a two-sets-to-love lead it might be enough to push McNeill over the edge. Bobby dug in and gave it everything he had, winning the set, 8-6. But the effort clearly drained him. His game fell apart, and McNeill blasted his way to win the third and fourth sets, 6-3, 6-3.

By now, the crowd was completely involved in the match, shouting and clapping at the efforts of both players.

Bobby changed gears. In an effort to catch McNeill off-guard and to save what little energy he had, Bobby decided to quicken the points by coming to the net at every opportunity. With the score tied at 4-all, McNeill saved two break points to make it deuce. He served and rushed the net, hitting a sharply angled crosscourt volley into Bobby's forehand court. At first, the linesman indicated the ball was out, and a simultaneous cry from the gallery followed:

"Out!" But then the linesman held down the "safe" signal, indicating the ball was good. Bobby, his back turned to the linesman, did not know of the change until umpire Ben Dwight called the score: "Advantage McNeill." Unbelieving, Bobby walked up to the linesman and cried out, "For the love of Pete!" This was the harshest language fans heard from Bobby on court. But the linesman held firm, and Bobby, without any show of disappointment, accepted the decision and walked back to return serve. He put McNeill's service in play, rushed the net and was passed by a beautiful shot from McNeill, 5-4.

After Bobby held serve to knot things at 5-all, new balls were brought out—an advantage to the server because new balls fly through the air more quickly. McNeill saved a break point after two brilliant passing shots by Bobby and held serve. With Bobby serving at 5-6, McNeill returned serve with a scoop shot that dropped just over the net with lots of backspin. Bobby rushed to the net and managed to put the ball back in play, but it was so close to the net when he hit it that he had trouble stopping in time. He used body English to keep his shorts from grazing the net, but umpire Dwight announced the point was McNeill's because Bobby's foot had touched the net. To the hisses of the gallery, Bobby walked over to the chair to ask exactly what happened, and when informed he calmly walked back to serve, love-15.

McNeill slammed Bobby's next serve far beyond the baseline, drawing cheers from the fans, who assumed McNeill intentionally threw the point in a gesture of good sportsmanship (McNeill would later say that he thought about throwing the point, but the miss was simply a dreadful shot.). Score: 15-all.

The game went to deuce. McNeill got his first match point with a sharp attacking volley after a powerful drive that pulled Bobby out of court. Bobby saved himself by coming in behind his serve and volleying behind McNeill on his forehand side, causing McNeill to fall flat. Deuce again. Two points later, McNeill saved game point by running down a volley to his forehand side, catching it just before it hit the turf and flicking it for a brilliant crosscourt pass. It was, recalled McNeill, an "impossible" shot, "the best I'd ever hit in my life." And "it couldn't have come at a better time, as it so unnerved Riggs that he missed two difficult low volleys coming behind his serve at deuce and match point. I got the feeling he was desperate."

Match point. The final ball rose off Bobby's racquet, a half-volley off his shoe tops. For a moment, it looked as if it might just drop over the other side of the net, but then it caught the tape and fell back to Bobby's side. Game, set, and match. Beaten and exhausted, Bobby managed to leap over the net to congratulate the new champion.

Bobby never made excuses, he never complained publicly about the two calls that may have cost him the match, or about his illness. With nothing but sincere congratulations for the man who vanquished him, he said, "Don played great tennis that day, and deserved everything he got."

The match was trumpeted as one of the finest ever at Forest Hills, comparable to the epic battles of Tilden and "Little Bill" Johnson in the Twenties. Moreover, wrote *American Lawn Tennis*, "never did a champion lose his crown more gracefully than did Bobby Riggs."

But it was a bitter loss, more so than his loss to Adrian Quist in the Davis Cup final the year before, as it cost him a spot on the pro tour against Budge. But his heroic effort and the complete dignity with which he carried himself had earned him something perhaps even greater, something he had never had up to that point: respect. Before the match he was the ruffian, the villain. When he walked off, he was a hero.

Wrote the Associated Press: "When Riggs walked off the court after Dwight Davis presented the championship trophy to McNeill, the crowd gave him a burst of prolonged applause. Partly because he had been beaten, but more because they knew that in the past year of his reign he hadn't been treated as a champion should be. And, heartsick as he was, Bobby walked off in that Charlie Chaplin manner of his, with a big grin on his face."

Back from the brink. A relieved Bobby relaxes for a photograph after winning back the national championship trophy at Forest Hills in 1941 against his arch-rival, Frank Kovacs.

9

Of Nerve and Endurance
1941

The train ride from New York to Chicago the day after Forest Hills was dismal. The feeling on board was akin to a wake. In a sense, someone had, in fact, died. After all, amateur tennis was supposed to be "a stepping-stone" for Bobby. His ultimate goal, turning professional, appeared shattered by his loss to Don McNeill. Without the national title, he didn't have the drawing power to turn pro. In his mind, he might as well go back to his dog food account at the ad agency or get a job teaching tennis to country club kids. "It seemed as though all my years of work had been wasted," he said.

Before boarding, Bobby blew up at his wife Kay, telling her it was all her fault that he lost, arguing that if she hadn't left the window open the night before he would not have gotten sick.

Bobby was just blowing off steam. He had been sick with the flu the entire week leading up to the final. The open window had nothing to do with his loss. Besides, he had a difficult time getting truly mad. His tantrums were almost comical. "For anger, the best he could do would be to literally foam at the mouth. When he got worked up and started screeching in that little voice of his, small flecks of spit would form at the corners," recalled Kramer.

Still, it was an unusually glum Bobby who boarded the train with Kay, Ted Schroeder, and Jack Kramer. The two youngsters were scheduled to play an exhibition in Chicago later that week.

During the overnight ride, while Kay slept, Kramer and Schroeder kept Bobby company, trying to take his mind off the crushing defeat. As the three men absentmindedly played cards, Kramer and Schroeder made small talk—about girls, cars, baseball, the war, anything but tennis. Bobby joined in the chitchat, but clearly his mind was stuck on the stadium court at the West Side Tennis Club and his uncertain future. To Schroeder's and Kramer's amazement, not once did he gripe about the loss, or even mention it.

Back home, however, the loss hurt Bobby as no loss ever had before. He replayed the match in his head compulsively. He had trouble sleeping, sometimes waking up in a cold sweat, so exhausted he would roll over and sleep in half the morning. He was depressed, confused, and angry. For a brief moment, he even considered quitting tennis altogether.

Kay quickly brought Bobby back around. "Look Riggs," she said, "We'll win it back. We'll stay in the amateurs and win it back." Bobby had beaten McNeill three out of the five times they played leading up to nationals, so McNeill was not a superior player. He had been better than Bobby on that specific occasion, and that was all.

Though he lost the title and his chance at the pros, Bobby had not lost his status as a gate attraction. At the Pacific Southwest Championships, Perry Jones forked over an until-then unheard of amount of $800 in expense money to entice Bobby to play. After a relatively easy straight-set victory over Jack Kramer in the semifinals, Bobby again faced McNeill, who by then was on a more than 20-match winning streak. McNeill quickly went up two sets to love, and it again looked bad for Bobby. But with a great attack, cool defense, and grim determination, Bobby hung in and defeated McNeill, 5-7, 2-6, 6-0, 12-10, 6-3. After over three hours of play, McNeill was, according to *American Lawn Tennis*, "literally staggering from fatigue."

It was an important victory for Bobby, if only to prove to himself that he should continue, a feeling confirmed the following week at the season-ending Pacific Coast Championships in

Berkeley, which Bobby won in the final with a four-set victory over Frank Kovacs.

By the end of 1940, Bobby lost the No. 1 ranking. He was No. 2 behind McNeill, with Kovacs in the third position. Even so, Bobby played more matches and won more tournaments than any other top player (13 of 19 tournaments in singles alone). He also posted winning records over both McNeill (4 of 7) and Kovacs (2 of 3). Still, Bobby's disappointment at losing the national title only fortified his determination to regain the No. 1 position the following year.

For her part, Kay completely embraced Bobby's career, taking personal charge of his comeback. She imposed a strict training regimen and made sure he stuck to it. The program included everything from conditioning and diet (he must have consumed "ten thousand" milkshakes with raw eggs in them, she said) to his grooming and wardrobe. Gone were the greasy locks and the ill-fitting shorts. Before meeting Kay, Bobby never paid much attention to his appearance. Before hitting the road, he simply packed his tennis clothes with a pair of baggy slacks and a V-neck sweater. That was all about to change. Kay wanted Bobby to start looking like a champion.

"I had a friend in California who was a seamstress and made beautiful shorts for Bobby," Kay recalled. "I decided he needed to have a cool haircut. He had to have something different than everybody else, so I had him get a crewcut so he'd stand out." Kay also had Bobby buy some fine tailored suits for those nights during a tournament when he was expected to appear at a party or reception.

Bobby entered every event he could—not to pad his bank account with expense money as he had the previous year, but to toughen himself. Starting in December with the Sugar Bowl tournament in New Orleans, the southern winter circuit proceeded to Tampa, then Orlando, St. Petersburg, Coral Gables, West Palm Beach, Ft. Lauderdale, Jacksonville, and Pensacola. At first, Bobby thought his primary competition would be McNeill. But as the season progressed it became increasingly clear that Kovacs, since dubbed the "Clown Prince of Tennis" by sports writers, posed his biggest challenge. Though Kovacs could be his own worst enemy, when he was "on" he was nearly unbeatable. During the trip, Bobby lost to Kovacs four straight times.

Dealing with Kovacs' dazzling shotmaking was one thing. Contending with his completely unpredictable behavior was another. Although Bobby was not above gamesmanship on court, he always played within the rules. Kovacs pushed them beyond the breaking point. If things were not exactly to Kovacs' liking, or perhaps even if they were, he was liable to simply walk off the court.

Gardnar Mulloy recalled a match at Newport in which Kovacs was having a difficult time against a low-ranked player. Playing in ninety-degree-plus heat, Kovacs suddenly decided he'd had enough. He dropped his racquet, held his head in his hands, and claimed to be suffering from sunstroke. Defaulting the match, Kovacs was carried off the court into the dressing room, where he was laid down. He immediately sat up and quipped, "Thanks for the lift, boys," and left the grounds.

It seemed that whenever Bobby and Kovacs faced each other, Kovacs went out of his way to devise new ways to upset Bobby. In Miami, Kovacs and Bobby were set to face each other in the best-of-five-set final. A shaggy-looking Kovacs, who decided to let his beard grow during the course of the tournament, goofed off initially, mugging it up for the crowd, hitting trick shots, and basically handing Bobby the first two sets. After deciding to play seriously, Kovacs put up a fierce struggle to pull out the third set, 8-6. At this point the players were given a 10-minute rest break.

As they walked off the court to take their break, Bobby, wary of what Kovacs might pull, warned the umpire, "I'm going to stay right here during the rest period. This tournament has a ten-minute rule for intermissions, and I'll be ready to play in exactly ten minutes. You'd better tell that to Kovacs."

The umpire leaned over and notified Kovacs that he had to be back on court in 10 minutes. Kovacs listened carefully and nodded, then walked off the court, presumably to go to the locker room.

Ten minutes passed and Kovacs was nowhere to be seen. Bobby reminded the umpire of the rules, but was convinced to wait a couple of minutes longer. More time passed and there was still no sign of Kovacs. Someone in the gallery came forward to say that he saw Kovacs leave the grounds, get in a car, and drive off.

Fuming, Bobby turned to the umpire to ask for a default, but was asked to be patient. "But Bobby," they pleaded, "it will look very bad to default the match now. All these people paid a lot of money to see you two play. They'll raise hell if the match isn't finished."

After a half-hour, Kovacs bounded onto the court. "Well, I'm ready!" he announced cheerfully, bowing apologies to the gallery. A seething Bobby refused to acknowledge Kovacs, but with nothing left to do but play, he returned to the court. By now, however, Bobby was so angry it affected his game. Kovacs jumped to 3-0 lead in the fourth set. Bobby briefly fought back to even the set, but Kovacs' fierce hitting prevailed, 8-6. In the fifth set, an infuriated Bobby ceased trying, and let Kovacs run away with the set and match, 4-6, 1-6, 8-6, 8-6, 6-1.

The one-upmanship between the two players spilled off the court. Throughout the season, Bobby needled Kovacs over the incident in Newport in which Kovacs defaulted after feigning an injury. For weeks, he taunted Kovacs about quitting, saying that he would never abandon a match under any circumstances. The rivalry between the two reached a low point at the National Indoor Championships in Oklahoma City in March, where Bobby and Kovacs were seeded Nos.1 and 2, respectively, and were expected to fight it out in the final.

As recalled by Gardnar Mulloy, throughout the week Kovacs kept telling Bobby what a great player he was and how he admired his character and intelligence; how wonderful it was that Bobby never defaulted a match, no matter how injured or ill he felt. Mulloy recalled Bobby beaming with each compliment.

As expected, Bobby and Kovacs reached the final. The night before the big match, the players were all at dinner, where Kovacs continued his flattery. Suddenly, Bobby became violently ill and immediately left the table to return to his room. He was up most of the night in pain, and woke up the next day with a splitting headache.

Before going on court, Kovacs told Bobby how sorry he was, telling him it was too bad he would need to default, and wasn't it a shame to break such a splendid no-default record.

Bobby was in no condition to play tennis, but this was a final. He would not default. In an attempt to reduce the painful glare of the overhead lights inside the auditorium, Bobby rubbed lampblack under his eyes. He also decided to end points as quickly as possible by charging the net at every opportunity. But each time Bobby rushed forward, Kovacs passed him at will, leaving Bobby to shake his head despondently after each point.

On the changeovers, Kovacs solicitously asked, "Are you sure you don't want to default Bobby? You sure are pale." Bobby never answered, but painfully continued. By the time Kovacs won the match, 6-4, 6-0, 6-2, Bobby could barely stand.

Months later, Mulloy said, Kovacs admitted that he spiked Bobby's drink the night before with a Mickey Finn to make him ill. Bobby, however, never made much of the incident, even though it became common knowledge among the other players. Perhaps Bobby refused to believe Kovacs was venal enough to do so, or perhaps he decided to take his revenge out on the court.

Whatever the case, Bobby knew Kovacs' brilliance was matched by his tendency to self-destruct. Taking careful mental notes after each loss to Kovacs, Bobby prepared himself for what he expected to be an ultimate showdown with the "Clown Prince." On pure tennis ability, he felt reasonably sure he could hit the ball on even terms with Kovacs, but he was dead sure he could outthink and outfight him.

Off court, Bobby's troubles with the USLTA persisted. The association's watchdogs began pressuring him about his so-called advertising job in Chicago. The rules committee at the USLTA informed Bobby that, because the United States Advertising Corp. handled the Wilson Sporting Goods account, it suspected the job was a dummy and that Bobby didn't do any actual work. Recalling his door-to-door dog food survey during the cold winter of 1939,

Bobby was tempted to put up a fight. He declined, but not because of what the tennis establishment thought of him. Rather than embarrass his benefactors at Wilson and risk a suspension in the midst of his quest to regain the national title, Bobby decided to quit the ad agency and accept a job as an assistant to the public-relations director of Presbyterian College in Clinton, S.C.—another job set up through his friend L.B. Icely at Wilson.

Long before Ilie Nastase and John McEnroe became known as the game's most famous brats, Frank Kovacs (right) earned the nickname "The Clown Prince of Tennis" for his oncourt antics. His rivalry with Bobby sometimes spilled off the court.

Bobby arrived in Clinton in the spring of 1941. To welcome the newest addition to their staff, the college threw a banquet for Bobby and Kay. Bobby's collegiate hosts assured the couple that the school would make the two of them feel at home. This included, of course, allowing the town's newest and most-famous resident all the time he needed to play tennis. Bobby smiled appreciatively and told the gathering how happy he was to be there and how much he and Kay looked forward to becoming a part of the community.

No sooner had the hors d'oeuvres grown cold, than Kay returned to Chicago. Hospitality aside, for a city-born and -bred woman such as her, living in a backwater like Clinton was like living in a cave. Besides, Forest Hills was just a few months away, and with a full slate of tournaments in between, Bobby would be spending little time in Clinton himself.

By summer, Bobby was playing the finest tennis of his career. He drew even in his rivalry with Kovacs at four matches apiece, and during the grass court circuit made history by winning at Seabright and Southampton for a fourth time (over Schroeder and Kovacs, respectively), an achievement unmatched by any player, even Budge.

No longer considered a retriever, Bobby had turned into an all-court player. He mixed his incredible touch and finesse with power and a dead-on instinct for the kill, moving to the net without hesitation and decisively putting away balls. Tactically, he was unequalled. He could match his opponents shot for shot, neutralize their biggest weapons, frustrate them with a mind-bending variety of shots, and surely and steadily break them down. Not only that, but Bobby could adapt to any surface.

"The play of Riggs at Seabright and Southampton cannot be praised too highly or have attached to it too much weight," crowed *American Lawn Tennis* editor Stephen Wallis Merrihew, who two years before denounced Bobby's game as "monotonous" and "uninspiring." Said Merrihew, "A brain of the first order dominated Riggs' game and raised it to a pinnacle that has not often been equaled in recent years."

McNeill, meanwhile, who had started 1941 as the nation's No. 1 player, had fallen from contention. Up until the event in Newport the week before Forest Hills, he had not won a single tournament. He lost all of his matches against both Bobby and Kovacs, the latter of whom he had previously "owned," going undefeated against Kovacs the year before.

For Kay, there was another benefit to having Bobby reach so many finals. As the crowd of players dwindled over the course of the tournament, she got to spend plenty of time with Bobby alone. Years later, she pleasantly recalled having spent many days with

Bobby at the movies, sometimes sitting through two or three features in a row to kill time.

One aspect of Bobby's life that Kay left alone, in spite of what she and Bobby told the press, was Bobby's need to gamble. While tales about all-night poker marathons and fortunes won and lost were largely exaggerated, she later said, Bobby continued to play cards and dice. To give it up would be like asking him not to breathe. Besides, it kept his competitive fires burning, exercised his mind, and focused his concentration.

During the early rounds of a tournament, when the competition was light and all the players were around, it was easy to find a game. Typically, Bobby would leave for the evening, telling Kay he would be back no later than midnight. If he was lucky enough to get involved in a high-stakes game with one of the club's wealthy members, he might then send a runner up to Kay's room to say he would be back by 2:00 a.m. If that didn't buy him enough time, Bobby would send another runner up to tell Kay he would be back no later than 4:00 a.m.

To win in high-stakes gambling requires two things: nerve and endurance. That is, the nerve to risk it all yet remain composed in the face of imminent disaster, and the endurance to keep playing—all night, if necessary—until things turn your way. Bobby understood this.

At Rye in 1941, a big-shot movie executive, Gradwell Sears, showed up wanting to play some craps. At the Westchester-Biltmore, a Ping-Pong table was quickly converted into a playing surface. As the stakes rose, it didn't take long for most of the players to quit or be cleaned out, leaving just the movie executive, Bobby, Bitsy Grant, and Grant's friend, Champ Reese, holding the dice. A group of others, including Kramer and Schroeder, stood around the table looking on. As the game went deep into the night, Sears' losses started to mount. He began to panic, and tried to make up for his losses by wagering larger and larger sums. Schroeder and Kramer looked on in amazement as Bobby matched the producer bet for bet, cheerfully luring him in for the kill, almost goading him to raise the stakes even higher. Every so often, Bobby remembered Kay, and sent Schroeder up to her hotel room to say he would be finished soon. "He's up $1,000… He's up $3,000," Schroeder excitedly told Kay about Bobby's progress. By around 3:00 a.m., it was over. Bobby won $5,000; Grant won $3,000, and Reese won $800. Sears took out his checkbook and wrote out the checks. Dead tired, Bobby decided he needed sleep, but not before asking Kramer if he would drive Kay to New York that very morning to the bank in order to cash the producer's check. This was one debt Bobby intended to collect.

Despite his rapacious nature, many remember Bobby as very generous. As one of the few players able to make ends meet playing tennis, Bobby enjoyed helping other players out: offering rides, places to stay, or money, often with little or no expectation of being paid back. Years later, Bobby showed a similar soft spot for people down on their luck, offering total strangers money, time, advice, or a place to stay—allowing them to become part of his motley entourage. Perhaps it was because of his religious upbringing, a sense of "There by the grace of God go I." Or perhaps it was for the attention, the self-inflated passing of grace by an emperor upon his loyal subjects. With his gang beside him, Bobby could bask in the ego-massaging adulation. Whatever the case, it made him feel good. Bobby might have been a lot of things, but he was not cold or malicious.

With his $5,000 in winnings safely in the bank after Rye, Bobby set about reclaiming his national title at Forest Hills. Yet, despite his fine play leading up to the championships, and despite being the top seed ahead of Kovacs, No. 2, and defending champion McNeill, No. 3, Bobby was far from the fan favorite. There was, in fact, a palpable sense of disappointment when it was revealed that Kovacs and McNeill were in the same half of the draw. There would be no final between the hard-hitting McNeill and the erratic though vastly entertaining, Kovacs. Also, because of the war, it was a small draw, just 64 players instead of the usual 128.

Bobby played with grave seriousness the entire tournament, which was the culmination of a yearlong mission. There was no mugging it up for the crowd, no all-night poker marathons. Nothing was going to distract him from his goal. During his first three matches, he did not drop a set. In the quarterfinals, he rolled past

Frank Parker, 6-4, 6-3, 4-6, 6-2, setting up a semifinal match against Schroeder, his quarterfinal opponent the previous year. Bobby had never lost to Schroeder, and twice that season had defeated him without dropping a set. Unlike their previous meetings, this match was a dogfight, with Bobby eking out a victory in five sets, 6-4, 6-4, 1-6, 9-11, 7-5.

In the other semifinal, Kovacs dismantled McNeill, and most experts predicted he would go on to win the tournament. On a blustery day at center court at the West Side Tennis Club, Kovacs wasted no time trying to get under Bobby's skin.

"Does the wind bother you, Bobby?" Kovacs asked as the two walked onto the court, remembering his straight set win over Bobby at Southampton the year before on a windy day.

"No, I love it," Bobby answered, throwing Kovacs' provocation back at him.

Actually, Bobby hated the wind. He struggled to adjust to the conditions, allowing Kovacs to take the first set, 7-5. After settling down, Bobby started mixing slow, spinning floaters with deep, hard-hit groundstrokes and acute angles to disrupt Kovacs' rhythm. The tactic worked. Kovacs' game began to come apart. After each miss, Kovacs pressed harder, but his forehand kept missing, and he couldn't get to net without it. Meanwhile, Bobby started taking advantage of Kovacs' short, undercut shots to come into the net, where he cut off Kovacs' pass attempts with unbeatable volleys. The crowd, which had backed Kovacs from the outset, started to get more vocal, but the cheers did little to help him. Bobby ignored the gallery and calmly won the next two sets 6-1, 6-3. The umpire then called for the customary 10-minute intermission.

Bobby knew if Kovacs went to the locker room his coach, George Hudson, would have a chance to advise Kovacs to slow down his game and reduce his errors. Bobby knew Kovacs was high-strung, but that given a good rest and a quiet talk with Hudson, he likely would come out a different player.

Bobby walked to the umpire's chair, next to which Kovacs sat. While Kovacs sipped from a bottle of soda, Bobby picked up a towel and dried his hands and face.

"You look tired, Frankie," Bobby said pleasantly. "Probably want to go in and lie down a while, don't you?"

"Who's tired?" snapped Kovacs. "Not me. Let's get out there and finish this."

The ploy worked. Back on court, Kovacs' game continued to unravel. Occasionally, the "Clown Prince" pulled off an incredible pass or world-beating drive, but most of the time Kovacs seemed bewildered and dejected. He struggled to hold his serve, and Bobby kept him constantly under pressure. With Bobby serving up 5-3 in the fourth set, Kovacs fell behind love-40. Tired, frustrated, and desperate to end the match, Kovacs did Bobby the favor of hitting his next return far up into the stands, conceding the title. For once, Bobby had gotten the best of Kovacs.

Afterwards, Hudson told the press, "I'll swear I've been playing and coaching tennis for 35 years and that Bobby is the smartest player I ever saw. There have been greater players, but not smarter. He had no right in the world to lick Frank like that, but he did it, and you've got to give him credit. What a brain that little rascal has."

"Riggs came back to win the title he held in 1939 by beating a player who would have been a 2-1 favorite if there had been a bookmaker within the sacred precincts of the West Side Tennis Club," reported the Associated Press. For once, the press was not entirely wrong, Bobby said, because 2-1 was what he got.

The trick now was to turn that glittering trophy into cold cash. The $25,000 guarantee he'd missed out on the previous year was gone, with nothing in its place. In fact, following Vines' retirement, and Budge's domination over Fred Perry in 1940, professional tennis had been in a slumber. Tour promoter Jack Harris put together a brief tour that pitted Budge against Bill Tilden. Tennis's equivalent of Babe Ruth, Tilden was 48 and way past his prime, but he could still play a good game (the players said he was still the world's best player—for one set) and was a popular gate attraction. The sentimental favorite, however, was no match for Budge, then at the height of his game. Tilden won just six of 61 matches.

Following Bobby's victory at Forest Hills, Harris was hesitant to back a tour featuring Budge and Bobby, at least on the terms that Bobby wanted (the same $25,000 guarantee). He wanted Bobby to sign for a straight percentage of the gate, perhaps because he doubted Bobby's drawing power and needed a hedge. Bobby traveled to the West Coast to play in the Pacific Southwest Championships and Pacific Coast Championships, during which time he gave Harris's offer some thought. He lost in both tournaments, which did little to brighten his chances of getting a good pro deal.

Meanwhile, Don Budge was also angling to arrange a tennis tour. He talked to Alexis Thompson, wealthy owner of the Philadelphia Eagles football team, and sold him on the idea of promoting a round-robin tour featuring Budge, Bobby, Fred Perry, and Kovacs, who was also looking to turn pro. A deal was signed. Budge, certain the tour would be a sure-fire success, signed for a flat 60 percent of the gate, while Bobby and Kovacs each signed for a $25,000 guarantee. Arrangements were made for the tour to open in Madison Square Garden on December 26, 1941. Bobby was to play Perry, while Budge played Kovacs.

Once again, outside events intruded. On December 7, the Japanese bombed Pearl Harbor, and suddenly nobody cared much about tennis. Thompson ended up buying $5,000 worth of tickets for the tour's opening just to fill seats, giving them away to taxi drivers and pedestrians on Eighth Avenue. Of the 11,237 people in attendance that night, a significant proportion got in compliments of Thompson.

As for the matches, Budge let Kovacs' antics get the best of him ("Hey Don, how's it feel to have the second-best backhand in tennis?") and lost 6-4, 2-6, 6-4. Bobby, in his first-ever match against Perry, split sets with the British champion, winning the first 6-3 and losing the second 6-4. In the third, Bobby led by 5-4, 30-15, when Perry fell hard on his elbow. Too injured to continue, Perry was carried out of the hall.

Gene Mako replaced Perry when the tour went on the road, but the whole affair seemed to be jinxed. Attendance was light and some nights had to be cancelled. The tour closed early that spring, with the players playing just 72 matches out of a scheduled 90. As expected, Budge wound up the overall victor with a 54-18 record (15-10 over Bobby). But the tour lost money. Because he was paid on a percentage basis, Budge collected 60 percent of nothing. "Congratulations, Don," cracked Bobby, who pocketed his $25,000 check.

Placing second with a 36-36 record, Bobby was happy with the experience. Despite the rigors of playing every night, traveling town-to-town, and the strain of trying to be both best friends and arch-rivals with the people he was with 24 hours a day, he felt at last he was doing what he wanted.

That summer, Bobby worked as a tennis pro at the Edgewater Beach Hotel in Chicago. The hotel set up Bobby and Kay in a comfortable suite. Bobby taught tennis to the hotel guests and then hosted special exhibitions on Sundays, corralling whatever good tennis player might happen to be in town that week (more and more of whom happened to be in military uniforms). In August, Bobby played the U.S. Professional Championships at the West Side Tennis Club. In a tournament noticed by few, Bobby defeated Kovacs in the semifinal before being trounced by Budge, 6-2, 6-2, 6-2.

For the winter, Bobby took a job with a manufacturing company in Minneapolis as an expediter. ("You're probably wondering what I was expediting, and it's a good question," Bobby wrote. "It will have to remain that.")

When they left Chicago for the drive up, Kay was nearing the end of her pregnancy. The day after they arrived, February 18, 1943, Kay gave birth to their first child, Bobby Jr. Both mother and child were perfectly healthy, but were unable to return home from the hospital the next day because Bobby decided to enter the Minnesota state table tennis tournament, where he had reached the final. "He left me in the hospital while he finished up playing that," Kay recalled. "Believe me, I wasn't thrilled about that, [but] that's just the way he was."

But Bobby's free and easy days were coming to a close.

In April, Bobby got a letter greeting him cordially in the name of the President of the United States and drafting him into the Navy.

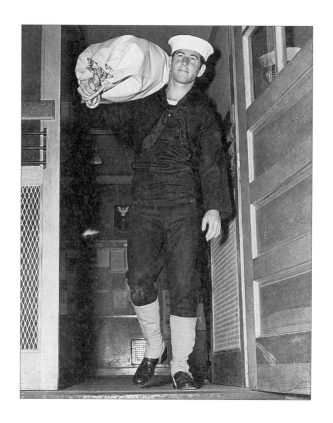

Seaman First Class Bobby Riggs. "He looked so silly,"
recalled one shipmate, "like a cartoon character."

10

A Wonderful War

April 1943-September 1945

To a man obsessed with tennis, anything else seemed a waste of time, even a world war. Being drafted into the Navy meant Bobby faced the possibility of being the target of something distinctly more lethal than a wool-covered ball. But worse for Bobby was the drab and regimented existence of a military inductee. Used to the free-and-easy life of the tennis circuit—where he bent, or even broke, the rules to get his way—Bobby had good reason to worry. After all, if any place should dispose the tennis champion of any notion that he was special, it was boot camp.

Sent to the Great Lakes Naval Training Center near Waukegan, Illinois, 25-year-old Bobby cut a ludicrous figure in his Navy bell-bottoms and cap. After his induction, Bobby's wife Kay returned home to Chicago. There was nothing to keep her in Minneapolis. Her family lived in Chicago, she had friends there, and Bobby was stationed, if only temporarily, 20 miles to the north. In his first few days at Great Lakes, Bobby sought to take advantage of this fact, and cheerfully asked his chief petty officer, "Hey, Chief, how's chances of going to Chicago for the weekend?"

The CPO was in no mood for jokes, especially from a scrawny grunt. He pulled Bobby close enough so he could feel his breath and let him know in no uncertain terms that his chances of a weekend pass were not only nil, but that if he persisted in asking such stupid questions he might find himself in several other very unpleasant places. Nobody leaves until boot training is over. Nobody. So don't ask. Don't even think about it. The CPO went on to say that whoever Bobby was in civilian life, the Navy considered itself better off before it ever obtained his services. That said, Bobby returned to his barracks, no doubt resigning himself to six weeks of drudgery.

Later, Bobby received a message that there was a phone call for him. After saluting what seemed a dozen admirals, ensigns, chief petty officers, and seamen second class to get to the phone, Bobby picked up the receiver. It was *Chicago Daily Times* sportswriter Irv Kupcinet (better known later as columnist and city gadfly for the *Chicago Sun-Times*).

"How would you like to play tennis with Henry Wallace over the weekend?" asked Kupcinet.

"You mean the vice president?" Bobby said.

"Sure. Who else?" answered Kupcinet. "Mr. Wallace is staying at the Blackstone [Hotel] over the weekend, and he wants to play with you. All right with you?"

"I'd sure like it," Bobby answered. "But, Irv, I already tried to get a pass to Chicago for the weekend, and they just about took off my head. I got the idea that I made a mistake even asking. They told me that nobody gets out of here until boot training is over."

"Well, suppose you let the vice president worry about that. He's generally credited with a little influence, you know. Anyway, I'll tell him that you'd like to play and let him take care of getting you out of hock."

Bobby walked back to his barracks, which he shared with about 200 other recruits. Seizing an opportunity when he saw it, he announced he believed he could get a weekend pass. In fact, he was willing to bet on it. His barracks mates, some of whom had just witnessed Bobby's run-in with the CPO, must have figured, "How stupid can this guy be?"

Falling into line, they put up their money—$20 here, $15 there. One can imagine a grinning Bobby, gladly taking all the action they could handle.

About an hour later, an excited officer ran into the barracks. "Riggs!" he shouted. "Get dressed right away. The commander will be around to pick you up in fifteen minutes," he ordered. "You're going to Chicago. And make sure you look right."

"To Chicago? What for?" Bobby asked, knowing full well what was happening and milking the moment for maximum effect.

"The vice president of the United States wants to see you!" the officer shouted. "Get a move on!"

Out of the corner of his eye, Bobby saw his CPO standing nearby, his jaw dropping to his chest. It was an expression no doubt shared by the rest of Bobby's barracks mates, all of whom realized they had just been had. They watched in amazement, probably mumbling under their breath a few choice descriptions for their puckish bunkmate.

Ordered to hurry, Bobby threw together his tennis gear and some clothes, not bothering to change out of his Navy dungarees. The base commander, who was to accompany Bobby to Chicago, entered the barracks. He wanted to make sure Bobby was presentable for the vice president. After being roundly saluted, the commander looked at Bobby.

"My God," he screamed. "You look like a character out of Gilbert and Sullivan. Get those clothes off! You'd disgrace the whole United States Navy in that outfit!"

While Bobby stood at attention in his underwear, the commander—like a mother dressing a small child—picked out a proper naval dress uniform for him to wear. After tying Bobby's tie for him and adjusting his hat, the commander shooed him into a large staff car waiting outside.

After briefly meeting with Vice President Wallace that evening at the hotel, Bobby was driven to a homecoming with Kay and his infant son, Bobby Jr. The next morning, he reported to the South Shore Country Club, racquet in hand. To Bobby's surprise, the vice president turned out to be a very good player. In fact, the 55-year-old vice president was a longtime tennis enthusiast and one of the best players among high-ranking Washington officials, known to show up for important cabinet meetings still sweating after a rigorous midday workout.

He insisted that Bobby not hold back. "Hit 'em as hard as you can," he ordered the champion. "I want to see if I can handle your serve."

At the end of the session, Bobby expected to be told to report the next day for another session, but the vice president said he wouldn't have time. So with a three-day pass in hand, Bobby spent the rest of his weekend at home with Kay and Bobby Jr., relishing the sweet deal and thinking about the winnings he'd collect once back on base.

It was a temporary reprieve, however. Life in boot camp was a monotonous routine of menial tasks and petty rules for Bobby. To help get through it, he talked Kay into doing his laundry, one chore he considered "real torture." Every few days at a pre-arranged evening hour, Kay drove from Chicago to the camp, where she picked up a bag of dirty laundry that Bobby tossed over the fence. The next night she'd return and throw a bag of freshly laundered and folded clothes back over. The arrangement gave Kay a chance to see Bobby, if only briefly. For the rest of the recruits, it was always a mystery how Bobby managed to have such clean and freshly ironed clothes, but never seemed to do laundry.

One time, Bobby went AWOL. Simply put, he was "tired of the Navy," so he decided to take in a nearby college football game, Great Lakes versus Purdue. It was an enormous risk, but risks were something he was used to taking. Besides, he assumed his escapade would not be discovered. At the stadium, he ran into Bill Stern, a sports announcer who was doing the national radio broadcast of the game. Invited into the broadcasting booth to watch the second half, Bobby congratulated himself on getting such a great seat. Suddenly, he overheard Stern say into the microphone, "And now we'll have a word from Seaman Bobby Riggs, the former national tennis champion, who is right by my side." Bobby's stomach jumped into his throat. He managed to stammer a few nervous lines, but was barely able to watch the rest of the game, certain some officer had heard him over the radio.

Lucky to a fault, Bobby's stunt went unnoticed, and for the duration of his training he somehow managed to muddle through without landing in the brig or getting his teeth knocked out.

Upon graduation, the Navy decided it would be better for everyone involved to keep Bobby out of harm's way. Besides, his status as a tennis star could be put to better use. Assigned as a sports specialist, Bobby did a brief stint at ex-boxer and Commander Gene Tunney's school in Bainbridge, Maryland, then was shipped off to Pearl Harbor. While many of Bobby's other tennis friends and rivals saw hard action in Europe or the Pacific, Bobby spent the war giving tennis exhibitions and clinics to the troops.

Despite his aversion to Navy life and his shortcomings as a soldier, Bobby found an ideal environment in the military—lots of men with free cash and plenty of spare time. It was never hard for Bobby to find a craps or poker game full of suckers willing to hand over their money. By the time he got to Honolulu, Bobby had already built up a bankroll of several thousand dollars shooting craps in specialists' school and playing poker on the voyage over aboard the light cruiser *Birmingham*.

Initially stationed at Aiea Barracks at Pearl Harbor, Bobby joined a group of other famous athletes, including major league ballplayers Johnny Mize, Elbie Fletcher, Johnny Rigney, and Buddy Blattner, along with boxers George Abrahms and Fred Apostoli.

Robert "Buddy" Blattner, a former two-time world champion in table tennis and then-second baseman for the St. Louis Cardinals, spent most of the war with Bobby. Recalling the first time they met, Blattner said he and a few of the guys, including Rigney and Mize, were outside the barracks playing basketball. As usual for mid-summer on the island, recalled Blattner, it was windy and hot as hell on the beat-up concrete court when Bobby walked up— short, duck-footed, his hat cockeyed.

"My God, you had to see it," Blattner said. "He looked so silly, like a cartoon character."

"What are you doing?" Bobby asked.

"What do you think we're doing?" shot back Rigney.

The group stopped playing. After a brief round of introductions, Bobby suggested a foul-shooting contest. It would be a way to break the ice, a chance to bond with "the guys." Why not put up a small bet "just to make it interesting?" Bobby added.

Sure, they said. After all, this was a group of professional athletes, men gifted with size, strength, and great hand-eye coordination; men who were proud of their athletic ability and who hated to lose. This little scamp didn't stand a chance. Bobby, after all, "didn't look like he could drop a marble down a well," Blattner said.

They agreed to shoot 10 free throws apiece. Bobby insisted on going last.

"I tell you," Blattner said, "it was tough getting that rubberized ball through that bent rim." By the time it was Bobby's turn, the most anybody had made was four baskets. Bobby got up, holding the ball two-handed and throwing it up between his legs.

"I tell you, it was the silliest-looking thing you ever saw," recalled Blattner.

Before anyone knew it, Bobby had made four baskets and still had three shots left, Blattner said. Stunned, the group watched as Bobby sent all three through the net without touching the rim. Nobody could believe it. They played again, and Bobby shot six free-throws, in the process winning the contest and taking their spending money for the month.

To the other athletes, Bobby was a freak of nature, a guy who didn't look like, walk like, or talk like a world-class athlete.

"If you were to line up a hundred people," Blattner said, "just ordinary rank-and-file, and say one of these men is the number one tennis player in the world, I guarantee you [Bobby] would probably be the ninety-eighth pick."

But what Bobby lacked in size, strength, and speed he made up for in hand-eye coordination, touch, anticipation, guile, and, more than anything, raw competitiveness. Bobby had an absolute confidence in his ability; a confidence derived from a refined understanding of his own limitations.

The other ballplayers never gave up trying to beat Bobby. "It was a fascinating thing," Blattner said. "[Bobby] loved the challenge, but he never cheated anybody. He didn't have to." If they wanted to take Bobby on at his own game, he was happy to oblige. If not, they could think up their own game, and Bobby would say, "Fine." They might change the rules, but the outcome was always the same. Tossing cards into a hat, lagging coins, throwing a football into an empty barrel, bouncing a ball into a wastepaper basket—whatever the contest, Blattner said, Bobby always won.

While stationed in Hawaii, Bobby, Blattner, and a couple of other men got to stay at a vacant house taken over by the Navy. For transportation, they commandeered a military Jeep to get around the island to put on their clinics and exhibitions. In general, Bobby put on between three and five tennis exhibitions a week at hospitals, recreation centers, camps, and clubs, his opponents rotating among those near the top of the base tennis ladder, including Norman Brooks, the fourth-ranked player in Northern California, and Jack Rodgers, the second-ranked player in Texas. Every Sunday, Bobby was part of a tennis exhibition put on at the Royal Hawaiian Hotel in Honolulu.

The rough asphalt courts on the base were a long way from the carefully manicured lawns of Forest Hills. Rackets and balls were also in short supply with most materials, especially rubber, diverted to wartime use. Instead, the players used either old balls that were overplayed, without any bounce and with the covers worn thin, or reclaimed balls that were lively but lost their covers on the tenth hit. Still, the game proved incredibly popular on base, with long waits for courts and most play limited to just a single set. A base tournament in 1945 drew 158 singles players and 67 doubles teams, and good crowds always turned out for Bobby's exhibitions. He had no difficulty keeping himself occupied and his game reasonably sharp. Bobby and Blattner also put on table tennis exhibitions.

As a person, Blattner said, Bobby was nice enough: friendly but not forceful, cordial but never demanding or obnoxious. He liked to joke around and was a very good storyteller, spinning long tales about life on the tennis circuit, the great matches he'd played, and the Hollywood stars he'd met. Unlike many of the guys, Bobby didn't drink much, and didn't smoke. He enjoyed a night out, but at some point during the evening he inevitably got involved in a game of some sort. And always, always for money.

For example, Blattner recalled, one time they all went into a bar and Bobby said, "You know what'd be fun?" And the next thing they knew they were all at one end of the bar trying to lag an ashtray by sliding it along the length of the bar. As far as Blattner knew, Bobby had no special insight into the ashtray's physics, or knew whether the bar was bumpy or grainy or wet or sandy.

Once again, Bobby insisted on going last, watching while half the guys slid the ashtray over the edge, automatically eliminating themselves from the game. The others, afraid of going over, ended up way short. Then Bobby got up. He carefully lined up the ashtray, made a couple of practice strokes, and— zip—sent it inside the others. Someone then said, "Okay, let's put some sand in this thing," and for the next round, they insisted Bobby go first. This time, they only did worse, Blattner said, while Bobby slid the ashtray to within a half-inch of the edge the bar and collected the money.

By the end of the war the other ballplayers were ready to throw Bobby off a cliff, not because they didn't like him, but because they just couldn't beat him at anything. Bobby's personality wouldn't irritate them, but he would beat them, and after enough losses it would drive them crazy. They just refused to believe that this wag with his "aw-shucks" manner could beat them, much less at anything athletic. But Bobby proved them wrong. "He was just great at everything he did," Blattner said. "It just amazed me."

Typically following an exhibition at a base or military hospital the commanding officer invited Blattner and Bobby over to the officers' club for beer, not only as a courtesy, but because they were eager to talk to a couple of genuine sports stars. Bobby enjoyed regaling them all with tales of his on-court and off-court exploits.

During one of these bull sessions, Blattner said, an officer turned to Bobby and said, "Well, Bob, this is quite a departure for 'ya, being in the service and the glamorous life of living on the tennis tour."

"Well, yes, I do miss tennis," Bobby said. "But you know, the thing I miss more than anything else, besides the competition, is that on the tennis circuit we play cards. I love to play cards."

To which one of the officers answered, "Bob, you know, every Wednesday night we play poker. And boy, you're invited to come on over."

"And boy," Blattner recalled, Bobby "gave 'em a story."

"Well, gosh, if I can," Bobby said. "You know, I think maybe I can get transportation. But tell me, what are the stakes?"

Told the game was a two or three dollar ante, $50 limit for two rounds of betting, and pot-limit on the third and last round of betting (meaning you can bet the total in the pot for that round), Bobby shook his head. "Oh boy," he said, "that's really stiff for me. But tell you what: Give me some time and I'll get some money together and I'll call you."

Of course, Bobby had plenty of money. In fact, he probably had more money than any of the officers. He was just baiting the hook. For him it was all a part of the game, putting them at ease, massaging their egos so they would be more likely to raise when they should call, hold on to hands they should throw away, or stay in a game when they should just go home to bed. Bobby knew better than anybody that those who think luck has anything to do with winning are just suckers. According to Blattner, Bobby "was very, very clever." He had a plan to win this game before the cards were even dealt.

A couple of weeks later, before the game, Bobby gave Blattner $300 and told him to hold onto it until he asked for it. The game was seven-card stud, and Bobby's plan was to ante, then only stay through the first round of betting. "Golly, that's too damn rich for me," he'd say, throwing in his hand.

In a ruse to further bait the trap, Blattner said, during play Bobby again folded. He laid his cards face down on the table so they were overlapping. He then hit them as if by accident so they all flipped over, showing that he had, say, a pair of eights. He then apologized and covered the cards up, but not before making sure everyone saw what he had. This way, he lulled them into thinking they could always bluff him out.

Hours passed, and like a wily predator waiting for precisely the right moment to strike, Bobby threw away hand after hand, watching as the pots grew bigger and bigger. Finally, he drew a "hellish" hand, Blattner said, a sure winner. The moment had arrived, and Blattner handed over to Bobby the $300 bankroll, with Bobby reassuring Blattner that he'd "pay it all back" the first chance he got.

"He's watching every card that's coming out. And they're raising fifty dollars to fifty dollars." At the last round of betting, it cost $250 to stay in the game.

"Everybody put in," Blattner said. "I think there were five guys in the game, and everybody stays in. And Bob, he's got it nailed, and he's giving them all that romance: 'Oh, gosh, this is gonna wipe me out,' and so forth."

The player next to Bobby ran out of money, so he turned to Bobby and asked what kind of collateral he would accept.

"What do you have?" asked Bobby.

"Well, I got this Packard," he said. He turned to the others and asked, "What do you think the car's worth?"

They put it at a thousand dollars or more.

"Okay, throw in the title," Bobby said.

"And don't you know it," Blattner said. "We drove home in that Packard. We had the thing the whole time we were in Honolulu."

B y now, Kay had moved to California to be closer to Bobby. She was pregnant with their second child, conceived during Bobby's three-day pass to play Vice President Wallace. For a while, she stayed at the home of Bobby's parents, Gideon and Agnes, though she never felt particularly welcome. The couple lived a reclusive life, she said. Gideon, nearly blind, kept to himself in his upstairs office. On his desk, he kept an oversized Bible in Braille that he used to help work on his sermons. His grandchildren would amuse themselves by running their fingers over the pages.

Agnes, meanwhile, rarely left the house. She joined a group called the Wednesday Morning Women's Club, where the group studied Shakespeare, but after raising seven children and years of taking care of the house, she seemed a "beaten-down woman" to Kay. She felt uncomfortable, more like an intruder than a part of the family, and decided to move out. With the help of Bobby's brother, Luke Riggs, who lived in the area and worked for the telephone company, she found a place of her own. While she waited for the war's end and Bobby's return, her husband dutifully mailed home a portion of his gambling winnings.

Officially, Bobby had other duties besides playing tennis and rooting out poker games. He'd give tennis lessons or put on exhibitions, but no one can remember him participating in any sort of military exercise. "He'd probably shoot off his foot," Blattner quipped.

During much of his time in Hawaii, Bobby was content to blithely move from one hustle to another, driving around in the Packard he'd won, seeking out card games or "scouting trips to find a movie I hadn't seen." Sometimes, he could find a "virgin" tennis court on which he could work an old hustle from his boyhood days in Los Angeles.

Bobby once mentioned an incident that happened near Pearl Harbor in 1944 when a young man challenged him to a game of tennis for money. The stranger did not recognize Bobby, and when he suggested they play for higher and higher stakes, Bobby obliged. In two hours, Bobby relieved the man of most of his savings. After doubling the bets, Bobby then proceeded to win the man's car and his bungalow outside Honolulu. Distraught, the man slunk from the court. Bobby summoned him back, and after telling him who he was, warned him, "Let this be a lesson to you. Never play strangers for money. At any game." Then, in a rare gesture of munificence, he handed back the money—minus $500, which he kept for the advice.

Bobby's time in Hawaii was relatively short, just a few months. Even before he arrived at Pearl Harbor, the United States and its allies were well on the way to regaining control of the Pacific following Japan's attack on Pearl Harbor. Victories in the Battle of Midway in June 1942 and the campaign at Guadalcanal that same summer gave the United States crucial momentum as it started to sweep across the island chains strung out across the Pacific.

By the summer of 1944, U.S. forces had retaken the Marianas, including the islands of Saipan, Tinian, and Guam. From airfields hastily constructed on these islands, just 1,350 miles south of mainland Japan, U.S. bomber squadrons began the campaign that eventually would bring Japan to its knees. After a naval base was established on Guam, Admiral Chester W. Nimitz transferred his headquarters there, bringing with him Bobby, Blattner, and a few other athletes. Their job was to entertain battle-weary troops from the bloody campaigns at Guadalcanal, the Solomon Islands, and the Philippines.

Once stationed on Guam, Bobby became Vice Admiral John Hoover's permanent doubles partner. Every afternoon at four o'clock, Bobby reported to a tennis court to play the admiral. Occasionally, Vice Admiral Charles A. Lockwood, commander of submarines in the Pacific, would join in. Careful not to break rank, Bobby made a point of hitting the balls directly to the admiral, who enjoyed seeing how much he could make the champion scurry around. It became a standing joke on the base that "the only time Admiral Hoover smiles is when he's running Bobby Riggs' tail off on the tennis court."

Meanwhile, down the road near Nimitz' compound at Island Command, Blattner put his Marines on alert. "Don't play cards with him," he said about Bobby. "Just take it from me. Don't play cards with him." But his troops saw Blattner's warning as a challenge. After all, from their first day at boot camp, all Marines are drilled to believe they can do anything better than anyone else.

At first, the hapless suckers might play for small stakes, Blattner said, but after they started losing or, worse, after Bobby let them win a little ("advertising money," as Bobby called it), they inevitably would say, "Come on," and ask to raise the stakes.

"Well, if you want to," was Bobby's standard reply.

"It just got to be ridiculous," Blattner said. "It would start out we'd play a game and somebody would say, 'That damn Riggs. He took ten dollars off me the other day.' So the other guy would say, 'Oh, come on. I'd like a part of him... Hey, Riggs! You want to try me?' "

"Yeah, I'll try." Bobby would answer. He might not know how good the new challenger was, but he was absolutely confident he was at least as good, and probably better.

Not only that, Blattner said, but Bobby "would nurture them to a point where they thought they were world champions and he was just a stumble-bum." Often, Blattner said, Bobby would have to hold back, lose a bit, just to make it look competitive.

But after winning, Bobby never gloated and never rubbed the loser's nose in it. It was always, "Man, I had a great day" or "I know you can play better than that" or "You were tougher than I ever thought you'd be." Bobby never it made it personal. It was just money. In this way, Blattner said, Bobby "would keep you in his camp, or his web at any rate."

"Oh Lord," Blattner said, "Bobby wiped out the entire platoon. He just absolutely wiped them out."

In 1945, with the war winding down, the Army and Navy brass agreed to stage a series of Davis Cup-style matches between the two services. All the best athletes in the world were now in military uniform, and the tiny island of Guam was now home to four of the best tennis players on the planet. Don Budge and Frank Parker were both stationed at the Army compound on Guam. Not far away, the Navy had Bobby and his old doubles partner, Wayne Sabin.

Despite his off-duty escapades, Bobby still took his tennis very seriously. Though the results of the interservice matches would be meaningless, Bobby saw them as a test of how well his game had held up since going into the Navy. He also knew that once the war was over he would have to fight it out to stay in the pro ranks, and that his stiffest competition would likely be J. Donald Budge. Three years older, Budge had so far dominated Bobby in their numerous matches. Like everybody else, Bobby stood in awe of Budge's power and was more than a bit demoralized. He had lived under Budge's shadow for years, and even those who thought well of Bobby considered him the player who could beat everybody but Budge. If Bobby was to wrest the tour away from the great Budge, he had to prove to Budge that he could beat him. Moreover, he needed to prove it to himself. Now that he had time to reflect on Budge's game, Bobby began devising a plan of attack.

Bobby knew Budge had a terrific all-around game, but he also knew from experience that if there was a single weakness in Budge's arsenal, it was his forehand. Unlike his beautiful, flowing backhand, Budge's forehand was not a natural stroke, but an "educated" shot he adopted later under the coaching of Tom Stow in Oakland. Because of this, Budge's forehand was apt to break down under stress.

Bobby also knew Budge was a bit vain about his game, and that he would never admit—even to himself—to the possibility he could lose. Because of this, Bobby suspected he might also be a bit lazy and possibly let his training regimen slip while in the Army. "I said to myself that the difference between Don Budge and me is who is going to come out of the service fit. So I said that I am going to work on my game and become a better player than I was before. And knowing Budge's personality and how proud Budge was, I knew that he would consider that he was so good that he would not have to practice. So I studied Budge's personality, and I knew that if he did not practice, he would go backward."

Bobby was absolutely right. While in Officer Candidate School at a base in Wichita Falls, Texas, Budge blamed "a certain lack of conditioning" for an injury he suffered. While working out on an obstacle course, he tore a muscle in his shoulder. Though largely healed by the time of his interservice matches with Bobby, Budge said his service motion and overhead had developed hitches as a way of compensating for the injury.

As for himself, Bobby decided he faced two tasks if he was to defeat Budge. First, he had to quit looking at Budge as if he were invincible. Second, he had to improve his conditioning so he could endure a long match with Budge. Thus resolved, Seaman Bobby Riggs was careful to stay in shape and keep his strokes sharp.

For the interservice matches, the players from each side took on one another in both singles and doubles over a weekend of play. The first match was scheduled on Guam and received island-wide publicity.

Given the rivalry between Budge and Bobby—the two best players in the world—and the rivalry between the two services, the matches took on the atmosphere of a heavyweight prizefight. Still, everybody thought Budge would win. According to Blattner, thousands of dollars were bet. "Everybody from the Army would come over to the Navy installation and say, 'We got two thousand dollars on Budge, can you handle that?'" Blattner recalled. "And they'd say, 'Oh yeah, we can handle two thousand dollars.' " As for Bobby, Blattner added, "I don't know how much Bobby bet on himself. I didn't want to know. But I know it was many thousands of dollars."

Thousands attended the matches, with many more listening to Blattner's play-by-play broadcast over military radio. Unlike

Troops on Guam, 1945, watch one of the interservice matches featuring Army versus Navy. Unlike the polite, well-tended galleries of the All England Club or Forest Hills, the bois- terous spectators at these matches seemed better-suited to the bleacher seats at Yankee Stadium.

the polite, well-tended galleries of the All England Club or Forest Hills, the boisterous spectators at these matches seemed better-suited to the bleacher seats at Yankee Stadium, whistling at the players, shouting encouragement to their favorite, applauding missed shots, and taunting an opponent.

The conditions for the matches were equally brutal, played under a blazing sun on courts carved from the island coral and surfaced with a mixture of broken rock and sand. Because of the intense heat and humidity, Bobby and most of the other competitors played shirtless and in shorts, but the ever-proud Budge insisted on playing in the traditional white shirt and white flannel pants.

In the first match, the smart money definitely was behind Budge, who picked up right where he left off before the war, cracking his serve, hitting blistering groundstrokes, especially off the backhand side, and pushing Bobby all over the court. As always, Bobby hung tough, scrambling all over the place, answering Budge's tremendous pace with his characteristic soft touch. But Budge was clearly in command. Near the end, after Budge passed Bobby once again, Bobby simply shook his head and muttered, "Ah, you're too much." Budge won 6-2, 6-2.

On the island of Peleliu, the next match was closer, but Budge won again, 6-4, 7-5. A disheartened Bobby came off the court thinking he'd had some chances, but simply could not capitalize on them. Frank Parker, Budge's Army teammate, went up to Bobby afterwards to congratulate him, saying that he really had Budge going, and that at one point Budge came off the court white, actually shaking. Parker told Bobby that Budge had had to bear down with everything in order to win.

Parker's comment made Bobby look at the match in a different light. Perhaps he simply did not take advantage of the chances he had because of an inferiority complex. He accused himself of not trying hard enough, and decided that from then on he would treat every point as if it were a championship point in a national championship final.

With this new outlook, Bobby won the next two matches, played on the islands of Ulithi, 6-1, 6-1, and Saipan, 6-3, 4-6, 6-1. Afterwards, Budge confided in Parker his disbelief at losing two in a row to Bobby. The fifth and final match was scheduled for the first week of August on the island of Tinian. Both Bobby and Budge knew this one had broader implications than just the pride of their respective services or entertainment for the troops. Whoever won would have a psychological edge over the other in any post-war contest.

Before going out, Sabin asked Bobby, "Do you think you can do it?"

"If I beat him today," Bobby replied to his teammate, "I'll know for sure I can beat him any time."

On a brutally hot and steamy day, the two went at each other in a tense, seesaw affair. Knowing that he could not outgun Budge, Bobby took advantage of the conditions, working to make the points long to wear Budge down. Nothing was given away. Bobby hit his shots deep and to the corners, using his fine touch to vary the pace of the ball and keep Budge off balance. The two split the first two sets. Budge took the first, 8-6, and Bobby the second, 6-1. As the match wore on, Budge did begin to tire. As Bobby had predicted, he started to benefit from errors off Budge's forehand side.

To anyone watching it was dead even, 6-6 in the third. But Bobby's plan was working. After more than two hours of chasing down balls, reaching for overheads, and dashing after dropshots, Budge could barely move. Bobby won 8-6.

"You couldn't believe that this little guy... it was like David and Goliath," Blattner said. For the first time, Bobby had beaten Budge in a series he knew the great man badly wanted to win. Bobby had proven that Budge was human, that he did make mistakes. He knew then he was at least Budge's equal.

While the Navy lost the series, 4-1, Bobby won six of his 10 singles matches, posting a 3-2 record against Parker. The matches with Budge, he would later write, gave him much-needed confidence that carried over when he returned to the States.

At about the same time Budge and Bobby were playing that final match, technicians on the other end of the island reassembled the parts of America's newest secret weapon inside four nondescript buildings near the end of Tinian's runway. On August 6, 1945, the device was loaded onto the Enola Gay, one of three B-29 bombers that lifted off the tiny island's airstrip bound for the Japanese port city of Hiroshima. Within days, Japan surrendered, ending the war.

Blattner returned home to renew a career in baseball and later in broadcasting in St. Louis. While with Bobby in the Navy, he said, the only time he ever saw Bobby lose were those tennis matches to Budge and Parker.

Inside the Pan-Pacific Auditorium, Bobby needed to lob the ball just below the large clock. Too low, and the ball would fall short, only to be put away by one of Budge's smashes. Too high, and the ball would hit the clock, and Bobby would lose the point.

11

The Quest for the $100,000 Plum
1945-1947

Amid the rubble and devastation of World War II, history was left to ponder what might have been. Had there been no war, would Thomas Dewey have become president? Would baseball's Bob Feller have pitched 30 wins in a single season? Would Bobby Riggs have won back-to-back Wimbledons? It was only natural to speculate.

In the United States, tennis limped along from 1942 to 1946, encouraged by President Franklin D. Roosevelt as a morale booster for the home front and the troops overseas. Still, some tournaments were cancelled for the duration; others played with reduced draws and shortened schedules, or were limited to women. Newport, the nation's oldest tournament, was suspended until war's end. At Forest Hills, the men's matches were cut from best-of-five sets to best-of-three until the semifinals. At Seabright in 1945, the tournament was held with a field of just eight men and four women.

The end of hostilities left the rest of the tennis world to pick up the pieces. Only after some debate did the All England Club decide to stage Wimbledon in 1946, despite a shortage of racquets, balls, and court equipment, and with a large section of the still-damaged Centre Court cordoned off. Wartime passions led the International Tennis Federation, the organization that oversaw Davis Cup competition, to temporarily expel nine countries from the organization, including Germany, Italy, and Japan. The Cup itself remained locked in a bank vault in Australia.

Of course, none of this mattered to Bobby. In September 1945, home on a 30-day leave, he arrived at the Alameda Naval Station in Oakland, where he was greeted by Kay, Bobby Jr., and the newest Riggs, Larry, born June 14, 1944, while Bobby was in the Pacific. After a year and a half apart, Bobby was nervous about the effect of such a long separation. Kay quickly reassured him. "Where've you been, Riggs? Your hair looks awful."

Naturally, his first order of business was to make up for lost time. Moving to Los Angeles, Bobby returned to the Los Angeles Tennis Club, which had changed little since he was last there. Joining him was a familiar crowd: Bill Tilden, Don Budge, Gene Mako, Frank Parker, Frank Shields, and Fred Perry. While awaiting his discharge, Bobby was able to work on his game, rustle up money matches, and mingle with the Hollywood set— Errol Flynn, Douglas Fairbanks Jr., Humphrey Bogart, Claudette Colbert, Gary Cooper, Charlie Chaplin. He might find himself thrown in a match with some of the up-and-coming juniors at the club, which then included a temperamental kid from East L.A. named Pancho Gonzalez.

Without a professional tour, Bobby, Budge, Perry, and the other players cast about for something to do. Tilden suggested staging a big professional tournament in Los Angeles. Why, he said, they could even play it at the L.A. Tennis Club. Always one to prefer the grand gesture over practical or personal necessity, Tilden then proposed, "Maybe we could play it for some charity."

Terrific idea, they agreed, but forget the charity. They had been away for a long time and needed to resume earning money.

Billed the World Hard Court Professional Championships, the event was held at the L.A. Tennis Club the first week of December, four weeks after Bobby's official discharge from the Navy on November 3, 1945. Tilden acted as tournament director, promoter, and participant. Though 52 years old and way past his glory years, Tilden was still a monumental figure in the game, admired by players and beloved by fans. Not only that, but his 52-year-old game was nothing to sniff at.

Before enthusiastic crowds, Tilden amazed everybody by reaching the semifinals, dispatching big-hitting Lester Stoefen 7-5, 6-0 in the quarterfinals, a feat made more remarkable by the fact that the old man had been down 5-2 in the first set. The next day, Tilden returned to earth, getting trounced by Budge, but in a third-place playoff, he again surprised the gallery by defeating Perry in a tough three-set match. Like the Tilden of old, he hit aces all over the court, and seized every opportunity to send his forehand drives deep into the corners for winners.

The final pitted Budge against Bobby, the two players most fans expected to slug it out for the title of world's professional champion. With the public largely ignorant of Bobby's victories over Budge in their Army-Navy series, Budge remained the overwhelming favorite. Few knew that the Budge who walked out on the court that day was not the awe-inspiring Budge who had dominated Bobby in both the amateur and professional ranks.

Up a set and 3-1 in the second set of the best-of-five-set encounter, Budge looked like he would maintain his dominance, but then Bobby roared back. He kept the ball away from Budge's backhand, attacked Budge's second serve, and lobbed at every opportunity to take advantage of Budge's lingering shoulder injury. Bobby took five straight games to win the second set and then went up 5-2 in the third set. Budge started grasping his right arm. He called time and had a doctor summoned to the court. Budge complained of cramping in his arm, and the doctor gave him a quick rubdown before letting him continue. After Bobby served out the third set, 6-2, the players were given an intermission, during which Budge retired to the locker room, where he received a complete rubdown, took a shower, and changed his clothes. It was of no use. Bobby ran through the fourth set, 6-0, to win the match.

Eventually, after collecting from the losing bettors in the crowd, a jubilant Bobby spoke to the press. "I'm sorry that it happened that way," he said, alluding to Budge's arm troubles, "but I'd have beaten him anyway. I'm champion today. I've always wanted to be the champ and I've worked and struggled all along towards that end. I caught up with Budge today. Shake hands with the new champion, boys."

But few were ready for a new champion to be crowned. Most fans refused to believe Bobby could defeat Budge on even terms. The newspapers speculated Budge's ailing arm was behind the defeat, and Budge himself suggested as much. To settle the issue, a rematch was scheduled for the next month, January 1946, at the Pan-Pacific Auditorium in Los Angeles. Sixty-five hundred people packed into the hall, the biggest turnout yet to see a match on the West Coast. Thousands were turned away at the door.

"No one could believe that a little runt like me had a chance against the great Don Budge," Bobby said. "The time before had been a fluke, the master had been wounded and out of condition. There wasn't a tennis expert in the country who would make it even money. Which was fine with me, since I got terrific odds. That night in the dressing room before the match, Errol Flynn came in with some friends and they bet me twenty-five hundred dollars each at odds of two-to-one that I would lose. It was terrible. Even my supporters were worried. I got all the pre-game bets I could handle."

Inside the Pan-Pacific Auditorium a large clock hung from the ceiling some 35 feet above the center of the court. From the opening game, Bobby started lobbing. He figured that to get just the right depth, the ball had to be lofted about three inches beneath the bottom of the clock. Too low, and the ball would fall short, only to be put away by one of Budge's overhead smashes. Too high, and the ball would hit the clock, and Bobby would lose the point.

Budge played with the heaviest racquet in the game, $17\frac{1}{2}$ ounces, a fact he was openly proud of and that only added to his reputation as a power hitter. "Budge was a straightaway smasher," Bobby said. "He killed the ball, never to the right or to the left, but directly down the middle. When he was fresh they were almost impossible to return. But how fresh will a man remain when he has to rely on his overhead for ninety percent of his game? Just about a set, I figured."

Budge played impressively that night. He took the first set, 6-4, and jumped to a 5-2 lead in the second set, winning with his big serve and attacking volley. His fans were screaming wildly and waving pennants in the air. While toweling off at a changeover,

Bobby looked up and saw Errol Flynn sitting in a sideline box a few feet away, smiling broadly and making dollar signs at him. The odds had skyrocketed by then, but Bobby continued to make bets using hand signals. Recalled one fan sitting behind Clark Gable and Groucho Marx: "Whenever Riggs changed sides in the match, he placed bets on himself by holding up fingers to the crowd. Gable held up one finger. Riggs shook his head and held up two fingers. Gable held up two fingers and nodded. That meant that Riggs bet Gable $2,000 that he would win that set, even though he was behind, 5-2. He also placed bets with Groucho and others the same way." On the other side of the court, his brother John Riggs was doing the same. Together, Bobby and John were able to get odds as high as 10-to-1 against Bobby's winning. This, however, was no set-up. Cool and composed, Bobby stuck to his game plan. He started to throw up lobs.

"Every time I lobbed I could hear the crowd holding its breath to see where the ball would go," Bobby said. "Most of them fell within six inches of the baseline. Only three of them actually hit the clock. I must have lobbed him about seventy times during that match." In the second set, Bobby saved two set points, pulled even, and took the set, 9-7. "It was obvious to me," Bobby said, "that Budge was getting tired. That racquet of his was beginning to feel as though it weighed twenty pounds. But I figured that much out before the match."

"By the middle of the third set," Bobby said, "Budge was getting sick of those lobs. He was deathly ill. At one point in the third game of that set I gave him seven straight lobs, all of which missed that clock by a hair. He smashed them all back, except the last one, and after that it was all downhill. I took the last two sets, 6-4, 8-6, and Budge retired to the dressing room with a steel elbow."

In his own mind, Bobby felt vindicated. He had completed his mastery over Budge. Never again would he feel intimidated by the Great One. Others took notice, too. The great Tilden, who scoffed after Bobby's victory at Wimbledon in 1939, wrote: "Once more Riggs proved himself the champion of the world. Once more Budge, greatly to my regret, showed he is no more the player he was… What has gone? I can only explain it by saying that Budge now plays not to lose. He is no longer playing to win." The supreme confidence that had served Budge so well had wilted. The Great One, who for so long seemed so far above everybody else, had returned to earth. Joining the company of mere mortals, he was now vulnerable.

Buoyed by the success of the World Hardcourt Professional Championships, Tilden was convinced there was a market for a series of professional tournaments. Enlisting players such as Bobby, Don Budge, Fred Perry, and others, he formed a new organization, the Professional Players Association. Tilden, a veteran of early professional tours, understood that the head-to-head format was flawed. Without the threat of elimination, the competitive element was missing and the matches were always susceptible to accusations that the results were either fixed or the players lacked incentive. Tilden's idea was to create a professional league with tournament play.

Over the years, calls had gone up to open tournaments to both amateur and professional players, but the ruling amateur establishment staunchly opposed all such proposals, arguing that to do so would sully the "purity" of competition. Honor and purity, however, had little to do with it. The system of under-the-table payoffs that amateur officials defended was simply *de facto* professionalism. What really was at stake was power and control over the game, which amateur officials clung to through their stranglehold on the major tennis events—the national championships and the Davis Cup—and their clever manipulation of the divisions between the players, the fans, the media, and each other.

Few clubs would risk the wrath of the amateur establishment by hosting a professional tournament during the amateur season. For example, when Perry and Ellsworth Vines took their tour to Europe in the summer of 1937, the tour nearly died when the British Lawn Tennis Association forbade any affiliate club to host the matches. The tour was rescued by the hasty construction of a portable wooden court that was hauled around to various outdoor football grounds rather than tennis clubs.

The resulting logistics of touring made it impossible to host full-fledged professional tournaments. As a result, the tours evolved into head-to-head contests between the reigning professional champion and the top amateur challenger. Usually a warm-up match between two lesser players preceded the feature match—the "animal act," as it was known inside the tour. To avoid competing head-on with the more recognized amateur game, the pro tours took place primarily during the winter months. After the tour, the next top amateur player would be signed for the next year.

By his sheer energy and presence, however, Tilden managed to put together what no one before could: a series of six professional tournaments, starting in Southern California and the Southwest, then moving to the Midwest and East. Tilden did the negotiations, made the deals, got the player commitments, arranged the draw for each tournament, and acted as referee. The players included Bobby, Lester Stoefen, Fred Perry, Wayne Sabin, John Faunce, Frank Kovacs, Gene Mako, and Welby Van Horn. Among the bigger events was a $10,000 tournament in 1946 in Philadelphia sponsored by the *Philadelphia Inquirer*. Tilden also managed to land a five-year contract for the World Professional Grass Court Championships to be held at the country's premier tennis venue, the West Side Tennis Club in Forest Hills.

Tilden's perseverance paid off, as many of the events were successful. Some players complained when they learned that Tilden rigged the draws to ensure he advanced to the latest possible round, but Bobby defended the practice. The way he figured, it was less a matter of fairness than good business, as Tilden was still a major gate attraction. After all, professional tennis was largely an extension of the entertainment business.

The tour might have succeeded, too, had not a couple of events intervened. First, in February 1946, after Bobby and Budge's match in the Pan-Pacific Auditorium, Jack Harris, who promoted the two players' prewar tour, convinced them to participate in a 25-match head-to-head tour. With that, the tournament tour lost its top two gate attractions. Second, and more important, was Tilden's conviction and imprisonment on a morals charge in 1947, an event that shocked and saddened the entire tennis world. His arrest in

Los Angeles after being caught with an under-aged male youth made public what had been an open secret among the players. Though Tilden "never made passes at fellow players, as far as I know," Bobby said, "he was overly fond of ball boys." Without Tilden, the driving force for the tour was gone. Though a few tournaments he organized continued on their own, without Tilden's missionary zeal to keep the tour going, plus his ability to bully into line such a diverse group of personalities and egos, the dream of an organized professional tour died. Wrote Bobby: "Pro tennis owes a tremendous debt to Bill."

B obby and Budge's tour in 1946 was billed as a classic battle of styles: the slugger, Budge, versus the clever boxer, Bobby. To the winner of the tour went the title and the opportunity to headline the next tour. The loser would be left on the sidelines. Budge, 31, knew he was in the twilight of his career and that this could be his last real chance to cash in on his legendary status. But without his accustomed power on the serve, and frustrated by errors on his overheads, Budge found balls he used to put away with ease against Bobby coming back. It unnerved him and he changed tactics, trying to rally with Bobby from the baseline, exchanging drop shots and lobs. Instead of outslugging Bobby, he wound up trying to beat Bobby at Bobby's game.

Opening March 9, 1946, in Chicago before 7,811 spectators, Bobby won a tense five-set match. As the 25-match tour moved east, Bobby charged out to a 13-2 lead, leaving Budge no chance of overtaking him. Bobby's dominance worried promoters in the lucrative East Coast markets of New York, Philadelphia, Boston, and Pittsburgh, who saw interest in the tour wane and their gate receipts collapse. "What the devil is happening?" they complained to tour publicity director Jack Miller. "Tell Riggs to ease up on Budge. Good gosh, man, do you realize such successive beatings are killing the gate?"

A fellow player approached Bobby after a stop in Providence, R.I. "Bobby, why don't you let Don win a couple of matches? You're leading him eleven matches to one. It's killing the crowds, and you're not being fair to the other members of the foursome [Wayne

Sabin and John Faunce played the preliminary match], who stand to get a handsome bonus when the series is over—that is, if good crowds make it possible for promoter Jack Harris to have any of that folding money to pass around."

After reportedly telling this person to mind his own business, Bobby agreed to extend the tour to 46 matches. Meanwhile, Budge cast off his vanity and started wearing glasses on court. He also adjusted his playing style. He whittled Bobby's lead, ending just two matches back, 22 wins to Bobby's 24. Still, the tour was only a moderate financial success, with an average attendance of 3,425 per stop.

For Bobby, all that remained was to win the season-ending U.S. Professional Championships at Forest Hills. This, he figured, would be the crowning jewel of his ascendancy as world pro champion. It was a moment for which he had planned since Budge dismantled him at the professional championships in 1942, and no one could have been more motivated. On the other side of the court, however, Budge figured that if he could win the title at Forest Hills, he might salvage what remained of his standing as defending champion, or at least keep himself in contention. Besides, he was still an immensely popular figure and the heavy sentimental favorite going into the tournament.

As expected, both Budge and Bobby reached the final, with most fans still expecting Budge to win. Despite the tour results, the years off during the war, and Budge's injury, "Big Red" was still considered the all-conquering king, the irresistible force, while Bobby was, as always, seen as the pesky upstart.

In less than an hour, it was over. To the stunned disbelief of the 10,000 spectators packed into the horseshoe-shaped stadium at the West Side Tennis Club, Bobby dismantled Budge in straight sets, 6-3, 6-1, 6-1. For three games in the opening set, Budge looked ready to prove himself the same indomitable player people had known, turning a 0-2 deficit into a 3-2 advantage. But things then went badly awry, as he made error after error: missed overheads, netted volleys, drives hit wide or beyond the baseline. For his part, Bobby played solidly and with purpose, but this was not the Budge the fans expected, or even the Budge Bobby expected. Fans could hardly believe their eyes. At the awards presentation, Budge made a brief speech. He told the fans how sorry he was that he had let them down so badly, and promised to come back the following year and reward their dedication. Years later, recalling that year and his disastrous 2-13 start against Bobby on that tour, Budge said he preferred to remember that in his last days as pro champion he won 20 matches to Bobby's 11.

Despite his success, Bobby's mastery over Budge mattered little. With Tilden's dream of a series of professional tournaments falling apart and the amateur game yet to get back on its feet, there was nothing for him to do. Until a legitimate amateur champion emerged, there was no one for him to play against, and the U.S. public had little interest in another tour between him and Budge, leaving Bobby to bide his time.

At the National Indoor Professional Championships in Philadelphia in the spring of 1947—the tournament organized by Tilden the previous year—Bobby crushed Budge again, 6-1, 8-6, 6-3. Afterwards, the two agreed to a series of head-to-head tours in South Africa and Europe by promoter Jack Harris. Bobby again edged Budge, 12-6. Upon returning, Bobby himself sponsored a brief tour with Frank Kovacs, still a powerful player and a popular gate attraction. But after turning professional, Kovacs had lost his sunny good nature. The "Clown Prince" had since become more bitter and caustic, intimidating ball boys, showing up late for matches, and offering to fight heckling spectators. At the Philadelphia tournament, Kovacs swigged from a large soda bottle full of Rum Collins mix during the changeovers. When he finished the bottle, he sent a ball boy out for a refill. When the boy came back with plain soda, Kovacs held up the match while he waited for the youngster to go out and retrieve the requested libation. Bobby finished their brief tour on top, four matches to three.

By 1947, with the amateur game reorganized, the eyes of the tennis world were on a hot young player named Jack Kramer. One of Perry Jones' "golden boys" back at the L.A. Tennis Club, Kramer was tall and handsome. Moreover, like Budge and Ellsworth Vines, he had a big game, an attacking, serve-and-volley style that was exciting to watch. Forget Bobby's dominance over Kramer when the two youths played against each other at the L.A. Tennis Club. (Once, after having won 27 straight games against Kramer, Bobby told his frustrated friend: "Look, kid. I know you're gonna be a player sometime and we're gonna meet and I just want you to know now who's boss.") Forget that before the war Bobby could beat Kramer nine times out of 10.

In 1946, Kramer lost just two matches. He won Forest Hills and anchored the United States team in its dramatic victory over Australia in Melbourne to regain the Davis Cup. He likely would have won Wimbledon that year had blisters not hampered him on his racquet hand. In 1947, Kramer was expected to win both Wimbledon and Forest Hills. It was clear he would be the star of the next pro tour, which was expected to make a fortune.

Bobby was the reigning professional champion. By all rights, the tour was his. But the public and the promoter, Jack Harris, clearly had their sights set on a tour that pitted Budge, the Great One, against Kramer, the second coming of Budge. From a commercial standpoint, Budge was so well known, so popular, and had such a terrific record that promoter Harris decided to tip the scales in favor of Budge by declaring that the winner of the 1947 U. S. Professional Championships at Forest Hills would get the opportunity to tour with Kramer. With all the marbles riding on that one tournament, Bobby called it "the $100,000 plum." The winner got the tour and the $100,000. The loser went home with nothing.

On a hot, muggy day on the grass at Forest Hills, the two men met in the final for what turned out to be one of the most important matches of their careers.

The tennis, however, failed to live up to the magnitude of the event. Both players came out tentatively, neither willing to take chances with so much at stake. The result, wrote Bobby, was a display of "mediocre" tennis in which the pair traded the first two sets. Budge won the first comfortably, 6-3. Bobby took the second, also at 6-3. In the third set, Bobby jumped to a 5-2 lead, and for a moment it seemed that Budge might be ready to fold up his game and go home. But he dug in, raised his level of play, and broke Bobby's serve to even the set, 5-5. Serving at 5-6, Budge then saved two set points to knot the match at 6-all. Holding serve to even the set again at 7-7, Budge then broke Bobby's serve to go ahead 8-7, giving him the opportunity to serve out the set.

But then Bobby dug in. He broke Budge's serve to even the set, 8-8, held serve, then broke Budge again to win the set, 10-8.

After a 10-minute rest, the players emerged from the locker room after a shower and a change into fresh clothes, Budge jumped to a quick lead and held out to win the fourth set, 6-4.

With everything riding on how well he performed over the next few minutes, Bobby clenched his teeth and gripped his racquet. It was now or never. "I thought of all that money and I swore I'd run my legs off before I'd let it get away from me," he later wrote.

After two and one-half hours, his arms cramping, Bobby used every shot he had—volleys, lobs, drop shots, service aces, and groundstroke placements—to keep Budge at bay. Serving at 3-5 and 0-40 in the fifth set, Budge made a final surge, fighting off three match points. But he followed this with three successive errors, giving Bobby the game, set, and match, 3-6, 6-3, 10-8, 4-6, 6-3. Bobby, not Budge, would tour with Kramer.

Years later, Bobby called this his single greatest moment in tennis.

To his fans, Budge said, "A year ago I told everyone present I'd be back this year and try to make amends. I believe I have. And I'll be back next year."

He did return, but there would be no more chances for the fallen king.

The match-up was billed as a classic contrast in styles and temperaments. Bobby boasted that he could beat Kramer (at left) any time, anywhere and on any surface. Here, the two smile before playing the opening match in Madison Square Garden.

12

Duel of the Decade

1948-1949

New Yorkers, who tend to think of weather as something that only happens to other people, paid little attention to the snow that was falling the morning of December 26, 1947. An almost mild 29 degrees, the sky was a conservative shade of gray and there was scarcely a breath of wind. The snowflakes themselves descended in a silent and orderly procession, and not until mid-afternoon did the average citizen begin to notice how heavily it was falling (it would average 1.8 inches per hour).

An eerie silence settled over the city. Traffic stopped. Fifth Avenue was white and vacant. Side streets were choked with thousands of stalled cars, busses, and trucks. Parkways were dotted with white mounds, each of which marked an abandoned automobile. Broadway's enormous electric signs gave only a wan glow in the gloom.

By five o'clock, New Yorkers had finally realized the full impact of what was happening. The heaviest snowfall in 76 years had buried the city. In just over 18 hours, 25.8 inches of snow had fallen. Central Manhattan subway stations were jammed with pushing, flailing throngs. At Grand Central Terminal and Pennsylvania Station, crowds stormed train gates until extra police details herded them into order. The thousands who fought their way into commuter cars soon regretted their triumph, as the trains got stuck soon after leaving the city. The Long Island Railroad shut down completely, its electric trains stalled as well as the steam locomotives sent out to rescue them.

Hotels were besieged, and a sea of the stranded headed for bars, all-night movies, and the apartments of friends.

From his room at the Hotel Lexington, promoter Jack Harris stared out into the bleakness and glumly said, "No one will go out to see a tennis match in this weather." For weeks, the press had hyped the series between Jack Kramer and Bobby Riggs as "the most widely discussed topic in the game for the past year" and the "Duel of the Decade," the biggest attraction since pre-war days when Don Budge ruled the courts. Now the tour seemed doomed before it began. It was too late to postpone. More than 16,000 tickets had already been sold. They had to play. Suddenly, Harris lamented, the "Duel of the Decade" was about to be the "Bust in the Blizzard."

Just getting to Madison Square Garden proved a challenge. Even if a taxi could be found, the streets were impassable by car. From their hotel just a few blocks away, the four players—Kramer, Bobby, Pancho Segura, and Dinny Pails—hiked cross-town to the arena. As they clambered over snowbanks with racquets in hand, the foursome had to wonder why they bothered.

Across the East River in Queens, John Frankenheimer, a young college student home for the holidays, tried to get through by telephone to the Garden to see if the match had been cancelled or rescheduled, but the lines were jammed. A star on the Williams College tennis team in Massachusetts and a former ranked junior player, Frankenheimer followed the game like other kids followed baseball. He idolized Jack Kramer, and every year went to the national championships at Forest Hills, having witnessed Kramer's comeback against Frank Parker from two sets to love down in the 1947 final a few months earlier and Don McNeill's upset over Bobby in the 1940 final. This, Frankenheimer reckoned, was the equivalent of the heavyweight championship of tennis and, blizzard or no blizzard, he was not about to miss it. He put on his winter coat and a heavy pair of boots, and grabbed a pair of cheap wooden skis. "I took the subway; got off at like 48th and 8th, and I skied for about six blocks," recalled Frankenheimer.

When Frankenheimer and the players arrived, they were amazed to find that more than 15,000 other fans had also trudged, skied, or snowshoed their way to Madison Square Garden. Of 16,052 tickets sold, only 938 people failed to show up. Columnist Jimmy Powers of the *New York Post* called it "the greatest tribute to an indoor athletic event in the history of sport." The $55,730 in gross receipts was second only to $58,120 taken in at the opening of the Vines-Perry tour in 1937.

Like most fans, Frankenheimer, who went on to fame as a film director of Hollywood thrillers, such as *The Manchurian Candidate, Seven Days in May,* and *Ronin,* expected Kramer to demolish Bobby. For two years, "Big Jake," as players and fans called Kramer, had been nearly invincible. He lost just one match in 1947, ending his amateur career on a 41-match win-streak that drew inevitable comparisons to giants such as Bill Tilden, Ellsworth Vines, and Don Budge. He played the kind of game—aggressive serve-and-volley tennis—that was popular with fans. He was also tall, blond, and handsome, with the sort of easygoing manner and healthy glow that was associated with Southern California. Here at last was a hero the nation could get behind.

The son of a brakeman for the Union Pacific railroad, John Albert Kramer was born in Las Vegas, Nevada on August 1, 1921. In 1935, the family moved to Los Angeles, in part to nurture young Jake's (or Big Jake, as he was later to be called) burgeoning interest in tennis. After being dispatched in the opening round of his first tournament, someone suggested that Jack see a man named Perry Jones at the L.A. Tennis Club. By the following year, Kramer had won the national boys' singles and doubles titles at Culver, Indiana.

While learning to play the game at the club, Kramer received the help of an older club member, Clifton Roche, an automotive engineer whose work led to the development of the automatic transmission. His invention made him rich, and Roche retired young, became a tennis enthusiast, and with an engineer's eye started diagramming tennis courts, investigating shot angles and looking at point scenarios to analyze risk versus reward. "Coach" Roche, as he was called by his protégés, calculated the "mathematical unsoundness" of hitting the ball to certain spots in certain positions.

He called it "percentage tennis," and while the phrase is now hackneyed in the game, it was revolutionary to Kramer. The key element to Roche's theory was learning the difference between a good shot and a smart shot. From this, Kramer came away with the knowledge that a player positioned at the net not only creates more angles with which to put the ball away, but cuts off more angles to his opponent. This puts an opponent under greater pressure, making it more likely he will miss.

Taking these lessons to heart, Kramer charged in at every opportunity. He followed his first serve to net, used his big groundstrokes to drive an opponent off court, and positioned himself at the net for a putaway volley. Roche was also a fanatic on psychology and fitness, and taught Kramer how to pace himself, how to conserve energy (a finite commodity in the days of five-set matches with no tiebreakers), and how to "play to the score." That is, thinking beyond the point being played, knowing when to play hard, when to let up, and when to make a sacrifice play.

Kramer, who enjoyed playing poker, described the technique: "Put the ball in a certain spot, and then put yourself in a certain spot, and the chance of the other player getting out of that spot would be the same as drawing a third king or to a straight or whatever."

Bobby, too, liked to think of tennis in terms of percentages, probabilities, and tactics. Describing his game of "Airtight Tennis," Bobby wrote: "Eight out of ten points in tennis are not won but are lost... Errors, not clean winners, account for most of the points in any tennis match." The pressure Bobby applied was more psychological than physical. Instead of cutting off angles, he worked at opening them up. Instead of just defeating his opponents, he worked at breaking them down. His game was one of anticipation, consistency, footwork, and endurance. He set out to exploit an opponent's weaknesses and to make them hit uncomfortable or off-balance shots. He might also change tactics midstream, moving from defense to offense. Instead of forcing errors, he lured opponents into making errors, gradually working on their confidence and getting them to doubt themselves.

Despite their contrasting styles, Bobby and Kramer approached the game with a similar philosophy. At its core was the application of pressure, an ability to use the geometry of the court and a gambler's sense of the odds. The biggest difference was that, against Kramer's unrelenting attack, the loser could come off the court with the consolation of knowing he had been beaten by a superior player. Against Bobby, an opponent came off the court shaking his head, frustrated at how he lost and how he could have missed all the chances given to him, convinced he had never played so badly in his entire life.

That night in the Garden, Bobby's pre-war dominance over Kramer mattered little. In the intervening six years, Kramer had gotten bigger, stronger, and more mature. Kramer was married with children, and the formerly high-spirited and reckless youth had become a tennis perfectionist. His good looks and laid-back demeanor belied a seriousness and unwavering sense of purpose that he took onto the court every time he played. Kramer now overwhelmed opponents, and most experts figured Kramer's "big game" simply packed too big a punch for Bobby, a player many still considered just a scrappy baseliner.

As preparations got under way, media hype for the big match snowballed. As with the Budge-Riggs tour, this was billed as a classic contrast in styles and temperaments. Bobby boasted that he could beat Kramer any time, anywhere, on any surface. Then, borrowing a line Frank Kovacs used seven years before, Bobby said of Kramer, "I'd like to play him every day of the week and twice on Sunday."

When asked, Kramer said he considered Bobby a purely defensive player, and that he didn't think such a style could hold up against his withering attack.

Bobby had a couple of advantages going into Madison Square Garden that night. One was experience. The lights, the pressure, the crowds all were familiar to him. Another advantage was the element of surprise. He and Kramer had not played against each other in years, and although he was fairly certain how Kramer would play, he was counting on Kramer figuring him strictly as a baseliner, a backcourt player reluctant to come to the net. In practice matches leading up to the big event, Bobby did nothing to undermine this impression, losing unimpressively to both Segura and Pails while Kramer handled them both with ease.

But Bobby had been planning this match for weeks, approaching it as if it were a chess match. He outlined his strategy, scouted Kramer, applied his psychology, and choreographed exactly how the match would unfold.

When the house lights dimmed and master of ceremonies Alice Marble introduced the players, a weak smattering of applause greeted Bobby as he breezed onto the court with his usual grin and cocksure walk. The crowed roared when Kramer stepped onto the court. Well aware of the reception he'd receive, Bobby had spent the previous hour working the crowd, cajoling fans into betting $10, $15, $100, and giving odds to back their hero Kramer. After all, Bobby was familiar playing the role of the villain. By the time play started, he was still negotiating courtside.

While the fans settled in their seats, Kramer promptly dropped the first three games. In 20 minutes, Bobby had won the first set, 6-2. In a surprising role-reversal, Bobby was the aggressor and Kramer the counter-puncher. "I made up my mind to lob him and go to the net every time," Bobby recalled. "He also had a faulty backhand and so, unless I had an open court, every shot would go to his backhand. Not most of them, all of them." At times, Kramer had to stoop to his shoetops to scrape Bobby's heavily sliced shots as they skidded off the court. Watching Bobby, "it seemed that each one of his strokes was a definite part of a well-organized plan," noted an astute observer from *American Lawn Tennis*.

Broken four times in the first two sets, Kramer showed flashes of brilliance. In the second set, at 4-all, he had Bobby down 15-40. But Bobby wriggled out of that and won the set, 10-8. After winning the third set, 6-4, Kramer went up a break in the fourth, but Bobby broke back twice to take the set and match, 6-2, 10-8, 4-6. 6-4.

For every spectacular shot off Kramer's racquet that drew cheers from the audience, there were twice as many misses. He over-hit, pushing the ball beyond the baseline or into the net. He missed approach shots and simply could not pass Bobby at the net. Even his much-feared serve failed him when he needed it most, double-faulting on crucial points.

Afterwards, Kramer admitted he had been nervous, and said he had trouble adjusting to the indoor conditions and the canvas court. "But that's no alibi," he said. "I got jittery and missed the easy ones."

The next day, flush with victory and $20,000 in collected bets, Bobby demanded a meeting with Kramer and Jack Harris. As they sat on a train bound for Pittsburgh, the second stop on the tour, Bobby announced he wanted to renegotiate his contract. The original deal signed by the two players called for Kramer to get 35 percent of the net profits and Bobby to get 17½ percent. Logic and fairness might dictate that Bobby, the reigning champion, receive more than the challenger, but tour economics dictated that the challenger get the big money because the amateurs retained all the power and publicity in tennis. Bobby understood this. What he argued was that if he kept beating Kramer, or that if they played so close that interest in the tour allowed them to double back through New York and other major cities, then he rightfully deserved an extra share. It was a typically shrewd argument for Bobby, whose talents as a negotiator were second only to his abilities as a tennis player. Reluctantly, Harris and Kramer agreed to give up 2½ percent of their share of the profits over $100,000.

For Kramer, having been beaten on opening night in New York in front of the big-city press and now beaten out of 2½ percent of the profits, the stakes of the tour became immediately clear: He was fighting for nothing less than his survival. "I sat there thinking that I had better win this tour," he later wrote. "If I did not I was as useless in tennis as yesterday's newspaper. Wimbledon, Forest Hills, the Davis Cup—none of it would mean a damn. Budge lost one tour by a couple of matches and he is buried. It made me struggle. There is no greater incentive than the threat of extinction."

Gradually, Kramer made adjustments. From Pittsburgh to Cleveland to Dayton, a series of one-night stands took the tour across the Midwest, then over to the Northeast and down the Atlantic Coast to Florida. The format for each night was the same: first Segura and Pails played the preliminary match, then Bobby and Kramer played the main event, followed by a doubles match, usually Kramer and Segura against Bobby and Pails.

As was tradition, the tour took place over the winter months. At first, they traveled mostly by train. Then, as the distances grew greater and the train schedules less convenient, promoter Harris found a couple of DeSoto station wagons. If Bobby and Kramer bought the cars, Harris offered to kick in for the gas. This allowed the players to leave a town at their convenience. Bobby owned one car, Kramer the other. Generally, Kramer, Harris, and Pails rode in one car, Bobby, Segura, and, occasionally, Kay in the other—every so often switching traveling companions to break the monotony.

Often the ideal time to travel was right after the evening matches, when the players were too keyed up to sleep anyway. This meant driving in the dead of night, often in bad weather. Occasionally, the players flew, but it would be a few years before the players could travel by air regularly. Playing an average of four to five matches a week, the tour moved first from city to city, playing arenas in major cities, then to smaller cities and towns where they played in cramped auditoriums or high-school gymnasiums.

A one-ton panel truck carried the canvas court, the net, the balls, and the souvenir programs. The court was split into two 800-pound sections that took six men to handle. When they arrived at a new city, the court had to be rolled out. The halves were laced together at the net. It was then pulled tight by ropes fed through 22 eyes on each side of the court and anchored to the stands. More than once, a player chased a ball off the court only to trip on the ropes.

The truck driver was a regular member of the tour, paid a small salary plus a commission for each program he sold. The arenas hired six or so workers to help put down the court under the driver's supervision. Players then scouted the court as standard operating procedure. If the court was loose, players might slide and be injured. At the end of the night, the court had to be rolled up precisely to fit back into the truck.

The long hours, overnight drives, and often freezing weather made it a tough way to make a living. "It was backbreaking work," recalled Bert Brown, a former player hired as a driver for the 1949-50 tour. It was also dangerous. One time, Brown said, he fell asleep at the wheel and woke up having driven into a snowbank. "I told myself I gotta get out of this," Brown said. He found someone to take his place, a kid he knew from the Los Angeles area, Bill Sullivan. Brown spent a couple of weeks breaking Sullivan in, then quit. "I was ruining my health," Brown explained. Later, he heard Sullivan did the same thing, and fell asleep at the wheel. Only Sullivan wasn't as lucky. He was killed.

Improvisation was crucial. The players had to play in dark, sometimes unheated, arenas. At a hockey rink in Canada, the court had to be laid over the ice, but the boards around the ice left nothing with which to anchor the court. Bert Brown, driver at the time, pounded large spikes into the ice to secure the ropes. "I didn't want to ruin their ice. But I did it anyway," Brown said. Otherwise, the matches would have been cancelled.

Bobby congratulated Brown for his ingenuity. "You did the right thing," Bobby said. "You saved the tour."

In Little Rock, they had to play on the stage of a high-school auditorium. The space wasn't big enough for the canvas court, so they painted a facsimile of a tennis court on the stage floor. In Saratoga, New York, they played in an opera house with the back wall 18 inches from the baseline. Near Springfield, Massachusetts, they played in a gymnasium in which the players had to run around basketball stanchions set two feet behind the baseline. Forced to avoid the obstacles, "you could be sure that both players used a back-and-forth strategy—nobody was hitting any drop shots," Kramer quipped.

It was a grueling routine: the constant traveling, the unpredictable conditions, the hassles and isolation of being on the road. Unlike amateurs, who got to hang around cushy country clubs for a week, this world consisted of cheap hotels, gas stations, and all-night coffee shops. And unlike tournament play, there were no easy early-round matches. Every match was hard-fought.

More difficult, perhaps, was convincing the fans that the matches were on the level. The head-to-head format drew inevitable suspicions that the matches could be fixed or that, at the very least, the players might not be motivated to play their very best. "At each stop we had to convince everybody that we played for real, that we weren't some damn circus," Kramer said.

At least Bobby and Kramer had the gratification of being paid well. Segura and Pails, who played the preliminary match, received just $300 per week apiece, and they had to pay their own expenses. The $8,800 Kramer collected on opening night in New York was more than those two together earned for the entire tour. No, it wasn't fair, admitted Kramer, "but if you wanted to play professionally, it was the only game in town." For a while, Segura lost more money playing cards than he was earning playing tennis. Bobby taught him how to play poker, but not very well. "Bobby stole my money," Segura complained. "He was playing poker with wild cards, and I didn't know what I was doing." Banned from the card games until he was solvent again, Segura recalled occasionally having to sleep in the car because he couldn't afford a motel room.

When it came to cards, every player had his own favorite game. Kramer preferred five-card draw, jacks or better to open the betting—a conservative game in which the odds are simple and winning is a matter of patience and a little knowledge. Bobby liked to play a game called Indicators: five cards dealt to each player and five cards dealt face down in the middle. The middle cards are turned over one-by-one, indicating which cards are wild. This is a wide-open game, in which the rules on sound poker strategy go out the window. The pots build quickly and winning is more a matter of chance and chutzpah than skill.

Life on the tour was tough. But considering the players were more or less quarantined with the same guys who were trying to beat them out of a job, they all got along remarkably well. "After the matches we would relax with each other, have a few beers, play cards, because often as not we were somewhere alone and all we had for good company was each other," Kramer said.

Segura (born Francisco Olegario Segura) was a three-time intercollegiate champion at the University of Miami from 1943 to 1945. He grew up on the dirt floor of a sugar-cane shack in Guayaquil, Ecuador. A non-aristocrat of Inca heritage, Segura's father was the caretaker at a local tennis club and let his son use the courts after hours. A sickly youth, Segura suffered a bout of childhood rickets that permanently deformed his legs, leaving him bowlegged and pigeon-toed (other children teased him, calling him "parrot foot"). He was so weak he had to hold the racquet with both hands. Despite his handicap, Segura displayed extraordinary talent. With the help of some wealthy club members he quickly

Though he never got the recognition he deserved, Pancho Segura was a staple of the early pro tours and a crowd favorite because of his amazing ability and big-hearted nature. Kramer called his two-handed forehand "the best shot in the game."

developed into a fine player. Not only was he fit and agile, but his two-fisted forehand evolved into what Kramer called "the best shot in the game," able to deliver both considerable power and a wonderfully delicate touch. He won his country's national championship as a 17-year-old in 1938, and followed that with a series of titles in South America.

He arrived in the United States in the summer of 1940 with an English-speaking friend, a straw bag, and two racquets. Entering Forest Hills that year, he lost in the first round to Frank Parker. Gardnar Mulloy quickly recruited Segura to play for the University of Miami, where Mulloy still ran the tennis team. But because Segura knew so little English, he became the butt of practical jokes.

"The football players took him over like they did Bobby Riggs," recalled Mulloy.

At a bar or a party, one of the football players might lean over and tell Segura, "See that girl over there? Boy, she's warm for your form, you know. She wants to make love to you. Go over and say, 'I want to fuck you.' "

Segura, in his broken English, would ask "What's that mean?"

"Just go say it."

So, Mulloy said, Segura "would go over and say it and the girl would either whack him one or run away." Perhaps as a consequence of such experiences, Bobby said, Segura's conversation was liberally sprinkled with profanities.

Nevertheless, Segura, or Segoo, as he became known on the circuit, became a beloved figure in the game, not just for his amazing tennis ability but for his big-hearted nature and disarming sense of humor. Unfortunately, because of the war and the fact that he turned professional early in his career (1947), his achievements in tennis went largely ignored. But he was a staple of the professional tour for 20 years, winning the U.S. Pro Championships three times in a row, 1950-52, and was a longtime crowd favorite. "The fans would come out to see the new challenger face the old champion," Kramer said, "but they would leave talking about the bandy-legged little sonuvabitch who gave them such pleasure playing the first match and the doubles. The next time the tour came to town the fans would come back to see Segoo." A shrewd tactician, Segura later became a coach and mentor to players such as Jimmy Connors and Andre Agassi.

Like many athletes of his era, good-natured Australian Denis "Dinny" Pails lost his best years to the war. A fine stylist with a big serve, he spent the war years working in an Australian airplane factory, after which he won his national championships in singles. Pails reached the semifinals at Wimbledon, played Davis Cup, and ended up ranked No. 6 in the world in 1947. Deciding to go after bigger things, he turned professional, and caught Harris' eye.

After a month and a half, Bobby and Kramer had played to a virtual dead heat. By the time the tour reached Los Angeles in the middle of February, Kramer held a 15-13 lead. Not only were they nearly tied in terms of matches won, but the matches themselves were tough, closely fought contests. Troubled by Bobby's aggressive tactics, Kramer had to adjust his game. "His strategy was to smother me," Kramer recalled. "That sounds ridiculous, given my larger size and greater power, but Bobby had the confidence, the speed and the agility. When we first started touring, he came at me on his first serve, on his second serve, and on my second serve. He could come to the net on his second serve by lofting a high bouncer into the far corner of my backhand service box. I couldn't generate any real power, and with the high bounce, he also had time to get into the net."

Kramer found that if he missed many first serves Bobby was all over him. "My second serve didn't kick like Bobby's, so he could return that deep enough and follow into the net. Unless I was getting an unusually high percentage of good first serves in, I—the big server—was more vulnerable to service breaks. It was a crazy situation, and it forced me to learn to hit a high-kicking serve down the middle to his backhand in the deuce court. It forced me to think attack constantly. I would rush in and try to pound his weakest point—his backhand, which had control, but not much speed—pound it, pick on it, smash it 'til it broke down. For the first time it was kill or be killed. So the style I am famous for was not consciously planned; it was created out of the necessity of dealing with Bobby Riggs."

By improving his second serve, Kramer started to get the results he needed. At the Pan-Pacific Auditorium in Los Angeles, the site of Bobby's first big win over Budge, courtside seats for the players' two matches sold for $12.50 apiece, a small fortune in 1948. Before big hometown crowds, they each won a match, but shortly afterward the tide turned. Kramer then went 10-1 in matches from California across the West and into Texas. At first, Bobby tried to respond by slugging his service returns, a gamble that gave him little margin for error. He could win only when he played his very best.

As Kramer's lead grew, Bobby became demoralized and gave up trying. "I hated it and fell apart," Bobby later explained. "I'm not a grind-out man. That [Madison Square] Garden match was a clutch match, a natural for me. I'm always up for those kinds of matches. I'm only really good when we play for all the marbles. Who's got the nerve? That's my game. I can't play a grind-out, a match a day for two months. I'm no good at that. I'm a now-or-never guy. Always have been." Bobby felt he could always rise to the occasion for a big match such as his defeat of Budge in the final at Forest Hills the year before. What he could not understand was why Kramer, even after he wrapped up the tour by stretching his winning streak to the point Bobby had no chance of coming back, "just poured it on harder and harder… Sometimes I wouldn't see him for two weeks except on the court," Bobby wrote. On the rare occasions that he lost, Kramer angrily kept to himself, recounting the match in his mind and berating his mistakes. In his merciless determination to win, Kramer's dominance started hurting the gate. True, they were competitive athletes, but they were also entertainers, and no one wanted to pay to see a blowout.

In Fort Worth, Bobby hit bottom. According to Bobby, he had the flu. According to others, he was out all night playing poker. In any case, he was in no shape to play tennis. Before their match he approached Kramer in the locker room: "Look, you gotta give me a break. Carry me a bit. Make it look it competitive. Your winning streak is killing interest in the tour, not to mention costing us a lot of money. If for no other reason, do it for the fans, who paid good money to see us. Please."

Kramer listened silently and then went out on court, whereupon he handed Bobby his most humiliating loss of the entire tour, finishing him off in less than an hour without the loss of a single game. More than half the audience got up and left at the intermission. "Those who stayed did a good deal of heckling and belittled the finish of Kramer's 6-0, 6-0 victory with a lusty burst of booing," wrote one columnist. "As far as they were concerned, Riggs hadn't been trying for anything that didn't come right at him." Afterwards, Kramer went up to Bobby and sternly said, "Don't ever ask me to do something like that again."

In the face of such a trouncing, Bobby came away with the consolation that at least the audience knew the results weren't fixed to keep the scores even.

After going into Los Angeles with a slim 15-13 match lead, Kramer went 54-7 to finish the North American tour 69-20. As his lead lengthened, interest in the tour diminished and the crowds thinned. From a spectator and financial viewpoint, the tour was a huge success, attracting 332,977 fans and grossing $503,047—the most yet for a professional tennis tour. After deducting expenses and local promoters' cut, Kramer's 35 percent share came to $89,000; Bobby's, $45,387. It was the payoff of a lifetime for a lifetime devoted to the game. Appearances in South American and Europe subsequently earned another $135,000 for the tour.

Facing the prospect of becoming an instant has-been, Bobby's last and only hope was to win the U.S. Professional Championships at Forest Hills that July, the only American professional tournament of any consequence. If he could beat Kramer there, he still could claim to be a valid contender and perhaps prolong his career (Budge, too, figured that a win there might revive his wilting prospects).

It was not to be. Kramer was simply too strong. On the carefully manicured turf at the West Side Tennis Club, Kramer first took out Budge in an epic semifinal. Against the aging warhorse, Kramer came back from two sets-to-one and two service breaks down in the fourth set to win, 6-4, 8-10, 3-6, 6-4, 6-0. Against Bobby in the final, Kramer withstood a steady barrage of shots by Bobby to win 14-12, 6-2, 3-6, 7-5.

Bobby had his chances. He had an easy putaway volley to win the first set, but, perhaps trying too hard, missed it. Years later, he remembered that shot, wondering if, had he won that point and the set, he might have won the match and turned his fortunes around.

Instead, like Budge the year before, Bobby faced forced retirement. From the pinnacle of tennis success—his mastery over Don Budge, his ascendance to world champion, and his top billing in the most successful professional tour ever—Bobby appeared out of a job. The harsh reality of head-to-head tours meant a new challenger needed to be found. Angry and frustrated, Bobby quit training, gave up trying on court, and let himself go. He hated losing, hated being next to best, and saw his future crashing around him. Bobby had to deal with a predicament that eventually faces any career athlete—the grim inevitability of life without sport.

Pancho Gonzalez was a tall, handsome, brooding young man with a volatile temper. He was considered just a kid with promise when he came out of nowhere in 1948 to win the big one, the national championship at Forest Hills.

13
The End of the Road
1950-1952

From its wartime doldrums, professional tennis emerged stronger than ever—popular, profitable, and no longer the neglected stepchild of the amateur game. The best tennis was now played in the professional ranks. And though hostility still abounded between the two camps, even stalwart defenders of the amateur game had to admire Jack Kramer's dominance over Bobby. The old guard no doubt took satisfaction in seeing Kramer, their former golden boy, send the game's impudent "bad boy" into tennis oblivion. "They wanted to see him beat me soundly, partly because of their personal affection for Jack," Bobby said, "and partly because in some obscure manner they thought it would represent a victory for the forces of clean amateur tennis over the forces of hardboiled professional tennis."

From champion to chump, the all-or-nothing nature of head-to-head tours meant Bobby was history. No, it was not fair, but Bobby understood the rules as well as anybody. Ironically, for the second-best player in the world, there weren't a lot of options left. He could go out and find a "real" job, perhaps giving tennis lessons at some resort for $20 an hour. Or he could continue to tour as part of the "animal act." Neither held much appeal for a man of Bobby's ego—a player who had mastered Budge and who had grown accustomed to the mantle of "world champion." Bobby felt he was still one of the game's greatest players and, moreover, one of its greatest entertainers: "Being number two after fighting for years to defeat Budge to be number one, I wasn't happy being number two."

At the United States Professional Championships at Forest Hills in June 1949, Bobby won the title for the third and last time, defeating Budge once again. But this was not the same Bobby who fans were accustomed to seeing. Noted *American Lawn Tennis* magazine: "An older and more subdued Bobby Riggs proved that he is still the second best professional tennis player in the world by defeating an older and slower Don Budge in the final of the national professional championships to take over the crown vacated by Jack Kramer." Kramer, who had obligations in Europe at the time, could not play. "Even in absence," wrote *ALT*, "Kramer was the dominant figure of the tourney. Riggs won the title, but no one present doubted for a moment that Big Jake is still the pro ruler, national professional championships notwithstanding. The regular whippings that Jack handed Bobby during their 18-month tour have taken their toll. Not only has Riggs been played down to a walk physically, but his personal ego and supreme confidence have been badly mistreated by the smiling Kramer... In none of the six matches that brought him to the final round did Riggs behave with that easy nonchalance and confidence that were his trademark in years gone by."

Years later, Bobby would say he threw in the towel too early, that he could have remained competitive for a few more years. But he was burned out. His 18-month tour with Kramer had been the longest and most grueling tour of any to date. In all, Bobby had been on the road nearly four years straight, leaving him physically and emotionally drained. "I was fatigued. I was tired. After playing Budge for four years, I misled myself. I told myself youth will be served, you can't stay on top forever—nobody does, nobody ever has, and neither can you. Kramer's come along and he's number one. It's time to move on to something else. I sold myself on that." At 31, Bobby decided to hang up his racquet.

As luck would have it, a new opportunity presented itself, one that would allow Bobby to stay in the game. While finishing up a tour of South America, Kramer, Bobby, and the other players had grown dissatisfied with promoter Jack Harris and fired him. Taking over the tour themselves, the players divided the responsibilities between themselves. When it was over, Bobby suggested to Kramer that Bobby step into the role of promoter. After all, he had experience through his work with Bill Tilden and the Professional Players Association in 1946, and had promoted his own brief tour with Frank Kovacs in 1947. On the basis of their close friendship—that and a hefty offer of 35 percent of the gate to Kramer, twice what Harris had given defending champion Bobby the previous year—Kramer agreed.

"I could still make deals and smoke big cigars," Bobby later reflected. "Be in the act in some way. My ego was still being fulfilled. It made it easier not to be the champ."

It would be billed as Bobby Riggs' World Championship Tennis Tour, but it was essentially a partnership between Bobby and Kramer. When it came to major decisions, nothing was done without consulting Kramer.

Their first task was to find a new challenger. But scanning the ranks of the amateur game the summer of 1949, the pickings looked slim. Of the possible prospects, the top two appeared to be Ted Schroeder, Kramer's friend and former doubles partner, and Pancho Gonzalez, a fiery, big-hitting kid who had come from obscurity to win Forest Hills the year before.

Schroeder, or "Schroed," was the same age as Kramer and another alumnus of the Los Angeles Tennis Club. A scrappy, fearless serve-and-volleyer, Schroeder had been tutored by Cliff Roche, and shared Kramer's belief that the key to winning was to take over the net. Yet in Schroeder's case, this belief was based less on Roche's theory of "percentage tennis" than on the fact that Schroeder simply lacked the consistent groundstrokes needed to win from the backcourt. Whereas Kramer's athletic serve-and-volley game was smooth and graceful, the wiry Schroeder's relentless charges seemed almost desperate, with all the artistry of a leatherneck storming Omaha Beach. Nothing stopped him.

Against Kovacs in the quarterfinals at Rye in 1941, Schroeder followed every serve to the net, only to watch Kovacs blister the ball past him, one service return winner after another. At one point,

Schroeder got up to serve and, once again, furiously followed the ball to the net. This time, instead of ripping the ball past Schroeder, Kovacs caught the ball in his hand (surrendering the point in the process) and proclaimed for everyone to hear, "Ted, you've got to be kidding."

What Schroeder lacked in style, he more than made up for in courage. No matter how overmatched or how far down he was, he never gave up. Opponents and fans marveled at his drive and tenacity, as time and again he turned lost causes into marathon victories. No wonder Kramer made him his permanent doubles partner. And no wonder Schroeder became one of the truly great Davis Cup stalwarts.

In 1942, Schroeder won the national amateur championships at Forest Hills, defeating Frank Parker in a tournament overshadowed by the escalating war. After that, he refused to play the national championship because of his disdain for the eastern tennis establishment and the hypocrisy of amateur officials.

His commitment to Davis Cup, however, was unshakable. In 1946, he helped return the Cup to the United States after a seven-year sojourn in Australia. Overall, he played for five Davis Cup squads and compiled an 11-3 singles record. Brusque and opinionated, Schroeder rubbed a lot of his fellow players the wrong way, but his on-court heroics made him a fan favorite.

Perhaps most amazing about Schroeder was the fact he was only a part-time player. While attending Stanford, he played only a few tournaments during the summer, and never took the time or expense to play Wimbledon. During the war, he served as a Navy pilot, after which he worked at Kelvinator Refrigeration Products near Los Angeles, never playing more than a few summer tournaments as well as the Davis Cup.

In 1949, on his first and only trip to Wimbledon, Schroeder earned the nickname "Lucky" after a series of narrow escapes en route to the final. In the first round, he came back against Gardnar Mulloy after losing the first two sets. In the quarterfinals against Australian Frank Sedgman, he was again down two sets to love, trailed 0-3 in the fifth, and saved two match points before taking the set and match, 9-7. Against South African Eric Sturgess in the semifinals, Schroeder came back after being down two sets to one, and in the final against popular Czech player Jaroslav Drobny, he played his fourth five-setter in seven matches, winning the title, 3-6, 6-0, 6-3, 4-6, 6-4.

Pancho Gonzalez, Schroeder's Davis Cup teammate, washed out early at Wimbledon in 1949, falling in the fourth round. This fueled speculation that his championship run at Forest Hills the year before had been a fluke and led some to call him the "cheese champ" (he was then nicknamed Gorgo, as in Gorgonzola cheese). Both Kramer and Bobby knew Gonzalez had championship potential, but at 20 years old he seemed too raw and undeveloped to turn professional. During a series of practice matches against Budge in Los Angeles, Gonzalez won only one set out of 25 matches. "I was over the hill at that point," recalled Budge. "I said, 'Pancho, you can't even beat me now. How in hell are you going to beat Jack?'"

Born May 9, 1928, Ricardo Alonso Gonzales (he later dropped the "s" in favor of a "z"), Pancho was another product of the L.A. Tennis Club "pipeline." A tall, handsome, brooding young man with a volatile temper, Gonzalez never quite fit in. As a 15-year-old, he became the top ranked player in Southern California. But he refused to attend school, leading Perry Jones to bar him from tournament play. He joined the Navy at 17, emerging 16 months later in 1947. He surprised many by beating a number of higher-ranked players with his blistering service and attacking style of play. Ranked 17th nationally, he was considered just a kid with promise when he won the big one, the national championship at Forest Hills.

As far as Kramer and Bobby were concerned, Gonzalez' win had a flaw: Schroeder had skipped Forest Hills. Schroeder held a 7-1 edge over Gonzalez in tournament play, making him the obvious pick to be the new pro challenger. Before Wimbledon ("The only reason I went to Wimbledon was to turn professional," Schroeder confessed years later), Bobby and Kramer met with Schroeder to strike a deal at the Atheneum Court Hotel in London. Schroeder would play the next pro tour for a straight $25,000 guarantee (a laughably small amount considering Kramer's take the previous tour). Kramer recalled urging Schroeder to take a smaller guarantee against a percentage of the gate, but Schroeder insisted on the $25,000. "I kept telling him [it] was stupid until Riggs told me to shut up and let the kid have what he wanted. We signed a letter of agreement to tour the next winter, [and] Bobby went back to the States to start lining up arena dates."

Two weeks later, in Scarborough, England, Kramer received a call. It was Schroeder. He wanted out. Kramer argued with Schroeder: The deal's been signed. It's too late to back out. Besides, it's the opportunity of a lifetime. What would the fans think? All to no avail. Schroeder kept telling Kramer he was just not up to the grind of a pro tour, and that he could not bear the thought of getting up and playing a match every day.

Kramer tried to convince him otherwise, but finally Schroeder ended it, saying, "Don't make me unhappy, Jack." In order to allow another player to rise and take his place, Schroeder told Kramer he would stay out of competition that summer. At the time, Kramer believed this meant Schroeder would skip Davis Cup and Forest Hills.

A couple of weeks later, Kramer got another call, this time from Bobby.

"That little sonuvabitch has double-crossed us again."

"What sonuvabitch?" asked Kramer.

"Schroeder," whined Bobby. "He's agreed to play Davis Cup."

Not only that, but Schroeder's heroics in retaining the Cup that year would end up stealing the spotlight from the other U.S. singles player, Gonzalez, who figured to be the best alternative to Schroeder. Bobby was furious. When Schroeder then announced he would play at Forest Hills, Bobby placed another frantic phone call to Kramer.

Kramer told Bobby to take it easy. This could work out. If Schroeder were beaten, a new hero would rise to take his place. On the other hand, if Schroeder won, he would face even more pressure to turn pro. They could then offer him a deal he could not possibly turn down.

Though seeded first and second, Schroeder and Gonzalez were hardly shoo-ins for the final. Neither dominated the field the way

Kramer, Budge, or even Bobby had when they were favorites. Schroeder had played only two matches since his Wimbledon victory two months earlier. Meanwhile, Gonzalez had shown he could lose to just about anybody. Nevertheless, Schroeder and Gonzalez managed to eke their way into the final, and Kramer and Bobby simply had to wait for the outcome.

Given their record against each other, no one gave Gonzalez much of a chance. But in one of the great Forest Hills comebacks, the tenacious 21-year-old clawed his way back from a two-sets-to-love hole to defeat the favored Schroeder, 16-18, 2-6, 6-1, 6-2, 6-4. The first set alone took more than an hour to complete, the longest ever in a Forest Hills final. When the five-hour match was over, Kramer went into the locker room. A spent Schroeder said, "Now, I guess everyone will be happy."

Soon afterward, Bobby flew to Los Angeles with Gonzalez. By the time they landed, Bobby had Gonzalez' signature on a contract to tour against Kramer, with each player to receive 30 percent of the gate. Segura and Parker signed on for the animal act. In the finals of the Pacific Southwest tournament a couple of weeks later, Gonzalez secured his position as the top amateur by again defeating Schroeder.

On Oct. 25, 1949, the tour opened in Madison Square Garden. Before a crowd of 13,357, some paying a top price of $8 a seat, Kramer won the opener with relative ease, 6-4, 3-6, 6-3, 6-2. In terms of gross receipts and attendance, it was a solid turnout, though nowhere near that of the Riggs-Kramer debut.

For this tour, Bobby gave Kay a job doing advance work— traveling ahead of the players to the next stop to promote the match and meet with the newspapers. She missed the excitement of the circuit and hated not having her husband around for most of the year. Besides, she knew what life was like on the road, and Bobby was never very discreet. She figured that perhaps by working with him she could renew their closeness and avert disaster. So she left her sons at home in California with her father and brother.

As a promoter, Bobby was a natural. He was good-natured, energetic, and fast-talking—a born deal-maker. He handled everything: booking the arenas, arranging accommodations, handling publicity, introducing players to the audiences, and signing the checks. He worked hard. "He was on the ball all the time, because he understood he was fighting for his financial life," recalled Kramer. "And he was great at selling tennis. I mean, he was tireless. He would go on shows, he would talk to sports writers every place. He was as much of a story himself as Gonzalez or myself. He was a hell of a great interview. The hard thing was how to shut him off."

Bobby's biggest problem, Kramer said, was a lack of selectiveness. To Bobby, "Tour dates were like women—he would take a shot at them all. If Riggs saw three guys standing around a gas station kicking tires, he'd try to sell them a date on the tennis tour." As a result, Bobby tended to overextend himself and the players. "Scheduling five matches with travel in one week was a pretty rough thing," Kramer said. When Jack Harris had managed the Riggs-Kramer tour, he tried to give the players a couple of days off each week. This way, Kramer said, "you'd be a little more fresh, and you'd also be able to promote the match in the city in which you were gonna play." Bobby, however, "scheduled Gonzalez and me to play ten nights in a row all around New York in little places— the amphitheaters and all that kind of stuff—and God, we were worn out."

The bigger problem, however, was Gonzalez. The youngster was simply in over his head against the stronger, more seasoned Kramer. For one thing, Gonzalez's training habits were horrendous. He ate poorly, slept little, and was hooked on cigarettes and soda pop. Insisting on traveling by himself, Gonzalez would sometimes drive all night to the next stop, walking onto the court sunken-eyed and exhausted.

Following the Madison Square Garden opener, Kramer won 22 of the first 26 matches, including a 6-0, 6-0 shellacking in Waterloo, Ontario, that took less than a half-hour. Lacking the self-discipline needed to compete night after night, Gonzalez seemed incapable of managing himself, Kramer recalled. Moreover, the intensely proud Gonzalez took each loss as a personal affront. And when he started losing, he got mean. He raged against opponents, linesman, photographers, newsman, and even spectators. Off the court, he was just as difficult, arguing over money, blowing up over perceived insults, refusing to sign autographs or work the crowd, and being rude to the press.

"As a professional competitor, Gonzalez never comprehended that when you joined a tour you became, in effect, a major

The circus comes to town. A banner hung across an avenue in Queens, New York, advertises the arrival of Bobby Riggs' tennis troupe to the national championships at Forest Hills in 1949.

stockholder," Kramer said. "The more publicity, the bigger everybody's cut. Even though he was usually the top name, he would almost never help promote. The players could have tolerated his personal disagreeableness, but this refusal to help the group irritated them the most." Furthermore, as the competitive gap widened between Gonzalez and Kramer, Gonzalez's disposition worsened.

If Gonzalez seemed hostile and overly suspicious, he did have his reasons. His dark skin and Mexican-American heritage made him a frequent target of racism, particularly in the South. At times he was refused service in restaurants or would pull into a motel late at night only to have an office clerk click off the lights. Once, somewhere in Texas, the group stopped for a bite to eat at an out-of-the-way diner after the night's matches. They had barely sat down when someone in the restaurant made a bigoted remark aimed at Gonzalez. Tired, hungry, and in a dark mood after once again losing to Kramer, Gonzalez exploded. He stormed to his car. The other players followed. By the time the group caught up to him, he had a pistol in his hand and was about to go back inside the restaurant. Only after the others physically restrained Gonzalez and wrested the gun away did he cool off. Segura also encountered racism on occasion, but he kept his composure. "I was smart enough to know when to back off," he said.

Kramer's lead over Gonzalez steadily widened. A 22-4 win-loss record in November grew into a 42-8 margin in January, 59-18 by the end of February, and 71-21 in May. Interest in the tour waned. The matches drew smaller and smaller audiences. At times, between the players, linesmen, and the referee, there seemed to be more people on the court than in the stands.

But they kept going, driven by Bobby, who had promised Kay a mink coat if he earned $50,000 from the tour. To make that happen he had to keep adding dates. What was supposed to be a 100-stop tour through the U.S. and Canada kept growing and growing. Eventually Segura left, and Bobby stepped into his place to play Parker.

After 123 matches, Gonzalez and Kramer were both physically and mentally exhausted. Sore and homesick, they approached Bobby and told him the tour had to stop. Reluctantly, Bobby agreed. On May 21, 1950, in Dayton, Ohio, the tour ended. Plans for a European tour were scrapped. Kramer and Gonzalez each collected $73,000, but at a cost. Kramer, who had been suffering from a sore neck and back, was diagnosed that summer with arthritis. A new drug, cortisone, would keep him playing two more years. Gonzalez, however, seemed washed up, a has-been at 22.

Kay's plans for saving her marriage had not panned out. Her job doing advance publicity put her one or two stops ahead of the tour, which meant she saw Bobby even less than before. Whatever intimacy they previously shared was lost. Before, she could at least travel with him for short stretches of the tour. Now, her contact with Bobby was mostly via telephone or telegram, and even then mostly dealt with business matters. She was isolated, frustrated, and lonely.

Meanwhile, Bobby started travelling with another woman. Her name was Judy, and she was "a straight twenty-dollar tipper," Kramer said. "Buy a Coke, she'd tip a twenty." Whereas the rest of the players drove from town to town, Judy and Bobby sometimes flew to the next stop, then were chauffeured around town. Clearly, the attraction was more than physical, Kramer said, as he suspected Bobby was priming her to bankroll a South American tour.

Afraid about his future after tennis, "Bobby was always looking for a rich girl," said Gloria Kramer, who accompanied her husband during part of the tour. Jack had grown used to girls coming and going from Bobby's room, but for Gloria, who was close friends with Kay, the spectacle was too embarrassing and hurtful to bear. Finally, she cornered Judy and told her straight out, "Judy, would you please take your money and go home?" Which Judy did, leaving as quickly as she had come. Later, while waiting for the players to go on court, Bobby approached Gloria and asked her if she had told Judy to leave. "And I said, 'Yes, I did,' I thought I was being altruistic."

"What'd you do that for?" Bobby asked, honestly surprised.

The way he saw it, he was only having fun. Judy was simply a "friend," someone who might be able to help out with the rest of the tour. He didn't try to deceive. He felt he had nothing to hide. He didn't sneak around, and he never meant to hurt anybody. He still loved Kay, and moreover, he knew she still loved him.

Bobby lived in a world of moral ambiguity of his own construction. With an almost childlike sense of right and wrong, he never wrestled with ethical dilemmas. For him, there was no connection between action and intent. Like the notorious "insanity defense," Bobby operated on the philosophy that how could he be blamed if he didn't know the difference?

During the Riggs-Kramer tour's stops in Europe and Australia the year before, Bobby went "crazy," recalled Kramer and Segura. By then Kramer's lead was insurmountable, so Bobby devoted most of his energies to partying and women. While on the road in the Pacific, Bobby traveled with a beautiful girl whom he endowed with the title of "personal secretary," but whose real job was simply to keep him company. Newspapers splashed racy shots of the couple holding hands or cavorting on the beach. Bobby boasted in interviews to the press under headlines such as, "Look out girls, here's Bobby."

"Let's face it, in a business like a tennis tour, marriage is a high-risk proposition," Kramer said. "Maybe it was because they were separated so often from their wives, and maybe because of the separations there were other women. Probably it was both."

Kay knew there were other women. She also knew that for their marriage to survive, Bobby would need to shape up. As it was, he barely knew his two boys. Even when Bobby was home, she recalled, he wasn't really present. "He would get up in the morning, have breakfast and go over to the Los Angeles Tennis Club to play tennis. He wouldn't want to leave… sometimes he'd force himself to come home for dinner." He was never cruel or vindictive, she explained, just careless and childish.

As for Bobby, he too had been unhappy with his marriage. No doubt part of it was due to the long separations from Kay—two full years in the Navy in the South Pacific, then the tours with Budge and Kramer. But a lot of it had to do with his own restlessness. "I wanted to stay out and play gin and poker and different games, and I was late to dinner and she'd raise hell about it," he admitted. Not that he didn't love Kay. He did. But love and romance were never priorities in his life. "My big play was always the games, the tennis, the golf, the gambling," he said.

"I don't think he had any roots any place," Kramer said of Bobby. "He was only happy on the road because he was meeting fresh people." As for women, they were just part of the game, part of the fun—"the icing on the cake," Bobby once said.

Kay, however, could not continue this way. After the tour closed in May, she asked Bobby for a divorce. It was, she admitted later, as much a scare tactic as anything. "I thought if I said, 'Let's get a divorce,' he'd come around and become a wonderful father," she said. "But he called my bluff."

By the end of July 1950, a judge in Los Angeles made it official, ordering Bobby to pay Kay $700 a month alimony and granting Kay custody of their two boys. After the hearing, Bobby told reporters outside the courtroom there were "no hard feelings" and that Kay would continue working for the tour. He meant it. The two remained lifelong friends.

No longer a player, Bobby found more time to pursue his off-court interests, which invariably led to trouble. "He used to try to find people to do some gambling while he was in town," Kramer said of Bobby. "He figured, 'Why waste a night?' "

For example, in 1951, while the pro tour was in Miami, recalled Kramer, Bobby had fouled up the schedule, leaving the group with four days off. Gardnar Mulloy, who was living nearby and trying to raise money for a trip to Wimbledon, approached his old friend Segura about playing a friendly exhibition to help him out. Segura agreed. Arrangements were made at the Hollywood Beach Hotel and the necessary publicity released.

Hearing of the match, Bobby saw an opportunity to make some quick cash, so he asked Mulloy if he could help line up some bets. Mulloy had a wealthy acquaintance, Dan Orenstein, a street-tough millionaire who owned the Terminal Cab Company in New York City. He had a palatial estate in Miami where Mulloy would be invited to play tennis with him and his wife. Before the match, he asked Orenstein if he wanted to bet with Bobby.

"Well, Gar, do you think you can beat him?" asked Orenstein of the match with Segura.

"Well, I don't know," answered Mulloy. "I have in the past. But he's been on this tour and is supposedly pretty tough." After some consideration, Orenstein agreed to bet.

The day of the match was brutally hot, and a good crowd formed. With $3,000 already on the line, Bobby sat next to Orenstein. As the match got under way, he continued to pester Orenstein, angling for further wagers. Finally, Orenstein got irritated and said, "Bobby, look, let's make one bet and forget it. I'm tired of you. I want to watch the match. Let's make one big bet and forget it."

So Bobby answered, "Okay, we'll make one bet."

"How much?" asked Orenstein.

"I don't know. How about thirty-five hundred," Bobby offered.

"Ten thousand dollars," countered Orenstein.

Bobby gulped. "Ten thousand?"

Figuring Orenstein was bluffing, Bobby said, "Well, you don't have ten thousand dollars."

Orenstein got up indignantly and walked into the hotel, soon emerging with $10,000 in cash, and plunked it down. "Cover that, Bobby." Bobby wouldn't do it. He couldn't. The other bets stood pat. The two watched the match.

Bobby noticed that Segura's two-handed forehand lacked its usual ferocity, and that he did not seem upset after making uncustomary mistakes. After Segura and Mulloy split two long sets, Bobby was sure he smelled a rat. He went on court during a changeover and told Segura there was some heavy action riding on the match. Bobby demanded Segura start playing on the level. Segura told Bobby to get off his case, saying it was only an exhibition match, not the Wimbledon final. Besides, Segura was only playing to help out Mulloy, to whom he felt indebted for getting him into the University of Miami. Segura had secretly decided beforehand to play just well enough to lose.

After Mulloy won the match in a third set, Bobby stormed over to Mulloy and Segura and started yelling, accusing Segura of throwing the match, fuming over how the two of them had colluded to rob him of a small fortune. Bobby slapped a soda out of Segura's hand and screamed, "I was going to give you a bonus. Well you can forget that." Afterwards, Bobby told anyone willing to listen that Segura threw the match and that Orenstein paid him off. Naturally, word got back to Orenstein.

The next year, Bobby was back in Miami. While at the Miami Coliseum to watch Mulloy play another exhibition match, Bobby once again approached Mulloy to see if Orenstein might want to bet on the match.

Seemingly oblivious to the events of the previous year, Bobby visited Orenstein in his private box.

"Hi Dan, how are ya?" asked Bobby.

"Fine," answered Orenstein, who was surrounded by some equally tough-looking friends.

"Would you like to bet on it?" Bobby asked.

"Yeah, sure, I'll bet," answered Orenstein, "What do you want to bet?"

Prepared this time, Bobby offered, "How about your ten thousand?"

"Okay," Orenstein said. "Let's shake on it."

Bobby stuck his hand out and Orenstein grabbed it, squeezing Bobby's hand hard and pulling him close.

"Listen, you little punk. You've been going around telling everybody I paid off Segura to throw the match. I had nothing to do with it. Now, I tell you one thing. I'm going to pay off and Gar's gonna play. And I don't care how much money it takes, if he wins, you're gonna have cement shoes in Biscayne Bay. Nobody's telling me I fixed something." While Orenstein talked, Bobby's eyes widened and he started to pull away. When Orenstein let go, Bobby ran out of the room. That, and all other bets between the two, were off.

The 1951-52 tour would be Bobby's last. If the Gonzalez-Kramer tour had given Kramer doubts about Bobby's management ability, the subsequent tour confirmed them.

In 1949, the biggest name in tennis was a leggy bombshell named Gertrude "Gussy" Moran. A 26-year-old from Santa Monica, California, Gussy was a player of some promise, rising as high as No. 4 in the country and winning the national indoor singles and doubles titles that year.

But it was Moran's wardrobe more than her tennis ability that set her apart. She walked onto the courts at the staid All England Club wearing a pair of suggestive panties trimmed with a half-inch of lace, causing an immediate sensation. Dubbed "Gorgeous" Gussy Moran by the press, she was surrounded by photographers wherever she went that season, and became a favorite of gossip columnists everywhere. *Life* magazine devoted four pages to her. *Sports World* magazine featured a color spread of Gussy Moran photos. The

Los Angeles Examiner ran a story on the phenomenon of Gussy's popularity.

The lace panties had been the brainchild of Teddy Tinling, a fashion designer who later created the dresses worn by both Margaret Court and Billie Jean King in their matches against Bobby. Not since French tennis star Suzanne Lenglen shocked the tennis establishment 20 years earlier by abandoning the traditional petticoats and corsets for more comfortable (and practical) calf-length dresses had there been such a scandal. Tennis suddenly became sexy.

Betting that Gorgeous Gussy's publicity would translate into paying customers, Bobby and Kramer signed Moran to headline the next tour, giving her a hefty $35,000 guarantee against 30 percent of the gate. For her opponent, they signed Pauline Betz, 1946 Wimbledon singles champion and four-time national amateur champion at Forest Hills ('42, '43, '44, '46). Betz might have achieved more, but her amateur career ended in 1947 after an incident involving Elwood Cooke, a friend and husband of Sarah Palfrey Cooke. Cooke sent a letter to various tennis clubs to see if there was any interest in a series of matches between Betz and his wife. Getting wind of the letters, USLTA officials declared Betz a professional and barred her from amateur play, this for simply thinking of turning pro. The controversial and unprecedented action ended Betz's amateur career while she was at the top of her game.

Pancho Segura was cast in a supporting role as Kramer's opponent for the tour. Segura was much improved since he had first turned professional two years before. A crowd-pleaser, Segura earned his spot on the tour by winning the national professional championships in Cleveland that summer, defeating Kramer in a five-set semifinal and Frank Kovacs in the final.

For the first time, Segura was given a stake in the tour: $1,000 a week plus five percent of the gate. It was slim, but for Segura significant. Kramer cut his share to 25 percent in order to sign Moran, while Bobby took the lion's share with 40 percent of the gate. Betz, meanwhile, was paid a straight salary.

Having two women headline the tour was a novel idea, and might have worked had the pairing been more competitive.

Unfortunately, Betz thoroughly dominated Moran. Perhaps the most underrated woman ever to play the game, Betz was an all-court player, able to get to net quickly and volley decisively. She could run down balls and pass opponents at the net, and she had a penetrating backhand. She might have gone down as one of the greatest if her amateur career had not been cut short by the USLTA's arbitrary ruling. Gorgeous Gussy was simply no match for her.

When Pauline Betz (right) took to the court against "Gorgeous" Gussy Moran (left) on the opening night of their tour in 1950, she not only outplayed her, but outdressed the tennis siren, wearing a silver lamé skirt.

At the tour's opening in Madison Square Garden on October 28, 1950, Betz outplayed Moran, defeating her 6-0, 6-3 in just 30 minutes. Not only that, she outdressed Moran, walking on court in a shocking pink sweater with a black and silver lamé zebra-stripped skirt. Despite fantastic publicity in New York and in every city they played, few people actually came out to watch the tennis. Only 6,526 filled the Garden, the smallest opening-night attendance for any tour to date.

"Kid," Bobby said to Kramer midway through the tour, "we have got a problem." Their solution was to dump Betz. At a hotel in Washington, D.C., the pair cornered Betz in her room. With little preface, Bobby asked, "Isn't there something we can do to get you to sprain an ankle?" A disbelieving Betz, not knowing what to say, simply returned a bewildered look. Bobby, figuring she was holding out for more money, replied, "All right, Kid, we'll give you a car if you'll sprain an ankle." At this point, Betz broke down and cried.

Bobby apologized to Betz for being so blunt and told her to forget everything he had said. But as the two left, Bobby added, "But look, Kid, at least try and make it close."

Betz tried, Kramer recalled, but whereas Moran might have had a chance on an off-night when Betz was going for the lines and making mistakes, a more deliberate Betz became more consistent, making the scores even more lopsided. "Now Pauline was concentrating and was damn near unbeatable," Kramer explained. Nobody was happy—Betz, Moran, Bobby, the other players, and, least of all, the fans. When Moran finally did beat Betz in Milwaukee, recalled Kramer, Betz left the court in tears, screaming at Bobby, "Well, I guess you're happy now!"

Bobby tried everything to revive the tour's sagging fortunes. At one point he even sneaked into Moran's dressing room and secretly slit her famous lace panties with a razor blade. As she prepared to take the court, he told her, "When you stand in front of the press seats, bend over and that'll start some action." Moran, who had started taking a shot of bourbon to calm her frazzled nerves before taking the court, quickly realized what Bobby had done and angrily refused.

The tour was a financial disaster. By the time it closed in March 1951, it had grossed only $94,396, barely a third that of the Riggs-Kramer tour. All the publicity had never translated into paying fans. "If I had any doubts, I learned from this experience that tennis fans come out to see tennis," Kramer said. "Exploding scoreboards and giveaways are not going to work in tennis."

Frustrated, Kramer decided to promote the next tour himself. Though the two were good friends, Kramer decided that Bobby was "just not thorough enough to make a good promoter" and told him so.

On top of everything else—his failed marriage, the tour fiasco, and the loss of Kramer's confidence—Bobby also ran into money troubles. Before their divorce, Bobby had agreed to promote a series of post-season baseball exhibitions featuring the National League All-Stars and the American League All-Stars. They put up $250,000 of their own money to launch the idea, and signed some of the biggest names in the business, including future Hall-of-Fame pitcher Bob Feller.

Barnstorming baseball tours, however, were a thing of the past. When Jackie Robinson broke baseball's color barrier in 1947 with the Brooklyn Dodgers it undermined the longstanding post-season competition between Negro League stars and major leaguers. As Robinson was followed by Satchel Paige and Roy Campenella, the Negro leagues faded. Moreover, once the football season began, no one was interested in baseball.

Adding to Bobby's woes, opening night in Chicago during the fall of 1951 was rained out—a total bust. Kramer recalled Bobby coming to him and saying, "Jack, I made a damn stupid deal and I'm short on money, and I hope you'll carry me for a little bit, and I'll get it to you as fast as possible." At that point, Bobby owed Kramer about $38,000. Kramer gladly agreed to defer payment until the end of the tour.

Bobby briefly toyed with the idea of promoting another tour himself. But while in Florida in the fall of 1951 he met the girl of his dreams, a wealthy New York socialite named Priscilla Wheelan. He also discovered a new passion: golf.

Golf provided the perfect marriage of Bobby's favorite pastimes—sports and gambling. "The second worst thing in the world is betting on a golf game and losing," Bobby was fond of saying. "The worst is not betting at all."

14

"Give me a millionaire every time."
1952-1954

During their pro tours, when the weather was nice, Bobby and Jack Kramer took up golf. They'd hack around, bet a little, and then get ready for that night's matches. It was a nice way to kill time—relaxing, sociable, and not too strenuous—yet still challenging enough to maintain the interest of such highly competitive individuals.

After quitting tennis and moving to Florida, Bobby learned what golf was really all about. When he saw ordinary golfers shooting eighty-fives and nineties and betting all kinds of money, it was like discovering a rich uncle he never knew he had. "How long has this been going on?" he asked himself.

Evolutionary cousins in sports, golf and tennis share a long and sometimes uneasy kinship. Both date back to ancient times. Both have a deep respect for tradition and etiquette. Both were popularized in the U.S. around the turn of the century. And both have reputations as pastimes for rich snobs, a reputation reinforced by the fact that the two often share the same exclusive clubhouse.

In the age of television and big-time professional sports, the two are seen as rivals for the same fan base and sponsors, each using the other as a measure of its own relative success.

Golf, however, never carried with it the stigma of being a "sissy" sport, in part because although women played golf, they generally didn't play with men. In golf, the sexes were kept separate. Clubs that admitted women usually restricted them to certain tee times. Tennis, meanwhile, has long been promoted as a way for people of both sexes to get exercise. Women have always been part of the game, and mixed doubles makes tennis one of the few international sports in which men and women compete against each other on the same field.

This inclusiveness earned tennis the reputation of being effeminate, despite the fact the game is both more dynamic and a truer test of fitness and athleticism than golf. It has also made tennis a harder sell to new fans and participants over the years. For example, in 2000, while the tennis establishment pondered ways to revitalize the game and attract new players, golf enjoyed a boom the likes of which it had never seen, particularly among young people. One poll showed that among young adults golf was considered the "coolest" sport, surpassing such rugged events as mountain biking and snowboarding.

Unlike tennis, golf long ago opened itself to professionals, recognizing the fact that career athletes needed to earn a living. In 1901, nearly a half-century before Bill Tilden's abortive attempt to form a professional tennis league, the Professional Golfers Association was founded in Britain. And while tennis took strenuous measures to separate amateurs from professionals, golf nearly always allowed amateurs and professionals to compete against each other.

Playing for money was no disgrace in golf because it had nearly always been played for money, particularly after the adoption of the handicapping system in 1912.* By giving lesser players strokes, everyone could compete on even terms regardless of skill level, a distinct advantage when it came to wagering.

Competitive to a fault, Bobby had tinkered with various forms of handicapping in tennis over the years. At the L.A. Tennis Club when he was learning to play, he spotted an opponent games or

---

* In golf, a player's handicap is the average of his or her most recent scores. This is then compared to the number of strokes for par. The difference is the number of strokes to be deducted from his or her score at the end of the round.

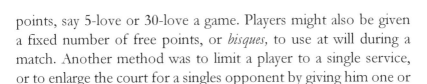

points, say 5-love or 30-love a game. Players might also be given a fixed number of free points, or *bisques,* to use at will during a match. Another method was to limit a player to a single service, or to enlarge the court for a singles opponent by giving him one or both of the doubles alleys.

Over the years, Bobby devised his own unique ways of handicapping—precursors to the more elaborate hustles he became famous for later. He might restrict himself to hitting only backhands. Or he might, as he did one sweltering day at the L.A. Tennis Club, take on an opponent while wearing a heavy winter overcoat. During tennis parties at studio executive Jack Warner's Hollywood estate, Bobby and other top players played against movie stars such as Groucho Marx or Randolph Scott with the single provision that the stars had to keep the ball inside the fences surrounding the court.

The problem with handicapping in tennis, however, is that the better player still almost always wins. Even after spotting opponents five games, Bobby said, "You'd be amazed how many people think a lead like that is insurmountable. It's only when the score is 5-5 that that crazed look comes across their faces, when they realize they're never going to win." Moreover, evening a score doesn't make the points any more interesting.

In golf, the challenge is not necessarily beating the other player. It is to play the course and to shoot to your handicap or better. The opponent, in essence, is yourself. This also makes golf a natural fit for betting, a perfect marriage of Bobby's favorite pastimes— sports and gambling. "The second worst thing in the world is betting on a golf game and losing," Bobby was fond of saying. "The worst is not betting at all."

Even with his high handicap, Bobby found he could beat many better players. "I just out-competed them," he said. "Fuck the tennis tour, I thought. Golf is easier."

Bobby got a token job as the tennis pro at the Roney Plaza Hotel, a large, pink, art-deco hotel in Miami, a place where movie stars mingled with mobsters. It was a job that gave him plenty of time to play golf.

Tagging along with good players, Bobby watched carefully and learned. Through imitation and practice, Bobby was breaking 100 consistently within a year. And not long after that, shooting in the eighties. He got his handicap down to 16, and started hanging around courses in Miami: the La Gorce Country Club, the Seminole, and the Bayshore public course.

He kept company with a cast of characters who went by names such as The Stork, Shaggy Ralph, The Dog Man, Charlie the Blade, and Three-Iron Ward—men with deep tans and a nose for action. This was 1952, the Golden Age of golf hustling, and South Florida was its center. The state's fine weather and abundance of courses made it a magnet for ringers, hustlers, and con men from around the country. They traveled the circuit, stalking the clubhouses and driving ranges, looking for action.

Working in concert or alone, they sought easy marks: tourists, businessmen on vacation, or millionaires from Texas—suckers, or "palefaces" in the parlance of the trade. Among themselves, they joked to one another about being "too tan." Many of these hustlers were terrific players, and might have played professionally, but found the money from hustling easier and more plentiful. At the time, a top pro might earn $30,000 a year, a sum elite hustlers might earn in a week. Asked if he would ever turn pro, the famous Alvin Clarence Thomas, a.k.a. "Titanic" Thompson of Evansville, Indiana, replied, "I could not afford the cut in pay."

In the heady post-war days in Florida, money seemed to grow on palm trees, and big action could be found at many of the courses. For golf hustlers, it was an invitation to steal. La Gorce, a posh club that boasted more than 150 millionaires, was known as Hustler's Haven. "It was like an open-air poolroom," Bobby said. "La Gorce was a den of thieves. All the ringers, hustlers and smart guys were there. If you didn't know what was happening, you wouldn't see an elephant if it jumped up on the table. But if you didn't let yourself get outmatched, you won. You've got to get into the right match-ups, know your own levels, and the other guy's."

Like all craftsmen, hustlers were individualists, each developing a routine or gimmick with which to lure their prey. After all, the essence of the hustle is to make the victim think he's getting an even break. Charlie the Blade used only one club, a four iron, but could do as much with it as most scratch golfers could with all 14 clubs. The Stork played every shot standing on his right foot with his left foot stuck up behind him. The Whiskey Drinker swigged from a flask he carried in his golf bag, growing more congenial and unsteady on his feet with every swing. By the time he reached the ninth hole, he tipsily demanded that all bets be doubled, after which his demeanor and game miraculously straightened out. Few suspected that the amber "Scotch" in the bottle was only tea.

And like all craftsmen, hustlers had their own hierarchy. Among top hustlers, men like The Whiskey Drinker were considered the lowest form in the trade, nothing more than cheap tricksters, and were viewed with the same disdain a banker might have for a pawnshop broker. The best were artists, men who turned the common hustle into an elegantly constructed con. La Verne Moore, alias John Montague, first appeared around 1930. A crack golfer and master of trick shots, he once challenged a sucker that he could pick off a sparrow sitting on a telephone wire with a ball hit by a mid-iron. He did. Another time, he bet that he could blast a completely buried ball out of a sand trap and onto the green with a wedge. He did that, too. He'd crack the window in his motel room six inches and chip balls through the opening over and over without breaking the glass. Legend has it he played entertainer Bing Crosby for high stakes and took him for a wad of cash, playing with nothing more than a rake, a hoe, and a baseball bat, while Crosby was allowed to use all his clubs.

Among Bobby's regular partners was Martin Stanovich, better known in golfing circles as The Fat Man. Weighing in at 230 pounds, Stanovich owned one of the most preposterous swings in golf. Feet planted apart, head hung low, he had a ridiculously short back swing and lunged at the ball like a man trying to kill a cockroach with crowbar. Even more remarkable was the fact that he almost always hit the ball a little farther and a little more accurately than anyone else.

"Look at that guy," top pro Lee Trevino once said to Bobby as the two watched The Fat Man tee off. "You'd say he couldn't beat his way out of a paper bag. But he'll sixty-eight you to death—a hell of a player." Trevino himself grew up hustling golf in Texas, later acknowledging his debt to Titanic Thompson's teaching skills. As a kid, he'd play against older, better-equipped players with a soda-pop bottle attached to the end of a stick and wrapped in tape.

The Fat Man was an equal opportunity gamesman, taking on pros, hustlers, and "nice people who just love to lose money." But being an amateur, he demanded three strokes from any pro as a matter of policy. "Then I don't have to work so hard," he told a reporter. A scratch golfer, against everyday opponents The Fat Man allowed a 12-stroke handicap but wound up taking their money anyway, clucking sympathetically and offering tips to improve their game during the round. "The Fat Man always gave you what you thought was a fair game," Bobby said. "Trouble was, you were usually wrong. He was treacherous, and I learned a lot from him. I got caught in the middle too often not to learn something."

From this rogue's gallery of golfing, Bobby said, "I learned all the angles, I mean *all* the angles." Earning what was called a "traveling handicap," Bobby legitimately acquired his handicap from the back tees at a very difficult course, but played his money matches from the middle tees, giving him the necessary "fair advantage" he deemed necessary. Though an average golfer compared to the other sharpies—not long off the tees and with a clipped, abbreviated backswing—Bobby had terrific touch around the green. Moreover, he was a superior competitor, becoming positively inspired when playing for high stakes.

"I always rise to the occasion for that big bet," Bobby said. "Pressure makes me produce. Kills most guys. Mortifies 'em. I love a contest, a game, a challenge. To be a winner, you've got to be an appraiser. You've got to be able to play at your best under pressure. And more money creates more pressure. Money is the finest fuel in the world. You see, if you're betting all the time, everything is just another bet. You don't even think about the money after you've made the arrangements. You're used to it. And you're usually playing with people who have more money than you do. Now that's an advantage, because they're thinking about the money and they play six strokes worse than they usually do. I play better under pressure." Bobby called himself the best money player of all time, a competitor immune to choking under pressure—a boast that pushed him to be ever more extravagant and grandiose in his challenges.

More than anything, Bobby was a supreme judge of ability—both his own and that of an opponent. "I was always pretty good about figuring a player's true handicap," he maintained. Cool and calculating, he enjoyed playing with men like The Fat Man, but almost always managed to come out unscathed. "I've played Riggs and beat him four times," The Fat Man once said. "Trouble is, he won't play for real money unless I give him half the golf course."

Bobby was a master at selling people a situation they really didn't want. Nine out of ten times they would buy it anyway, only to realize later that they had been had. His advantage in golf was that nobody knew how good he really was. While everybody would naturally be leery of taking on the Wimbledon champion in tennis, nobody was afraid to bet on golf against the funny little man with the squeaky voice and jaunty walk. By offering long odds or a big handicap—by appealing to "the larceny in everyone's soul"—he bragged he could get a $10 bettor to bet $100, forcing him to play for more than he liked and thus immediately putting him under pressure. By luring such bettors in over their head, he'd have them beat before they got to the first tee. To Bobby, it was about brains, competition, and out-smarting the other guy. The money was incidental, a way to keep score.

"He had an obsession with winning, and not with money," Bobby's son, Larry Riggs, explained. Recalling an incident at the La Costa resort when he was caddying for his father, Larry said, "He was playing with this high-rolling guy for a couple days and the guy had lost a substantial amount of money. We met out there and Dad was giving him all these bets they were going to play that day." The man stopped Bobby, and asked, "Bobby, how much do I stand to lose if I lose all bets all ways?"

"Well, you could lose maybe, uh, fifteen hundred dollars," Bobby answered. "But that would never happen, because if you were down you could press at the end and double up."

The man, who had been playing and losing for several days, pulled out his wallet and withdrew fifteen hundred dollars in cash and handed it to Bobby. "Here's fifteen hundred dollars. Let's just play and have fun."

Bobby gave the man a curious look, then handed back the money. "No. I want to play for it."

Said Larry, "He didn't care about the money. He just wanted to go out and beat the shit out of the guy. He hated guys who'd stop trying as soon as he started winning, because it took the victory out of it. Then they could say they quit, or didn't try, but that they didn't lose. No, Dad was interested in winning."

The standard bet in golf is the nassau, actually three bets in one. In a $50 nassau, $50 rides on the first nine holes, $50 on the second nine, and $50 on the lowest 18-hole total—for a total of $150. Bobby sometimes played with as many as 10 different nassaus going on at the same time: one at even, one with a one-stroke handicap, then two strokes and three, four, five, six, seven, eight, and nine strokes. Additional bets were made as the round progressed. A "press" started a new bet for the same dollar amount on remaining holes of a nine-hole leg. Bets would be declared on individual holes, including bets for the longest drive, the straightest drives, "greenies" for hitting the green on par 3 holes, "sandies" for making par from a sand trap, or "Paul Bunyons" for making par from deep in the woods. Sometimes there were so many bets going on at the same time, Bobby might not realize he had forgotten to collect on all of them until he was driving home.

Another popular form of betting in golf were Calcutta pools, in which tournament competitors were auctioned off to the highest bidders according to their declared handicaps. Some pools ran as high as $250,000. (The name originated from England's Calcutta Turf Club, sponsor of a large horseracing sweepstakes.) The money raised was pooled, and at the end of the tournament the "owners" split the winnings with the tournament victors. But cheating was rampant in such pools, with some golfers turning in falsified handicaps and others taking bribes to lose. Following a scandal in 1955 at the Deepdale Country Club on Long Island in which two hustlers made off with $16,100 in a $45,000 pool playing with phony handicaps, the U.S. Golf Association outlawed Calcuttas at all golf clubs. Bobby, who lived nearby at the time, admitted playing in the match at Deepdale, but said he knew nothing about the two golfers who won it.

Playing for as much as $100,000 a round, such matches became spectacles. Crowds gathered to watch the action, and as the players made their way from hole to hole, caravans of golf carts trailed the participants—club members, golf fans, fellow hustlers, and the merely curious. The noise, the crowds, and the commotion drew the ire of many other club members. Bobby was often at the center of the action. Over the years, a few clubs asked him to keep his activities more subdued, and more than once he was suspended or barred.

In addition to bets with the other players, Bobby often had a half-dozen other bets going with bookmakers who followed the group around the course. "These guys would try to distract me when I was about to make a shot," Bobby recalled. "Just as I leaned over the ball, they'd crash two golf cars together. They'd move around me on the tee or the green to disturb me. But I knew what they were up to and I never let them bother me. They'd make all kinds of noise. I just played the ball."

Some didn't stop at noise. "I've played with guys who had a pal watching the match way out in the fairway, about where our tee shots would land. If I happened to hit a ball into the rough, 240 yards or so from the tee, the pal would kick my ball behind a tree or even pick it up and put it in his pocket. This meant a lost ball and a stroke penalty." They might also bribe caddies to give bad advice—or pay off the greenskeeper to change the pin placements. Bobby sometimes found himself on the butt end of such accusations, for improving a lie or duping a player into making a foolish bet. Such antics became a part of the game for him. As in other forms of gambling, this was more a battle of wits than skill.

As much as the golf itself, Bobby enjoyed the negotiating beforehand. As someone once said, "Golf matches are not won on the fairways or greens. They are won on the tee—the first tee." Like a medicine show barker, Bobby, or "Squeaky" as he came to be known around the Florida golf circuit, took over the dialogue, trying to dictate terms. "Tell you what I'm gonna do," he'd chirp. "I'll give you a stroke; a half-stroke and play you even on this hole, three bets for fifty dollars each... You know, I haven't picked up a club in a month... Man, you're stealing me blind. Tell the man that's a good bet... I just want action." If he couldn't win through persuasion, Bobby would succeed through perseverance, often holding up the tee as other club members lined up behind them impatiently.

Only the strongest-willed opponent could prevail. Once, in the early 1950s, Welby Van Horn ran into Bobby while playing in a tennis tournament in St. Augustine, Florida. The former tennis rivals and doubles partners started talking about golf. Agreeing to play a round the next day, the two started talking about how much to bet and how many strokes to give. Having reached no conclusion, the two met for breakfast the next morning and renewed the bargaining. Again, nothing was decided, and the haggling continued as they got into a cab and rode out to the golf course. Still unsettled, the negotiations continued as they went into the pro shop and bought balls. The two kept talking as they approached the first tee. The talking continued even after both teed off and started down the fairway. Finally, with no deal reached, Bobby got mad, accused Van Horn of trying to take advantage of him, picked up his ball, and stormed off the course. "I was a good friend of his," Van Horn recalled. "But I said to myself, 'He's not going to hustle me.'"

With a sixth sense for money and a knack for being in the right place at the right time, Bobby's biggest coup came in 1953, about a year after he took up golf. The match was played over the course of a week at the Greenbrier Country Club in White Sulphur Springs, West Virginia, then Sam Snead's home course. The participants included Bobby, Dan Topping, owner of the New York Yankees, Jose Dorelis, called "The Count" because he wore a monocle, and Ray Ryan, an eccentric oil tycoon and real estate developer from Evansville, Indiana who was reputed to have mob connections.

Bobby had played with Ryan earlier that year in Florida and was at Greenbrier after a Calcutta pool. He had not played well and decided to stay over at the hotel to practice when Ryan showed up.

A mediocre golfer who loved to bet high, Ryan usually traveled with his own pro, but on this trip he decided to chance it on his own. Bobby gave Ryan a stroke a hole, two on the par fives, and sometimes two on the par fours. "I started out playing for what I could afford to lose," Bobby said. "Now Ryan, he thought he could win. He thought he had a license to steal, a real bargain, but that week he went completely crazy and shot above his game." Ryan's usual 100 game blew up to around 135.

"He was hitting the ball sideways he was so bad," Bobby recalled. "He was pressing bets with both hands, and by the time he got to the eighteenth tee the first day he was deep in the hole. I'll never forget. He pressed again on that hole and by three-putting he lost one hundred thousand right there. Boy, they were big times. At the end of that week he owed something like five hundred thousand dollars. Now, you bleed a lot of rich guys and you oughta hear 'em squawk, like they'd been stabbed for chrissakes. But not Ryan. The next day he asked us boys to stop by his suite. We arrived and he was sitting behind a card table with a suitcase full of thousand-dollar bills. We lined up and he paid us off without flinching. With a smile. He was a great high roller. None better. All he said was: 'Boys, If I win tomorrow, I want to get paid in the same way.'" In a postscript to the story, Bobby said he lost all the $180,000 he claimed to have won back in a gin game against Ryan the next week in New York.

Of course, not everybody lost as magnanimously as Ryan, particularly when high stakes were involved. Bobby tried to be careful in choosing the people he played with, and was so genial that, according to one friend, "you'd practically think he was doing you a favor by taking your money," but a lot of opponents did not take losing so gracefully. Bobby had a drawerful of bad checks to prove it. But deadbeats weren't the only hazards. South Florida was then a second home to many mobsters, tough guys who didn't like smart-asses, particularly those who made off with their money.

At Bayshore Country Club in Miami one day in 1955, Bobby's nephew Dave Riggs agreed to caddy for his uncle. Dave, son of Sanders Riggs, was a junior pilot with Pan American based in Miami. During his days off, he enjoyed hanging out with Bobby. On this day, he said, "We were playing with a guy named Jackie and a couple other guys, and I noticed that Jackie's caddy is wearing an overcoat." It was a bright, sunny day, Dave said, but "Who knows? It might rain." As the round progressed, Bobby's lead widened, and Jackie, a stout, bald man who spoke in strings of profanities, grew angrier and angrier, at one point deliberately driving his cart over Bobby's ball in the fairway. Bobby ignored the offense and played the buried ball, still managing to win. Jackie cursed, but paid up.

The next day, Dave saw Jackie's picture in the paper. Jackie was John "Jackie the Lackie" Cerone, a top boss in the Chicago Mob. The story accompanying the photo talked about how the City of Miami had asked Cerone to leave town. "Then it dawns on me why his caddy had on an overcoat," said Dave. "He wasn't just carrying the clubs."

Vic Braden, a friend of Bobby's who worked on the tennis tours and later became a tennis writer and coach, recalled a day working at the posh El Mirador Hotel in Palm Springs, then owned by Ryan. A "friend" of Ryan's came up to him and asked, "Do you know Bobby Riggs?"

"Yeah, he's a good friend of mine," Braden answered.

"Could you give him a message?"

"I'd be happy to. I understand he's coming into town tomorrow."

"Just tell him he's got 24 hours to get out of town."

Recalled Braden: "At first, I thought it was a joke, but this guy was serious."

To his misfortune, Ryan himself learned how serious his "friends" could be. In 1977, he was killed when a bomb blew up his Lincoln Continental in Evansville. The blast was so powerful it knocked out power to a section of the city. The assassination was believed to be revenge for testimony Ryan gave a decade earlier over an attempt by the Chicago Mob to extort $60,000 a year from him in protection money.

Bobby was oblivious to such dangers, however, even when confronted with threats head-on. He believed his celebrity status and good nature made him immune. Longtime friend and protégé Lornie Kuhle recalled a late-night poker session in Florida in which, after losing yet another hand to Bobby, his frustrated opponent leaned back and pulled up his shirt to expose the butt of a large handgun. The man then said menacingly, "I think it's time for you to leave." Kuhle went bug-eyed and started tugging at Bobby to get up and go, but Bobby shrugged him off and cheerfully said to the man, "Oh, you're not going to use that. Put that thing away. We still got some cards to play." Shocked, the man obliged, and continued to lose.

For Bobby, it was just the action, that adrenaline rush of taking on all comers and proving himself supreme. The bigger the foe, the sweeter the victory.

"People misunderstand the mentality of a hustler," he explained. "It doesn't matter how well you do things, it's how you negotiate the handicaps. I found out long ago to always gamble up. Play rich guys and knock 'em in. It's no fun playing guys who go broke if they lose. How do you collect? Jockey for position to get to the big people.

"Let me tell ya. Listen. I love millionaires," Bobby said. "I really do. Give me a millionaire every time. There were a lot of them around then. Beautiful, the salt of the earth. Wherever I went, they were lining up waiting for me. They loved playing with me. It was a challenge. They liked being taken by the best."

Although the bigger the foe the sweeter the victory, action for Bobby didn't have to involve large stakes. "He'd rather hustle a bum out of a dollar than pick a hundred dollar bill out of the gutter," Ted Schroeder said. "That's just the way he is. He couldn't sit still. He always had to have action. He'd bet on anything, anything."

For example, one longtime friend told the story of being in a car with Bobby when Bobby asked if he would like to come over that evening and play Ping-Pong.

"No," he answered, "My wife and I are playing bridge with some people."

"Oh, do you play for money?" Bobby asked.

"Yeah, we play for a little money."

"Well, maybe you'd like to come over and play with Priscilla and me."

"Sure," the friend said. "Do you play a lot of bridge?

"No," Bobby answered. "But if you play for money I'm willing to learn."

With his marriage to Priscilla, Bobby seemed to have it all.
She was beautiful, funny, adventurous and, best of all, rich.

15

"There's no winning here."

1952-1971

Given the scant importance Bobby gave to the women in his life, he might have been better off finding himself a trophy wife: beautiful and undemanding. Too bad his taste in women ran to those who were smart, funny, and complicated—women who had higher expectations from a partner and husband. When it came to the give-and-take of marriage, Bobby simply wasn't up to the task. This was something Kay had learned the hard way.

The way Bobby saw it, however, his marriage to Kay was a victim of circumstances rather than neglect: the war, the tours, the long absences, and life on the road. Considering all that, it was a testament to his and Kay's love that their marriage lasted as long as it did.

In 1952, Bobby was just getting out of tennis, living in Miami and playing golf, when he met Priscilla Wheelan. Like him, she was freshly divorced, and at the time was living at her parents' villa on North Miami Beach. When he first saw Priscilla at the LaGorce Country Club in Miami, Bobby said it was "instant chemistry, love at first sight." Priscilla seemed to have it all. She was beautiful, funny, adventurous, and, best of all, rich.

Priscilla was the younger of Dorothy and Robert Brown Wheelan's two daughters. Robert Wheelan, or "R.B." as most friends called him, was a self-made millionaire, a gruff, charismatic, hard-drinking, hard-working man who never forgot a name and had a nose for business. A born entrepreneur, he sneaked across enemy lines in World War I to sell chocolate to German soldiers. In 1927, he founded Wheelan Studios, which later went on to become the American Photograph Corporation.

Photography had become ubiquitous since its invention almost a half-century before, and framed or wallet-sized portraits of loved ones had become a popular custom. Hand-held cameras, however, especially for indoor use, were complicated and expensive. For most families, the alternative was to have portraits done in photographic studios. A few years after founding Wheelan Studios, R.B. came up with the idea of putting photo studios inside department stores. This way, families could have portraits done more conveniently during family shopping trips downtown. By the end of World War II, American Photograph grew to more than 360 outlets nationwide and took in as much as $20 million a year. A shrewd businessman and a tireless worker, Wheelan expanded the concept to include traveling studios for high-school or college yearbooks, and seasonal enterprises such as photographing children's visits with Santa Claus. For millions of American children, getting one's picture taken on Santa's knee became a ritual of growing up.

In addition to American Photograph, Wheelan had numerous real estate ventures, including hotels in Florida and New Hampshire. The family had an apartment in Manhattan and a large house in an affluent section of Great Neck, Long Island. He was also a noted philanthropist, creating the Wheelan Foundation and helping found the Cornell-North Shore Hospital on Long Island. The family moved in the highest circles of New York society. For the two daughters, Patricia and Priscilla, growing up a Wheelan meant the best of everything—private schools, grand vacations, summers in the White Mountains, and winters on Miami Beach. Nothing was too good for R.B.'s girls.

Following a ceremony at Priscilla's parents' home on Great Neck, Long Island on September 11, 1952, Bobby and his bride took a month-long honeymoon in Europe. They then settled into the family's townhouse at the Archway Ocean Villas in Miami.

Now that he was out of the game, Bobby figured it would be different. He'd have the time and energy to devote himself as fully to his marriage as he did to tennis.

On March 8, 1952, Bobby's father Gideon died, ten days before his 85th birthday. By then the old man was senile, completely blind, unable to walk, and living in a convalescent home. He had suffered a broken hip three years before and never recovered, wasting away in bed. Bobby never said how he reacted to the news, but given Gideon's condition, his passing was likely a relief.

The service was held at Forest Lawn cemetery in Glendale, California. Hugh Tiner, a former protégé of Gideon's at the Sichel Street church who was then president of Pepperdine College, a school affiliated with the Church of Christ, officiated. Though a true religious pioneer, Gideon seemed to have outlived all those who could remember his achievements. When he died, the *Los Angeles Times* published only a brief announcement.

Bobby's mother, Agnes, lived another 18 years, dying in 1966 at the age of 84. Like Gideon, her final days would be spent in a convalescent home. She never remarried, kept to her routine of housework and chores, and rarely socialized outside the regular visits by her children and grandchildren.

Priscilla had an infant son, John, by a previous marriage at the time she met Bobby. R.B. had never trusted the boy's father, however, and had warned Priscilla against marrying him. After Priscilla's divorce, R.B. arranged to legally adopt the boy in order to cut the birth father off from the family. This would make for a clean break, without any issues of custody, visitation rights, or possible claims to the family fortune. When Priscilla married Bobby, custody was returned to Priscilla and Bobby became the boy's legal father, so John grew up knowing Bobby as his father.

At first, Bobby convinced his bride that they would travel the world together, do tennis promotions, exhibitions, and live the high life. But soon afterward, Priscilla became pregnant with her second child, and within 11 months of that her third child. (In addition to John, born November 13, 1950, Bobby and Priscilla had three children: James, born July 3, 1953, Dorothy, born June 18, 1954, and William, born July 31, 1956).

While living in Florida, Bobby played golf constantly. Priscilla wanted more. To better provide for her children and to get Bobby away from Miami and all the gambling, the hustling, and the occasional mobster, Priscilla talked him into moving to New York. Bobby would get a job at the family company, and with R.B.'s help, they bought a big house on 4½ acres of land at Plandome on Long Island, not far from Priscilla's parents' house.

By then, R.B. was in his mid-sixties and starting to ease himself out of the day-to-day running of American Photograph in preparation for the day his daughters would inherit the business. Today, this would mean grooming them to take over the reins. After all, they were both capable and intelligent. Instead, the times and tradition within the masculine world of American business in the 1950s meant giving their husbands high-placed jobs in the company. Daughter Patricia's husband, Mike Crimi, gave up a career as a lawyer in Florida to move to New York and take a position as executive vice president with the company. "My father-in-law became ill at times and needed someone to help him," Crimi recalled. "So I came up and went to work." It was, he said, "a family obligation."

Like Crimi, Bobby was given the title of executive vice president, an annual salary of $80,000, a sprawling office with a private bathroom and shower, his own secretary, and a secretary for his secretary—Priscilla made sure of all of this. "Priscilla was very protective," Bobby and Kay's son Larry Riggs remembered. If Patricia's husband had a big office, Priscilla demanded "my husband is going to have just as big an office. And if you have a bathroom in your office, we're going to have a bathroom in our office." Never mind the fact that Bobby had no real training or affinity for the job. "Priscilla wanted him there every day because she owned half the company," Larry said. "She was protecting her interests and her kids."

So Bobby did the husbandly thing. He slicked back his hair, put on a suit and tie, took the commuter train to work every day, and worked nine to five. He played the other guy's game. He went straight and tried to obey the rules. It was just possible he could prove himself in the world of business as he had on the tennis court. At least, he thought, he'd give it his best shot.

Was this the result of a compromise between Bobby and Priscilla? Did he agree to give up his itinerant lifestyle, settle down, do the nine-to-five thing, and in return did she agree to put up with the gambling, the absences from home, and the carousing? Though they probably never thought about it this way, they should have spelled it out, because in the end it didn't work.

For one thing, the success that came so easily to Bobby in sports eluded him in business. Gone were the glory, the crowds, the applause, the fans, and the reporters seeking hot copy. The adjustment was difficult because the truth couldn't be more plain. Tennis was fun. Board meetings were boring. Not only were there few tennis fans at American Photograph, few of his colleagues even knew Bobby Riggs as someone other than the boss's son-in-law. And though Bobby came into the job from a position of privilege, R.B. decided that if Bobby were going to grow into the job he would have to learn the business the same way R.B. had—from the ground up.

"I came into the company after having been a celebrity," Bobby said years later. "I was Riggs, the star, welcomed anywhere. And now they wanted me to start at the bottom, sweeping floors or something. Well, I wouldn't do that."

On the surface, R.B. and Bobby had much in common. Both were outgoing, self-made, and charismatic. R.B. might even have hoped Bobby would one day take over the business. But whereas R.B. was diligent and serious about work, Bobby was carefree and almost never serious, and this difference proved to be a source of tension.

"He just wasn't R.B.'s type," Crimi said of Bobby. At best, Crimi said, R.B. "could tolerate him, I guess." R.B. had no choice. The same obligation that required his sons-in-law to work for the family company required R.B. to put up with Bobby and keep him on the payroll.

As a result, Bobby was never a very happy businessman. Though he worked for American Photograph for nearly 25 years,

"I never had any initiative or drive to be a success in business," Bobby later said. Yes, he stayed partly out of an obligation to his family, but also because the job offered him a good salary and plenty of freedom to do what he wanted—play tennis or golf, or just goof off. But these would be lost years for Bobby, that time in the life of an athlete—or anybody who peaks before the age of 30—when everything that follows is anticlimactic. "One day," wrote journalist Jon Bradshaw, "he had gone to a party or walked into a bar—he couldn't quite remember—and no one, not one of them, remembered his name. 'Heck,' he thought, 'Gosh, you mean? Gosh, I'm Bobby Riggs, goddamn it,' and they had given him those infinitely quizzical looks, as though he had said something they had not quite understood."

Luckily, Bobby got along well with his brother-in-law, Mike Crimi. Quiet, cautious, and methodical, Crimi was the exact opposite of Bobby in terms of personality. And though the two were thrown into a situation rife with the potential for rivalry and animosity, the two sons-in-law grew to be good friends. Bobby let Crimi run the company, while Crimi let Bobby do pretty much what he wanted, assigning him tasks that gave him plenty of time to travel and play golf—jobs such as fieldwork or giving pep talks to the troops at sales conventions. By all outward appearances the two jointly ran the company, sitting in on board meetings and co-signing all the checks. But while Crimi spent most of his days dealing with bankers, lawyers, and accountants, visitors to Bobby's office would likely find him leaning back in his chair with his feet up on his desk, a cigar clenched between his teeth, a newspaper in one hand folded open to the latest sports betting line, and the phone in the other hand with his bookie on the line.

"We put Bob in charge of several things," Crimi said, "but you had to put someone there along with him because Bob's mind just wasn't on those things. That wasn't his interest."

Not surprisingly, Bobby would later say he felt "there was always this undercurrent of resentment" toward him at American Photograph, a feeling by the company's rank-and-file of " 'Wait 'til you leave the nest, you'll get yours.' Whispers like that."

Being a parent was also a stretch for Bobby. It was work. "I was not the kind of father who would gather the kids together on a Saturday and take them to Jones Beach, or out somewhere for a picnic," he said. While other kids' enduring memories of their fathers might be of trips to ball games or being taught how ride a bicycle, Bobby's children remembered trips to the golf course and meeting men who went by names such as The Fat Man and Charlie the Blade, or lessons from Bobby on how to correctly figure the odds.

"One of the regular memories that I have is of my dad soaking in the tub," John recalled. The phone would ring and a gruff voice shouted, "Yeah, is Bobby there? This is Mike." Mike had a voice that sounded like a tow-truck winch.

"My dad liked to bet on football," John said. "I would recognize the voice of my dad's bookie and I would say to my dad, 'Hey dad, Mike the Bookie is on the phone.' My dad would ask me 'to get the line on that Sunday's games,' and I would write down on a pad of paper the betting line for that day's NFL games. So I'm on the phone with Mike, giving Dad the line on all the games—Colts five over the Dolphins, whatever—and my dad's telling me, 'Put two units on this' or four units on that, where a unit is a hundred dollars. And for me it was like normal. This is what all American kids do for their dads."

In his own way, Bobby may have aspired to become the ideal husband and father, but he had no idea how to do it. "I tried to help my wife," Bobby said. "We had a Sunday school for a couple of years together and we used to have them back to the house and I'd be games-master for them, play tennis and softball with them and take them to see the Knicks or a table tennis exhibition once in a while. And I would go to Cub Scout meetings. But these were attempts. I suppose a really mature person does these things naturally, but I'd have to think about doing the right thing, about not going out and playing gin and poker again tonight."

More often than not he simply didn't think about it. It was nothing for him to spend a Saturday playing ninety holes of golf, the final putt sunk in darkness, the players' cars turned so their headlights illuminated the green. It was not unusual for Bobby to become so engrossed in a game of gin rummy or poker that he never made it home for dinner, or he might call and say, "Dear, I'll be home in half hour," then call back again a couple of hours later to say it would be another half-hour.

"It seemed more like he was a visitor in the house, a houseguest," daughter Dorothy Riggs said. "But I do have good memories," she said, recalling times Bobby would play paddle tennis with the children, take them to the golf course, or organize sports contests between them. Though time with their father could be boundlessly entertaining, Dorothy said, "it was always on his terms, around his schedule and day. It was everything wrapped around him."

For example, in the mid-1960s, recalled son Bill Riggs, "I remember my dad telling me when I was six or seven, 'I'm going to play tennis with you every day. I'm going to give you lessons. You're going to be a world-class player. You're going to be great.'" Terrific, Bill thought. "I got all dressed up. This was before we had a tennis court at our house. We went to the Port Washington Tennis Academy, and he played with me. Then, we were supposed to meet there the next day. I got all dressed up but he never showed up, and he never played with me again. I thought, 'What bullshit.'" Not only that, Bill said, "He never took any interest in other aspects of my life."

No wonder, Bill said, "I could never really connect with him."

To know Bobby was to play with Bobby, so the children who grew closest to him were those who played golf or tennis, who hung out with their father and watched sports on TV or played cards. "Unless you were into that, you couldn't spend any time with him," Dorothy said.

Even then, however, Bobby had a difficult time knowing how to be fatherly. "When we played our dad in tennis," John said, "the tradition was the first time you won a set you got a hundred dollars. Of course, this never happened against my dad. But I remember one time playing him when I was a teenager and I was 'on.' I was up 5-2 the first set and if I won the next game, I'd win the $100. At the changeover, my dad takes out his wallet and pulls out a hundred-dollar bill. He then takes that and places it in the alley under a rock. Then he says to me, 'I want you to think about that.' Of course, I fell apart and lost five straight games. Looking back, I think if that was my son, I'd be happy to see him win. I might even go out of my way to let him win, just to give him the satisfaction. But my dad just couldn't do that."

Larry recalled the same $100 bet: "He hit all these undercut spin shots, and they're bouncing all kinds of ways on the clay and I had tears in my eyes. And I told him, 'Please, I'm not used to these spins. Just play normal.' He said, 'No. Learn how to adjust to them.' He knew it was bothering me. He didn't care. We were playing. I was trying to win. He was trying to win. If I couldn't adjust to the spins, it was my problem. Once you step on the court, that's it. That I was his son didn't mean shit... When he's playing, he wants to win. He's not interested in playing for 'fun.' There's no fun involved."

Bobby hated to lose money, no matter how little and to whom, but he might also have been trying to teach his sons a lesson in competitiveness, in handling pressure and maintaining composure. Nevertheless, once engaged in a game, Bobby treated his children as just another opponent, an adversary to be sized up, toyed with, and eventually destroyed.

Not surprisingly, measuring up to their father came to be an impossible task for Bobby's children. There was too much pressure, too much aggressive infighting. The best way to deal with it, John discovered, was simply not to try. So he gave up tennis, studied hard, got good grades, and in 1968 entered Yale as a freshman. "He used to tell my mom, 'Priscilla you're ruinin' that kid with all your poetry and books,'" John said, adding that he thought his father would have been happier to see him go to Stanford, where he might have been able to play tennis all the time. "That was just his way of seeing things," he said.

John added, "I decided I needed to strike out on my own, make a place for myself, and in the end I think my father respected that. Besides, by not playing tennis and everything, it eliminated a lot of competitive tensions." Almost in spite of Bobby, John followed the path of his grandfather, going to graduate school in theology, becoming a minister and later a professor. Bobby's other children also found their own paths through life. Bobby Jr. became a businessman. Dorothy became an artist. Bill became a student of Asian philosophy.

Of Bobby's six children, only Larry took up tennis seriously. He went on to become a top college player and coach at Pepperdine University near Los Angeles. But he had his own problems with Bobby. When he moved out West, he tried to hide the fact that he was the son of Bobby Riggs. At the height of the "Battle of the Sexes" furor, Bobby told a reporter, "Larry's always been rebellious. He's been resentful of me and what I've done because he thinks he can do everything better than I can."

In the end, John said, "I came to realize that my dad was better as a pal than a father. And once I was able to understand his limitations, and not to expect him to be someone he really could not be, I was able to have a better relationship with him. Because he was fun to hang out with, and I always enjoyed going with him to the golf course, or to watch tennis together or just hang out."

Though Bobby had a way with people, he was clueless when it came to being a father. "He could say no and make you feel better than most people could saying yes," recalled friend Doug Dean. "He knew how to make someone feel very good. He would compliment them, and on that level he understood human nature in terms of treating someone with respect. I guess you could say he was sensitive." On the other hand, Dean added, "He was a guy who could be as insensitive as anybody I've ever seen." For whatever reason, this was especially true with his children, and nearly all of them went through periods of estrangement from Bobby.

In 1973 Larry was working as a stockbroker in Los Angeles. Bobby was at the Beverly Hills Country Club, eating lunch with Jimmy Connors, Lornie Kuhle, Pancho Segura, and Dean Paul "Dino" Martin, son of singer/actor Dean Martin and a former ranked tennis professional. "They're all talking," Larry said, "and Dad ends up making a bet that I was better than Dino. Sure enough, I get a call from Dad. 'You gotta leave right now and get your tennis stuff and come over.'"

"But Dad, the market isn't even closed yet."

"Don't worry about that. Just get your stuff and get down here."

Larry arrived as told. An audience gathered to watch, and Bobby went up to Larry to tell him he had a thousand dollars riding on the match.

"A thousand dollars!" Larry said. "You got to be kidding!"

A Riggs family Christmas portrait, circa 1961. From left: John, Bill, Jim, Dorothy, Bobby and Priscilla.

"Anyway," recalled Larry, "we start playing and it's a long, hard match, but I win—barely. I'm dripping in sweat and Dad tells me, 'Good work. I'm gonna take care of you. Now go take a shower.'" The way Larry understood it, Bobby would give him his share of the winnings afterwards, but when he returned from the clubhouse Bobby and Kuhle were on the court warming up against Martin and Connors.

"Don't worry," Bobby told Larry. "I got the whole thing covered in this match."

"Is he kidding?" thought Larry, realizing that Bobby might be slightly better than Martin—maybe—but that Kuhle sure as hell wasn't better than Connors. Disgusted, Larry just got into his car and left, learning later that Bobby and Kuhle lost all the money that he had fought for.

Part of Bobby's problem as a father was that, in many ways, he was a child himself. "They say some men mature earlier than others, and I don't know if I've ever shown any degree of maturity when it comes to this ability of fatherhood and being a husband and a Rock of Gibraltar," Bobby said. "I doubt very much whether I really matured past the stage of a teenager, or a young twenty probably at best."

On his own since 13, a star in an inherently selfish sport, doted on by his brothers and constantly surrounded by an entourage of friends and "handlers," it is little wonder Bobby was immature. Certainly, to reach the level of athletic perfection he achieved Bobby needed to be self-consumed. Athletes, like artists or politicians or anyone driven to achieve a singular goal, are not particularly well-rounded. "Narcissistic" is how many who knew Bobby describe him. In Bobby's case the term meant he was too self-absorbed to really experience sympathy for others—even his own children. It also meant he never considered anything he did to be wrong. The way he saw it, "What is good for Bobby is good for the world." Or at least he convinced himself of this. Whatever the case, the trait had a habit of coming out in some very inappropriate ways.

In 1970, when Bill was 14, he recalled, "My mother decided Bobby should take me to Wimbledon. He was going to play the seniors tournament. They have it every year, and they play the final on Court One. So in the weeks leading up to this trip Bobby started saying to me, 'Bill, when we get to England, I'm gonna have to get you a little English muffin. And when we get to France, we're going to have to get you a little French wench.'"

Bill thought Bobby was teasing him. After all, his father often used sexual innuendo around the house to goad his boys. Things like, "Hey Jim, did you get any last night?" Or taking note of his daughter's emergence into womanhood by pointing to Dorothy's breasts and saying, "Doll has TB... two beauts."

When they arrived in London, Bobby arranged for them to have separate rooms. Just as Bill was settling in, the phone rang. "I have someone here who wants to say hello to you," said a voice. The next thing Bill knew, there was a knock at his door. He answered to find a 22-year-old drunken Scottish prostitute. "That was my initiation into sexuality," Bill said. "I was like, 'Oh, my god.' I was terrified." Afterwards, Bobby said nothing. "He didn't want to be associated with it, in case it got back to Priscilla," Bill explained.

While living with her father around the time of his challenge match against Margaret Court, Dorothy said it got to the point where she wouldn't bring her girlfriends around to meet Bobby because she was afraid her father would slap the make on them.

Another time, Bill recalled, at Bobby's home in Leucadia in the 1980s, "I was kind of dating this girl, not really dating her but just getting to know her a bit, and I think she was a little, manic depressive or something, and maybe she wasn't taking her medicine. She was an out-there kind of girl. One evening she came over and I was out—I spent the night some place else—and Bobby asked her to play backgammon. When I came back the next morning, she had left and I said, 'What happened there, Dad?' And he said, 'Oh, I bet her if she won I'd give her $20 and if she lost she'd have to fuck me and suck me all night. She lost.' " Perhaps conditioned to such behavior from his father, Bill did not react strongly at the time. "She wasn't like my girlfriend," he explained. And Bobby? Well, Bill said, "he was never really a father." Nevertheless, looking back, he commented: "I'd like to think he wouldn't have done it if he knew she was my real girlfriend and we were serious."

What could Bobby possibly have been thinking? After all, he could have lied and told Bill the girl had simply left. But he didn't. He had no shame about what he had done. He might have even thought he was being funny.

Bobby's lack of boundaries was not quite as outrageous with all of his children. Bill seemed to bear the brunt of it, perhaps for no other reason than Bobby knew he could get away with it. Bobby always pushed the limits. He sized up Bill in much the same way he sized up an opponent on the tennis court—figuring out Bill's weaknesses and vulnerabilities. But in this case Bobby's talent had horribly warped consequences. Though not intentionally cruel, Bobby was simply a poor father. He may well have known this and figured it was enough to try and be their buddy. In Larry's case, it meant ensnaring him in his gambling schemes. In Bill's case, it meant treating him like a frat-house pledge.

While his unshakable confidence in himself and his ability to deal with people and situations served him well on the court, Bobby's inability to deal with his children left them struggling to understand their family and their relationship with their father.

"There was a lot of trauma growing up, and a lot of confusion and a lot of things to sort out," Dorothy said.

As a husband, too, Bobby fell short, though not because he didn't love Priscilla. "I guess I always thought the wife was supposed to be the mother and the homemaker and that she should maybe cater to the man more than he would cater to her," Bobby said. Certainly his parents were role models for this, as Bobby's mother, Agnes, never conceived of a life beyond taking care of her house and family. "I think deep-rooted in me is the notion that a woman's responsibility is to keep the guy happy," Bobby said. "The man's role basically, I suppose, is to be the breadwinner and bring home bucks and be the head of the household and not cheat on her and be strong and give them the feeling of being loved. I always thought I was pretty good, at least about the money." Of course, money was the one thing Priscilla didn't need.

As it was, she and sports were total strangers. She didn't know the names of major sports teams, never looked at the sports pages, and didn't enjoy watching games on TV. She also found card games, backgammon, and other forms of gambling distasteful and undignified, in part because of her strong religious background. She particularly never understood Bobby's compulsion to gamble. On New Year's Day, when Bobby watched all four major college bowl games, with bets riding on each one, Priscilla would not even approach the television room. Maybe, like Kay, she thought she could mold Bobby into the ideal husband and father—that a stable routine, secure home life, and the cushion of her family's millions would wean Bobby of his need to gamble.

But between his job, his buddies, and his games of golf, tennis, gin rummy, backgammon, and everything else, Bobby never seemed to be around. Priscilla increasingly found herself in the big house at Plandome alone with the children. The family had some household help, but the real burden of parenting fell upon Priscilla. The doctors' appointments, schooling, discipline, driving around, and attending sporting events and recitals were all Priscilla's responsibility.

She felt trapped, a homemaker living in the shadow of her husband with no life of her own. After all, she was smart (graduating cum laude with a degree in psychology from William and Mary College), she had talent, she thought she could have done more. Worst of all, she was terribly lonely. She craved Bobby's attention and love, but Bobby's first love, his only true love, was always the big play, the competition, being on stage and winning. And this she grew to resent.

To ease the pain, Priscilla drank, and for her children the predominant memory growing up would be of their mother's spiraling alcoholism. As they got older, she started drinking more and earlier in the day. "By the time I was in junior high school [in the early 1960s], when I got home she was usually already drunk," John said. "Not stumble-down or passed out or incoherent—that was to come—but drunk. It's funny how kids can tell these things, too. They have a sort of intuition. I could tell just walking in, maybe by a certain smell, or the way the house was left or the sounds that she'd been drinking.

"For some reason, perhaps because I was the oldest, I became her confidant. What happened is I'd get home and she'd want to talk. She'd get very emotional and talk about her problems and her life. I wasn't sure how to react to all this. On the one hand, a part of me might have felt special at having this relationship. On the other hand, I didn't know what to do and grew to dread it. Now, all I can remember is just how much I hated coming home."

When sober, Priscilla was sweet, funny, and sensitive. But she underwent a complete metamorphosis after drinking, "a real Jekyll and Hyde transformation," according to John. Drunk, she was vicious—both verbally and physically. The nights seemed a never-ending routine of screaming, insults, throwing things, and breaking dishes. Bobby might come home and find all his clothes strewn across the front lawn.

But Bobby continued as if nothing were the matter. He played his games and hung out with his friends. He would bring his buddies home and they would behave like the house was Bobby's bachelor pad. Recalled Larry, who with his brother Bobby Jr. used to spend summers at Plandome, "Priscilla couldn't stand it that all these people would come over and he'd just concentrate on talking to them." To get Bobby's attention, Priscilla would create a scene. "She liked putting on scenes because then she'd have his attention," said Larry.

Once, recalled Larry, they were all having dinner. Bobby brought home a guest, a golfing buddy. While Bobby's friend peppered him with questions about Wimbledon and his golf exploits, the rest of the family continued with the meal. But Bobby was really the only one talking. After a while, Larry said, Priscilla picked up a big bowl of mashed potatoes and stood up, as if she were planning to serve them. From one corner of the table, she walked slowly around, past Bobby, past all the kids, and right up to Bobby's friend. Having gotten the attention of everyone, she took the bowl and dumped everything unceremoniously on the guest's lap. "He was asking all these questions, and it just pissed her off," Larry explained.

Another time, in late 1963, Jack Kramer, though officially retired the year before as the tour promoter, arranged for the pros to appear in New York to show off their latest star, Rod Laver, a hot-shot Australian lefty who had just become the first man since Don Budge to win the Grand Slam, all four major tournaments in a single year. The event was part of three-city tour that pitted Australian stars against American stars in a Davis Cup-style format. For the New York stop, Kramer tapped Bobby to be the referee.

When the gang got to town, Bobby invited Kramer and the others to a party at his house on Long Island. Kramer gladly accepted, but unknown to Bobby, Gladys Heldman, publisher of *World Tennis* magazine, and a strong figure in the game, was hosting another party at her Long Island estate. Suddenly, Bobby's party lost its allure. Only four people showed up at Bobby's house: Jack Kramer, his wife Gloria, and two representatives from Wilson Sporting Goods. Having prepared for a dozen or so guests, Priscilla blew up. She grabbed a large pair of scissors and calmly went upstairs and into Bobby's closet, where she proceeded to shear an arm and leg off each of Bobby's suits before throwing them out the window. "That was her way of getting even with Bobby," Kramer later recalled with a laugh. "Poor Bobby hadn't done a thing. Gladys just had more appeal with the players."

Although such tirades had their humorous side, Priscilla could also be frighteningly cruel. "She had a real knack for knowing exactly what someone's soft spot was," John said. And she was not beyond verbal humiliation. "One ritual she insisted on was eating dinner together," John said. "It was important for her to have that semblance of family unity. But as her alcoholism got worse, these dinners got to be awful because of the personality change she underwent from drinking. Everybody was afraid. I don't think she picked on me so much, perhaps because she considered me her friend. And I think Dorothy didn't get it so bad, but the others did, and especially my dad. He bore the brunt of it. She would go on about his sports friends, his gambling, whatever. And I remember him with his head down, just taking it, not saying anything. He'd just ride it out.

"Thursdays were the worst," John said. "That was when the help had the night off and my mother would cook, which is tough to do when you're drunk. So add this stress to everything else and Thursdays were just a nightmare. Everybody dreaded them. I remember one particular Thursday with my mom screaming at my dad in the kitchen. As she is yelling at him, she grabs his glasses off his face and crushes them under her foot, and my dad doesn't do anything. He just stands there with tears welling up in his eyes."

Added Dorothy: "I was terrified growing up. There was no way to stop it, nowhere to go, no way to fix it, no one to talk to, and nobody helped us."

Despite the rancor, Dorothy said, Bobby "never raised his voice to my mom." For all his competitiveness, for all his sexist bluster later on, he never got angry or fought back. "He couldn't do it," she said. "I remember talking to him about it. I said, 'Dad, why do you let her talk to you that way. Why do you just sit back and take it?' And he just said that there just wasn't any other way to deal with my mother. If he tried to fight back it would just get worse, because there was no reasoning with her. You can't reason with an alcoholic. His tactic was the quieter you stayed, the less it gave her to fight against. She wanted him to fight back. She was provoking him. He'd say, 'Don't talk back and don't argue with her because you can't win. There's no winning here.'

"It was very strange to me, too, because we'd have these big scenes at night with my mother and the next day my mother would act like nothing ever happened. Like everything was perfectly normal and okay. There was no saying, 'I'm sorry' or 'I didn't mean to upset you kids.' There was absolutely no acknowledgement or recognition that anything had even happened."

Could Bobby have helped Priscilla if he had understood her alcoholism on the same terms as his compulsion to bet? Probably not. Besides, he never considered himself a gambling addict. In his mind, gambling addicts were compulsive losers: people bent on self-destruction. Gambling addicts were people who wouldn't rest until they had gambled away everything—their paycheck, the mortgage, money for a spouse's birthday present— walking away from the table after that final bet with a sense of relief that they achieved what they had set out to do. Casinos, horse tracks, sports betting, and the like were all rigged to favor the house—how else would they make their millions? They were sucker's games. Sure, he might entertain himself by playing baccarat or betting on football, but his big play was games in which he felt he had the edge, the advantage, whether from athletic skill, competitive toughness, inside information, or chicanery. He needed to know going in the odds were in his favor. No, he was a compulsive winner, a competitor. He was, in the best sense of the word, a hustler, someone driven to succeed, a go-getter.

"We talked about this and he adamantly denied he had a gambling problem," Dorothy said. "There was no kidding around. He was furious at the suggestion. He was in total denial about it. To him, it was a fun activity that he thrived on. To him, he was just having fun. I remember my mom would plead with him, 'But Bobby, you don't need to gamble. There's more than enough money.' It was not that there was a need to go out and make money that way, but it was so much a part of his personality. The thrill of it, the thrill of a challenge, I guess. He would do that at the cost of their relationship."

"He didn't dwell on it a whole lot," said friend Doug Dean of Bobby, "but he did seem to have a tragic flaw in that the competition sort of owned him in the sense that it's really all he cared about, at the expense of relationships or parenting or anything."

While money helped fuel Bobby's competitive instinct, he was never greedy in the conventional sense. The cushion of Priscilla's wealth actually got to be a burden for him. "I never thought of my wife's money as half mine. The millions weren't mine. The $100 I won on the golf course was. That was a challenge, and I had won it on my own," Bobby said. "The only good shot is your own hustle, writing a poem, dropping a putt, making your own slice shot. All that money didn't mean anything if I didn't have to strive for it. So I never bore down. It was too easy. That's why I was not a successful father or husband or businessman. It was really pretty stupid of me, the situation couldn't turn me on."

This also meant Priscilla's money was family money: earmarked for the bills, the groceries, clothes for the kids, and gas for the cars. Bobby's money was all Bobby's. "He was so fucking tight," Bill said. "I remember one time: It was Jim, Dorothy, myself, my mother and Bobby. A couple of us needed some new shoes so the five of us went to Stride-Rite across from where we lived on the 'Miracle Mile' shopping plaza in Manhasset. So we're in there—and Bobby always carried around a big fat wad of money for his gambling, he was always counting it every night—and so a couple of us got shoes and Priscilla said, 'Bobby, can you pay for the shoes?' And he said, 'No. Use your credit card.' He tightens right up. He couldn't pay for a couple pairs of shoes."

Bobby, his son John admitted, "was tighter than the bark on a tree." He hated spending money he didn't have to. He wore the same suit for six years. He would throw a dinner party and serve a bucket of Kentucky Fried Chicken. After winning Wimbledon in 1939, he received a $150 gift certificate for tennis clothes. Ten years later, he bragged, "I'm still wearing three of the tennis shirts I got on that deal." In fact, Bobby's only real indulgence was the money he spent on gambling.

One Christmas, Bill recalled, while visiting Bobby over the holidays, his father handed him a package.

"Here, I got you a present."

Bobby handed over a lumpy, hastily wrapped package with no ribbon, no card.

"So I open it up," Bill said. "And it's a bunch of used T-shirts and tennis shirts, some them with holes in them and bleach stains. I think there was a pair of old shorts, too."

"I thought you'd like these," Bobby said in all sincerity.

This was not a gag gift. "He was probably just cleaning out his closet and he hated to throw stuff away," explained Bill. "He thought I could use them or like them." Bobby was never much on shopping for Christmas presents. "I think one or two Christmases he gave us a hundred bucks," Bill said, "but that was about the extent of it."

As his home life deteriorated, Bobby's solution was to escape—to the golf course, to the tennis courts, to card games, to tennis exhibitions, to any place but home. Still he was miserable. This was not the life he had envisioned. His generally cheerful disposition gave way to bouts of depression and moodiness. One day, while driving around with a visiting friend, Bobby looked out the car window as they passed a cemetery and said gloomily, "That's where I belong—I am dead."

Among those who joined Bobby's weekly matches at the Mid-Town Tennis Club in New York were Arthur Ashe (left) and Gene Scott (center). Invariably, Scott said, the matches would involve a wager and require one or more of the players to be handicapped in some manner.

16
The Greatest Salesman of All Time
1952-1971

L eather-bound photo albums from the period portray a life of prosperity and contentment. Among the pictures, Bobby sits on an overstuffed couch next to a glittering, tinsel-covered Christmas tree, dressed in plaid golfing pants and V-neck sweater, his wife beside him and the children gathered around. In another, a graying, paunchier Bobby stands stiffly in a suit and tie among a group of businessmen, a wan smile on his face.

With slicked back hair and horned-rimmed glasses, Bobby could dress and look the part of the all-American family man, the button-down executive, and a pillar of the community. But it was an image he could not sustain. His turbulent home life aside, he was never cut out for a settled, nine-to-five existence. After all, he had been on his own since he was 13—playing tennis, hustling, constantly on the go, meeting people, and scouting out action. Like many who grew up in the Depression, he had a deep-seated anxiety over money and a drive for financial security. But once he had amassed enough wealth to put those fears aside, all the trappings of his genteel existence—the mansion, the rich wife, the four children, and the high-paying job—all that made him uneasy. Despite pronouncements that everything was "wonderful" or "beautiful," Bobby was clearly out of place. "You've got to stay in action," he joked. "It's good for the arteries."

"It was nothing for him to have 30 or 40 bets a day on everything," recalled Joe Fishbach, who knew Bobby from their days on the amateur circuit. "He'd bet on basketball, baseball, football, golf, tennis. Whether he was involved or not involved, there were bets... It really didn't matter how much the bet was, as long as there was a bet. How he kept track of it all, I don't know." To argue whether it was an escape from Bobby's troubles at home or the cause of them is moot. This was his way of life.

Bobby's wife Priscilla attempted to mold him into the kind of husband she needed. At first, she gave him time, and when that didn't work, she pleaded with him. When that failed, she threatened him. At one point she told him that if he didn't get counseling to treat his addiction, she would leave him. Bobby complied, and found a psychiatrist. For nearly a year, he dutifully went to the doctor's office each week. What he didn't tell Priscilla was that after a couple of sessions, he had the doctor flicking cards into a hat. The rest of the time, Bobby said, they played gin rummy.

Clearly, nothing was going to change. Bobby was going to do whatever he wanted. That's not surprising. That he could get a doctor to abandon his Hippocratic oath to gamble with him was simply a measure of his extraordinary gift for hustling. "If you never bet in your life and you hung around him for two days he'd talk you into a bet of some kind," Fishbach said. Indeed, Bobby bragged that he could turn small bettors into big bettors and get money out of guys who normally would never part with a penny.

"He had more fun getting someone to bet than actually making the dollar," said John Nogrady, another amateur-circuit veteran. "It was the trick of getting it, of getting someone to do it."

Tony Vincent, another longtime friend of Bobby's and a New York City tennis pro, called Bobby "the greatest salesman of all time. He could have done anything he wanted."

To others, he was simply a nudge, refusing to take no for an answer. "He'd break down your resistance," Fishbach said.

Friend and former champion Bob Falkenburg remembered one marathon session with Bobby in the late 1960s that began on the Westchester Country Club golf course and proceeded to the practice green, where the two first putted against each other, then competed at rolling the ball into the hole. From there they went to the clubhouse, where they pitched golf tees into an ashtray. They finally ended up in Falkenburg's hotel room, tossing cards into a hat. It was late, recalled Falkenburg, and Bobby was irked at being out $800, saying he needed another chance to win his money back.

"We'll play tomorrow," Bobby insisted.

"No," Falkenburg told him. "I'm leaving for Florida."

"Okay, I'll see you there."

Astounded that Bobby would even suggest following him to Florida, Falkenburg said firmly, "No, Bobby, you can't. It's for business. I won't have time."

"Well, then, when?"

Exhausted and annoyed, Falkenburg told Bobby he didn't know. By now, he needed sleep more than he needed the $800, so he insisted Bobby leave without paying.

"Now I don't see him for seven or eight years," Falkenburg recalled. "And I saw him at Wimbledon and the first thing he does he comes rushing up to me and says, 'Bob, Bob, I know I owe ya. I'm gonna pay ya.' And I say, 'No, forget it, Bobby. It wouldn't be fair now because I've already told everybody that you welshed on the bet. You don't need to pay me.' Bobby rationalized that the reason he hadn't paid was that the bet really wasn't over. He had to have one more chance."

Another time, in the late 1970s, Bobby lost a couple of hundred dollars on the golf course at the La Costa Resort and Spa near San Diego to Bob Lutz, another former top tennis player. After collecting the debt, Lutz returned home to San Francisco, happy to have won, perhaps thanking his good fortune at making such a clean getaway. But when he arrived home he found that Bobby had hopped on a plane and followed him, and for several days hounded Lutz into giving him another chance to win his money back.

"Bobby would run it into the ground with anybody," said friend Doug Dean. "It would start out being fun, but he couldn't let it go. He'd keep saying, 'We'll do it again tomorrow,' and he would take your last nickel. Finally, guys would just dodge him when they saw him coming. He had a problem at being able to shut it off."

Football coaching great Vince Lombardi once said after a tough defeat that his team didn't really lose, they just ran out of time. Similarly, in Bobby's mind no game was truly over until he had been given a chance to win his money back. Thus, while winning a contest against Bobby was one thing, getting him to pay off a bet was quite another. "He never paid you when he lost, unless you forced him," said Nogrady. "He would always say, 'We'll play it off.' But he did it in a nice way. You didn't get angry with him." Once, after his partner collected a check from Bobby for ten dollars in a game of doubles, Nogrady turned and joked, "Frame it."

"I think Bobby's forte in betting was he never intended to pay," said Fishbach. "Not that he wanted to cheat you, but in the back of his mind he figured he'd get you with another bet, a bigger bet. You can be a hell of a gambler if you play with the intention of not paying. It's a great attitude."

Following his retirement from the tours and his marriage to Priscilla, Bobby wrote that he "hardly touched a racket for the next sixteen years." True, his days as a competitive tennis player were over, and he could more often be found on a golf course than a tennis court. But Bobby continued to play. Each week, he lined up money matches at one of several country clubs on Long Island, on one of the three courts at Rip's on Manhattan's West End, or at the Tennis Center, whose two courts were laid out on the rooftop of a 13-story commercial building in mid-Manhattan. The Tennis Center's courts stood in the shadow of the smokestacks of a Con Ed plant along the East River. Depending on the wind, the players might find themselves playing in a swirl of billowing smoke, the balls turning black from soot before they even finished a set. It wasn't Wimbledon, but these places had other attractions.

The players, Bobby wrote, were an "argumentative gang of brokers, professional men and businessmen, mostly middle-aged and fair to middling tennis players." But their passion for action compensated for their lack of tennis talent. "To a man, they are born bettors who wouldn't think of taking to the court without backing themselves with a modicum of cash." Among them were Jack Dreyfus, the "Lion of Wall Street" and the multimillionaire founder of the Dreyfus Fund, and Hank Greenberg, the burly former slugger for the Detroit Tigers. All were intensely competitive and hated to lose. Playing mostly doubles, Bobby would lead this motley crew in contests for as much as $500 a set.

Recalling the scene at Rip's, where he used to teach, Nogrady said he would walk in and "they would be laying out bets: two-to-one on this doubles team; three-to-one on that team. And I used to say six-to-five they don't finish the match, because they all cheated and broke their racquets and walked off the court. They were terrible... they all thought they were smarter than each other."

It was these matches that gave rise to some of the wackier handicapping schemes against Bobby. To make their tennis matches fair against Bobby, the group came up with elaborate ways of reducing his advantage. On various occasions—and with substantial bets going—they required Bobby to play with a variety of handicaps, including carrying an umbrella in his left hand, even while serving; carrying a weighted suitcase in his left hand, also while serving; burdened by weights around his waist, wrists, and ankles; holding a leash with one or two dogs at the other end; tied with a rope, chain-gang style, to his doubles partner; or requiring them to alternate shots while sharing a single racquet.

On other occasions, stars such as Don Budge, Arthur Ashe, Ken Rosewall, and Pancho Segura would join the group, in which case Bobby might be the one demanding a handicap. In Ashe's case, recalled one regular, Bobby would take a bucket of tennis balls and dump them on Ashe's side of the court, creating a minefield of potentially career-ending obstacles. But Ashe, then a cadet at West Point who needed the practice—not to mention the money—would coolly stand behind the baseline and take a couple of minutes to concentrate on the haphazard pattern of balls. Once satisfied that he had committed it to memory, he would proceed to play.

Gene Scott, a former Top-10 star of the early Sixties who went to Yale and became a lawyer and later publisher of *Tennis Week* magazine, said Bobby was tennis' original handicapper. "I played him 25 times and each time he would handicap the match in some way, where he would take one alley or two alleys and give me one serve—not bothering to put chairs on the court as he did later for gags.

"By giving the alley he would know what it would do for you or not do for you because he had been doing it all his life. There's no genius about it other than you had to do it to understand what the rewards were and how it changed the dynamics of a game. It was like a muscle that he developed better than anybody else. A lot of us learned to do it better because of Bobby, but he knew it better than you did."

Bobby always ingratiated himself to every potential victim. "He was a very warm person," said George Gondolman, another pro and a regular player at the club. "Hey, how ya doin'? Good to see ya," Bobby might say. "You're playing great tennis… We gotta get out there and play once in a while, you know? Come on. Let's do something."

"He gave of himself every time he saw you," Gondolman said. "He was always prodding you, complimenting you, saying things like, 'Hey I didn't know how good you were… You're terrific.'"

Before he built his own court at Plandome in 1964, Bobby also played at the Great Neck Tennis Club in Manhasset, a small private venue. Here Bobby met a young ophthalmologist named Richard Raskind who had a powerful serve and an aggressive game. "There wasn't much of a clubhouse," recalled the Yale-educated physician, who had played several years on the amateur circuit in the Fifties and who later would become one of the most controversial figures in the game. "Just a place to change, but it happened to have all the best players in the New York area playing there. Bobby would drive by in his car in the spring and yell down to the courts, 'Hey, Doc, you look pretty good this spring. How about a practice match?' And by a 'practice match' Bobby meant a match you were going to bet on."

"Bobby was a master psychologist," continued the doctor. "He could play on people's egos. He could get people he could beat six-love, six-love and get them to give him games. He used to do that at Great Neck. He would play on their egos. And they would be stupid enough to give him games. And of course he'd beat them, but he'd keep it close. So then they'd say, 'I can't give you any games, Bobby, but I'll play you even.' So he'd play them even, and then win again. But he'd never beat anybody badly because if he did, he'd never get them to play again." After all, as the great poker champion Amarillo Slim would later say: You can skin a sheep only once, but you can shear him again and again.

During the winter, the action would move indoors. But indoor courts were rare in the mid-1950s. In New York, the only public indoor courts were at the Seventh Regiment Armory at 69th Street and Park Avenue, an immense Gothic structure that occupied an entire block. The hardwood floor inside could accommodate up to 14 tennis courts. The surface, however, was slick and unforgiving. The balls ended up covered in splinters and the players likewise came off the court pulling splinters out of their hands. The city's only other indoor tennis courts were all private, part of huge estates belonging to wealthy families such as the Phipps, the Fairchilds, and the Lowes.

Two scions of Eastern tennis society, Esmund and Alastair Martin, heirs to the J.P. Morgan fortune, also had an indoor court, an immaculately groomed clay court enclosed in a beautiful brick building with a glass ceiling. Esmund was an above-average player who enjoyed hitting with the best and was willing to pay for it. Each week, he'd invite local stars to play with him, and among the regulars were Bobby, George Gondolman, and John Nogrady. For the sake of fairness, it was agreed that if Esmund hit a ball off the wall and it was good, the ball was in play.

Big money matches in tennis were rare, but when they occurred Bobby usually had a hand in things. In the late 1960s, recalled Vincent, he and Bobby traveled to Paradise Island in the Bahamas to play an exhibition with a couple of European players—an English pro from London whose name Vincent could not remember, and Jean Noel Grinda, a former French star of the 1950s and a well-known hustler himself. The arrangement was for Bobby to play with the Englishman and Vincent to partner with Noel Grinda. On the side, Bobby and Noel Grinda agreed to a $10,000 wager. But before taking the court, Bobby convinced Vincent to throw the game in exchange for a share of the winnings. This required some finesse on Vincent's part. If he made it too obvious, the jig would be up and the bet called off. He had to be selective about which shots he missed.

Unknown to both Bobby and Vincent, Noel Grinda had made the same arrangement with the Englishman. This meant that half of each team was playing to lose. To the large gallery assembled to watch the match, nothing seemed amiss as the match continued: 2-all... 3-all... 4-all... 5-all... 6-all. Serving at 6 games to 7 and 30-40, Vincent had a chance to lose the match. "I had to serve to the English guy in the ad court," he remembered. "I could have lost the match," he said. "I could have double-faulted. But that would have been too obvious," so he put the ball in play. In doubles, the returner generally tries to hit the ball back to the server so it won't be picked off by the man at net. But "this English player kept hitting balls to my partner at net [Noel Grinda], who was putting the ball away," Vincent said. "I was trying to lose and my partner was trying to win."

Finally, at 10-all, everyone on court realized what was happening. "It was getting ridiculous," Vincent said. To save face as well as dignity, Vincent said, "Listen, I hurt my back. Can we quit?" Right away everybody agreed. In a show of indignation, Bobby stormed off the court, acting as if he was the one who had been wronged.

"Look, I don't want to just play," Bobby explained to Bob Barker, another in Bobby's tennis group. "For me, the closest thing to playing in a tournament is to bet."

Inducted into the International Tennis Hall of Fame in 1966, Bobby was honored to be included among the game's all-time greats. But given the chance, he would have preferred to be playing tournaments. By the 1960s, a few of his old friends and rivals, including Bill Talbert and Gardnar Mulloy, were competing on the senior-tournament circuit. But because he was still classified as a professional, Bobby was barred from sanctioned competition.

Since Bobby's retirement from tennis in 1951, Jack Kramer took over the tours. A bad back forced him to quit playing in 1952, but his success at promoting the pro tour and siphoning off the top amateur talent each year had helped make him a millionaire and gained him the unyielding enmity of the amateur authorities. Dubbed "The Czar" for his iron-fisted control over professional tennis, Kramer was nonetheless frustrated. Despite having proven the public's appetite for pro tennis, the game seemed no closer to going open than it did in the 1930s. When the International Lawn Tennis Federation (the world governing body for the game) got together for its annual meeting in 1959, the British pushed for a vote on open tennis, but the measure fell five votes short of the 139 (out of 209) votes needed to pass. Kramer felt sure that bad feelings toward him made his presence the major stumbling block to change. In 1962, with the game's popularity at an all-time low, Kramer got out. "I tried everything: star tours, round-robins, traditional tournaments, different rules, different scoring, different serves," Kramer said. Nothing worked. Convinced the amateur authorities would never agree to open the game as long as they had to deal with him, Kramer quit. Still, it would be six more years before Kramer's dream became reality.

Disorganization, a lack of a stars, and waning interest in the game left pro tennis struggling after Kramer's departure. Not until 1967, when a half-dozen of the top men bolted the amateur game in order to join the new World Championship Tennis pro circuit bankrolled by Texas oilman Lamar Hunt, did pressure on the game to open itself reach a head. Left with the realization that the major tournaments no longer featured the game's top players, the British and staid Wimbledon—the game's bastion of tradition—led the revolution. At its year-end meeting after the 1967 season, the Lawn Tennis Association of Britain decided unilaterally to open that nation's tournaments to professionals in 1968. The ITLF threatened to expel the British, but soon after the USLTA followed suit and the ITLF caved in. Finally, if somewhat reluctantly, tennis went "open."

Of course, Bobby followed all this with great excitement, not only because it ended the hypocrisy of the old "shamateur" system he had fought against his entire career, but because it meant he could once again play competitively.

For Bobby and other champions who had their memberships at the All England Club stripped when they turned professional, the inaugural open at Wimbledon in 1968 was like a homecoming. His membership reinstated, he planned to celebrate by entering the senior men's doubles tournament with old friend Pancho Segura. But the night before their opening match, Bobby accidentally put his hand through a plate glass window at his London hotel and severely cut his thumb, forcing him to withdraw.

Appropriately, the winners of the fortnight's first open singles titles were Billie Jean King, who went on to become the event's all-time champion, winning a total of 20 titles, and Australian Rod Laver. At the inaugural U.S. Open, U.S. Army 1st Lt. Arthur Ashe became the first open era winner of the title and the first black man to win a major singles title.

Once healed, Bobby returned to tournament tennis with a vengeance, traveling the country and world to compete in senior events. Bobby's game was tailor-made for senior tennis. At 45, the age that demarcates the senior division, few players have the stamina or strength to play the smashing, serve-and-volley game of young pros. A typical senior match is a duel of soft lobs and gentle cuts, drop shots and delicate angles—a game of patience, strategy, and placement.

This, of course, was Bobby's bread-and-butter, and made him almost an instant success in the seniors. He may have lost a step or two, his stamina may have faded. He now wore glasses and his hearing had started to go, but he still had the shots, the terrific touch, and the supreme confidence.

"There was a sense that being Bobby Riggs was worth at least a point or two every game because he was this king of angles and dinks and strategy," said Gene Scott. "He didn't hit the ball very hard, but he could lob with immaculate precision and he could basically do whatever he wanted with the ball. He was the world's champion and the impression was he could certainly do all that again, regardless of his age."

Though Bobby compared the play to "the younger game in slow motion," the quality was high. "What we lack in speed in senior ranks we make up for in grim determination," Bobby said. "I've worked harder on the court in senior play than I ever did in my life before. One reason may be that the rallies are so long. We don't use tie-breakers, and sets can run on forever." A match between two deftly confident senior players "can achieve high excitement and produce the kind of shotmaking a great many weekend players might do well to emulate," wrote a *Sports Illustrated* writer.

Against Bobby, opponents would come off the court after a match dripping in sweat and gasping for breath. The contests often turned into interminable backcourt exchanges. A linesman at one of Bobby's matches counting the number of times the ball crossed the net during one rally left off at a mind-numbing 147 times. Bobby also told the story about a spectator at one of his matches who went to the bar for a drink. When he returned to the match about 20 minutes later, Bobby and his opponent were still playing the same point.

"I look at Riggs and I say, 'there's no way that little guy can beat me; he's nothing: he'll be easy,'" Hugh Stewart told a reporter after a match against Bobby. "Then, when I get out there with him, he suddenly gets very big. Everything comes back and it's hard to handle. It's…" Stewart's voiced trailed off and he walked away from the interview, shaking his head.

Bobby was having the time of his life. "Letting me back into tennis was like giving me a new toy," Bobby said. "I'm having more fun playing senior tennis than I ever had as a junior champion or on the amateur and pro circuits."

Given the time and resources, a senior player could enter 20 to 30 tournaments a year against top-flight international competition. In addition to major events at Wimbledon and Forest Hills, there was an international team competition modeled on Davis Cup play.

In 1969, Bobby swept the courts—grass, hard court, and clay— and went undefeated in every major national or sectional senior tournament he entered, including the U.S. singles title. Over the next three years, he won four national singles and four national doubles titles. Though the crowds were smaller and there was nothing at stake other than personal pride, it was a thrill for Bobby to get back into the game and renew old friendships and rivalries. In 1970, he won the senior doubles event at Wimbledon with

1954 singles champion Jaroslav Drobny, a stocky lefty from Czechoslovakia who made his home in London. For Bobby, this was his first time back on the grass since winning his hat trick in 1939.

Undiminished by time was Bobby's furious desire to win and his skillful gamesmanship. Ploys he used to catch his breath or delay a match could still infuriate opponents, such as when he bounced the ball as he prepared to serve, then "accidentally" let it hit his shoe and roll into the court, whereupon he slowly would walk over, pick it up, walk back, and start the whole ritual over again. Or when he stopped play and knelt down to deliberately and painstakingly retie his shoes while his opponent waited impatiently.

One of the great psych-out artists of all time, Bobby could "talk you out of the game before the match," said Torsten Johannson, a former Swedish Davis Cup player and one of Bobby's top rivals on the senior circuit. "When I played him in the 1969 championship in Philly I won the first set 6-1 and began wondering if I was the best player in the whole world. Riggs convinced me I was. He told me I played a fantastic game and fed me that line of talk. I lost the match 6-1, 2-6, 3-6."

Since his return to the game, Bobby realized not only how much he missed competition and winning, but also how much he missed being the center of attention. Sure, the galleries were smaller and made up mostly of friends and family, but Bobby loved to ham it up, hitting trick shots and joking around.

Open tennis had reinvigorated the sport. The marriage of professionalism, commercialization, and television—along with the emergence of a crop of marketable stars—gave the sport energy and exposure it never had before. And with that came money—big money.

Given the high level of play in the senior game and how entertaining it was, Bobby contended the seniors deserved a share of the riches and recognition open tennis had brought to the game. It irked him that while he played his heart out in virtual privacy on the outer courts, women were getting paid top dollar and playing to near-empty stadiums. Or, as Jack Kramer said at the time, "people get up and go get a hot dog or go to the bathroom when the women come on."

"I knew we were playing far better tennis on the senior circuit than you could see anywhere in women's tennis," Bobby claimed. While he had to pay his own travel expenses and hotel bills, the girls "were raking in the loot" and, perhaps even more bothersome to Bobby, "getting all the glory."

With interest in tennis gaining, Bobby decided to write his autobiography, a book in which he would detail the game's past glory; his great rivalries against Budge, Kovacs, and Kramer; his days as a golf hustler and businessman.

George McGann, a tennis journalist and New York correspondent for Australian newspapers, agreed to work with Bobby. As a journalist, fan, and a recreational player himself, McGann no doubt knew Bobby's reputation, and felt this could be a plum assignment.

Beginning in late 1970, the two started meeting at Bobby's house in Plandome, but when Priscilla found out about the project she flew into a rage. Nobody knew Bobby as well as she did, she screamed. "Get out of here," she yelled at McGann. "I'm going to write this book. You don't know how to write it."

"I'm sorry," Bobby said to McGann. "I guess we can't meet here. We'll have to go to your house." McGann lived near Forest Hills, where he also worked as press liaison for the U.S. Open.

But McGann faced a bigger problem. What Bobby would say in private and what he would say for the record were two entirely different things. One day, after Bobby had left, McGann turned to his wife and lamented: "You know, there's no book here. Bobby knows everything about everybody, but he won't say a damn bad word. He could blow the whistle on everybody—the officials, the players, everybody—but he won't do it. He's too good-hearted. He won't say anything that would hurt anybody. There's just no bite to this book."

Nevertheless, McGann glumly pressed on. One day, at a loss, McGann asked, "Bobby, what lowest ranked men's player do you think could beat Billie Jean King?" Bobby stopped for a moment, then breathlessly answered, "Oh, anybody ranked about a hundred could beat the women's champion… any guy around a hundred… Hell, I could beat Billie Jean!" Then, his eyes lighting up, Bobby added, "As a matter of fact, I will. I'll challenge her."

At the time, it would have been natural to write off Bobby's response as typical bravado, but he knew a good idea when he stumbled on it. Shortly afterward, in January 1971, *Sports Illustrated* printed an interview with Bobby about the growing activity in senior tennis. In it, Bobby took his challenge public, saying he could beat Billie Jean King or Margaret Court, the top two female players in the world.

"It would be close on grass," he said, "but on any other surface I could take them in a one-set match, two out of three or three out of five… It would be close. Maybe they're better than I think they are." Whatever the outcome, it would be a good show. Moreover, he added, "I'm willing to put my money where my mouth is."

The *media hysteria surrounding the match was a phenomenon* Bobby *(center) could not comprehend, explain or control. But if nothing else, he understood cause and effect, and he was going to ride it for all it was worth.*

17

Hype of the Century
1972-1973

From La Jolla to Las Vegas, Acapulco to Puerto Rico, Monte Carlo to Grand Bahamas, and Forest Hills to Wimbledon, Bobby was doing what he loved best: playing tennis every day, being constantly on the go, meeting new people, and looking for action. Though still formally employed by American Photograph at a salary of $100,000 per year, Bobby was rarely at the office. Truth be told, he was not really missed.

At home, however, Priscilla was feeling more like a housekeeper for an itinerant tenant than a wife. She was still drinking heavily, in poor health, and struggling to find an identity for herself. But most of all, with the children nearly grown and out of the house, she was terribly lonely. After 20 years of frustration and threats, she decided to change her life.

In November 1972, while in La Jolla playing in the national 45-and-over championships and the national father-son championships with his son, Larry, Bobby got a call from Priscilla.

"Oh, hi. Hi honey. How's it going?" Bobby asked.

"I'm divorcing you," she said. "I'm not getting any younger, and you aren't either. You're not going to change and I don't want you to change—that wouldn't be fair. So you go do your thing and I'll start over." She didn't want to explain her decision, she didn't want to argue. She didn't need time to think about it, and she didn't want to give Bobby any chance to talk her out of it. It was over.

"You'll be getting papers out there and then you're out of my life," she said. "I moved all your clothes out and sent them to California."

She made arrangements for Bobby to travel to the Dominican Republic, where the whole thing could be done in one day. Bobby reluctantly agreed, and in February 1972, he arrived in Santo Domingo to finalize the divorce.

As Priscilla later explained to her children, "I could live with the absences. I could live with the gambling. I didn't even get mad when he gave me crabs." (Bobby's on-the-spot excuse for this was that he got them from wearing Pancho Segura's jock strap. As his punishment, Priscilla repeated the story to whomever would listen.) "But I drew the line when he starting gambling with my children's money." Whether or not this was true her son John Riggs wouldn't say, but clearly Bobby's gambling was an issue. "It was a maternal thing for her," John said. "She was protecting us." The irony of course was that "she couldn't stop drinking for us, but she was going to protect our inheritance."

As for Bobby, he never saw it coming.

"He was shocked, crushed," Larry remembered. "I mean, they had been putting up with each other for years and years and years. He had a normal life going. He had his kids and his family and a job in downtown New York and a regular haircut. He took the commuter train back and forth every day. So he's out there playing in this tournament and she says, 'You're done.' "

"I felt lost," Bobby later recalled. Despite everything—the years of arguing, the accusations and bitterness—he still loved Priscilla. Though he would be the first to admit he was far from the ideal husband and father, he always believed she loved him.

Despite her feelings, she felt things could not go on as they had. "She questioned my capability as to how much I could love anybody," Bobby later reflected. "She had all kinds of patience with me for twenty years and gave me all kinds of time and all kinds of chances to make the adjustment, to be the kind of husband she would really like to have. I just didn't have it, and she realized it."

As a settlement, Bobby sold back to the family a block of American Photograph Corp. stock that Priscilla's father had given him worth about a quarter-million dollars. He took his clothes and trove of trophies and moved into a $400-a-month townhouse at Park Newport in Newport Beach, California, an upscale apartment complex and health spa 10 minutes from the Orange County airport. The complex was built by wealthy developer and close friend Gerson Bakar, who let Bobby stay rent-free in return for taking the position of tennis director for the complex's six courts. Bobby and actress Racquel Welch were the development's two celebrity tenants and were used in promotions. A trophy case in the clubhouse held a few of Bobby's more prominent prizes, including the Renshaw Cup awarded to him for winning the gentlemen's singles at Wimbledon in 1939.*

But it was a difficult adjustment. "I felt out in the world and all alone," Bobby said. "I just didn't know what the hell it was. I had been married from the time I was twenty-one until I was fifty-five... that's most of my life." He also felt angry and betrayed. To his son, John, Bobby said, "You know, I tried. I really tried to be the husband and father she wanted." He took a regular job and lived in the suburbs. In his mind, he had given up a part of himself to do it, and in the process lost twenty years of his life. "You know the grass always looks greener on the other side," he said. "If she thinks she can do better, then let her try."

Settling into Park Newport, his townhouse clustered in among the apartments, Bobby was joined by his brother, Dave Riggs, then 67 and a widower. Dave moved in, did the housekeeping, answered the phone, kept Bobby's language in line, and drove Bobby around the golf courses. Meanwhile, Bobby continued to hustle tennis and backgammon games, play "sociable" golf, play cards, flip coins, and "exchange cash with everybody around." But it was joyless and indifferent, done merely out of habit and instinct. In the evenings, Bobby later confessed to a visiting reporter, "he would sit with his brother Dave in their townhouse and sometimes drink 10 Heinekens

---

* The case was broken into and the trophy stolen in 1978. Several years later, Bobby got a call from a man who found it at a yard sale. He noticed the name on it and offered to return it, but only if Bobby picked it up in person.

a night, slurring his words, growing loud, acrid and cruel; falling as he would later say, 'completely out of it.' "

Without a family, without a job—a job in which he never felt very appreciated anyway—Bobby needed something to get himself back into circulation. To begin his transformation, he changed his hair, abandoning his slicked-back, graying executive look. He tinted his locks to an auburn brown (or "Moonlit Brown," as advertised on the Miss Clairol box) and let his hair grow out so that his bangs fell boyishly over his brow. He decided to live the lifestyle of a "swinger" and surround himself with, as he put it, "a bevy of beauties." (Actually, Bobby had always been a "swinger," but in the "free love" atmosphere of the early 1970s, sleeping around no longer seemed taboo, and had taken on the more fashionable and innocuous moniker, "swinging.")

Bobby also had something to prove. He may have lost 20 years, but he knew he could make things happen, earn a million, be a star. He was going to show them, all of them: Priscilla, the people at his old job, all those who resented him or considered him just another has-been athlete with nothing left but a collection of dusty stories to tell. He could still think big.

A couple of years earlier, in 1971, following his publicized challenge to play Margaret Court or Billie Jean King, Bobby got a call from his old friend Jack Kramer. Kramer told Bobby that another mutual friend, Lake Havasu developer Bob McCulloch, had read about the challenge in *Sports Illustrated* and was interested in staging the match. McCulloch was always looking for offbeat ways to promote his resort development. In 1971, he bought London Bridge and moved it brick-by-brick to the Arizona desert. For Bobby, he offered to put up $5,000 in a winner-take-all purse for a Riggs-King or a Riggs-Court showdown. Similar offers were floated, but a deal could never be reached, either for lack of a sponsor or a television agreement or a challenger for Bobby.

Not long after Bobby's challenge was published in 1971, he accosted Billie Jean King at Forest Hills. He wanted to sell her personally on the idea. So he hopped over a little fence surrounding the clubhouse court where she was practicing.

Bobby had good reason to pick Billie Jean. She was not only the top-ranked female player in the world, but a scrappy fighter whose feisty personality and outspokenness made her a natural target for Bobby's chauvinist barbs. A heroine of the women's rights movement, she led a drive for better treatment and larger purses on the women's tour, whose players were paid a fraction of what the men earned.

"Why don't we play a fun match—for five thousand dollars to add to the fun—on any surface you like," Bobby said.

Billie Jean smiled, perhaps thinking that such a match might be a lot of fun, but she turned him down cold.

Bobby pleaded, "You've got to play. How can you not want to play?" What great hype the match would be for the women's tour, he reasoned.

But the way Billie Jean saw it, the fledgling Virginia Slims circuit she helped lobby to create was already struggling. If she lost, it might prove to enough people that women couldn't make it on their own. In so many words, she told him that if women's tennis couldn't stand on its own, it didn't deserve to succeed. Women's tennis didn't need him and, moreover, neither did she.

Bobby might have persisted, but soon afterwards his divorce from Priscilla threw his life into turmoil. A few months after moving to Park Newport early in 1973, Bobby ran into Tony Trabert at the L.A. Tennis Club. Trabert, a former Davis Cup star and a television commentator for CBS Sports, had just been appointed tennis director at a new housing-resort development called San Diego Country Estates, built by another developer-friend of Bobby's, Ray Watt. Trabert asked Bobby what became of the proposed challenge match with Billie Jean King.

"I'd like to see you revive that," Trabert said. "It's a great idea." Then, borrowing a line from the 1972 hit movie, *The Godfather,* Trabert added, "Why don't you make her an offer she can't refuse?"

Bobby put up $5,000 of his own money, Watt kicked in another $5,000, and in February, Watt called a press conference. Before a bank of microphones, Larry Laurie, the public-relations man for the Estates, announced, "Bobby Riggs, that old campaigner, ex-champion, has-been, claims that women's tennis stinks. To prove his point, he has put up five thousand dollars. Here's his certified check. Billie Jean King gets first crack at it but will have to answer within forty-eight hours. Otherwise, Bobby will send wires to Margaret Court and four or five other women, and he will play the first one to accept the offer."

Bobby then stood up. Employing the same line he had used against Kramer 25 years before, he goaded Billie Jean: "I'd love to play her every day of the week and twice on Sunday. Indoors, outdoors, on cement, clay, grass, whatever, I think I can beat her on any and all surfaces… You insist that top women players provide a brand of tennis comparable to men's. I challenge you to prove it. I contend that you not only cannot beat a top male player, but that you can't beat me, a tired old man." They may not have remembered when Bobby won Wimbledon and Forest Hills, or that he had played and beat legends like Don Budge and Kramer, but they'd remember him now.

Again, Billie Jean turned him down. "We didn't need him," she later explained in refusing Bobby's challenge. "We were making it on our own merits."

But when Margaret Court heard about it, she was annoyed, not because Bobby put down women's tennis, but because of his manifest preference to play Billie Jean King. "She might make more noise than any other woman in the game," Court said of Billie Jean, "but she certainly wasn't the best player."

On paper, at least, she was right. Margaret Smith Court was—and still is—the most successful player in tennis history, male or female, racking up more of the four major championships than anyone else. The mild-mannered and gracious Australian won 62 major titles in singles, doubles, and mixed doubles in her 15-year career. Only Martina Navratilova, with 57 titles, would ever come close.

In 1970, Court became the second woman after Maureen Connolly in 1953 to win a singles Grand Slam, sweeping the four majors (Steffi Graf became the third in 1988). Nearly six feet tall and powerfully built, Court played an athletic serve-and-volley game, prompting other women on the tour to call her "The Arm" because of her terrific reach and strength. Since returning from a year off to have her first baby, Danny, in 1971, Court had swept 12 tournaments in a row and won 89 of 92 matches. What's more, she had a winning record over Billie Jean, winning a total of 22 matches to Billie Jean's 10 over the course of their careers.

Matching their intense on-court rivalry, Court personally disliked Billie Jean. No women's libber, Court was shy, soft-spoken, and deeply religious (she went on to become a lay minister). She resented Billie Jean's egocentric grandstanding and the way she used the game as a soapbox to promote her political views. She was offended when Billie Jean publicly announced she had had an abortion in 1971, and even more so when Billie Jean carried on a lesbian affair with her assistant, Marilyn Barnett, while still married to husband Larry. The affair didn't break into the press until 1981, when Barnett sued Billie Jean for palimony, but it was an open secret among the other players.

Court's feeling was that if anyone should defend tennis, womanhood, and righteousness from Bobby's insults, it should be her, not Billie Jean. "Once I admired Billie Jean a lot but I don't anymore," Court said in 1975.

When Billie Jean balked, Court decided to take on Bobby's challenge, even though she had little reason to believe she could win. After all, battles between the sexes did not originate with Bobby Riggs. In 1921, Bill Tilden played a one-set exhibition against the great Suzanne Lenglen in France, winning 6-0. When asked about the result afterwards, Lenglen answered, "Someone won 6-0, but I don't recall who it was." Similarly, in 1936, 15-year-old Jack Kramer, then the national boys' champion, played Helen Wills Moody, perhaps the best female player ever, and beat her easily.

Court figured the match would be an entertaining lark, a fun exhibition to help publicize a real estate development and an easy way to pick up $10,000, "a kind of breather for me on the women's tour."

At a tournament in Detroit, Court excitedly announced to the other players in the dressing room that she was going to play Bobby for a $5,000 guarantee and another $5,000 if she won. Over the collective groan of the others, Billie Jean stood up and warned Court she wasn't being paid half-enough for what she was about to go through. "It's not just a one-day deal, Margaret," she said. "It's gonna be a six-week deal. So whatever you do, get ready for the atmosphere. He'll try everything, so be prepared for it all. Bobby's going to be rough." More than anything, she urged, "Please beat him so we can just get this over with."

Sure enough, once Court signed on, the match generated instant media interest. Soon afterwards CBS agreed to televise the event in a deal that included $10,000 to Court and $7,500 to Bobby. Even if Bobby lost, he'd be $2,500 in the clear. CBS scheduled the match to air nationally on Sunday, May 13—Mother's Day—a date that played straight into Bobby's hands, as Court was the most famous mother in tennis.

Giving Bobby a television audience was like throwing chum to a shark. With his gift for mangled hyperbole, Bobby quickly started playing to the press, calling it "the match of the century between the battle of the sexes." He taunted Court with his sexist banter, saying that there were "an awful lot of women looking to Margaret to salvage their honor," and that "she'll have that snarling pack of women's libbers at her heels saying, 'Please, please, don't let that cocky old pig beat you.' "

In unguarded moments, Bobby might have professed as much surprise as anyone over the resulting hoopla. He later said, "We didn't even think about television. We just wanted to stage the match at San Diego Country Estates for a few hundred spectators, for the publicity it would bring to the development through the press." After all, he knew as much about women's liberation as he did about quantum physics. But he couldn't help notice that even those with little interest in tennis were intrigued. It was a phenomenon he could not comprehend, explain, or control. But if nothing else, he understood cause and effect, and he was going to ride it for all it was worth.

Contrary to what many believed, Bobby's primary motivation was not money. Creature comforts: cars, clothes… he could care less about all that. He had worn the same suit for six years, and since leaving the world of "big business" his preferred wardrobe consisted of a clean jogging suit. No, he just wanted the publicity. "Heck, I haven't had any attention for twenty-five years," he said.

"And I love the limelight, an old ham like me, I really love it." If he needed to play the raving male chauvinist pig to put himself in the spotlight, so be it. Ride on the back of an elephant in his underwear? No problem. The match became his obsession, and Bobby, the entertainer, took over.

Situated in the rocky hills about 30 miles northeast of San Diego, the town of Ramona seemed an odd choice for a media event. Though now just another sprawling exurb for commuters to California's second-largest city, Ramona in 1973 was little more than a dusty farming community. Wedged between the desert and the Barona Ranch Indian Reservation, it was a place that had not "been so perturbed since the summer of '72, when the temperature soared to 117 degrees and all of the chickens died." But there, nestled between the boulders balanced precariously along the hillsides, was a man-made oasis, complete with a golf course, swimming pool, and three tennis courts, the beginning of a developer's dream and an old man's last stab at reclaiming lost glory and youth.

No less unusual was the pairing itself. Court, broad-shouldered and quiet, with a fierce serve and a blistering serve-and-volley game, played a man's game. Her husky stature elicited comments such as that from a spectator at Wimbledon: "Look at those legs. The lady is a man."

Bobby, on the other hand, was physically soft and delicate, and nearly two inches shorter than Court. He didn't use power, but stayed in the backcourt—he played like a woman. Despite all his shrill pronouncements, it would be hard to find two more unlikely representatives for the "battle of the sexes."

For her part, Margaret did her best to play down the sexist angle, portraying the contest as a lighthearted exhibition. "I am not carrying the banner for women's lib," she said. "I've never said we deserve prize money equal to the men. I'm playing this match for me. A woman is not supposed to beat a man, so I've nothing to lose."

This did little to assuage her colleagues on the tour, who were disappointed she had accepted Bobby's challenge in the first place. "Why should we have to justify ourselves against an old, obnoxious has-been like Riggs who can't hear, can't see, walks like a duck and is an idiot besides?" said Rosemary Casals, doubles partner and good friend to Billie Jean King. She then suggested Court wear "psychedelic ear plugs" to combat Bobby's jabbering.

Billie Jean King, however, knew the stakes were much higher than anyone was willing to admit. "If Margaret loses, we're in trouble," she said. "I'll have to challenge him myself."

With just eight weeks before the match, time was short. Overnight, Bobby's Park Newport townhouse turned into Riggs Central, an all-purpose residence, business office, and media center. An assortment of family, friends, and hangers-on surrounded Bobby, fielding phone calls and running errands, watching to make sure he ate right, got enough sleep, and stuck to the program. His brother Dave acted as a buffer, regulating the flow of traffic into the townhouse. Bobby's 19-year-old daughter Dorothy moved in, helping her father and lending moral support (although, as a member of the National Women's Political Caucus, she found herself torn between her support for the cause and her love for her dad).

Joining them also was Lornie Kuhle, tennis pro at the Las Vegas Country Club, as well as Bobby's longtime friend, hitting partner, protégé, and kindred spirit. Kuhle, 29, grew up in Decatur, Illinois, and first met Bobby through his friend Larry Riggs, Bobby's son. When Kuhle was 18 and trying out for a tennis scholarship at Pan American University, which Larry also attended, Bobby agreed to play Kuhle under the watchful eye of the school's tennis coach. Before going on court, Bobby told Kuhle to get to net and watch the lines. Kuhle did as he was told, "and of course I know the ball's going down the line, so I go over and, *boom*, knock off the volley. The coach goes, 'Whoa.' I win the first set. Then the second set Bobby says, 'Okay, this time I'm going to give you a couple of short lobs, so bounce them over the fence. That'll look real good.'

"So just like we planned, I come into net, he gives me a couple of short lobs, and I go *boom* and bounce them over the fence. The coach goes, 'Oh my god, this guy's great.'" The scholarship was in the bag. "It was," Kuhle said, "the all-time tank job."

Close ever since, Kuhle subsequently immersed himself in all things Bobby: traveling with him, carrying his racquets, driving him around, placing bets with his bookie, and basically being a handler, all-round friend, and ready-made foil for whatever scheme Bobby devised. Joked Bobby about Kuhle: "He has a Ph.D. in Riggsology."

Bobby's first order of business was to get into shape. One morning, he looked at himself in the mirror, gazed over the flaccid body, and said to himself, "Gosh, I won't last a set with that Amazon." At 160 pounds, he was about 15 pounds over his "fighting weight" from his pro tour days. Determined to get into shape, he put down the Heinekens, started jogging daily, and watched his diet. It was at that time a friend introduced him to Hollywood nutritionist Rheo Blair.

Blair, born Irvin Johnson, knew nothing about tennis. His specialty was body development. During the 1960s he had made a name for himself as a consultant to body builders and weight lifters. He went on to become a nutritional guru to the stars, listing among his clients Liberace and Lawrence Welk. A short, muscular man of indeterminate age, with his hair molded into a permanent Fifties pompadour, Blair theorized the proper combination of vitamins could cure schizophrenia. He had a taste for heavy jewelry, bright polyester suits, and José Greco shirts with bell sleeves.

For a fee of $5,000, Blair promised Bobby that if he followed his "rejuvenation program" to the letter, adhered to the diet, did the exercises, and took all the pills, he would not only get back into shape, but actually feel ten years younger. In fact, Blair said, he could give Bobby a body like Mr. America in five weeks, so Bobby could pose nude in *Cosmopolitan* or *Playgirl* if he so desired.

Bobby assured him that wouldn't be necessary. He just wanted to win a tennis match. After checking with his personal physician to make sure nothing in Blair's program could harm him, Bobby returned to the guru. When Blair asked for a down payment, Bobby handed him $2,500 and said, "You'll get the rest Rheo, *if* I win the match. If I lose, you get no more money. If you think your technique can help me that much, you should go along with this proposition."

Blair's face fell before recomposing itself into a shrewd look. "We'll see, dear," he said quietly. "We'll see."

He sent Bobby home with a valise filled with pills of all shapes and colors. Bobby was to imbibe 415 of them every day. This included 100 black pellets of soybean-wheat germ concentrate, 75 liver extract pills, 75 plastic vials of pure powered protein, smaller quantities of vitamins E, C, B1, B2, and B-complex, and calcium, amino acids, wheat germ concentrate, and one vitamin A pill. Much like acupuncture was reputed to change the body's energy flow, the pills were meant to alter the chemistry of Bobby's body and make him younger.

Another component of Blair's program was the "blood push," a two-hour rubdown that he claimed pushed the blood through the body's tissues and revitalized the muscles. Blair told Bobby the procedure would "supercharge" him by "pushing" the blood through every capillary. Though skeptical, Bobby enjoyed the massages ("It's a blood push, Bobby, not a massage," Blair kept telling him.). Each day, Bobby dutifully reported to a small, white stucco house off Hollywood Boulevard—Blair's laboratory. From the ceiling, a series of horizontal bars hung down like an elaborate jungle gym. Those in training were required to use the bars to get around the house. From the moment they entered, clients had to swing on the bars to move from one room to the next. Need to go to the bathroom? Use the bars. Blair's theory was that, while under his supervision, every moment needed to be devoted to physical fitness.

Inside the darkened main room ("to promote complete euphoria," Blair claimed), one of Blair's trainers administered Bobby's "blood push." This was followed by a soak in a whirlpool bath.

B obby needed no help promoting the match, and he relished fanning the flames of male chauvinism. "Women's tennis?" he ranted. "Sure, I think it stinks. Sure, they hit the ball back and forth. They have a lot of nice volleys, I guess, and you can see some pretty legs… sometimes. But it's night and day compared to men's tennis. Women play about twenty-five percent as good as men, so they should get about twenty-five percent of the money men get" (which was roughly what they got at the time).

The strategy worked. Soon, Bobby couldn't leave his townhouse without having a camera, a microphone, or a reporter's notebook suddenly thrust in his face. Male chauvinist pig, banner-carrying hero to senior players, arch villain to women's libbers, high-spirited rogue, and all-round oddity, Bobby could not go anywhere without being surrounded by people who wanted to shake his hand, wish him well, get him to say something funny, tell him to drop dead, or simply bask in the reflected glow of his dervish charm.

Bobby held court like the recently elected mayor of a small town, his head and hands moving in time to the endless flow of words. He replied to the simplest question with an expansive monologue, his answers a rambling stream of consciousness that may or may not have addressed the original question. He talked brokenly, leaving one sentence unfinished as he rushed into the next one; an idea repeated once, twice, or even three times while his mind raced to catch up, at times working himself into a state of apparent delirium. "It was," described journalist Jon Bradshaw, "as though the manic flood of his words swelled, only to crash against some invisible reef in his mind, before gathering speed again." Not having anything to say was no reason for Bobby to stop talking.

But he kept people listening, the reporters writing, and, moreover, himself in the spotlight. People might love him, they might hate him, but the one thing they could not do was ignore him.

Somehow, between the workouts, the rubdowns, the phone calls, and the interviews, Bobby found time to keep up a steady schedule of personal appearances, performing his wacky handicap matches in front of delighted crowds, signing autographs, and generally keeping the publicity machine humming. He even took a day off to "scout" Court during a Virginia Slims event in Richmond, claiming afterwards to a cluster of reporters that, on straight tennis ability, his chances looked slim. "She has a better serve, a better volley, a better forehand, a better backhand," he said. "But the question is, can you pull that game out when you need it? Can you play your best when the money's on the line? Margaret's a great player and a great sport. But in this kind of contest, you know, battle of the sexes, match of the century and all that, she's out of her depth."

Meanwhile, Court did her best to ignore Bobby. She continued to play and win on the Virginia Slims circuit, capturing 10 of 12 tournaments. She was looking ahead, not to her match with Bobby, but to the French Open and Wimbledon championships.

A true hustler doesn't beat the odds, but controls them. To Bobby, this meant winning the psychological battle before the match. Bobby "was what is known in the trade as a conniver—the sort of man who ostentatiously juggles a kind of charming conceit with sharp self-deprecation, in order, it happens, to keep his options open. He had, in fact, only one straightforward role to play—that of the evasive innocent," wrote Bradshaw. For all his braggadocio and brash exclamations, Bobby insisted on playing the underdog. "I play like a woman, she plays like a man," he said. "She's younger and faster and bigger and stronger. She's absolutely ferocious. She's got a bigger serve, a better volley and a stronger overhead. She's got me beat in every department, except maybe thinking, strategy and experience."

By playing down his own abilities, Bobby managed to put all the pressure on Court. Those who attended Bobby's practice sessions saw a man who looked, Bradshaw said, "like an account executive who had been advised by his doctor to take some exercise once in a while." Bobby looked helpless while Kuhle pounded serves at him, overpowered him from the net, and chased him from corner to corner along the baseline.

Bobby magnified the smallest issues as he sought the psychological upper hand. The best-of-three-set match was scheduled for one o'clock, a time Bobby realized would have Court looking straight into the sun when trying to pick off his lobs. A few weeks before the match, Bobby convinced the event organizers to resurface the court, ostensibly to improve its worn appearance. This was done, but the effect was to make the court slower, an advantage for Bobby that had some in the press crying foul. Another controversy erupted over the type of ball to use. Bobby had been practicing with lighter, faster Spalding balls. When Trabert, the event's chairman, informed Bobby that the heavier, slower Wilson balls preferred by Court would be used, Bobby protested. A compromise was reached when Trabert arranged for a coin-flip to determine the balls. A small, amused crowd watched as the coin was tossed. Bobby called tails, and lost. He appeared disconsolate to the journalists gathered around and referred to it as "the flip of the century."

While workers in Ramona tacked up posters on trees and telephone poles to direct the anticipated hordes to the match site, television electricians and carpenters scurried about: wrestling with wires, building platforms for the television cameras and hanging colored banners around the stands. Back in Newport Beach, Bobby held open practice sessions at his condominium complex, inviting the media and anyone else interested to come, watch, listen, and be part of the scene.

On the Friday before the match, Bobby drove his large Lincoln Continental to Ramona to begin final preparations. Between the handshakes, the autographs, the mugging it up, and the non-stop interview requests, Bobby squeezed in time to work out on the red and green court on which the match would be played. While a throng of press snapped photos and scribbled frantically, Bobby practiced his trademark assortment of high lobs, chips, dinks, slices, spins, and junk shots, all the while muttering to himself, "reciting the grim list of his deficiencies: his overhead lacked power, his serve lacked speed, his lobs lacked depth and accuracy, his ground strokes had no pace, his volleys were forced, the balls were too heavy, his legs too old and his elbow, he feared, would never loosen in time for the match."

After serving another ball into the net, Bobby shook his head, adjusted his glasses, and ambled over to the sidelines to towel off. "Hey, how do I look?" he said to no one in particular.

"Terrible," answered a spectator.

"Terrible, huh?"

"Clapped out."

"As bad as that?"

"Worse."

Bobby toweled his face and grinned. "Heck, I'm fifty-five years old. I've got one foot in the grave."

"Which one, Bobby?"

He grinned again. "The one I'm not going to need."

Informed that a pool of reporters had picked Court to win, Bobby gave a quizzical look. "You don't say?" he said. "What experts? Those reporters out there? Those guys? Those guys from papers I never heard of? Those experts? Let me tell ya. I'll tell ya about experts. They've been saying that all my life. Right from the start. All the way back. Riggs is gonna lose, he's gonna lose. The loudmouth's gonna get what he deserves. They take one look at me out there, those guys, and whatta they see? I'll tell ya what they see. They see what I want 'em to see. A tired old man, who's past it, dead 'n' gone, always moaning and groaning, they see an old guy living in the past, who can't serve, can't volley, can't even see the ball without glasses, much less get it across the net. And what does he do? He keeps on talking and boasting and bragging, he keeps on... Sure. They wanna see me get my brains beat in, served up like a pig with a tennis ball in his mouth. That's what they want.

"Heck, I *am* old. I'm practically a grandfather, maybe several times over, and sometimes the flesh won't do what the mind tells it to. And maybe it won't. Who knows? Experts. What can I tell ya? It's even money. You can cut it both ways. What a beautiful deal. Beautiful. You can see for yourself, day after tomorrow, right here. You watch. You'll see. Sure, the old skippiness is gone, the old zing. The way of all flesh, right? But I always rise for the big occasion. I get right up there for it. Heck, you know that, you know that. You know that much."

Yes, but could he win?

An informal survey of experts showed Bobby the heavy favorite. Harry Hopman, former player and Australian Davis Cup captain, told the *New York Times*, "The only way Riggs could lose would be by breaking a leg." To the same question, the great Fred Perry succinctly said, "She won't win a game."

Indeed, Bobby wanted nothing more than for Court and the rest of the world to believe he had them all played for suckers, that it was all part of his elaborate game plan. But to his closest confidantes he professed concern. The lethargy and dispiritedness he felt were no put-on. Since starting Blair's program, he had never felt so tired in his life. After four and a half weeks of choking down hundreds of pills two hours a day, Bobby had to wonder if he, for once, was the one being hustled. "Do you think that blood-pushing fag knows what he's doing?" Bobby confided. Every so often he got on the phone and screamed abuse at Blair, to which Blair calmly reassured him, "Gosh, Bobby, you're responding well, really well. You look so much younger, you really do."

Joked Kuhle, "At the rate you're taking pills, Bobby, you'll be four years old by Sunday."

Bobby's regimen of pills included more than just vitamins. Like many Americans at the time, he got his family physician to write him a prescription for Dexedrine. At the time, the amphetamine was considered relatively safe, and prescribed to millions of housewives under the pseudonym "diet pills" or, in Bobby's case, "pep pills." (Remember, this was an age of American "innocence," before the death of Elvis, before the Medellin Cartel and the "war on drugs.") Bobby found the drug boosted his energy level and lifted his game when he needed it. For him, it was just another training aid. After a particularly sluggish workout, Bobby said, "If this keeps up, I'll have to take some pep pills on Sunday morning. For extra zip."

O n Friday evening, Court finally arrived at San Diego Country Estates, accompanied by her husband, Barry, and 14-month-old son, Danny, who wore a large button on his shirt that read, "Bobby Riggs—*Bleah.*"

Court knew to expect a media frenzy, but she was ill-prepared for the scene at the Estates. More than a hundred reporters from news outlets all over the world had descended on the resort. Amid the crush of reporters, film crews, and photographers, Bobby pressed forward to warmly greet Court and her family. While Bobby whispered, chattered, and played to the crowd, Court pushed her way through to the relative safety of her suite.

The next morning, Court went through her first warm-ups, hitting against Tony Trabert and Vicki Berner, another Slims tour player. While Court banged away at groundstrokes and sent Trabert lurching to the sidelines to try to return her serve, Bobby sat a few feet away in the stands, awaiting his turn to take the court. He appeared overwhelmed, claiming she had not looked that sharp in Richmond.

"Did you see that forehand?" he said to anyone within earshot. "Gosh, Look again. Gosh, I didn't know she could serve that strong. Look, can you believe that overhead? Boy."

"Come on, you hit them that hard, Bobby," said Kuhle.

"Yeah, but I can't bounce them into the stands," Bobby continued. "Maybe she's having an unusual day, huh? Look, look at that reach on her. Did you ever see anything like it? I won't have a prayer if she plays like this tomorrow. She's making Tony look like my father."

To himself, Bobby secretly gloated. Court's hard-hitting exchanges might impress the tennis writers watching, "but to my mind she was practicing all wrong for the match." From the beginning, he made no secret that he planned to soft-ball Court to death with short angles, high floaters, and various kinds of spin.

An hour later, Court completed her practice and sat in the stands while Bobby sparred with Kuhle. She seemed to pay little attention to Bobby while he hit, continuing his running commentary to no one in particular while Kuhle drilled balls at him. But at one point, when Bobby served, she laughed out loud at the weakness of the shot and the way he shuffled about the court. She seemed relaxed and confident, and Bobby's pathetic display gave her every reason to remain so.

After the warm-ups, the reporters watching were allowed to ask the players a few questions. Court was asked if she would change her game plan should Bobby start making passing shots. She shrugged and said, "Lots of women have passed me and it didn't make me change."

"You mean you wouldn't change a losing game?" asked Bobby, who had walked up behind her.

"I'll let you know when we play our match tomorrow," she replied.

"Listen, Margaret," said Bobby, leaning in and becoming chummy and confidential, "why don't we just stay back on the baseline and have nice long rallies? We can have a lot of fun. We don't want to finish the match too fast."

Court smiled.

"Come on, Margaret. Just think of how many women are counting on you."

"Get off it, luv," she said, forcing a smile.

"Do you think Mother's Day is a definite advantage for you?" Bobby pressed on, practically shouting. "It's not fair. You have only one child and I'm the mother of six."

Court gave another exasperated smile.

"You would agree that this is an important match," he said.

"No," she said. "I think Wimbledon is more important."

"Gosh, Margaret. I don't understand that. I really don't. This is the most important tennis match in a hundred and fifty years. It's the match of the century."

Court stood by for a moment—watching Bobby immersed in his routine, his voice rising and falling like a medicine show barker, his arms gesticulating with every word, the crowd smiling at his comic posturing—before quietly walking away.

Her outward calm belied an inner turmoil, a growing irritation with the crowds, the press, the scrutiny, the constant demands to answer the same stupid questions, and, most of all, the relentless presence of Bobby himself. Once, while returning to his suite, Bobby walked into a room he suddenly realized wasn't his. There was Court, sitting there playing with her son, Danny. Bobby apologized and backed out, claiming later that it was an honest mistake.

"Can't you do anything about the loudmouth?" she asked Trabert.

"Not unless I can make you deaf," he said.

The final night in the clubhouse dining room, Bobby held forth surrounded by his entourage, the press, and anyone else who cared to join in. Between mouthfuls of avocado from a salad Blair had specially prepared, Bobby expounded on the match, its epic implications for sports and humanity, his ever-dimming chances, the existence of God, and anything else that popped into his head. A few tables away, Court and her family quietly ate dinner, trying their best to ignore the commotion nearby. At one point, unable to resist, Bobby picked up a plate of pills and carried them over as an offering to Court. She smiled and refused.

On Sunday, Mother's Day, as the morning fog that hugged the hills around Ramona slowly burned off, Kuhle awoke Bobby for the first of their planned three practice sessions before the match. He had exciting news.

"I dreamed about the match," Kuhle said. "And you won it 6-2, 6-1. It was very clear."

"That is a dream," Bobby said sarcastically. Still, it was a good omen. Later, Bobby called up his friend Jack Dreyfuss in New York, asking him to put a thousand dollars on Court to win.

"No, Bobby," Dreyfus said. "I know you can take her."

But Bobby insisted, explaining that the bet was simply for good luck. Besides, if anyone could afford to make the gesture, Dreyfus could. If that's what it took, Dreyfus said, he was happy to oblige.

Unlike Bobby's customary betting action before a big match, this was his only bet. While the rest of the world spoke of the match in terms of odds, percentages, and Las Vegas prices, Bobby stood pat. "I had too many other things going for me on this match," he said. "I had all the incentive I needed, without my usual big action on the side."

For Margaret, the morning's portents were not so auspicious. Danny had woken early and thrown his mother's favorite tennis shoe into the toilet. To her husband, Court glumly said, "I'll certainly be glad when this is over."

Walking through the clubhouse lobby back to his room Bobby ran into fashion designer Teddy Tinling, the man behind Gussy Moran's famous lace panties. Tinling had flown in from Tokyo to see that the yellow and green dress he designed for Court fit correctly.

"Are you going to win, Bobby?" asked Tinling, exquisitely garish in his mod outfit and shiny, bald head.

"It's a mortal lock," deadpanned Bobby, his cherubic mirth displaced by a calm intensity.

"Crazy boy," said Tinling, putting a hand on Bobby's shoulder. "You crazy boy."

As the fog gave way to brilliant sunshine, a crowd of 4,000 waited impatiently as the appointed hour drew near, sensing something big was about to happen. Exactly what, they weren't so sure.

A t precisely one o'clock the players entered from opposite sides of the court. To the wild applause of those in the stands and millions more watching on television, the two players slowly descended the grandstands, Bobby in a powder-blue warm-up suit, carrying a bouquet of roses, Court in her custom-made dress with her name stitched in big letters on the collar. Meeting at the net, Bobby handed Court the bouquet. "For the nicest mother in tennis," Bobby said with a grin. "Happy Mother's Day."

Court went along with the gag and gave Bobby a curtsy. Bobby then turned to television announcer Pat Summerall and asked, "Do you think these flowers will soften her up?"

"I don't think so," Summerall replied.

Because of the television timetable, the players were allowed only a three-minute warm-up. They had only hit a few balls back and forth when chair umpire Ben Press called, "Players ready. Play." This didn't matter to Bobby "since I had been practicing with Lornie Kuhle all morning," but Court seemed surprised. She didn't like being rushed. It also didn't help that Bobby won the toss and got to serve first. She took her position to return serve, leaning forward on the balls of her feet.

Standing at the baseline, Bobby pulled his white visor cap down over his forehead and adjusted his glasses. He wanted to test his game plan early, just to get a feel how she responded. He bounced the ball twice off the edge of his racquet frame, stood for a moment briefly, and gently lifted the ball into the air. Slicing the ball, he served it wide to her forehand. Court seemed momentarily stunned, then moved awkwardly to the ball and drove it into the net. 15-love.

Pleasantly surprised at the results, Bobby stood on the baseline, repeated his routine of bouncing the ball off the frame, and served another slice out wide, this time to her backhand. Again she drove it into the net. 30-love.

The crowd murmured. *Piece of cake*, Bobby thought. He looked across the net at Court, who again prepared to return serve, her crouch lower this time, more determined. Bobby decided to do something he generally never did in a match.

He served up a high, slow blooper that floated up and across the net. Court took two steps in and crushed the ball to the opposite

Margaret Court tried to force herself to the net, but any rhythm or confidence she could muster was destroyed by a steady succession of errors. By the end of the second set, Bobby stopped concentrating altogether, and was chatting amiably to the crowd and waving to his various girlfriends in the stands.

corner for a clean winner. The crowd cheered ecstatically. Bobby smiled, but he knew she understood the message he sent: This match is over. Two more sloppy errors by Court gave Bobby the first game, 1-0, and the players sat down before changing sides.

"Gosh, she's more nervous than I am," Bobby told Kuhle. "She's tight as a drum." Kuhle tried to keep Bobby focussed, prepared for anything, but Bobby had a sense the day was his.

On the opposite side of the umpire's chair, Court's coach, Dennis Van der Meer, told her what she already knew: serve, get to the net, and volley the ball away. But it wasn't working. Court lost her own serve at love, missing two easy overheads and double-faulting on the last point: 2-0. Bobby wondered why she didn't just try to keep the ball in play until she worked out her butterflies.

On his serve again, Bobby stuck with his game plan: serving out wide to keep Court from following her return into net and offering up a variety of floaters, lobs, spin shots, and drop shots. The strategy continued to work, 3-0. In all, Court had won just four points in the first three games.

In the fourth game, Court held, coming to net behind her powerful serve to make it 3-1, but to Bobby it was clear she had no confidence once she got there. "She's playing fast, too fast," Bobby thought. He decided to make his game go from soft to softer, concentrating on her backhand. Nervous and unable to get her first serve in, Court found herself stuck on the baseline, unable to attack Bobby's moonballs. She was playing his game. Bobby moved around the court at ease, anticipating Court's every move. He even got into net a couple times, finishing off the points with crowd-pleasing drop volleys.

At 5-1, Bobby was playing so loosely and confidently that he tried to hit a trick shot, a vicious slice designed to just clear the net, hit the court, and bounce back over to his side. But he mishit the ball, and it hit the court just in front of his feet and stopped dead. The crowd laughed, and Bobby grinned, kicking it away. He then double-faulted, allowing Court to break him. Bobby really didn't care. The set was his. This way he could break her to win the first set and then open the second set on his own serve, which he did: 6-2.

The second set was, for Court, mercifully short. At 1-1, she tried to force herself to the net, but Bobby's off-speed groundstrokes and eccentric spins forced her to retreat to the baseline again. Any rhythm or confidence she could muster was destroyed by a steady succession of errors. At one point, Bobby decided to stray from his game plan, and surprised himself by serving two aces in a row, one that Court didn't even move for. On the sidelines, Court slumped over, sullen and dejected, holding her racquet loosely between legs, her coach Van der Meer unable to offer anything that might snap her out it. Bobby, meanwhile, had stopped concentrating altogether, and was chatting amiably to the crowd and waving to his various girlfriends in the stands.

With Bobby serving at 5-1 in the second set, a few in the audience held out hope, as Court was able to take the game to five deuces, and had four chances to break Bobby's serve. Others suspected that Bobby was simply trying to prolong the match. After all, they had played less than an hour, and it was possible the ham in him was refusing to step out of the spotlight so quickly. But a final error by Court, a ball driven beyond the baseline, ended it exactly 57 minutes after it started: 6-2, 6-1— exactly as Kuhle had dreamed.

Bobby jumped over the net and put his arm around Court, trying to offer her a few words of encouragement, but she was in shock. At the awards ceremony, the promoters put the crowning touch on Bobby's victory. They arranged for the archetype of American manhood, actor John Wayne, star of numerous westerns and war epics, and known to many simply as "The Duke," to present the winner with two checks for $5,000—one of which was Bobby's initial stake being returned to him.

At one of several press conferences afterwards, Court admitted she had no rhythm or confidence, and professed surprise at Bobby's tactics. "I didn't expect so many soft shots," she said. "He kept changing pace, breaking up the rhythm. We girls are not used to that pace, that slow play." Incredulous, Bobby wondered exactly where Court had been the previous two months, especially "when I was telling the whole world exactly how I intended to play her. I had disclosed my game plan in detail and stuck to it."

He gave his own analysis of the match, going on for fifteen… twenty… twenty-five minutes, acknowledging that on any other day Court likely would have beaten him, that she may have been the victim of poor coaching, that she wasn't prepared for the media onslaught, and that everybody has a bad day once in while. In the end, however, he summed it up simply as "a classic case of El Choko."

As for what it proved, Bobby's old friend Jack Kramer said, "I guess it proves that the top ladies are about equal to a 15-year-old boy or a 55-year-old man, or maybe not as good."

To journalist Bradshaw, who had been tagging along for the week, Bobby said, "Oh heck, it was nothing, it doesn't really matter. Let's go back to the bar and have a beer and some fun. I've been a good boy too long."

*By the time she faced Bobby Riggs, six-time Wimbledon
singles champion and four-time U.S. singles champion Billie
Jean King built a reputation as a fierce competitor on court
and a crusader for the women's game off court.*

18

Both Separate and Unequal
1973

Billie Jean King didn't watch the Riggs-Court match. She was on a plane returning from Japan, accompanied by her companion Marilyn Barnett and fellow player and friend Rosemary Casals. During a stopover in Honolulu, the three raced off the airplane to try and watch the end of the contest, scrambling through the airport terminal to locate a television set. Finding a set of coin-operated TVs attached to a row of molded plastic chairs, they huddled around as Billie Jean furiously fed quarters into the thing and then spun through the channels in search of the match. Nothing. Because of the time difference, everything in Hawaii was delayed several hours. Casals pulled out a portable radio she was carrying and turned it on, catching the last part of a sports report: "…and Bobby Riggs has just beaten Margaret Court, 6-2, 6-1."

"Dammit," moaned Billie Jean, who for weeks had been hoping that Court would win and Bobby would simply go away, "now I'm going to have to play him."

Whatever she may have thought about Bobby's chauvinist prattle, Billie Jean knew the Riggs-Court match, watched by millions on national television, sent a clear message: Maybe women can't play tennis as well as men. Maybe they don't deserve equal prize money. With Title IX, the federal law mandating equal funding for women's sports in public schools and colleges just a year old, and with the Virginia Slims circuit that she helped lobby for struggling for survival, Billie Jean wasn't about to let this loudmouthed pipsqueak ruin things. The battle may have been symbolic, but the war was very real.

Women's liberation had taken center stage in politics and the media. In addition to Title IX, Congress passed the Equal Rights Amendment, and earlier that year, in what was probably the most controversial and biggest gain for women, the Supreme Court had legalized abortion in *Roe v. Wade*. Outspoken feminist Gloria Steinem had launched *Ms. Magazine* the previous year, and Helen Reddy's rendition of "I Am Woman" reached number one on popular music charts.

Women were asserting themselves as never before, and they had some concrete gains to show for it. Yes, women "had come a long way, baby," as the slogan for Virginia Slims cigarettes touted, but lest anyone be fooled, they still had a long, long way to go. On the playing field, female athletes were still getting a raw deal. A week after *Sports Illustrated* put Bobby on its cover for beating Court (under the tongue-in-cheek headline, "Never Bet Against This Man"), the magazine ran a sobering cover story that underscored the point. Reeling off reams of statistics, the three-part series, "Sport is Unfair to Women," detailed how women's right to play was severely restricted when it came to funds, facilities, coaching, rewards, and honors. In many places, absolutely no support was given to women's athletics. In some places, it was barred by law.

Tradition, regulation, long-held misconceptions concerning femininity and sexuality, as well outright male hostility combined to create an entrenched system that discriminated against women. At high schools around the country, girls interested in competitive sports were given few choices and even fewer resources. For example, in 1969 a Syracuse, N.Y., school board budgeted $90,000 for extracurricular sports for boys, and just $200 for girls. The following year, the board cut back on the athletic budget, trimming the boys' program to $87,000. Funds for the girls' program were simply eliminated.

Even schools that had programs for girls rarely extended them beyond the basic seasonal trio of tennis, basketball, and softball. In most cases, the coaches and athletes relied on candy sales, cooking contests, and raffles in order to raise money for uniforms and travel expenses.

Things were no better at the college level. At the University of Washington in 1973, where 41.4 percent of the 26,464 undergraduates were women, when it came to athletics, women's sports received less than one percent of the university's annual sports budget. Even at Vassar, a traditionally all-female college that began accepting male students just five years earlier, a budget of $4,750 was allotted to five men's sports teams in comparison to $2,060 for three women's teams. This when female students outnumbered males 2 to 1.

To many, sports seemed unladylike, and the girls who participated in sports opened themselves to ridicule, being called everything from "tomboy" to "butch" to "dyke." Young women were told to stay out of sports, that they would lose their femininity, develop bulging muscles, cause irreversible harm to their bodies, and be unable to have babies. There seemed to be a notion, commented one girls' basketball team coach sarcastically, that "we aren't supposed to sweat."

Consider the case of Susan Hollander, a student at Hamden High School in Connecticut. She had proven herself capable of competing on the school's varsity cross-country and indoor track teams, but there was no girls' squad, and she was prohibited by state regulation from participating on the boys' team. Backed by her parents, she sued the Connecticut Interscholastic Athletic Conference. The case was heard on March 29, 1971, in the Superior Court of New Haven and Judge John Clark FitzGerald ruled against Hollander.

In his decision, FitzGerald stated, "The present generation of our younger male population has not become so decadent that boys will experience a thrill in defeating girls in running contests, whether the girls be members of their own team or of an adversary team. It could well be that many boys would feel compelled to forgo entering track events if they were required to compete with girls on their own teams or on adversary teams. With boys vying with girls… the challenge to win, and the glory of achievement, at least for many boys, would lose incentive and become nullified. Athletic competition builds character in our boys. We do not need that kind of character in our girls."

Inequities such as these were what Title IX set out to correct, but even the most optimistic booster of women's sports knew it would take years to change the system and even longer to change public attitudes. The idea that fans someday might pay to watch professional women athletes play basketball or soccer seemed as far-fetched as, say, the concept of human cloning. On the rare occasion when the achievements of a female athlete got mentioned in the press, the article inevitably focused as much on the athlete's physical appearance as her athletic prowess.

A typical example of women's sports coverage appeared in the Aug. 23, 1971, issue of *Sports Illustrated*: "A cool, braided California blonde named Laura Baugh made quite a splash… her perfectly tanned, well-formed legs swinging jauntily. The hair on her tapered arms was bleached absolutely white against a milk-chocolate tan. Her platinum hair was pulled smartly back into a Viking-maiden braid." This was an account of a women's golf tournament.

Of course, 29-year-old Billie Jean King knew all this first-hand. Not only had she lobbied for passage of Title IX, she had been brought up within the same unfair system.

Born November 22, 1943, Billie Jean Moffitt grew up in a middle-class neighborhood in Long Beach, California, the oldest of Betty and Bill Moffitt's two children. Billie Jean and her younger brother Randy were both sports nuts (Randy went on to become a pitcher for the San Francisco Giants). The scrappy and outgoing Billie Jean loved playing football, baseball, and basketball with the neighborhood kids.

Though she more than held her own, when Billie Jean turned 10 her parents decided she needed to take up an activity more "appropriate" for a young lady. Her father, a fireman for the city, suggested golf, swimming, or tennis.

Billie Jean started taking tennis lessons at a nearby public park. Her first instructor, Clyde Walker, worked for the city, teaching tennis at various municipal parks on different days of the week. He taught Billie Jean the fundamentals of the game: how to hold the racquet, how to swing, and the importance of consistency. A proficient and eager student, Billie Jean immersed herself in the game, anxiously awaiting each lesson, reading up on the sport's great players, and talking tennis with anyone who cared to listen. Later, she would remember the stories Walker would tell his students, and in particular one "about this little punk who used to come out to the courts around Los Angeles and hustle matches when he was 13." That punk was none other than Bobby Riggs.

Within nine months, young Billie Jean improved enough to enter her first sanctioned tournament at the Los Angeles Tennis Club, still a center for tennis activity and a place where Perry T. Jones continued to rule with an iron fist. At the competition, Billie Jean advanced two rounds before losing a tough three-set match to a more experienced opponent. Billie Jean later wrote that she "could have cried" after losing the match, but the biggest disappointment she carried away from that tournament had little to do with the way she played. Jones, the same stickler for neatness and etiquette he had been 20 years earlier, refused to allow Billie Jean to stand for a photograph with the other junior girls because she was wearing a blouse and a pair of tennis shorts made by her mother rather than the mandated tennis skirt. It was at that point Billie Jean decided that if she ever had the chance, she would eliminate all the petty formality and snobbishness that permeated the game.

Billie Jean continued to improve. By the time she was 15 years old, she was the second-ranked 15-and-under girl in Southern California and fifth-ranked nationally. Recognizing potential when she saw it, a friend recommended that Billie Jean take lessons from Alice Marble, whose aggressive, serve-and-volley game many compared to Billie Jean's. For several months, Billie Jean's parents drove her the 40 miles to Tarzana, where Marble lived and taught on a private tennis court. "She helped me a lot technically," Billie

Jean wrote, "and worked hard on the advanced aspects of shot-making.

"What I got most from her, though, was the sense of what it was like to be a champion. She talked a lot about Don Budge, Bobby Riggs, Helen Hull Jacobs, Helen Wills Moody, and the other great players of her era." Among the stories Billie Jean likely heard were of Marble's and Bobby's workouts on Carole Lombard's private court under the supervision of Eleanor Tennant.

By 1967, the seven-time Wimbledon champion (two in singles and five in doubles) and reigning U.S. singles champion had built a reputation as a fierce competitor who excelled in big-match situations. Her heroics in Federation Cup play (the international team competition for women) between 1963 and 1979 helped the U.S. reach the final nine times and win seven through her 51 victories in 55 matches in singles and doubles.

Billie Jean (now Billie Jean King following her marriage to Larry King in 1965) was also becoming increasingly vocal in her criticism of the old "shamateur" system of under-the-table payments. During her run at Forest Hills in 1967, Billie Jean was pulled aside by USLTA president Bob Kelleher and warned that if she didn't tone down her opinions she likely would face suspension.

She didn't, but it hardly mattered. By the next year, tennis went "open," shedding the pretense of amateurism. When it did, Billie Jean realized she was now part of the entertainment business. The inequities that she accepted as a "shamateur" taking under-the-table payments no longer could be quietly tolerated now that prize money and endorsements were on the line. Female players got less money (generally a quarter of that awarded to the men) and had fewer tournaments available to them. In 1971, there were 34 tournaments available for male pros versus just 19 for women.

Billie Jean became the first woman athlete to break the $100,000 milestone in prize money in 1971. But the same year Rod Laver, the leading winner on the men's circuit, collected $290,000. Not only that, but to reach her total, Billie Jean had to win three times as many tournaments as Laver. The year before, she tried to orchestrate a boycott of the prestigious Pacific Southwest Tournament in a dispute with tournament director Jack Kramer over the disparity in prize money between male and female players. She subsequently lobbied to help found the fledgling Virginia Slims women's tour.

Billie Jean never argued that the best female players could beat the best male players. They couldn't. At first, she simply agitated for a better split of the prize money, perhaps 5-to-3 or 2-to-1. But that wasn't fair either, she realized, because it meant women as entertainers were still getting short-changed. "From a show-biz standpoint I felt we put on as good a performance as the men—sometimes better—and that that's what people paid to see," she said. "If our show was as entertaining as the men's, then we should have been getting equal pay. It was really that simple."

The conventional argument espoused by tennis officials (mostly male) and tournament promoters (also mostly male) was that the women didn't deserve it. For one thing, they didn't play as much. By tradition, women at major tournaments played two-out-of-three-set matches while the men played three-out-of-five-set matches. Secondly, and more subjectively, they played an inferior game. "In the long run," Kramer said, "the duller and surer that you play women's tennis, the better your chances of winning."

At this point, Kramer ran the Pacific Southwest Championships, the second-most important tournament in the country after the U.S. Open. Kramer offered $25,000 in prize money for the men and $2,500 for the women. In 1970, Billie Jean and a handful of other players, including Rosemary Casals, decided something needed to be done to make the situation more equitable. At first, they considered trying to organize the women players to boycott the tournament. Gladys Heldman, founder, publisher, and editor of *World Tennis* magazine, the country's leading tennis periodical, told them to wait. She agreed to represent them in negotiations with Kramer to try and give the women a larger share of the purse. Kramer remained adamant.

In his mind, the fact that women received only a fraction of the prize money earned by male players wasn't prejudiced, "it was just good business." Said Kramer: "The only prejudice practiced in tennis against women players is by the fans, who have shown repeatedly that they are prejudiced against having to watch women play tennis when they might be able to watch men play."

Billie Jean and the other players discussed their options. In the middle of a "long and loud discussion in the women's locker room at Forest Hills" a couple of weeks before the start of the Pacific Southwest in 1970, Heldman announced she had arranged for a women's pro tournament in Houston the same week as Kramer's tournament. With the help of Joseph Cullman, a tennis fan and chairman of cigarette maker Philip Morris, a purse of $7,500 was set and the tournament was christened the Virginia Slims Invitational. Soon afterwards, Virginia Slims and *World Tennis* announced a new women's tour with $309,000 in prize money to begin play the winter of 1971. Billie Jean, Casals, and 16 other women signed $1 contracts agreeing to play the circuit. A number of top players, however, refused to join the renegade circuit, among them Australia's Evonne Goolagong, as well as a rising young American star, Chris Evert. Many of the players were fearful of retribution by the USLTA or their national associations.

Like the old barnstorming days of the early professional tours, the players on the inaugural Slims circuit did everything from giving interviews and making public appearances to tout the new circuit, to selling tickets and working the crowds. The tour also instituted a few innovations to try and liven the proceedings for the fans, including new "No-Ad" scoring that reduced the number of long, dull matches, and encouraging greater crowd participation. The number of tournaments, which began in January and ran into the spring, expanded to 14 that first year, with a combined $189,100 in prize money.

Billie Jean won eight of the inaugural 14 tournaments and collected $37,000 in prize money. More to the point—and to everybody's surprise—the tour was off to a roaring start. Players, attracted by the $18,000 minimum purse per tournament, quickly got over their reservations and signed on (the next year, minimum prize money rose to $35,000 per event). Long-term survival of the tour, however, remained far from assured.

When Billie Jean heard the score between Bobby and Court, she feared that Court's poor showing reaffirmed what so many suspected about the disparity between the genders in athletics. She worried that Title IX, just a year old, was in jeopardy because, she said, "You know Congress. They're all men. It doesn't represent the country at all." She became so stressed on the flight, she said, that she got "lockjaw."

As soon as she stepped off the plane, the press surrounded her, interested not in the $8,400 she won at the Toray Sillook Tournament in Tokyo, but in whether she would play Bobby.

"Before, I kept out of it," she told them, "but I'm ready to challenge him now… The fans were really cheated by Sunday's mismatch. I understand Margaret played just terrible. I think I can beat him. I know one thing, I won't do worse than Margaret did."

All that needed to be decided was where, when, and, of course, for how much.

Bobby typically replied to questions from reporters with a rambling stream of consciousness that may or may not have had anything to do with what was actually asked. Here, he and Billie Jean King talk to the press prior to their match. (Looking over Bobby's shoulder in the white shirt is his friend and protégé, Lornie Kuhle.)

19

The Merchants of Tennis

1973

One of the estimated 30 million people watching the Riggs-Court match on television was Jerry Perenchio, the son of a winemaker who started his career booking bands and catering frat parties before founding his own talent agency. In 1971, he promoted the $20 million fight between Joe Frazier and Muhammad Ali in Madison Square Garden. Well-known and well-connected, Perenchio had a head for business and an instinct for what sells. In 1973, he and partners Norman Lear and Bud Yorkin were behind three of TV's biggest hits: *All in the Family, Sanford and Son,* and *Maude.*

Gathering with friends around a television set one weekend in Palm Springs, Perenchio became entranced by the Riggs-Court spectacle. "When it came on," he later told Bobby, "the whole town stopped. Everyone was turned on by the match. Women bet on Margaret Court. Men bet on Bobby Riggs. And I said to myself, 'This isn't tennis—it's something bigger.' "

Despite the lopsided score and the fact that Perenchio didn't know tennis from tiddlywinks, he knew a good fight when he saw one. Bobby's hyperventilated banter and comic bravado reminded Perenchio of Ali, a supreme showman who practically invented the art of trash-talking in sports. Riggs-Court had drama, it had humor, it had action. It was pure entertainment and great television. The numbers bore this out. Almost half of all TVs turned on at the time were tuned into the Riggs-Court match, earning it a whopping 39-point share of the audience. By comparison, the final of the World Championship Tennis series in Dallas, which started an hour and a half before Riggs-Court and featured the top two American male players, Arthur Ashe and Stan Smith, attracted a modest 4.5-point share of the viewing audience.

Determined to get a piece of the action, Perenchio set out to contact Bobby.

"I didn't know Bobby or how to get hold of him," Perenchio recalled. "But Tony Trabert [the former player and broadcaster who was affiliated with San Diego Country Estates] was a fellow member at the Bel Air Country Club and I knew Tony. So I called him and said, 'Look, Tony, if you can put me in touch so that I can get in a room with Bobby Riggs—and if I sign him—I'll give you $10,000.' Now Tony's a very nice guy. He says 'I'll do it for free.' I said, 'I don't want you to do it for free. I'd be happy to pay you a finder's fee.' He says, 'Okay, I'll be happy to do it anyway'." So he gave me Bobby's number."

Catching up with Bobby was another matter. Since his victory, he was busier than ever, juggling a never-ending barrage of requests for interviews, invitations from TV talk shows, and offers to endorse everything from dog food to baby bottles. Bobby kept the publicity pot boiling himself by, among other things, announcing his intention to enter a Virginia Slims event in Newport, R.I. that summer. He mischievously explained: "Why not? After all, there is no sex after 55. All senior players over 55 should be permitted to play in the ladies' events."

The phone at his Park Newport townhouse rang incessantly, and it now took two postmen to deliver all his mail. Wherever he went, people asked for his autograph, to have their picture taken with him, or just to shake his hand—many of them women. While driving along the Los Angeles freeways, people pulled up alongside his Lincoln Continental (license: R. RIGGS), honked their horns, and raised their fist in a victory salute. One day, he saw a bumper sticker: "Bobby Riggs for President." Promoters, agents, and con men beat a path to his door—all of whom Bobby welcomed and listened to as sincerely as a priest taking confession.

Then, of course, came the challenges. World Poker Champion Amarillo Slim announced in Las Vegas that he was prepared to tutor a woman to take on Bobby in poker. (He gave up after several attempts to reach Bobby on the phone. "Can't get through to the little bastard," he complained. "He's got himself surrounded by lawyers and them public-relations fellas.") Pool champion Willie Mosconi proposed a pool match with Bobby, and Margaret Clemons, president of the Girls Rodeo Association, invited Bobby to a goat-roping contest for a winner-take-all stake of $10,000. After she offered to give Bobby a five-second handicap Bobby wired back: "NOT MUCH EXPERIENCE AT GOAT-ROPING BUT HAPPY TO ACCEPT CHALLENGE. FIRST, NEED TIME TO PRACTICE. SECONDLY, WANT $25,000 PRIZE NOT $10,000. THIRDLY, WANT TEN SECONDS HANDICAP NOT FIVE." He never got a reply.

Relishing all the attention, Bobby told one writer, "It's like being reincarnated. It's beautiful. It's by far the greatest thing I have ever done, bigger than Wimbledon, bigger than winning the pro tour. This is the highlight of my career."

To Billie Jean King's initial suggestion that they play a $10,000 winner-take-all match at her home court at Hilton Head, S.C., Bobby scoffed: "Imagine that. Billie Jean trying to get me to play at Hilton Head for a measly $10,000. She must be out of her cotton-picking mind. Doesn't she realize that my price now has gone up? Fifty thousand is a more realistic figure."

Exactly how much more money such a match could bring even Bobby might have had a hard time believing. That would be the job of Perenchio, who finally got through to Bobby and arranged to meet him at Caesar's Palace in Las Vegas, where Bobby was playing a tennis exhibition with Pancho Gonzalez.

By now Bobby's entourage had expanded to include brothers Luke, recently retired from the telephone company, and John, also retired after a 36-year career as a special agent for the U.S. Department of Justice in California assigned—ironically—to gambling enforcement. Also tagging along was Bobby's teenage son, Jim, who was given permission to stay with his father by his mother, Priscilla, who still lived at Plandome. For John and Luke, it was like the good old days of nearly 40 years before, both of them falling back into their self-assigned roles as managers and go-betweens, trying to keep baby brother in line. John kept track of Bobby's schedule, ran interference on the telephone, updated the master phone list, and monitored Bobby's whereabouts as best he could. Those seeking to talk to Bobby had to go through John.

In a suite at Caesar's Palace, Perenchio sat down with Bobby to pitch himself and the match he envisioned. Confident and direct, Perenchio was nothing like the legion of ten-percenters who had been hounding Bobby with grandiose schemes and pie-in-the-sky ideas. Here was a man who knew exactly what he wanted and how to get it. He wasted no time getting to the point, predicting that Bobby's next match could well bring in $2.5 million in ticket sales, TV rights, and endorsements—putting tennis among the big-money sports for the first time. "Everybody was after him then, Perenchio recalled. "But I told him who I was and what I did and we hit it off. I said, 'Here's what I'll do. We'll be fifty-fifty partners. I'll put up all the money and all you have to do is your job'."

At first, Bobby was reluctant, if only out of a sense of loyalty to Jackie Barnett, the small-time promoter who had produced the Riggs-Court match. Perenchio glanced at the contract Bobby had signed with Barnett, who was introduced to Bobby by a friend, and quickly pointed out that not only did Bobby put up $5,000 of his own money for that match, but he signed away the TV rights in exchange for a measly $7,500 from Barnett, not to mention all the lost endorsement opportunities. If anybody had been suckered, Perenchio told Bobby, it was the great hustler himself. Thus convinced, Bobby shook Perenchio's hand and signed a contract to co-produce this match and any future matches.

Afterwards Bobby confessed that in his haste to put together a deal, *any* deal, he got taken advantage of in the first match. But, he added, "who was to know it would shoot off like this?" Truth is, despite all his tough-talking bluster, Bobby never grasped the finer points of business. He naively took people at their word and was content to seal the deal with a handshake without consulting a lawyer or accountant. In this case, he was lucky to have Perenchio.

Perenchio's first task was to sign Billie Jean. In late June, he met with Larry King, her husband, who acted as both her lawyer and manager. Tall and blonde, Larry was as cool and dispassionate as his wife was tempestuous and outspoken. His stone-faced support of Billie Jean during the Marilyn Barnett palimony imbroglio in 1981 convinced many critics he must be gay, to which she answered that he was just congenitally—sometimes exasperatingly—even-tempered.

As outlined to Larry by Perenchio, the match would be billed as a $100,000 winner-take-all match, but each player would be guaranteed $150,000, with a $100,000 bonus going to the winner. Thus, with one match, Billie Jean would earn a minimum of one-and-a-half times the same landmark figure it took her a year and 31 tournaments to reach two years earlier.

And while in her public pronouncements Billie Jean insisted the match was about equal rights and dispelling stereotypes, there was no doubt in her negotiations with Perenchio that it was also about money... a lot of it.

It would be the single richest tennis match in history, Perenchio assured Larry, but for it to succeed it would need to be promoted like a heavyweight prizefight, with the build-up relying on the images of Bobby as the supreme male chauvinist pig and Billie Jean as the flag-bearer of women's rights. Larry King told Perenchio that Billie Jean had no problem going along with this, that she was as much a ham as Bobby, and felt that this could only be good for the game. Thus agreed, a deal was struck, and suddenly Billie Jean's decision to refuse Bobby's $5,000 a few months earlier appeared to be a pretty good hustle on her part.

Yet to be settled were details such as the site, the date, and the format. In the meantime, Perenchio promised to keep the whole thing quiet until after Wimbledon. This way Billie Jean could play the tournament without having to contend with the inevitable media crush that would surround the Riggs-King match.

But Perenchio did not tell Larry King about his agreement with Bobby to split 50-50 any remaining profits from the television deal, tickets sold at the gate, and fees from the site—a detail that, when it came to light, would cause Billie Jean to threaten to pull out of the match.

A deal in hand, Bobby jumped on a plane to London to scout King. At Wimbledon, he ran into his old friend Bob Falkenburg. "C'mon, Bob, let's go see Billie Jean play. I'm gonna play her in a big match, you know."

Why bother, Falkenburg said, "you can beat her any way you want."

"No, no, no," Bobby insisted. "She's tough." Not only was she faster on her feet than Margaret Court, Bobby argued, but she was more aggressive, a better volleyer, and, most of all, had nerves of absolute steel.

Nevertheless, Falkenburg saw no way Bobby could lose to Billie Jean, particularly given his terrific touch and ability to control the pace of a match. "I remember mentioning to him," Falkenburg recalled, "'Well, boy, you really got a great deal here. You're gonna beat Billie Jean, and then you'll play the next women's champion, and you'll be able to beat her and then probably have another three or four you'll be able to beat'." This could be turned into a franchise, Falkenburg said. Of course, Bobby had already figured this all out. In fact, he was counting on it.

On July 11, at a crowded press conference at the Town Tennis Club in New York, Perenchio got Bobby and Billie Jean together to announce the match, which still lacked a site and a date. "The Ali-Frazier fight was 'The Fight'," Perenchio announced to the throng of reporters and cameras. "This is 'The Match'." He then turned the stage over to the two combatants.

"Of course, we pretty much scripted the thing to give everybody an idea of what it was about," Perenchio later said, but even with all the good-natured banter, the event was not without some real tension. At first, Billie Jean politely smiled as Bobby gleefully talked up the match, spewing his sexist blather about "a woman's place is in the bedroom and the kitchen, in that order."

He predicted Billie Jean would lose because "she's a woman and they just don't have the emotional stability. She'll choke just like Margaret Court did." He then suggested that after dispatching Billie Jean maybe he would take on America's newest tennis darling, 18-year-old Chris Evert, whom Billie Jean had defeated in the final the week before to win her fifth Wimbledon singles title. "I'll even have the men against me in that one."

Propping up her head as she rested her elbows against the table, Billie Jean patiently listened as Bobby ranted, waiting for her chance to speak. When it came, she lashed out: "That creep runs down women; that's why my feeling is like... hate."

Upon hearing this, Bobby's face dropped, genuinely hurt. He was only having fun, trying to promote the match, *their* match. He turned to Billie Jean like a child who just had his hand slapped. "Please don't call me a creep. You don't mean it."

"Creep," Billie Jean repeated, "That stands."

After the press conference, a group of feminist writers including Nora Ephron of *Esquire* magazine and Grace Lichtenstein of the *New York Times* approached Bobby.

"We've got five hundred dollars to bet against you, will you cover it?"

"Is this jawboning or whipout?" asked Bobby. "Let's see the color of your money."

Ephron pulled out a fistfull of bills collected from a pool of women reporters, then demanded, "But we want odds of eight-to-five. That's Jimmy the Greek's line in Las Vegas."

Bobby protested, saying the match was no more than an even bet, but Ephorn stood firm.

"Okay," Bobby agreed. "You're gonna blow your dough anyway—what's the difference what the odds are?"

Billie Jean and Bobby ended by posing for a few publicity photos (in one, Bobby leaps over a tennis net while Billie Jean gives him a hand by pushing it down to give him some added clearance). The three then split up: Bobby to the West Coast to begin promoting the match; Perenchio to his office to nail down a site and date; and Billie Jean into seclusion to begin preparation for the U.S. Open and to try to ignore the media circus.

Never before had Vegas quoted odds on a tennis match, but then again nothing about this match was traditional in terms of tennis—not the way it was promoted, not the amount of money involved, not the attention it received, and, ultimately, its insignificance as a sporting event.

Perenchio understood this from the very start. Indeed, it was the reason he'd gotten involved. Bobby's little hustle, his male-chauvinist pig rant, had mushroomed into a national event. Perenchio commented later, "That moment was a stroke of genius and I was lucky to jump on the bandwagon."

Immediately after the press conference, the phones started ringing, and the more Perenchio talked, the bigger the sums grew. "The key to promotion," he joked at the time, "is getting everyone else to pay the tab. I love it." For example, an event usually pays a fee for use of a venue, but because of the huge interest in the match, Perenchio figured he could get a site to pay him for the privilege of hosting the event. In this case, he said, "we put the site up for auction." The contenders included the Astrodome in Houston, Madison Square Garden in New York City, Caesar's Palace or the MGM Grand in Las Vegas, and the Superdome in New Orleans. For $250,000, the Astrodome won, in large part because its 46,000-seat capacity could hold the throng of anticipated spectators. (Up to that point, the biggest live audience for a tennis match had been the 25,578 on hand for the 1954 Australia-U.S. Davis Cup final in Sydney.)

With tickets selling for as much as a then-unheard-of $100 per seat, Perenchio calculated the gate could bring in more than $600,000. The Astrodome gave ticket buyers the option of sitting on the Riggs side or the King side, and announced that the Riggs seats were going faster. Perenchio went so far as agreeing to provide two dozen celebrities at the event, and talked Caesar's Palace of Las Vegas into chartering a jet to fly them to Houston in exchange for televising 20 bra-less cheerleaders wearing Caesar's Palace T-shirts.

As for television, Perenchio first approached ABC, with which he already had a working relationship, and the network agreed to buy the TV rights for $750,000 (compared with a mere $58,000 paid by NBC for the rights to that year's Wimbledon). Foreign TV and ancillary marketing activities were expected to bring in another $500,000 or so. ABC also agreed to broadcast the match in prime time on a Thursday evening, foregoing the traditional Saturday or Sunday afternoon slot for tennis finals. It then sold more than $1 million worth of commercial time at $80,000 a minute, putting the match in a league with football's Super Bowl. To ensure the match filled the two-hour time slot (a genuine concern after Bobby's 57-minute rout of Court), Riggs and King agreed to a best three-out-of-five set format. Billie Jean preferred it this way. Women traditionally played best-of-three set matches, and she wanted to debunk Bobby's chauvinistic drivel about how women could not stand up physically to men in a long match. It would make her victory more convincing. Besides, she figured she was fitter than Bobby, and wanted to leave him no excuse if he lost.

Leaving no potential revenue source untapped, Perenchio planned to squeeze another $50,000 by charging spectators $5 a head (plus $1.60 for parking) to watch Bobby and King practice in the days before the match on a temporary court inside a plastic "bubble" erected outside the Astrodome. Other plans included manufacturing and marketing Bobby Riggs tennis clothing for men and women and Bobby Riggs tennis rackets. "I think we can sell one million racquets at $40 and make a $10 profit on each," he told one reporter. He also explored setting up a chain of Bobby Riggs tennis clubs, the first to be built next to the Astrodome itself.

A brief hitch emerged when CBS went to court seeking an injunction to stop the match on grounds that it had retained TV rights to the match under a contract with Jackie Barnett, who in turn sued Perenchio for not naming him executive producer of the Astrodome match. The matter was settled out of court, presumably with financial payments to CBS and Barnett.

While Perenchio cut the deals, Bobby hit the TV talk show circuit, appearing on the *Today Show*, *The Tonight Show*, and *60 Minutes*, among others. Playing the role of male chauvinist pig to the hilt, Bobby jubilantly launched into his extravagant sexist tirade with the energy of a fire-and-brimstone preacher. "I love women," he proclaimed mischievously. "I think every man ought to own two of them." Or, "Women should keep their biscuits in the oven and their buns in bed." As for Billie Jean, he promised to "psych her out of her socks." Remember the bouquet of flowers he gave Court? How about this: "I get the biggest funeral wreath you ever saw, and I wear black crape all over during the match and put a casket on the side of the court with a dummy in it. After she loses, I'll bury her once and for all." And while he claimed that "there is no way she can beat me," he also delighted in ticking off Billie Jean's ostensible advantages: a better serve, better agility, a better overhead, backhand, and forehand volley, more stamina. He claimed the best-of-five set format alone should be enough to drop the betting odds from 8-to-5 to even money. As with Court, he enjoyed playing the underdog who could not lose. "The last time I went five sets was 30 years ago," he said. "Five sets! I'll be killed. If I don't beat her in three sets, she'll have a great advantage."

Boastful, boorish, and unrestrained, Bobby was an irrepressible egomaniac. His television appearances were not interviews as much as verbal performances—sales pitches by a carnival barker. Given the time, he might offer to take on his host in a game of tennis while carrying a suitcase or a bucket of water, or he might put on a display of tossing cards into a hat or shooting baskets. Once the "On Air" light came on, the biggest problem was shutting him up. Even the motor-mouthed Don Rickles, the acerbic substitute host of *The Tonight Show*, admitted he had been out-talked by Bobby, who simply ignored Rickles' comic insults.

What Bobby said was often outrageous, even despicable, but as villains went, he was remarkably benign—particularly given the real-life villains being paraded before the nation during the televised Watergate hearings at the time. In his overblown pronouncements, Bobby made it clear his chauvinist shtick was just that, a put-on. He wouldn't know Gloria Steinem, wrote Grace Lichtenstein, if "she tap-danced across his chest in spiked heels." Moreover, Billie Jean knew it, and everybody else did too.

Part spectacle, part sociological phenomenon, the match nevertheless struck a nerve around the country. People who had no interest in tennis were suddenly talking about this match, voicing their opinions, taking sides, and laying bets. For a nation weary of the Vietnam War and the ordeal of Watergate being played out on television, the match offered a perfect distraction. It was a bloodless brawl, a cathartic release from the real-life conflicts that had been tearing at the nation—the war in Vietnam, the race riots, the assassinations of the Reverend Martin Luther King and Robert Kennedy, student protests, growing poverty and the decay of the nation's inner cities, inflation, and rising unemployment. While the issue of women's rights was serious enough, the real reason the match took off was that Bobby came along at a time when the country desperately needed some comic relief.

Many newspapers were unsure of exactly how to cover the event. Was it sports? News? Lifestyle? As an athletic contest, the match was destined to rank somewhere between professional wrestling and a demolition derby, especially when there were real sports stories to cover: Secretariat's run to horse racing's Triple Crown, Hank Aaron's pursuit of Babe Ruth's home run record, and the undefeated Miami Dolphins' march to a third straight Super Bowl.

At the *Boston Globe*, the sports editor told tennis writer Bud Collins in early September not to bother going to Houston for the match. A few days later he came up to Collins and said, "Gosh, you'd better go." The venerable *New York Times* previewed the match as if it were a prize fight, with a chart comparing King's and Riggs' height, weight, chest, wrist, bicep, neck, forearm, hip, and thigh size.

There was something alluring about Bobby, something vaudevillian... something uniquely American. He was a puckish P.T. Barnum in tennis shorts and horned-rim glasses; a perpetual adolescent, a middle-aged everyman in search of the Fountain of Youth; and, yes, a hustler, a self-made man of action who lived by his wits and made the most of every opportunity. Call it genius or dumb luck, Bobby was going to exploit the moment for all it was worth.

But just to make sure, Perenchio hired a couple of public relations firms to keep Bobby busy, scheduling a steady stream of appearances, interviews, and publicity shoots. Bobby's Park Newport townhouse became busier than ever, filled with family, friends, pretty girls, reporters, groupies, and deadbeats. Bobby's bedroom was like the Oval Office. He sat up in bed, a phone by his side, his briefcase opened up and all his cards and phone numbers spread out before him, shouting commands or calling in visitors as he needed them. Or he might be on the couch, grabbing fistfuls of vitamin pills with one hand from a big bowl like they were popcorn, holding a big glass of orange juice in the other, and with the telephone scrunched against his shoulder. He'd talk, take another handful of pills, and drink, then talk, then another handful of pills, and drink.

When he wasn't on the phone, he'd pore over some of the mail selected for him to read: endorsement offers, interview requests, challenges, love letters, and well-wishers. His celebrity status made him the sudden target of every lonely heart, nut case, and con man in search of a purpose. Once, recalled his son Bill, the phone rang. John or David picked it up, then shouted to Bobby, "It's the Grand Wizard of the KKK. He wants it known that they are endorsing you. You want to talk to him?"

"Hell no," answered Bobby. "I don't want anything to do with that asshole."

Another time, he cheerfully showed off a sweatshirt emblazoned with the acronym WORMS, a gift from the World Organization for the Retention of Male Supremacy. It came with a citation, the head WORM honoring him and describing the group's "disdain for effeminate men... and masculinity in women."

When given the chance, Bobby gave impromptu press conferences to expound on his grand schemes and the future of Riggsdom. No more small-time stuff, he promised. From now on, the only endorsement offers he'd consider would be "a Ford, a Chrysler, a Bristol-Myers, a Gillette," he said. "I'm talking to the William Morris Agency... Maybe five million in it. I don't know how much net. I'm still evaluating." At times, he could be found tearing out magazine ads as possible future endorsement references. After Billie Jean, he said, "it'll be hot-and-cold running women, it'll be the Super Bowl or the Rose Bowl of tennis, the Riggs spectacular once a year—the best woman player of the year, that's the one who'll have to play Bobby Riggs." Indeed, Perenchio was putting out feelers for a rematch with Margaret Court and had already contacted Chris Evert's coach and father, Jimmy Evert, to try and line up a match between Bobby and the high school phenom. No way, Evert told Perenchio. "She had no interest in getting involved in the hype," Perenchio recalled, particularly for a match she figured she was likely to lose. No matter, Perenchio figured, there would be time to work all these deals after Bobby's victory over Billie Jean.

Despite the flood of endorsement offers, Bobby and Billie Jean turned nearly all of them down, agreeing to maintain relative parity in their commercial exposure. Billie Jean did a TV commercial for Sunbeam hair-stylers, while Bobby picked up endorsements for Sunbeam shavers, Nabisco crackers, and Sugar Daddy lollipops. Bobby also received $75,000 for a Hai Karate aftershave commercial in which two tennis bunnies leap over the net to embrace him. In the closing shot, Bobby winks, tilts his tennis shade rakishly, and says, "Imagine, a 55-year-old sex symbol." By now, the tennis visor, the horned-rim glasses, the page-boy haircut were visual trademarks. Bloomingdale's department store in New York ran an advertisement for tennis gear featuring an unidentified tennis player with a visor and dark-rimmed glasses under with the tagline: "Never bet against this man." Bobby never endorsed Bloomingdale's, but he got a kick out of the copycat promotion. There would be more time to consider endorsement possibilities after the match. Perenchio said he figured Bobby might be worth $2.5 million. That is, if he won.

As always, his brothers tried to keep baby brother in line, to keep him focused on the main business at hand, and to get him to show the "proper decorum" of a champion. They resented Bobby's shameless posturing for the press. It grated them to watch their brother play tennis wearing a petticoat and bonnet, or to read about Bobby in the *National Enquirer*. Under the headline, "New Romance for Anti-Feminist Bobby Riggs," the *Enquirer* ran a large photo of Bobby groping B-movie actress Sandra Giles. *Time* magazine featured a photo spread of Bobby dressed in various costumes of male chauvinist pigs through the ages. In one, he posed as Henry VIII with nude model Susan Holloway on his lap.

Though he didn't practice much, Bobby played plenty of tennis. Between his promotional appearances, the goofy hustles and numerous money matches, he played so much tennis that he developed a painful tennis elbow. Here, he shows off during a tennis exhibition in Bear Valley, Calif., in July 1973.

In another, a shirtless Bobby played a pot-bellied Tarzan beside a supplicant Jane.

What bothered Bobby's brothers most, however, was Bobby's image as a cheap hustler, a cheat. At one point, Dave, a mild-mannered former school teacher, wrote out a press release that Bobby agreed to sign. "It's true Bobby has a compulsion for gambling," Dave wrote, "and this distresses me and other members of the family, but he has never taken unfair advantage of anyone."

In the meantime, Bobby was the toast of the town, invited to all the best Hollywood parties, and cruised around Beverly Hills. Never had he received attention like this: not after winning Wimbledon or his tours with Kramer. All the TV shows, magazine covers, and newspaper interviews made Bobby instantly recognizable. According to a poll conducted by A.R. Nelson Research, Bobby's frenetic efforts made him the fourth most-recognized sports personality in the country behind Joe Namath, Willie Mays, and Muhammad Ali, proving the maxim that any press was better than no press at all.

Everywhere he went there were groupies: young girls, pretty girls, poor girls, models, stewardesses, actresses... and he loved them all. Encouraged by his image as the nation's most prominent male-chauvinist-pig and dirty-old man, he felt free to live out his wildest fantasies, nuzzling and pawing over every young thing within reach, and pledging the "franchise" for a particular area to girls he met during his travels.

For much of the summer, Bobby stayed at the Los Angeles home of Steve Powers, a wealthy friend introduced to Bobby by Larry Riggs, who was then working as a stockbroker with Bateman Eichler, Hill Richards in Beverly Hills. Powers lived in a mansion formerly owned by Betty Grable that had its own tennis court and guest house. It proved a more convenient base of operations for Bobby's daily rounds than Park Newport, about 45 minutes away. Recalling the conversation in which Bobby invited himself to stay at his house, Powers said Bobby phoned and asked, "You play tennis up there on Sunday?" Yes. "Will there be girls?" Yes. Bobby moved in and within a few days took his host and several friends for more than $2,000 in betting tennis, Powers said. "He's been a great help in picking up girls in Beverly Hills. I get out of the car, then he comes up and babbles a lot of nonsense, and the girls figure that anyone who knows anyone that mad can't be all bad."

It was, recalled Larry, "just one huge party after another—getting laid, smoking big, fat cigars and drinking bourbon. Remember, this was the roaring seventies; it was unbelievable what was going on." After one hard-drinking evening, Bobby fell asleep, and the girl walked off with $1,800 in cash from his trousers pocket. "There wasn't even any sex," Bobby said afterward.

Every so often, Larry said, he would call up and tell Bobby, "Dad, you need to start practicing… May, June, July, August went by. Every day I'm telling him. And finally he goes to me, 'Larry. Listen to me. Don't forget, I'm the Godfather… I know what I'm doing. You don't. You don't tell the Godfather what to do or how to do it. He tells you. I know what I'm doing.'

"I said, 'Dad, how do you think you're going to beat her when you haven't played any?' He said, 'I told you earlier. Don't worry about it'."

B obby was playing tennis, sure enough, plenty of tennis. Between all his promotional appearances, the goofy hustles, and numerous money matches, he played so much tennis that he developed a painful tennis elbow for which a doctor prescribed an anti-inflammatory drug. "Bobby didn't practice," admitted Lornie Kuhle, his hitting partner, "but he never practiced, ever. He'd just play. That was his idea of practice." Besides, Bobby felt his primary task was promoting the match; defeating Billie Jean was a given.

He conceded much to Billie Jean to get this match, agreeing to the best-of-five-set format, allowing her to pick the surface—a fast Sportface carpet rather than the slower Supreme Court surface he preferred—and single-handedly taking on all the promotional chores. "I gave her everything that she wanted because I would have played her if they had asked me to put on roller skates," he later said. Victory was a sure thing. As he later explained: "You know, I didn't think I could lose. And the funny thing is, I wasn't sure I could beat Margaret in that first match. But after that I had no doubts about Billie Jean."

Meanwhile, Billie Jean was laying low, avoiding the press, refusing autographs, and concentrating on the one thing she knew she had to do in order to beat Bobby: play tennis. "I realized the one thing Bobby wanted me to do was get caught up in everything," she said. "He's a hustler, but in order to hustle you he's got to see you, know where you are, keep tabs on you. I felt if I hid from him, If I wasn't around physically, it would drive him nuts. And so I stayed out of sight." Besides she had tournament commitments: Denver, Nashville, New Jersey, Newport, the U.S. Open, and—the same week as her match with Bobby—Houston.

"Most people said I could not win. That was a given," Billie Jean said. And, truth was, "I really didn't know if I'd win... But I was going to do everything in my power to win by working out, just by being totally organized and ready."

Among other things, she began lifting weights to strengthen her legs and her knees, which had undergone two surgeries since her tennis career began. She had never played a three-out-of-five set match, but was determined to be ready. "I said to myself, 'That's fine, macho boy, let's see how you do'," she said. "I had trained hard. I could have gone 10 sets."

At the U.S. Open beginning the end of August, the first major tournament ever to offer equal prize money to men and women (thanks to a special grant by Bristol-Myers under its brand name, Ban deodorant), King retired in the middle of a third round match against Julie Heldman, daughter of publisher Gladys Heldman. King claimed to have the flu. The default spurred speculation in the press that Billie Jean had "tanked" the match, lost intentionally in order to pull out of a tournament the following week so that she could spend more time preparing for Bobby. When her husband told the press she might have hypoglycemia and that playing against Bobby was questionable, others wondered if perhaps the pressure was getting to her. *Newsweek* planned to put King on its cover the week before the Riggs match but decided against it after Billie Jean pulled out of the Open, fearing the Houston match would be cancelled. Margaret Court ended up winning the Open, her fifth Forest Hills singles title, but at the post-match press conference the only question the horde of reporters were interested in asking was who did she think would win between Bobby and Billie Jean.

Bobby wondered aloud if all of Billie Jean's antics were a ploy. "She's trying to get sympathy from the public and from me because she realizes this is the most important match of her life," he said. "Basically, what she's doing is appealing to the Virginia Slims people to let her out of the tournament so she can get ready for me... She's trying to psych me out but it won't work. I'm unpsychable."

A series of blood tests a couple days later revealed that Billie Jean was fine, that she had merely suffered a reaction to the penicillin prescribed to her for the flu. Her secretary, Marilyn Barnett, assured reporters that her match against Bobby was still on. Billie Jean then flew to Hilton Head, S.C., where, after playing an exhibition match against Chris Evert to be televised the next spring, she began her workouts for Bobby in earnest, surrounded by a small group of people that included her husband Larry and Dick Butera, a business associate turned good friend who was president of the Hilton Head Island Racquet Club and the World Team Tennis franchise Philadelphia Freedoms, on which Billie Jean played.

Working with resident pro Pete Collins, she practiced two hours a day. They worked especially hard on her volleying and her overhead. She knew Bobby's strategy would be to lift as many lobs as he could and hope she would lose a few in the Astrodome lights. To practice, she returned as many as 200 lobs a day to Collins. They also watched films of the Court-Riggs match to discover Bobby's weaknesses, although it was difficult to tell because the match was so one-sided. Earlier that summer, Billie Jean approached Court at a tournament in Nashville and asked for her advice on how to beat him. "I felt funny asking her about it," Billie Jean said later, given the bitterness of their rivalry. "I knew it would be a sore point with her. I really didn't know whether she wanted me to win or not." Court told Billie Jean she didn't remember much about the match, but that Bobby's backhand lacked power, that he didn't hit over the ball, and that he tended to rely on placement entirely. The information proved useful, as Billie Jean would relentlessly attack Bobby's backhand.

Edgy and intense, Billie Jean tried to calm her nerves and gather her focus by spending time alone every day in quiet meditation, listening to the soundtrack of "Jesus Christ Superstar" or to the music of her friend, Elton John. Once, while watching a football game on television between Stanford and Penn State, she broke into tears during the halftime show when the Stanford University band formed the letters BJK and played "I am Woman."

Twice she threatened to pull out of the match altogether. The first time was when she learned she had been cut out of the TV deal. "That's it. The match is off," she screamed. "Call Perenchio. I want to tell him." Perenchio immediately flew out to Hilton Head from Los Angeles. After hearing Billie Jean give him umpteen reasons why she shouldn't play, Perenchio agreed to kick in another $50,000 for her. "Think about it," she told Larry afterwards. "Without me, without us, they don't have this match."

Billie Jean subsequently told Roone Arledge, head of ABC Sports, that she would not go out on the court if, as planned, Jack Kramer was in the broadcasting booth opposite Howard Cosell and Rosemary Casals. After all the bad blood between Billie Jean and Kramer following her boycott of the Pacific Southwest tournament three years before, she did not want to give Kramer a national forum where he could further denigrate women's tennis.

Arledge balked at first, thinking she was bluffing. Only after sitting down with Billie Jean the day before the match, a meeting in which she told him dead on that she was serious about not playing, did Arledge relent, agreeing to have player Gene Scott replace Kramer.

Scott's and Casals' jobs would be to offer opposing viewpoints during the match, a verbal confrontation to complement the physical one taking place on the court. Meanwhile, although he had never before announced a tennis match, Cosell would do the play-by-play. The famously verbose sportscaster had risen to become one of the best-known personalities on television. His abrasive "tell-it-like-it-is" style made him both the most liked and disliked sportscaster in America, according to a *TV Guide* poll in the mid-Seventies. Initially making his reputation as a boxing commentator in the Sixties, Cosell's style was often confrontational and bombastic. A lightning rod for criticism, he became heavyweight champion Muhammad Ali's most vocal defender when Ali refused service in the Army following his conversion to Islam. The two had a great give-and-take relationship, and played off each other as if lifelong friends. After getting the call in 1970 to be an announcer for a new ABC show, *Monday Night Football*, Cosell helped attract a huge audience to the landmark series, which went on to be the longest running prime-time show ever.

Billie Jean, Barnett, and Butera left Hilton Head and flew to Houston the Sunday before the Thursday night match. Larry King had flown in earlier and arranged hotel suites for them and for Billie Jean's parents, who flew in Monday from Long Beach. The group stayed together in the posh Houston Oaks Hotel, about 15 minutes from the Astrodome and closer to the Net-Set Racquet Club, where Billie Jean was to begin play in a Virginia Slims event the next morning. Most important, however, it was away from the crush of media and fans.

At the Net-Set Racquet Club, an outdoor complex of courts nestled within a new ring of condominium apartments, only a handful of fans were on hand to watch Billie Jean in action. They paid $3 to see the star play her first-round match, compared with the $100 charged for courtside seats in the Astrodome. In fact, spectators were outnumbered by reporters anxious to interview the reclusive Billie Jean after her match. That, and to see if her physical condition was as grave as they had been led to believe. Billie Jean won easily. "I feel wonderful," she said, adding testily, "I did *not* have cancer, hepatitis or hypoglycemia. I wasn't on my deathbed. *You* people invented all that." As to rumors that she had withered under the pressure: "I don't think he's ever played a $100,000 match either. We'll see Thursday who can take the pressure and who can't."

Billie Jean pensively looked out over the sea of cameras, microphones, and notepads, and said, "You know, women's tennis started right here in Houston three years ago. But we never had press conferences like this. We never had press conferences, period." She then took a shower and changed her dress and went back on court to play a second round match, a concession by the tournament organizers so that she could use the rest of the week to prepare for Bobby. Any questions about her fitness were quickly put to rest after Billie Jean defeated Kristien Kemmer, 6-0, 6-2.

Determined to keep to her routine, Billie Jean hit for two hours a day with Dennis Van der Meer, whom she designated as her game coach for the match. She discussed strategy with Collins and reviewed the Riggs-Court tape again. She then changed her sleeping habits, forcing herself to stay up late and sleep in until 10:00 or 11:00 a.m. so that she would be fresh when she stepped onto the Astrodome court at 8:00 p.m. Other than a big press conference on Tuesday at the Astrodome with Bobby, she would do her best to avoid the hoopla, stay calm, and concentrate.

Bobby, meanwhile, arrived in town a week before Billie Jean, accompanied by his "touring medicine show featuring sons, relatives, land developers, starlet-models, and Bobby's favorite nutrition specialist, Rheo Blair." Booked into a large suite at the Astroworld Hotel across the street from the arena, Bobby strolled the lobby, making friends and giving interviews to everyone from Howard Cosell to the editor of the Fondren Junior High School paper. While Bobby talked, Blair hovered in the background, carrying a small white bag filled with brown bottles containing his vitamin concoctions. Every so often, he'd slip Bobby a few pills, which Bobby nonchalantly munched between questions.

After the binges in Los Angeles, Bobby meant to spend more time getting in shape and practicing. Begged by Lornie Kuhle and Blair to start taking the match more seriously, he moved to San Diego the week before going to Houston to go into full training mode, telling reporters he had sworn off booze and girls for the duration. He meant to practice, he really did, but in the swirl of activity, it seemed he'd never quite start, or once he started, something inevitably would interrupt him.

By the time he arrived in Houston things were crazier than ever—thanks in part to Perenchio, who arranged to have waiting for him six buxom Las Vegas showgirls who were to accompany him around town in skin-tight sweaters emblazoned with the legend "Bobby's Bosom Buddies."

Since Billie Jean's default at the U.S. Open two weeks before, ticket sales had dropped to near zero, and Bobby took it as his solemn duty to pick up the promotional pace. For the 10 days before the match he spent every waking moment promoting, scheduling up to five television tapings a day, numerous photo opportunities, radio and newspaper interviews, speeches to the local Rotary Club and other civic groups, cocktail parties and book signings. His publisher, J.B. Lippincott, decided to rush Bobby's autobiography to the printer following his defeat of Court. Writer George McGann said the book, *Court Hustler*, "made some sort of publishing history for getting a book out as fast as they did." As it was, "the book didn't have the strength to it until the match made it interesting."

Bobby's itinerary included trips as far away as Beaumont and San Antonio (three-and-a-half hours away) to drum up ticket sales. His nightly practices in the bubble adjacent to the Astrodome became public exhibitions in which he hustled games against three or four local celebrities, setting a few chairs out on his side of the court and giving his victims the alleys. Challengers included Texas Congressman Bill Archer, renowned heart surgeon Dr. Denton Cooley, and a stockbroker who brought along his own cheerleaders. He even hustled Billie Jean's husband, Larry King, spotting him four games and winning 6-4. He would then invite audience members to play him for $100 a shot. If you could win two out of three games, you got your $100 back; if not, you got a "I Was Hustled by Bobby Riggs" button.

Following the practices he conducted a mass interview with the public, all the while pitching for Hai Karate after-shave and Sugar Daddy lollipops. Then at night, he had fancy dinners (claiming each was his "last supper") followed by sessions in his hotel room, where he held court until 2:00 or 3:00 in the morning, telling anyone who'd listen why he would win.

While accompanying his father on one of his public forays, Bobby's 16-year-old son Bill was asked what his dad was like before he started making a living by challenging women at tennis. The boy, carrying a book titled *The Art of Meditation*, gave a detached smile and replied, "Ah, he was just like he is now, a big ego. Except nobody listened then."

With reporters in tow, wearing a tennis shirt and a sports jacket with deep pockets to hold the vitamins he continually gobbled, Bobby roamed the streets of Houston like a politician seeking last-minute votes. Crowds showed up wherever he went, and he gladly obliged them with tennis exhibitions in bank lobbies, parking lots, and on street corners.

At one stop, he tried to get away for lunch when he was besieged again by a new group of reporters and photographers. Would he burn a bra for a picture? Bobby will do *anything* for publicity, someone said. So a brand-new white brassiere was rounded up, along with lighter fluid and a match, and Bobby went to work, burning a finger in the process.

During lunch at a diner, Bobby caught two guys staring at him while he was at the cash register. Without missing a beat, he launched into his pitch: "Hey guys, I hope you'll come out to see me in the Astrodome." The men walked up and shook his hand. "There are too many women in Houston rooting against me and I need your help."

Later, in the car between appointments, Bobby was exhausted. He continued to talk, but the bravado was gone. To a reporter riding along, Bobby talked about his ex-wife, his children, and, in a moment of candor, about Billie Jean. Despite all the outrageous pronouncements, Bobby admired Billie Jean. He was attracted to her forthrightness, her determination, her gamesmanship, and her absolute conviction in herself—even her sense of humor. He could see in her so much of himself. Like kindred spirits, they were bound by the fates in this moment. It was why he was so hurt when she called him a creep at that first press conference.

"I wonder what she thinks of me?" he asked wistfully. "She really thinks she can win, you know. She sincerely does."

"Have I got time for an hour nap before my next appointment?" he asked an assistant, who told him he had two and a half hours.

"I've finally got time to work, and I'm too tired to jog. I've had so many interviews and such that I haven't had time to work or sleep."

"You want to start slacking off on those $100 matches?"

"Naw, fill up the $100 deals," answered Bobby.

"Well, you've got Congressman [Bill] Archer for a match. You want to drop the $100 deal?"

"Hell no. If he's a congressman he can afford $100."

"This guy from Dallas called long distance and wants to know if you will play him. Ever heard of him?" Kuhle asked, handing Bobby the scribbled message.

"Never heard of him. Call him collect and see who he is, and if I have to, I'll go to Dallas to play him. You never know, he might be one of those $15,000 bettors."

Speaking of the big match, Bobby said: "One hundred thousand dollars, a hell of a purse, huh? I never knew how big this thing would go over, but I knew it would have appeal and be a big event. It took me five years to get it to this peak... I've tried for five years to get Billie Jean into an arena, and finally the money was good enough to get her in one. I think I'll have two or three more matches like this for sure, and then I'll worry about something else later. Maybe I'll start challenging in golf or challenge the best women basketball players in free throws. This thing could go on for four or five more years.

"I might run out of tennis players. Chrissy Evert wants to play me. Margaret wants a rematch, and I imagine Billie Jean will want one. They'll never be happy until one of them beats me, and it may be until I'm sixty-five."

But the preparation for the biggest night of his life left Bobby grumpy, hungry, and worn out. The mountains of pills and regimen of small feedings that Blair had prescribed made Bobby sluggish and nauseous. "I'm taking so many pills I must have a glass stomach," Bobby admitted. After demonstrating to one television interviewer how he swallowed fistfuls of pills, Bobby gagged, rushing afterwards into a bathroom to throw them up.

He also complained about the advantages he had given Billie Jean in order to get her to play, accusing her of gamesmanship and peevishness due to her constant demands. "She's a damn good player, but she's pulled everything in the book on me at one time or another and I couldn't trust her not to pull another," he said.

He even considered demanding that the format be changed to best-of-three sets. "I'm disturbed over that part of it. She's younger and stronger. She has all the advantages in a long match. I've talked to my lawyers and they say that part can't be changed because the contract didn't specify how many sets it should go."

Nevertheless, Bobby refused to contemplate defeat. "Billie Jean's banking that I'm not in shape and not serious enough and she may be right. But I saw the girls at Wimbledon and they were so bad it confused me. I know I can play my game. The question is, can she play up to her ability under the pressure? Can she stay loose, hit out, be great on the tough points and win? I don't believe it. She'll fold. I make me a 17-point favorite.

"It doesn't matter," he continued. "I figure I can play her four or five different ways... I have a lot of options, but I'll probably let her start the action and I'll just find the answer to anything she does."

Others were not so sure. "He thinks this is such a lock, he can beat her at half-speed," Kuhle said the week before the match. "I think he's right, but... starting Sunday, we're going to have to really start working. We worked hard the last four days before the last match, and we'll do the same thing this time."

The day before the match, George McGann, Bobby's biographer, arrived in Houston to see Bobby and to follow up on the match for a subsequent edition of the book *Court Hustler*. Bobby's brother John greeted him.

"Listen, you're in for a shock," John said.

"What's that?" asked McGann.

"Bobby's not going to win tomorrow."

"Why not?"

"He's been a drunk for four months," John said angrily. "He's been running around with a bunch of girls he calls 'Bobby's Bosom Buddies,' screwing and drinking all that time and hasn't played a lick of tennis."

"What? You mean this?"

"Absolutely."

John had been beside himself for weeks. At one point, he called his nephew, Dave Riggs, and said he feared Bobby would embarrass himself on the court. Asking for his nephew's help in getting Bobby under control, John pleaded to Dave, "C'mon. We'll lock him up."

But for all their efforts, Bobby was unmanageable, an unguided missile. All his brothers could do was chide him, shake their heads, and apologize for his behavior. "Don't take him too seriously," Dave said quietly to a reporter. "He's not perfect. He's got his faults just like other people."

After hearing John's warning, McGann went straight to Bobby. "John said you have no hope tomorrow against Billie Jean," McGann said.

"What!? I'll kill that broad," Bobby answered. "I'll kill her. She won't stand a chance."

"Don't forget," McGann said, "we have an agreement with the publisher for a $75,000 bonus if you win," half of which was to go to McGann.

"Why are you so interested?" demanded Bobby. "You going to buy [your wife] a mink?"

"Yes," McGann answered. "That's right."

Hurt and disappointed, McGann could only hope Bobby was right. Maybe there was no way he could lose. Maybe he would magically rise to the occasion. Nevertheless, he looked awful—hyper and worn out—a man in dire need of a good night's rest and some time by himself.

Later that night, Bobby had another visitor to his suite, his old friend Gardnar Mulloy, also in town to see the match. Mulloy wanted to wish Bobby luck.

He knocked on the door, and Bobby's brother John answered. "Hey, Gar, come on in."

Recalled Mulloy: "The room was filled with smoke and about 10 young women along with a couple of other guys. Bobby was in his pajamas, sitting on the sofa, talking on the phone."

Upon seeing Mulloy, Bobby lowered the phone and greeted his friend. "Hey Gar, how are ya?"

"Bobby, what the hell are you doin'?" Mulloy said. "You got to play tomorrow night. What're you doin' with all these people?"

"Ah well, they're all my friends, Gar. I'm workin' out a contract for after this match."

"Bobby, you got to win it first."

"There's no way that broad can beat me," Bobby said.

Turning to leave, Mulloy answered, "That's famous last words, Bobby. Famous last words."

As he entered the Astrodome, Bobby looked grim, nervous, almost ashen. He did not seem to love it anymore. "How's it going?" he muttered to nobody. "Where is she?"

20

The Unthinkable Happens
1973

At the Los Angeles Tennis Club, the old gang, including Jack Kramer, Ted Schroeder, and Gene Mako, gathered around the club's television set on Thursday evening, September 20, 1973, to watch their old friend and rival take on "that broad." The general feeling was that there was no way Bobby could lose this match and that the 8-5 odds given him by Las Vegas oddsmakers grossly overestimated Billie Jean King's chances. But it would prove to be a very strange evening.

Interest in the match had reached a fever pitch. Three hundred press credentials were issued, more than for any of the Frazier-Ali fights. The match was to be broadcast to 36 foreign countries. In London, five theaters would pipe in the match over closed-circuit television live at 3:00 in the morning. CBS, which broadcast the Riggs-Court match, set to air the blockbuster movie *Bonnie and Clyde* in an effort to draw away from ABC some of the 40 million viewers expected to watch the match in the United States.

As promised, promoter Jerry Perenchio chartered a jet to fly in a contingent of celebrities from Hollywood, a group that included Andy Williams, Claudine Longet, Rod Steiger, Jim Brown, Desi Arnaz Jr., Glen Campbell, Janet Leigh, Robert Stack, heavyweight champion George Foreman, and Merv Griffin. During the afternoon, they played a series of celebrity exhibition matches before the evening's main event.

Earlier in the day, Billie Jean went to the Astrodome to get a look at the court, which could not be set up until after an Astros baseball doubleheader the day before. Stretched out over a wooden platform laid out between the second and third base line, the green acrylic fiber court looked like a postage stamp inside the cavernous structure. Anyone unfortunate enough to have bought seats in the upper tiers would be lucky to see the players, much less the ball. Around the edges of the court, workmen had set up rows of yellow folding chairs—the $100 ground-level seats. "It was such a huge building that the feeling of space was weird, not like a tennis stadium at all," Billie Jean remembered. Despite the vastness, the space between the court and seats set up around the court was very tight.

The bigger problem, however, was the dome's reflective mesh ceiling and the lights along its rim. Knowing Bobby's lobs, Billie Jean figured even if she could spot the ball, it would be nearly impossible to gain any depth perception. "I knew right away if a lob ever got up in there, forget it."

A few days earlier, designer Ted Tinling arrived with a pair of dresses he had designed for Billie Jean just for the match. She tried on the first, a magnificent creation covered with a shiny cellophane-like material, but found it itchy, so she went with the backup, a relatively plain white dress trimmed in blue brocade and rhinestones.

After a brief warm-up on the court, she had the Astrodome staff take her into the visiting team's locker room to show her where her brother Randy Moffitt would dress when the San Francisco Giants played in Houston the following week. Taken to locker 22 (the same number as her birth date—a good omen, she thought), she tacked a note to the locker: "Hi, Randy—BJK." She was ready.

If Bobby was nervous, he certainly wasn't showing it. Before his scheduled warm-up at the Astrodome, he spotted Gardnar Mulloy and asked if the old warhorse would go over and hit with him inside the arena. Sure, recalled Mulloy, who always dressed in tennis clothes, ready to be called to the court on a moment's notice. Mulloy started hitting with Bobby, he recalled, but after 10 minutes, Bobby suddenly left the court. After waiting some time for him to return, Mulloy gave up. He and a friend walked over to the practice bubble adjacent to the arena to see if they might hit a few balls.

"So we go over there and, low and behold, there's Bobby," Mulloy said.

Alongside the court was line of people waiting to pay $50 each to play a two-out-of-three game challenge against Bobby. With chairs scattered around the court, Bobby was wearing a big wig and an apron. Underneath he had a blue tennis shirt with holes cut out around the nipples. "I was gonna give this to Billie Jean King," he said mischievously. "She might look better in it than I would."

"Bobby, what the hell are you doin'?" Mulloy asked. "You're playing tonight."

Gene Scott, called in to replace Jack Kramer in the broadcasting booth that night, had run into Bobby the day before. Though Bobby was almost always ebullient, Scott recalled, this time he was positively jumping out of his skin. "I mean his eyes looked like pinwheels on a kid's cereal box," Scott said. "He was popping pills, and while I don't know what they were exactly, they were not vitamins. He referred to them as, 'I'm trying to balance my uppers and downers today… I'm a little too up,' or 'I'm a little too down.' The way Bobby behaved, it made sense. Bobby was so 'up' that one of his advisers may have told him, 'Bobby, you need to cool off. Here's something to relax you'."

The pills, the promotion, the running around, all of it had left Bobby wrung out. On top of everything, said friend and assistant Lornie Kuhle, "his tennis elbow was horrible… At one stage he couldn't raise his arm at all." And the anti-inflammatory prescribed for the condition upset Bobby's stomach. As the hour of the match drew near, the reality of what he had done, or rather failed to do, sunk in for Bobby.

Said Kuhle: "It was like Bobby finally realized that the final exam was here and he hadn't studied for it."

Bobby's son, Bill Riggs, who accompanied his father to Houston along with brother Jim, said that just before the match, his father opened a vial containing capsules of amphetamine. Usually Bobby would take one or two pills. This time, it was different. "He said this was the most important match of his life," Bill said. Bobby took five pills at once.

Inside the Astrodome it was stifling hot. As match time approached, the atmosphere was like no tennis match before or since. It seemed equal parts circus, political convention, championship prizefight, and tent revival. Some 30,472 people hooted and chanted as balloons floated to the rafters.

In the party-like atmosphere on the Astrodome floor, workaday Texas fans wearing blue jeans and T-shirts mingled with celebrities in evening gowns. White-gloved servers carrying silver trays cruised among the crowd, offering glasses of champagne at $1 each while chefs served up slices of hot roast beef from carving board carts located at either end. The 80-piece University of Houston Cougar band blared songs such as "Jesus Christ, Superstar" while a dozen majorettes wearing red hot pants performed a Rockettes routine out front.

Souvenir stands sold $5 commemorative racquet covers with cartoon drawings of Billie Jean and Bobby, sweatbands bearing the biological symbol for women, and even patches of Astroturf. From the upper tiers, fans hung an array of banners—"East West North South Ms. King Gonna Close Bobby's Mouth," or "Oconomowoc, Wisc. Says Beat Him Billie Jean." In a glass-enclosed booth at one corner of the court, a tuxedo-clad Howard Cosell offered this description to the more than 48 million Americans watching on television: "What a scene this is. The Houston Astrodome, where they've played every sport in the world, but never before tennis… It reminds me of a college football game. One of the most extraordinary things I've ever witnessed in all my years in sports. Incredible."

From his courtside seat, promoter Perenchio sat back contentedly and surveyed the glittering spectacle he helped create. He ran a hand over his Beverly Hills razor cut and proudly said, "It's the fight crowd. It's ancient Rome. It's the closest I've come to getting a woman and man in the ring together."

A flourish of trumpets heralded Perenchio's most ostentatious touch to the night's festivities. On a feather-adorned golden throne, carried aloft by four toga-clad Rice University track stars, Billie Jean entered the arena Cleopatra-like. Wearing a wool cardigan sweater over her white tennis dress, she laughed and waved to the multitudes amid shouts of "Right on, Billie Jean."

To the television audience, Cosell said haughtily, "She's a very attractive young lady, and sometimes you get the feeling that if she ever let her hair grow down to her shoulders, took her glasses off, you'd have somebody vying for a Hollywood screen test."

Another trumpet flourish, and from behind the stands emerged Bobby. Surrounded by a mob of photographers, he sat in a rickshaw with gold wheels pulled by his Bosom Buddies dressed in tight red and gold outfits, their chests, wrote journalist Grace Lichtenstein, "heaving against their sweaters like miniature dirigibles." Wearing a bright yellow warm-up jacket with the Sugar Daddy logo stitched onto the back, Bobby cradled a giant-sized caramel lollipop.

As Bobby made his grand entrance, Cosell commented, "Billie Jean's got the public's support, but he doesn't care. Deep inside, he's so confident about his ability to duplicate the effort against Margaret Court that sometimes when you're with him and he starts talking about the forthcoming match you almost think he's in a state of delirium."

What the television audience saw, however, was an unusually subdued Bobby. He was not laughing. He looked grim, nervous, almost ashen. He did not seem to love it anymore. "How's it going?" he muttered to nobody. "Where is she?"

From a few rows back, Billie Jean's father, Bill Moffitt, turned to a reporter and, pointing at Bobby, said, "I want him to shut up. If he tries anything funny I'm gonna punch him."

Near the center of the court, Bobby and Billie Jean met for a pre-planned exchange of gifts. Bobby handed the giant lollipop to Billie Jean, saying, "I think she'll be a real sucker for my lobs tonight." Billie Jean presented Bobby a live piglet named Larimore Hustle— a male chauvinist piglet, she told him.

"That's too cute for him," said television commentator Rosemary Casals, who seemed to be relishing her role as the anti-Riggs agitator. "He doesn't resemble that sort of a pig." A moment before, Cosell asked Casals what she thought the score would be.

Without hesitation, the audacious Casals said, "I predict Billie Jean will win in three sets, 6-4, 6-3, 6-3."

Behind Billie Jean all the way, the crowd cheered loudly every time Bobby made a mistake during the brief warm-up. The cheering continued when the match abruptly began.

At a meeting the previous day, the players and their representatives met with Roone Arledge, president of ABC Sports, and the Astrodome staff to go over the ground rules for the match and to review some of the pre-match hoopla, including the player entrances. After getting the players to agree to two-minute breaks on changeovers (rather than the customary 90 seconds) and a four-minute break between sets (a concession to television), Arledge turned to Bobby and warned him about his promotion of Sugar Daddy. The candy's manufacturer, Nabisco, he argued, was not an official sponsor and should be charged $80,000 a minute for advertising time like everyone else. Bobby told Arledge that the Sugar Daddy name was part of his image and as such he needed to wear the jacket. After some prolonged negotiating, Arledge agreed to allow Bobby to wear the jacket through the introductions, but that the free ride ended there: The jacket had to come off. Bobby, however, had one more hustle up his sleeve. "He always said whenever you make a deal with somebody give them more than they bargained for. You've got to give them good value," Kuhle recalled. "And he did." The jacket stayed on through Bobby's entrance into the arena and the introductions, through the players' warm-up, through the first game and through the first two changeovers. Meanwhile, an infuriated Arledge sat in the television command trailer, ordering technicians to juggle cameras or angles to cut off images of the jacket. It was to be Bobby's last association with ABC.

Billie Jean won the toss and served first, coming out aggressively, determined to prove to Bobby this would not be a replay of the Margaret Court match. Taking her time and playing very deliberately, a clearly nervous Billie Jean committed a couple of errors to allow the game to go to deuce, but still showed she was in control as Bobby struggled to move about the court. Watching another one of Billie Jean's volleys sail past him, Bobby clapped his racquet face and said, "Atta girl." To the wild applause of the crowd, Billie Jean won the first game with a crisp forehand volley.

Billie Jean could not believe how slow Bobby was, how softly he hit the ball, and thought he must be faking it, that he must have some trick up his sleeve. Perhaps he was playing possum, waiting for the right moment to unleash his bag of tricks. She turned and asked Dennis Van der Meer, one of her two designated courtside consultants (the other was companion Marilyn Barnett), "He's putting me on, right?" Nope, Van der Meer assured her, having previously sat courtside at the Court-Riggs match. She was seeing the real thing.

Bobby, meanwhile, instructed Kuhle to track down Billie Jean's friend, Dick Butera, in the stands. Before the match, Butera tried talking Bobby into a $5,000 bet at odds of 2 to 1. Bobby refused, demanding odds of 8 to 5. Now down one game, Bobby sent Kuhle to Butera's seat. "Bobby says he'll take 2 to 1," Kuhle told Butera. The wager was placed.

At first, Billie Jean and Bobby played cautiously, feeling each other out, probing for weaknesses, and looking to establish momentum. From the start, however, Billie Jean was more focused and determined. Sticking to her game plan, she refused to fall for Bobby's loopy topspin, a shot designed to tempt her into making errors as Court had. Instead, she simply chipped the ball back, concentrating on hitting to Bobby's backhand and on running him from one end of the court to the other.

Leading 2-1 on the next changeover, Billie Jean returned to her seat. She looked over at Bobby, who was slumped over in his chair between Khule and Blair. "He was hyperventilating and really nervous. I was nervous too, but I had it under control better than he did so I knew that was going to be a factor." Suddenly, the weeks of pent-up anxiety drained from Billie Jean's body. She felt confident. "All I ever feared was the unknown, and soon enough he was a known quantity to me," she wrote. "That was the first time I was able to truly believe that he was only a person, like me; he was just a man."

Seeing how sluggishly he was moving, Billie Jean decided to alter tactics. Instead of simply charging into the net at every opportunity, to blister the ball past Bobby, she decided to mix it up. She would answer his array of chips, chops, and spins with her own assortment. She would hit as softly as she could, keeping the ball in play, moving him from corner to corner and from up to back, running Bobby into the ground.

At the L.A. Tennis Club, one of those packed around the club's TV also noticed the difference between the two players. "As soon as I saw Billie Jean play that first game I knew she had it," Arthur Ashe said. "There was no choke there. She was moving so easily, and Riggs looked so slow, and there was no way he could overcome that with con, because she just wasn't scared the way Margaret had been. So I called out for a bet, and got the prevailing odds, 5 to 2, $50 to $20."

On the other side of the net, Bobby looked tense and confused, adjusting his glasses. Although it was early in the match, he already seemed to be tiring. The jacket came off, revealing a blue tennis shirt already soaked in sweat. Bobby returned to the court. From the broadcast booth, Cosell looked over at Bobby and stated the obvious: "The jacket comes off, and maybe the braggadocio a little bit reduced."

Bobby was having trouble getting his first serve in. Even more astonishing, he kept playing to Billie Jean's strength, her backhand. After a 28-shot rally in the third game left him gasping for breath, he started serving and volleying, a change that seemed more desperate than tactical, designed more to shorten the points and conserve energy than to throw off his opponent. Surviving a break point at 30-40, Bobby managed to hold serve to even the score, 2-2.

A poor service game and a missed backhand volley by Billie Jean in the fifth game allowed Bobby to break, going up 3-2. Though it was cause to celebrate, Bobby looked haggard as he sauntered back to his seat. Meanwhile, Billie Jean remained confident. "Up to that point I'd been trying to make my shots too good, but I realized I just didn't have to go for the lines every time. He was slow, he couldn't hit with a lot of pace, and I could take the net any time I wanted." She returned to the court looking more serious than ever.

Preparing to serve, Bobby stepped to the baseline and, after bouncing the ball a couple times off the edge of his racquet frame in his usual ritual, he paused, looked up, and could not believe what he saw. "She walked right up to the service line while I was serving. I looked up, saw where she was standing, and said, 'Is that girl crazy? She thinks she can return my serve from up there. Is she nuts? I'll blow her away.' I reached up and, *bang*, I hit my hardest ball and it just caught the tape. So now I have to come in with my good American twist second serve. But Sportface carpet wouldn't let the spin take hold. It was set up easy for her. Right on her backhand, her best shot."

Billie Jean broke right back to even the score at 3-3, a game in which Bobby failed to get a single first serve in, double faulting at 15-30 to give her two points to break back. His problems were compounded by his weak lob, which continually fell short, making easy pickings for Billie Jean. The hundreds of overheads she hit in practice at Hilton Head paid off. After each rush to the net, she smartly took two steps back in anticipation of the lob, which more often than not Bobby put obligingly within her reach. She won the game on a crushing overhead smash.

Bobby's game of Airtight Tennis was leaking precariously. Suddenly he wasn't playing his game, he was trying to play her game. But it was a game he didn't have. In a contest of pure athleticism, the 55-year-old Bobby was no match for the 29-year-old Billie Jean. He rushed himself, going for winners instead of keeping the ball deep into Billie Jean's court to keep her away from the net and her deadly volley. The errors piled up. Millions of people wondered exactly what they were seeing.

"I think Bobby looks a little bit nervous," commented Casals. "He doesn't look right to me."

Responded Cosell: "Funny, with this match I guess we all expected some high humor involved in it. Instead it's become a very serious, serious thing because the comedy has gone out of Bobby Riggs."

At the L.A. Tennis Club, recalled Kramer, someone captured the collective feeling of the place with the remark, "Looks like Bobby bet on Billie Jean."

Serving at 4-5 to stay in the first set, "the nerveless wonder, the man with all the angles, the guy who knew how to keep a hold on himself with the eyes of the world on him, choked," wrote Lichtenstein. Bobby double-faulted to give Billie Jean the set. The crowd roared its approval, drowning out the chair umpire's calling of the score, which boomed through the arena's public address system.

Arthur Ashe turned and called out for another bet from the crowd at the L.A. Tennis Club, claiming Billie Jean would not only win, but win in straight sets. The odds on Bobby were dropping fast. The best he could get was 3 to 2. "When you've got one player who can't move and the other can hit the ball and isn't nervous, you have got a sure thing in tennis," he said later.

Of the 34 points Billie Jean won in the 10 games of the first set, 26 had been clean winners, shots Bobby never even reached with his racquet. As usual, Bobby hardly ever hit winners. His game relied on forcing an opponent into errors, and right now he was making the most of them. Courtside, an entourage that included brothers, sons, friends, and advisors all hovered around Bobby, vying for his attention, but Bobby seemed lost.

"Come on, Dad, wake up," urged Jim, his 20-year-old son.

Agreeing before the match to a live, between-set interview with ABC's Frank Gifford, a wheezing Bobby gave the television audience his own courtside analysis: "She's playing very well. She's playing aggressive. This is a net player's court, and she's very good at the net. She's making a lot of wonderful volleys, and I missed a lot of first serves. She's getting the ball at my feet. And I'm having a lot of trouble on her return of serve. She's playing better than I am right now… and I'm in for a long afternoon."

But, he added, "It's just the first set. There's a long way to go. All I can tell ya is I'm going to have to pick the pace up, or change my tactics or play a little faster. She's awful quick and swift. I'd like it to be a set all after this next set."

Turning to the one thing that had always worked for him in the past, Bobby sent Kuhle into the stands to Butera's seat, looking for another $5,000 bet, this time at even money. Butera, suspicious that Bobby might be setting him up, losing the first set on purpose to sucker him, shouted down to Billie Jean, asking if he should up the ante. Annoyed, Billie Jean told Butera not to bet. "I figured I needed the extra incentive to lift my game," Bobby said afterwards. "But the man turned me down, so I'll never know whether the bet would have helped me or not."

During one of his pre-match rants, Bobby promised to jump off a bridge if he lost to Billie Jean. Now, as the two players rested, one Virginia Slims player who had taken the night off to see the match went through the audience, passing out small pink pieces of paper—tongue-in-cheek invitations to Bobby's bridge jump:

If I lose to Billie Jean King, I will jump off a bridge.
—Bobby Riggs
This certificate admits one person to the Bobby Riggs Bridge Jump.
Place, time and date to be determined.

Then, in smaller print at the bottom:

Odds that Bobby will con the bridge into lowering itself before the jump: 8-5.

Opening the second set on her service, Billie Jean quickly jumped to a 30-0 lead, but Bobby started running around his errant backhand return, taking the ball on the forehand side. The tactic worked, throwing Billie Jean momentarily off balance. That and a couple of uncharacteristic errors by Billie Jean gave Bobby an opening break of serve and a 1-0 lead.

But Billie Jean quickly regained her composure and the momentum. She broke Bobby's serve in the second game with her favorite shot—a running backhand that she drove crosscourt for the winner. She went on to win five of the next seven games to take the set, 6-3. Somewhere from the sidelines, one fan shouted, "Come on, Billie Jean, start acting feminine—miss a few."

Bobby tried quickening the pace between points, serving before she was quite ready to return, looking to break her rhythm. Nothing worked. Though Billie Jean coughed up a couple of service breaks, she easily broke Bobby right back, on one occasion at love.

Exhausted, flat-footed, and unable to anticipate what Billie Jean's next shot might be, he seemed lost, sometimes literally. "Where is Bobby Riggs?" Casals asked at one point. "Where did he go?" Apparently unaware of the score, Bobby started to return to his chair, thinking it was a changeover. Another time, he got caught too close to the net, and watched helplessly as one of Billie Jean's lobs floated past his head, falling just beyond the baseline. "I could hear that sigh of relief from Bobby here," commentator Gene Scott said.

Few believed Bobby could lose to Billie Jean, especially so badly, and many believed he could still turn it around. Who knows? Perhaps this was all part of a magnificent con. After all, he had done it before, dropping a set to heighten the drama and drive up the odds. So Bobby lost a set. No sweat. So he lost two sets.

"But as you kept watching his performance you thought, 'Hey, he just can't keep on doing this'," recalled Scott. By the middle of the third set, with Bobby grimacing, shaking his head, rubbing his elbow, and looking to the heavens for help, the drama of the match had been sucked out, replaced by an air of inevitability. There would be no comeback.

With King leading 4-2, Bobby stopped the action. His arm feeling like a lead pipe, he took a break to have his aching fingers massaged. Unknown to anyone, Billie Jean had also started to cramp in her legs, either from nerves or dehydration. While Bobby gulped down pills and cupfuls of water, Billie Jean got her left calf rubbed down.

The break changed nothing. Billie Jean rolled on to a 5-3 lead, just one game away from victory. Serving to stay in the match, Bobby stood at the baseline, stared across the net, and prepared to make a final stand. He reached deep down, recalling his matches against Don Budge, Jack Kramer, and Frank Kovacs, his battles against Perry T. Jones and the tennis establishment, and his struggle for tennis legitimacy. He was looking for something to turn the match around. He reached, but nothing was there. "I pressed on the gas and I found out I was already playing as well as I could. I had no high gear to shift into," Bobby said later.

The final game, the second longest of the match, went to five deuces, but not because of any eleventh-hour heroics by Bobby, who failed to get a single first serve in the court. For the first time all night, Billie Jean appeared to be choking. Holding two match points, Billie Jean missed a couple of easy shots, and was visibly angry with herself. At deuce on the sixteenth point of the game, Bobby double faulted to give Billie Jean her third match point. After again missing his first serve, Bobby came in behind a weak second serve. Billie Jean's return floated high to his backhand, an easy put-away. But Bobby hit it harmlessly into the net. Match over: 6-4, 6-3, 6-3.

Billie Jean threw her racket into the air and pumped a victory fist as Bobby jumped the net to congratulate her. "You're too good," he said as he draped an arm around her shoulders. Though much of the match would remain a fog for Billie Jean years later, the fact that Bobby had the energy to leap over the net stuck out in her mind. Then, like the end of the seventh game of the World Series, fans stormed onto the court, swarming around Billie Jean. Finally, she thought, it was over.

Despite the post-match pandemonium, recalled Scott, "all I remember is the celebration was not as gala as the build-up. There was a sense of anti-climax. You had this enormous build-up, and you had the match and you thought, 'Well, it's going to keep on exploding past that.' But no, the gala celebration was strictly a personal one for Billie Jean. The public celebration was not a galvanizing event. Later on, it became a sociological phenomenon as people started to write about the results in terms other than just winners and losers and what the score was. Then it became this signal event for women's rights and whether women can compete with men or deserve a place on the same platform with male athletes."

At a post-match press conference, Bobby offered no excuses. "Billie Jean was too good, too quick," he said. "She would make better shots off my best shots. She was playing well within her game and I couldn't get mine started. She deserved to win, no question about it.

"I know I said a lot of things she made me eat tonight. I guess I'm the biggest bum of all time now. But I have to take it. To the victor goes the spoils... At least I had enough gas left to jump over the net," he joked.

Bobby immediately added, "I would've given Billie Jean a rematch if I had won so I want a rematch. I think I can do better, but that will be up to Billie Jean."

Having accomplished what she set out to do, Billie Jean said, "I feel this was the culmination of 19 years of playing tennis. I love tennis. I've wanted to change it ever since I was 11 years old and wasn't allowed in a picture because I didn't have a tennis skirt on. I think this match will do great things for women's tennis. I've always wanted to equalize things for us. I don't care if this was an exhibition. I don't care what kind of match it was. A lot of non-tennis people saw it and they know we can play now."

As for a rematch: "Why should there be a rematch?" she said. "Women have enough problems getting to compete against each other at the high school and college levels. Their programs are terribly weak. Why do we have to worry about men?"

Then Bobby and Billie Jean posed one more time for photographers, who naturally demanded that they smooch. "I'm liable to turn you on," Bobby warned her. Billie Jean took the risk, responding, after several encores: "They're good kisses." At which Bobby jumped up, yelling: "Hey! She took it back! She says I'm not a creep any more."

To many of Bobby's old friends and rivals, his loss to Billie Jean King was more than just bad. It was calculated.

21

Tennis, Everyone

1973-1976

Billie Jean King may have been the sentimental favorite going into the match, but her victory left many suspicious, especially given Bobby's reputation. "A lot of men—especially around our age—were so stunned when he lost that they figured he must have tanked," said Bobby's old friend and rival Jack Kramer. Don Budge was not only convinced Bobby threw the match, but took it personally. "He really let the game down… it just wasn't a nice thing to do."

The rumors started before the match even ended. Bobby not only played badly, he played like a foil designed to make Billie Jean look good. By the time he double-faulted the first set away, those who knew and played against Bobby—Gene Mako, Don Budge, and much of the tennis old guard—figured his performance was more than just bad, it was calculated.

"I was looking at the match on TV," Mako said, "and in the middle of the second set, after watching for 30 or 40 minutes, I knew exactly what was going to happen… Here's the control player of the world. That was his game, [but] he hit the balls in the center of the court, short. So Billie Jean, who liked to volley, would hit as tough a shot as she could and come in. Any good club player wouldn't hit the ball up the middle and on the service line. And when he did come to net once in a while, he'd hit an easy volley into the bottom of the net."

As conspiracies go, it may not rank with the Kennedy assassination, the existence of UFOs, or even the Black Sox scandal of the 1919 World Series, but the belief that Bobby lost intentionally against Billie Jean proved just as enduring. The day after the match, Karl Kamrath, a Houston architect and a former competitive tennis player who was in the audience, sent a telegram to friend James Van Allen, founder of the International Tennis Hall of Fame in Newport, R.I. "The opinion of most of us, including Rod Laver, is that we all got 'hustled' by Riggs last night," he wrote. "It is felt he may have bet a bundle on King at Las Vegas at 7-2 odds three weeks ago. It surely appeared he didn't play his best but made King look real good."

Years later, in the dining room at the Los Angeles Tennis Club, Gene Mako laid out his version of the alleged fix. Stabbing the air with a fork between bites of salad, Mako made his case like a crusty courtroom lawyer. "Listen, this was a man who was willing to do anything for money, *anything.*" Bobby had been bugging Billie Jean to play for three years. But each time, she refused. "Finally, Margaret [Court] agreed to play, and he beat her 2 and 1," Mako said, "and very shortly thereafter, Billie Jean agreed." Was it because Billie Jean thought she could win? Probably not. After all, Court was better than Billie Jean. In 1973, Court amassed a 102-6 win-loss record, winning 18 of 25 tournaments, including three majors (Australian, French and U.S. Open). And while Bobby was 55 years old at the time, he could still play tennis. He was the top-ranked male player for his age, Mako said. "I wonder," he asked rhetorically, "why did she agree when she refused him 10 times before?"

The reason is simple, he explained. Billie Jean knew in advance that she'd win. It was, in fact, part of the plan.

Eighty-three and still brawny at the time of the interview in 1999, the intense Mako seemed a walking encyclopaedia of sports trivia, able to rattle off obscure facts as if they were the most intimate details of his life. What probably happened, Mako said, is that Bobby went to Billie Jean's hotel room somewhere, and said, "I've had enough of this. Would you play me if you knew you were gonna win?" And she answered, "Do I understand what you're saying?" And Bobby said, "It's very simple. All I want is a return clause in the contract." All Bobby wanted was the money and the publicity, Mako theorized. The rest, as they say, is history. Billie Jean agreed. Then, Mako said, "Bye-bye."

Joe Fishbach, another longtime friend of Bobby's, saw it the same way. "Against Billie Jean, he definitely threw it," he said. "I played tennis with him hundreds of times and there were three parts of his game that he never lost. One of them was the serve. People don't realize it, but he had a great serve, one of the best kick serves around—and he never double faulted. Against Billie Jean King he threw in a slew of double faults. The second thing, he had a terrific lob, one of the best. But she'd come up to net, he'd throw up a short lob and she'd smash it away. But the strongest part of his game was he had wonderful anticipation. But they'd have a rally and he'd hit the ball and run one way and she'd hit the other way for a winner, which for me was impossible to believe. It was so obvious it was laughable. But to the average person it looked like he was off his game, he was nervous, he was sick."

So the natural question remained: Why wouldn't Bobby, the consummate showman, at least make it look competitive, forcing it to go five sets and thereby creating a big build-up for a rematch?

"You have to know Bobby," Mako said. "You have to know the ego of the person. He couldn't stand to throw a match without making it look ridiculous. But he did it so deliberately, so methodically, like a tailor fixing a tear in your shirt, that it was scary." He wanted people to know that he threw it.

"Now, obviously, if you're going to do that, doesn't somebody understand it?" Mako asked. "Doesn't somebody pick up on it? But when my friends, so-called tennis experts, didn't know, I was shocked. How could somebody watch a match like that and not know it. It was that obvious. And it killed me that no one else saw it. People didn't pick up on it."

In closing, Mako offered, "Now, Rosie Casals made a prediction before the match about the scores," referring to Howard Cosell's question to Casals during the televised broadcast. "She said that Billie Jean was going to win 6-4, 6-3, 6-3." It wasn't just close, Mako said, "it was the *exact* score of the match. Now how does that grab you?" What might be the odds of guessing the exact score in a best-of-five set match? Very long, to be sure.

But what about the rematch?

After the match, Mako speculated, Bobby went to Billie Jean to demand a rematch and she told him to get lost. Call it poetic justice, call it just desserts, whatever, Mako said, "For once, somebody double-crossed Bobby."

Bobby, of course, denied all accusations that he threw the match. In an interview just two months before his death in 1995, he said, "There are no secrets... I made the classic mistake of overestimating myself and underestimating Billie Jean King. Anytime you do that, you're in trouble." In fact, the rumors had become so widespread that in 1983 Bobby went on the television show *Lie Detector*, hosted by celebrity lawyer F. Lee Bailey, in which he answered the question while attached to a polygraph machine. He passed. Not only that, but to silence those who would believe the great hustler could get the better of a polygraph machine, the test was administered not once but three times, according to Dr. Edward Gelb, a renowned expert in the field who was a consultant on the program—once on-camera and twice in preparation for the show.

"I passed the test," said Bobby. "I proved I didn't let Billie Jean win. I did bet on the match and I bet on Bobby Riggs and I lost. The truth of the matter is I did not play a good match. It was an uncharacteristically bad match. It was the kind of match I should thrive on—a big money match. I'm betting on myself and if I win I get somebody else or a rematch with her. It was a bitter, bitter defeat."

Bobby went on to address the accusations of his old colleagues: "But some guys were mad. They felt I had disgraced them, that I had disgraced the cause of men, and especially older guys—the over-the-hill gang. Some even accused me of throwing the match. Throwing it! I had expected to make it an annual affair, by beating the women's champion for the next five years or so, until I got so old one of them could beat me. Losing cost me money. Sure, I made $1.5 million on the match—after endorsements, personal appearances and TV rights—but I might've made more."

Remember also that Bobby offered Billie Jean's associate Dick Butera another $5,000 bet to the $10,000 already on the line after losing the first set. This fact, pointed out Bobby's good friend Lornie Kuhle, makes no sense if Bobby planned to lose the match. "Bobby *hated* losing a bet," Kuhle said, "and I bet $15,000 for him of his money. That killed Bobby to lose that [$10,000]. That was a huge bet. Huge."

To longtime friend Jack Kramer, the idea that a man of Bobby's ego would go out and intentionally look bad before millions of people seemed ridiculous, no matter how much money he stood to gain. Besides, added Kramer, who grew up in Las Vegas and knew a thing or two about gambling, "the whole world was focused on Bobby Riggs before the match, and it is inconceivable to think that he could have laid off big money against himself without it being discovered. Besides, while there was a lot of money bet on the event, it was almost all man-to-man stuff—or rather man-to-woman. The professionals wouldn't touch a gimmick competition like this one. In fact, in Vegas all they permitted was courtesy betting for good customers, what is known there as a 'thin market.' Even if Bobby could have concealed huge bets, he had no place to lay them. So a betting coup makes no sense."

Kramer, too, heard Mako's theory that Bobby promised to lose the match in order to get Billie Jean to play, a plan that would have required Billie Jean King's collusion. When asked about it, Billie Jean laughed. She said she wished Casals had told her the score beforehand. It could have saved her a lot of nervousness.

"No," Kramer said, "Bobby got beat head-up because after he clobbered Margaret Court he figured he could beat any of the dames without training," Kramer said. "Here he completely miscalculated Billie Jean, who has always risen to the occasion... Billie Jean beat him fair and square." The fact of the matter is Bobby had more to gain by winning than he ever did by losing to Billie Jean, no matter what the motivation, whether money or publicity. "Bobby Riggs, the biggest ham in the world, gets his greatest audience—and purposely looks bad?" Kramer asked. "There's no way. If he had beaten Billie Jean, he could have kept the act going indefinitely. Next they would have had him play Chrissie [Evert] on clay."

About Bobby and his pre-match shenanigans, Kramer joked, "It was more than one woman who took care of Bobby Riggs in Houston." He simply blew it. He was cocky and overconfident. He didn't train or prepare well and his game collapsed, the same way it had in other important moments in his career. He only had himself to blame.

Whatever the case, Mako said, "What difference did it make?" Exaggerating for effect: "At the time, there were 5,000 people around who could beat either one."

While personally devastated by the defeat, Bobby may have achieved more in losing to Billie Jean than if he had won. After all, 48 million people in the United States and more than 90 million worldwide watched the contest. ABC grabbed a phenomenal 52 percent of the viewing audience, making the match one of the biggest TV events of its generation, a cultural landmark alongside the Beatles on *The Ed Sullivan Show*, the Kennedy assassination, the moon landing and the Watergate hearings. While it is arguable whether or not Riggs-King changed the history of the women's movement (after all, it was well underway by the time Bobby started mouthing off), the shear visibility of the match did much to affirm it.

"You wouldn't believe the number of people who have got to tell me exactly what they did, wherever they were, as they watched the match," Billie Jean said. Recalling a press conference at the *The* (Philadelphia) *Evening Bulletin* about two weeks after the match, Billie Jean said, "I must have met everybody in the [newspaper] building, and I talked to most of them—just small talk, nothing serious. I found out later, though, that the morning after the match with Bobby, several of the women there had stormed into their bosses' offices, and demanded raises on the spot. I couldn't believe it."

More important, the match brought tennis to millions of people never before exposed to the game, and it did it in a way that made the game fun, helping erase its image as a stodgy pastime for the rich. The arrival of "open" tennis in 1968 created a new tennis boom as prize money and promotion drew in expanded advertising, television coverage, sponsorships, and a crop of marketable star players. The game also attracted legions of new fans and players. The Riggs-King match turned that boom into an explosion.

In 1960, the number of tennis players in the United States was put at slightly over five and a half million. In 1970, that number had jumped to 10 million, and by 1975, two years after the Riggs-King match, the number swelled to nearly 20 million players. Similarly, in 1960, there were fewer than 50 indoor tennis facilities in the United States. By 1973, the number had multiplied to over 600, and by 1977 increased to over 1,500 indoor clubs.

After the Riggs-King match, tennis was suddenly the "in" sport, surpassing golf in popularity to both play and watch. Demand for equipment and court time reached an all-time high. In 1976, Americans spent $555 million on tennis balls and equipment, up 33 percent from the $418 million spent in 1974. One giddy manufacturer at the time estimated it would be 10 years before the industry could catch up with demand for racquets and balls. And even with an average of 11,000 new tennis courts being built each year in the United States during the boom, people still could not find an empty court.

A typical example was Denver, Colorado. By 1974, the city boasted 112 public courts, twice the number it had five years before. In 1972, the city had only nine indoor tennis courts. By 1974, it had 45. According to Don Carleton, a representative for Wilson Sporting Goods at the time, demand for tennis equipment jumped 10 times since 1968, and at Cherry Creek High School, the boys' tennis team drew more prospects than the football team.

In 1971, of the total time allotted on television to sports by the three major networks, only 2 percent went to tennis. By 1976, that figure jumped to 13 percent, with some 70 tournaments covered. In terms of broadcast hours, the 107 hours of tennis televised that year put it fourth behind basketball (112 hours), baseball (157 hours), and football (332 hours).

The boom also brought about the game's most significant democratization since the widespread construction of public and municipal courts at the turn of the century. Dispelling the notion tennis was the domain of country club snobs, the results of one survey estimated that nearly half of tennis households earned less than $20,000 annually, and almost 30 percent of husbands in these households never went to college.

The single largest group drawn to tennis was women, and in the wake of the Riggs-King match the game that drew the most interest was mixed doubles. Billie Jean's victory had made tennis the great equalizer, and on courts across the country the hopes of the women's movement were being played out. Of course, there was more to it than that. Tennis was one of the few sports in which men and women competed on the same field of play. Sociability had as much to do with the growth in mixed doubles' popularity as competitiveness, a point made in a 1976 *Time* magazine cover story on the subject. "American men and women pursue on the tennis court such things as health and ego reinforcement, true love and sexual aggression, social status and a special vision of the good life." Said one woman quoted in the article, "Let's face it, I took up tennis so we'd be invited to the Saturday parties at the club." By the mid-1970s, tennis clubs had replaced discotheques as preferred pick-up joints and tennis instructors found themselves turned from simple teaching pros into "a combined guru, shrink, social worker, friend and sounding board."

This public interest in mixed doubles also had a direct effect on the professional sport. Though it had long been part of the game, a lack of interest in mixed doubles by fans had made it something of a neglected stepchild. Between 1975 and 1976, however, the U.S. Open increased the prize money in mixed doubles by more than 300 percent, and television took a freshly invigorated interest in such matches.

The flood of women who took up the sport following the Riggs-King match also helped secure the boom's financial viability. Indoor clubs that once struggled to survive as courts laid empty all day were now booked solid, mostly by women—housewives looking for some good exercise and a reason to get out of the house for a couple of hours. "I was a tennis pro at an indoor facility in Houston, Texas," recalled Jason Morton, who was also the chair umpire that night in the Astrodome, "and my business jumped 20 to 25 percent after that match, particularly with women. The sport exploded among women. My club, at midday, was all women."

At the same time, teaching pros who before worked part-time or at summer camps could now work year-round and actually make a decent living. Face it, said Doug Dean, a teaching pro and friend of Bobby's, "he helped pave the way for professional tennis, and his match with Billie Jean gave half-assed guys like me jobs."

Years later, as he looked back on his life and the match with Billie Jean, Bobby could say he was glad to be part of it. "That was the biggest thing to happen in tennis in 10 or 15 years. Women got more equal prize money. Hey, tennis just took off and that was one of the big catalysts, the big boom in tennis. It was satisfying to be the person involved in that."

Bobby once joked about the women playing on the pro tour, "They owe me a piece of their checks."

Though he figured he was washed up, Bobby discovered he could make a living just being himself. Losing wasn't so bad, after all.

22

The Happy Hustler

1973-1983

The day after the debacle in the Astrodome, Gardnar Mulloy went up to Bobby's suite in Houston to see how his old friend was doing. This time, nobody was there. For once, Bobby was alone.

"Where are all your friends, Bobby?" Mulloy asked.

"Gar, I really blew it, didn't I?" Bobby said. Mulloy didn't need to say anything. He was at the match and saw for himself how badly Bobby played against Billie Jean King. He had seen Bobby running and panting, gasping for breath. He could tell Bobby had tried, but just didn't have anything to give. He couldn't win.

"But," Bobby said, "luckily I have a contract that if I lose, I have a rematch... I'll get her next time."

There would, however, be no rematch. At the post-match press conference, Billie Jean vowed never to play Bobby again, saying one match was all history needed. She later repeated her pledge at promoter Jerry Perenchio's post-match party. It was a bitter pill for Bobby, and for years he would claim that Billie Jean double-crossed him.

"I'm very disappointed in Billie Jean," said Bobby in 1982. We played such a great match and when I lost I jumped over the net and congratulated her like a real gentleman. I didn't even mention we had an ironclad return-match clause in our contract. In fact, I let Billie Jean enjoy herself for two weeks and then I mentioned it to her and she said, 'You can take that return-match clause and you know what you can do with it'."

In fact, there was no rematch clause. "That was Bobby's wishful thinking," Perenchio said. What he and Bobby signed was a standard contract for the promotion of the Riggs-King match and future matches, *if* there were future matches. Bobby blew any possibility of perpetuating it beyond Riggs-King by losing to Billie Jean, Perenchio explained.

Bobby tried challenging other top female players in singles, but no one was interested, which led him to accuse Billie Jean of leading a boycott against him. With his characteristic mixture of grandiosity and self-pity, he said, "After she beat me, we offered any other woman $1 million to play me. And you know what happened? She called up all the top girls at that time—Chrissy Evert, Evonne Goolagong, Nancy Richey—and said, 'Look, Mr. Riggs has offered me a million dollars for a rematch.' Then she said to those girls, 'That guy is so tough. He's gonna play better next time. So help the women's cause. Don't anybody else play him. Let's freeze him out.'... A conspiracy was formed to keep me from earning a living in my invention of mixed-singles tennis."

On this point, Perenchio claimed Bobby was paranoid. "Billie Jean King said she wouldn't play him again. She knew it was over, [but] he just kept trying and trying to rekindle the flame," Perenchio said. "Nobody wanted it."

Bobby, however, was unwilling to let it go. "For years, he'd try and get it going again," Perenchio said. He would call up and say, "Now I'll play..." and Perenchio would interrupt him and say, "Bobby, it's not the same. It just doesn't mean anything now. You got to get it. You were able to capture a moment in the history of America with the women's lib movement and that was what you were riding on and the wave has crested. It's over. Nobody gives a shit anymore. It doesn't mean the same to say that you're a chauvinist pig."

The weeks and months after Riggs-King were not easy for Bobby. Not only had his grand plans come to a screeching halt, he had suddenly become an instant has-been. He was the most-recognized loser in sports. The public ridiculed him, his old friends felt he had disgraced them, and many figured he had thrown the match.

Bobby "went into a depression, really, for about six months," friend Lornie Kuhle said. He became quiet and morose, and he started to drink more than he should. Although not a chronic drinker (he sometimes went months between drinks), he binged. There was never just one beer, but four, five, or more. While generally Bobby was gentle, gracious, even fawning in social situations, when he drank he became loud, crude, and obnoxious. One friend of Bobby's recalled an evening at Caesar's Palace Casino in Las Vegas when he and Bobby were waiting for someone. Bobby ordered a beer to pass the time. Forty-five minutes and three or four beers later, Bobby had lost all patience.

"Where is this sonuvabitch?" he demanded. He walked over to a house phone, picked it up, and got hold of the guy, who he then proceeded to excoriate at the top of his lungs. "YOU'VE GOT SOME BALLS MAKING ME SIT AND WAIT... I DON'T CARE WHAT YOUR EXCUSE IS... I'LL TELL YOU WHAT... LOSE MY NUMBER... FOREVER!!!" By the time he was done, the casino floor fell silent. Bobby slammed down the phone and stormed out, oblivious to the hundreds of eyes now focused on him.

Despite his personal torment, Bobby kept up his public persona as the good-natured wise-guy and ageless pixie. He also kept up a busy assortment of commitments made during the pre-match hoopla. A couple of weeks after the match, Bobby traveled to Lake Havasu, Arizona to fulfill his promise to jump off a bridge if he lost. London Bridge, the ancient London landmark and object of the famous children's rhyme, had incongruously been moved to the middle of the Arizona desert and reconstructed as a tourist attraction. In 1971, developer Robert McCulloch, a friend and golfing buddy of Bobby's, paid $2.5 million for the centuries-old relic to the British government, which had planned to tear it down and replace it because it was sinking under its own weight into the bed of the Thames River. As a way of drawing attention to his resort development, McCulloch hired a corps of engineers to take the structure apart brick-by-brick, ship it in pieces, and reconstruct it over a manmade lagoon.

True to his word, Bobby arrived at the bridge, where he was met by a throng of excited fans along with the local sheriff and his deputies.

"Bobby Riggs, there's no way we're going to let you jump off this bridge," the sheriff informed Bobby, explaining that the bridge was 55 feet high and the water below only a foot and a half deep, making it likely Bobby would be killed or seriously hurt.

"Now if I did happen to get away with it, there would be other people trying to jump off the bridge and they would be hurt, perhaps killed, and they would have all kinds of suits on their hands," Bobby recalled. "So they thought it would be a very bad thing for Lake Havasu City." So as a compromise, Bobby floated under the bridge in an inner tube to the cheers of the crowd.

Though he figured he was washed up, Bobby soon discovered a new career. He found he could make a living by being himself. He could play celebrity tennis exhibitions, do his goofy challenges, travel the country, and hustle wherever with whomever over whatever came his way. After all, this was an age in which mass media and the cult of personality made being celebrity an end in itself. Losing, it turned out, wasn't all that bad.

Bobby was hired as tennis director and casino host at the swank Tropicana Hotel and Casino in Las Vegas, where not long after his match with Billie Jean King he played against the sequined king of Las Vegas, singer Liberace, in an exhibition before several thousand people.

As recalled by friend Lornie Kuhle, "Liberace showed up in rhinestone-studded hot pants, but he just stood around the court while a pro he hired hit for him. The pro would be running around and Liberace stood behind him, hamming it up with the audience."

Suddenly, Bobby had more demand on his time than ever. Nabisco, makers of the Sugar Daddy lollipop, were so impressed by Bobby's devotion to their product that they made him something of a permanent spokesman for the candy. His defiance of ABC Sports executive Roone Arledge's order that he not wear the Sugar Daddy jacket on court in his match against Billie Jean went beyond the call of duty. "It didn't do him any good to leave that thing on in that damned heat," said Edward "Ned" Bjornson, a former Nabisco executive. Not only that, but it made an enemy out of Arledge. As a result, Bjornson said, "We kept on with him long after he lost and it looked like he wouldn't be of any value."

In the long run, it worked out for both. Said Bjornson: "Actually, he was probably more valuable to us business-wise later on than he was before [the match]. We couldn't have afforded Michael Jordan or anybody like that, but we could afford Bobby Riggs. And he had a natural affinity for the product line. It became a sort of trademark for him. It worked out well for him, too."

Paid on an event-by-event basis, Bobby earned between $40,000 and $50,000 a year from Nabisco. "It was done on a piecemeal basis on a peanuts budget and was a way to get a little exposure for the product... But we got our money's worth. We never had written contracts with him. We just paid him by the event, or every now and then we decided it was time to give Bobby some money. He trusted us. But there's no question it helped. We could get Bobby to go anywhere, anytime. He'd drop other things. We tried to set things up for him that he enjoyed. He'd get to know our customers real well. He'd make the sales calls, he'd play golf with anybody and, if you insisted, he would try not to hustle. He'd go to state fairs or ride in parades. He was always good-natured about it, and he was never an embarrassment."

In 1975, Nabisco reported that sales of Sugar Daddy increased 47 percent during the previous year, an increase due in no small part to Bobby. "The Nabisco top brass loved him," Bjornson said. "He was a good guy, a loyal guy. Once you took him under your wing, he'd be a friend for life."

Of course, Bjornson admitted, "it could have backfired... There was always a risk that he might hustle a good customer too much," but knowing this, "we wouldn't put him with any customer who couldn't afford to lose money to him. They just knew they were going to get hustled, and it was always done with a smile."

At the time, Nabisco had another spokesman promoting another product, Chuckles jelly candies. Robert Craig Knievel was a former insurance salesman, petty thief, and con man. He got his start as a motorcycle daredevil in 1965, when he tried attracting attention to his motorcycle dealership by jumping a motorcycle off a ramp to clear a set of snake- and cougar-filled boxes laid end to end. He landed short, however, shattering the box full of rattlesnakes and scattering the slithering contents as well as the spectators. From there he took his show on the road, changing his name to Evel (a nickname first given to him by a prison guard, which he then changed by taking out the 'i' and replacing it with an 'e'). By 1973, he was as famous for his numerous broken bones and life-threatening injuries as he was for his death-defying jumps over cars, buses, and fountains.

Like Bobby, Knievel was a pop culture phenomenon. He was also a man who, like Bobby, enjoyed gambling and liked to view himself as a buccaneer. Beyond that, however, Knievel could not have been more different than Bobby in personality and temperament.

There was nothing sweet or comic about Knievel. He was a rough, surly, hard-drinking man with a menacing demeanor and explosive temper. In 1977, an unflattering book about Knievel written by his former publicist so enraged Knievel that he beat the man with a baseball bat, breaking both the man's arms. For that, Knievel spent more than five months in jail. Unrepentant, he emerged to say, "I should have killed the dirty little bastard."

"Evel was not a good person," said Bjornson "He'd beat up people... [He] was very difficult... You couldn't take him out with customers. He was hostile. If you rate Bobby at, say, 100, Evel was probably 25. And he cost us more money and more aggravation."

In September 1974, as Knievel prepared for his most spectacular stunt, a jump over the Snake River Canyon in Idaho on a custom-made, rocket-powered cycle, Nabisco arranged for Knievel to invite Bobby to a celebrity golf tournament he hosted in his hometown of Butte, Montana. The event was seen as a good way to promote the canyon jump and build up good will for their mutual sponsor. Having Bobby attend would also help increase interest and attendance at the tournament, as well as hype Knievel's preparations for the Snake River gig. Knievel sent one of his two Learjets to Las Vegas to pick up Bobby and his entourage, and even had them stay at his mansion.

Over the course of the weekend, Bobby and Knievel hung out together, mugged it up for the media, and, accompanied by a police escort, bar-hopped around Butte, making like they were best buddies. Given the situation and their disparate personalities, perhaps it was inevitable that tension would develop between the two. Recalled Don Rhodes, a friend and assistant to Bobby at the time, "You had two positives that are clashing. Bobby was taking away from Evel's spotlight and Evel from Bobby's, and so there

Evel Knievel and Bobby are all smiles at an impromptu press conference to announce their $25,000 bet on whether Bobby could ride a motorcycle from Las Vegas to Twin Falls, Idaho in three days.

was a bit of a friction going on between the two of them." This likelihood became a certainty when Bobby hustled Knievel for $5,000 on the golf course.

On the day he was to leave, Bobby, Knievel, and a group of others were eating breakfast at a restaurant on the way to the airport. "We were all sitting at the table eating and Knievel glared at Bobby," remembered Rhodes.

"You know, cocksucker, you took me for a lot of money," Knievel snarled. Suddenly all of the niceties the two had

maintained over the weekend in their public appearances
evaporated. Knievel was furious, Rhodes recalled. "And I'm
thinking what's this guy gonna do now?"

"I want my money back," Knievel said.

Bobby, perplexed and clearly nervous, started stammering,
"Well, you know… I, well, I don't know. What do you want? Do
you want to play dominoes? We could play backgammon, or
you know…"

"No, no," Knievel said, his eyes narrowing. "I'm not going to
play your games, you goddamn hustler."

With a sense of desperation, Rhodes spoke up: "Why don't
you guys have a motorcycle race?"

"And boom," Rhodes said, "Evel turned around to me and
said, 'What's that?'"

"Yeah, you know, a race, where you go from one place to
another and you give Bobby a lead."

This got Bobby thinking, and after a moment he excitedly said,
"Yeah, I'll tell you what. Why don't we go back to Vegas. I'll drive
a motorcycle from the Tropicana to the Snake River Canyon, where
you're gonna jump. Now, how fast do you think I could do it?"

Knievel thought for a moment, then said, "I'll give you three
days to do it." The two negotiated the terms and the stakes for a
minute longer, and then one of the group scribbled out on a piece
of paper: "Evel Knievel bets Bobby Riggs that he cannot ride a
Harley Davidson under 200cc from Las Vegas to Twin Falls, Idaho,
by 2 p.m. Twin Falls, Idaho, time Sunday, September 8, 1974 [the
scheduled time of Knievel's canyon jump]. If Bobby Riggs does,
he wins $25,000. If he does not, he pays $25,000 to Evel Knievel."

Suddenly, everything was okay. The two seemed best buddies
again, and Knievel gave Bobby a warm bon voyage back to Las
Vegas. The beauty of it was, no matter who won the bet, it could
be promoted to the hilt, making it a winning situation for both.
Knievel arranged with Harley Davidson to set Bobby up with a
motorcycle. Time was short, however. Bobby had just two days
to get the motorcycle and make preparations before leaving for
the 650-mile trip. Also, Bobby had never ridden a motorcycle

before. "Ah, don't worry," Bobby assured. "I'll learn how to do it."

Though one of the century's greatest athletes, Bobby was perhaps one of the world's worst drivers, which might be why he generally preferred to have others drive him around. When he did get behind the wheel, however, it was white-knuckle time, and as a driver he was compared to the clueless Mr. Magoo—oblivious to all hazards and obstacles.

Said Rhodes, "It amazes me that I never heard about him getting in a car accident. I mean, I'd be driving along and he'd grab the wheel and he'd yank it."

"Get in there," Bobby would say. "Move faster… slow down…hit those brakes."

"When you were in any kind of traffic," Rhodes said, "the guy was miserable to be with."

One time, recalled Bobby's friend and attorney Robert Johnson, Bobby was driving from his home near San Diego in Leucadia to La Costa to play golf. On the highway exit ramp Bobby failed to notice a truck bearing down next to him and, before he knew it, he was forced off the road and into a ditch. The car ended up on its side. Unhurt and unfazed, Bobby climbed out, dusted himself off, and headed for the nearest Lincoln Continental dealership. After making two calls—one to a Lincoln dealership in San Diego and another to a dealership in Las Vegas (just to make sure he was getting the best price)—he bought a new car on the spot and drove to La Costa to make his tee time, abandoning the wreck.

When Bobby was driving, said his first wife Kay, "People were always giving him the finger."

The Harley Davidson people showed up at Bobby's door with a 175cc motorcycle—legal for highway use, but under-powered and uncomfortable for long trips. Nonetheless, Bobby looked tiny beside the hulking machine, and as he made his first tentative maneuvers in an empty Las Vegas parking lot, Rhodes thought to himself, "Oh my god, what I have done. I've suggested something that's going to get Bobby killed."

After testing for his motorcycle driver's license ("I almost failed it," Bobby said. "I couldn't do figure eights very well."), a leather-clad Bobby hopped aboard his motorized steed, waved good-bye to a crowd of well-wishers gathered in the parking lot of the Tropicana Hotel that included fans, reporters, celebrities, and Vegas showgirls, and headed north toward Salt Lake City. Behind him followed his entourage in a motor home filled with fried chicken, ham and cheese sandwiches, and 24 cases of soda pop.

From the beginning, however, Bobby had problems. Several times he was nearly blown over by passing trucks. At the first gas station Bobby pulled into, he turned the throttle the wrong way, sending the bike lurching forward, just missing one of the pumps. "The gas attendants thought I was a daredevil," Bobby told a reporter. "I thought I was a goner." Moreover, the long hours and heavy vibrations from the road cramped Bobby's stomach.

After more than seven hours of riding, Bobby pulled into Salt Lake City just as darkness fell. His hands were so cramped his fingers had to be pried off the handlebars. He needed to be helped off the motorcycle. "I ache all over and probably won't be able to get up in the morning," Bobby told a waiting reporter. "My arms, my legs, my rear end, my whole body… I ache all over. I think Evel Knievel may have hustled me. This is a lot rougher than I thought it would be. But I'm gonna make it for sure. I'm gonna be there in time for him to take out his checkbook and hand me $25,000."

After a long, hot tub and a good night's rest, Bobby was up the next morning and ready to go. Having been alerted to Bobby's presence overnight, the Salt Lake City Police Department had a reception waiting for him.

"We walk out through the front of the hotel," recalled Rhodes, "and there must have been twenty or thirty police officers standing at attention beside their motorcycles, all of them lined up side-by-side, like a gauntlet. Bobby had to walk down between them. He had no idea this was going to happen, but everybody came up to him wanting to shake his hand and the media was filming and suddenly he was 'on' again. He works his way to the end of this line of police officers and there's his motorcycle. Overnight, somebody had cleaned it up and buffed it to a shine, and Bobby gets on and says a few words into the microphone and off he goes."

As Bobby rode off, the police officers jumped on their motorcycles. One by one, they pulled up behind Bobby, escorting him to the city limits, creating a diamond formation with Bobby in the lead and the motor home at the end. Along empty early-morning city streets, the parade worked its way through town, taking up all lanes of traffic with lights on and sirens blaring. Just before reaching the city limits, and after turning onto the highway, the formation broke off, all except for two motorcycles, which came roaring up behind Bobby. Passing him on either side, the officers stood on their seats and saluted as they passed. They then hopped down and disappeared in a roar.

Another long day took Bobby to Boise and another media reception. Though a detour more than 100 miles west of Twin Falls, Boise was a stop Bobby and Knievel agreed to in order to take advantage of the publicity. With just three hours left between him and Twin Falls, Bobby knew the $25,000 was his. The next day, just outside Twin Falls, Bobby passed a truck on the side of the road with a banner attached to it: "Hey Bobby, Billie Jean would have been there by now." By the time Bobby reached the rim of the Snake River Canyon, the countdown for Knievel's leap into the history books was well under way. Joined by nearly 30,000 people at the site and millions more watching on television, Bobby watched as Knievel blasted off the gigantic ramp toward the opposite side of the canyon some 1,500 feet away. But the drogue chute designed to bring Knievel safely back to earth inadvertently deployed on take-off. The rocket never made it as far as midway across, and as it floated beneath the canyon rim toward the rocks below, Bobby said, "Oh, my god! Evel is gone and my $25,000 with him." But Knievel survived, bruised, bloodied, and discredited—and paid up.

Like any proposition artist, Bobby thrived on these challenges. He carefully calculated the edge he needed to win, but at the same time made it seem his opponent had an even chance. Most important, he made it entertaining, creating the perfect publicity stunt. Following his loss to Billie Jean, Bobby devised a number of high-profile ventures to help keep his competitive juices flowing and satisfy his need to stay in the spotlight. Among them was an exhibition one-mile run against world-class distance runner Jim Ryun in Ft. Lauderdale in February 1974, a race in which Bobby got a half-mile head start. In December 1975, there was a 50-mile race against Australian long-distance runner Bill Emmerton across Death Valley in which Bobby got a 25-mile handicap. And in July 1984, Bobby competed against top female golfer Marilynn Smith in a round of golf in which Bobby got a chance to throw the ball on the green once each hole. In each case, Bobby won.

His biggest challenge, however—getting Billie Jean back on court for a rematch—went unfulfilled. But he never gave up trying. He hounded Billie Jean whenever he got the chance. Confronting her in 1983, he asked her, "Come on, you mean for $3 million apiece you wouldn't play an hour?"

"That's right," Billie Jean said.

Unable to let the gimmick die, however, Bobby did manage to put together a number of mixed-sex doubles challenges against other top female players, including a 1981 doubles match with partner Pancho Segura against female professionals Marita Redondo and Kate Latham (in which Bobby hired an actor to play a witch doctor in a grass skirt, feathered headress, and face paint to go on court before the match to cast a voodoo curse on his opponents); a 1982 "Love Match" with Pancho Segura against University of Southern California players Ana Mara Fernandez and Kelly Henry; and a Mother's Day challenge on the tenth anniversary of the Riggs-Court match in 1983 featuring Bobby and former Australian professional Mal Anderson against female professionals Wendy Turnbull and Rosie Casals. Bobby and Anderson took home the $50,000 winners' share, with $25,000 going to Turnbull and Casals.

In his last shot at the big time, Bobby teamed up with retired professional Vitas Gerulaitis in 1985 to take on the world's No. 1 female doubles team of Martina Navratilova and Pam Shriver in a $500,000 challenge match in Atlantic City. At 67, Bobby was older than the combined ages of Navratilova and Shriver—and it showed. Noted *Vogue* magazine: "Basically, Riggs amounted to a 67-year-old ball-and-chain shackled to the ankle of Gerulaitis. Riggs couldn't serve, couldn't return serves, couldn't hit overheads with any amount of force." Despite losing in straight sets, 6-2, 6-3, 6-4, Bobby pocketed $100,000.

Ever the opportunist, Bobby continued looking for ways to turn circumstance into cash. One of the most unusual presented itself in 1976 when he was still living at Newport Beach, California. While sitting with some friends on the veranda at the nearby John Wayne Tennis Club, Bobby noticed a tall, broad-shouldered woman practicing below.

"Who's that down there playing?" Bobby asked.

He was told she was a new member at the club, that she was a doctor who and had just moved her practice to Orange County from New York. Bobby continued to watch.

"Wow!" Bobby exclaimed as the woman smacked a ball into the corner.

Bobby became intrigued. Not only was the woman tall and athletic, she played aggressively, with a powerful serve and big groundstrokes.

"Look at that," Bobby said a minute later. "That's a killer instinct." But there was something else about her, something vaguely familiar. He couldn't put his finger on it, and he returned to his conversation.

A moment later, the woman batted away another ball.

"Hey, look at that!" Bobby said again. Determined to learn who it was, he waddled down to get a closer look, walking right onto the court and stopping play. He squinted through his glasses and, after a moment, broke out into a big smile.

"Oh my God. It's Dick!" Bobby said. "I'd know that backhand anywhere." Standing before him was Dr. Richard Raskind, the Yale-trained ophthalmologist Bobby used to play when he lived on Long Island at Plandome. Only now, "he" was a she. In August 1975, Raskind had sex reassignment surgery and became Renée Richards, then moved to Southern California, hoping for a fresh start in life.

"The guys said that you had the operation and moved out here," Bobby said, "but I didn't know where you were." Unfazed by his friend's new identity, Bobby gave Richards a big hug and insisted she join him and his friends to catch up old times.

"So we had a big greeting, and that was a wonderful reunion," Richards recalled. "Then he says, 'C'mon, Renée, we got to go down to San Vicente [Resort in Ramona, where Bobby played Margaret Court].' So I said, 'What's in San Vicente?' He said there's a club down there. 'It's not that far from San Diego. We'll go down there and play a practice match with these guys.'" Of course, by "practice match," Bobby meant money would be involved.

"Now, these guys bet for a lot of money," Richards recalled Bobby saying. "A lot of money."

"Well, I didn't care. I had just moved there. I didn't know anything. I was just happy for the friendship and to have someone to play with."

"This is Renée Richards," Bobby said to their opponents when they arrived. "She's a friend of mine."

Of course, recalled Richards, "They didn't know who I was. So they looked at me. I was tall. I wasn't on the tour or anything, and they were very skeptical."

"Well, what do you want to play for?" one of the men asked.

"Let's play $1,000 a corner," Bobby said ($1,000 per person).

"A thousand a corner?" the man said, a bit taken aback. "Let me see her hit a few first."

Bobby took Richards aside. "Look, these guys want to bet," he said, "but they want to see you hit a few. So hit a few, but not too good."

"So I hit a few," Richards recalled, "but not too good."

Agreeing to the wager, the foursome took the court. After winning, Bobby collected the money, and after handing Richards her share he told her, "Renée, get in the car."

"I didn't know any better," Richards said. "I just got in the car. I thought we were going to have drinks or something. But he drove out of there so fast you'd think the posse was after us."

Not long afterward, at a local tournament in La Jolla, another former acquaintance of Raskind's recognized her and tipped off a San Diego television sportscaster, who broke the story. Her secret out, the 41-year-old Richards found herself in the middle of a media furor, especially when she decided to try and play on the professional women's tour. Both the Women's Tennis Association and the USTA opposed her eligibility, as did most of the players, who felt that Richards' size (6-foot-2), strength, and experience (playing competitively against men) gave her an unfair advantage.

In the first tournament Richards entered in August 1976, all but seven of the 32 players entered dropped out, and the WTA withdrew sanctioning of the tournament. Nevertheless, because of public curiosity about Richards, the tournament drew a national television audience and massive publicity. The irony of the situation was lost on the majority of the players and the WTA, which continued to lobby for a more equitable share of the prize money. But it was not lost on Billie Jean King. She was about the only top female player to welcome Richards. She made a point of talking with Richards and even requested to play in a tournament in which Richards had entered.

Blackballed by the tour, shunned by players, treated like a freak by the public, and nearly broke, Richards persevered. When the USTA denied Richards admission to the U.S. Open, she sued. Offered $250,000 to play against Bobby in an exhibition at Caesar's Palace, Richards refused, afraid that participation in such a spectacle might hurt her chances of getting on the tour, even though she desperately needed the money. "This has been the most difficult year that I've spent in my life," she told a newspaper reporter at the time. "It's been brutal, absolutely brutal—from a financial standpoint, from an emotional standpoint, in every way."

A court order in 1977 forced the tour to admit Richards. By then, she had accumulated enough losses to alleviate fears she would dominate the tour. "It took them a while to understand that I wasn't a giant killer, that there weren't going to be five hundred people like me coming along to overwhelm women's tennis," she said.

That May, Richards also accepted an invitation to play in a paid exhibition with Bobby in Baltimore. She needed the money. Before 1,700 people in the Baltimore Civic Center, Richards and

Bobby lost to the team of Gardnar Mulloy and Billie Jean King, 6-1, 6-4, in just 42 minutes. According to Mulloy, who co-promoted the match, Billie Jean agreed to play on the condition she did not have to play with Bobby.

As it turned out, it would be the closest Bobby would come to getting a rematch against Billie Jean. Bobby lost to Richards in two more exhibitions that summer before modest-size audiences in London, Ontario. Richards played a couple of years more on the tour before returning to her medical practice and eventually moving back to New York.

Though he never got a singles rematch against Billie Jean, these were sweet days for Bobby: a life on the road, no long-term commitments, something new, something different every day. He was also a worldwide celebrity. He became a regular on television talk shows, appearing on Johnny Carson, Mike Douglas, Merv Griffin, with cameos in episodes of the *The Odd Couple* (playing Ping Pong against Billie Jean King), *MacMillan and Wife*, *Get Christy Love* (with Rosemary Casals), *What's My Line*, and *Love, American Style* (also with Casals). He got a bit part in the 1979 movie *Racquet* with Bert Convoy and Phil Silvers in which he played (appropriately enough) a debauched tennis pro. The movie was a magnificent flop.

In 1975, Bobby was named one of the country's "most beautiful men" by a group of women calling themselves Man Watchers Inc., alongside Hollywood stars Burt Reynolds, Al Pacino, Robert Redford, and Alan Alda. Hotels asked him to be their tennis director; conventions invited him to put on exhibitions; colleges wanted him to give speeches. Whatever the event, Bobby made sure he wore his Sugar Daddy jacket, handing out fistfuls of the candy wherever he went.

"I play 40 to 50 of these exhibitions each year now," Bobby said in 1978. "I play a lot of club pros, young girls, mayors, politicians, celebrities, disc jockeys, columnists. I'm doing exhibitions, grand openings, clinics about 50 weeks out of the year. I enjoy it. What else would I do? My kids are grown. I'm single. I like to travel places, experience lots of things."

And Bobby was good at what he did. A natural showman, he could entertain crowds with his banter for hours. Always the first to show up and the last to leave, the biggest complaint about Bobby was getting him to stop. A scheduled 30-minute talk would run into an hour and a half. Bobby figured if people were paying for him to appear, he was going to give them their money's worth, and refused to leave until he signed the last autograph.

"I make about $300,000 a year, I guess" Bobby said in 1978. "If there's any money in it, I get involved. For example, they're opening a new Sheraton Hotel in Kalamazoo. So I will go there and play a little tennis, sign autographs and go to a cocktail party and be a personality. For that, I get from $2,500 to $5,000 for one day. Then I'll go to Dubuque, Iowa, to open a shopping mall. I'll play table tennis or badminton or shoot free throws or whatever. Everybody in town can get to challenge me."

At times, his family despaired over Bobby's antics. The tennis strip-teases, the oddball challenges, the exhibitions while leashed to animals ("The worst partner I ever had was a donkey," Bobby said. "Most stubborn thing… I just couldn't move it."), all of it made him a clown in the eyes of the public, eclipsing his legacy as a true champion. But Bobby didn't care. He knew what he had done. "Do I expect people to remember that I won Wimbledon in 1939?" he explained. "The things I can do today mean much more to me than being remembered for what I did 40 years ago. I don't want to rest on yesterday's laurels." Besides, he was having the time of his life.

Though his genius for self-promotion served him well, Bobby had a knack for getting involved in some very stupid business deals. In fact, the great hustler was prone to be hustled. Used to sealing a deal on a handshake, Bobby was not one to read a contract before signing. And because he took people at their word, he was a sucker for a good sales pitch. As a result, he committed himself to deals in areas in which he had no business, such as his ill-fated attempt at an all-star baseball series after the war. Restaurants, dairy cows, tennis court equipment, bowling alleys, real estate—his family winced every time they learned of Bobby's investments.

Even if he did have an attorney or accountant review a deal, once sold on the idea Bobby was nearly impossible to dissuade.

"Bobby was a high-maintenance client," recalled attorney Robert Johnson. "As good as he was at handicapping sporting events and gambling matters, he was a little bit loosey-goosey on some of the things that he would bite for. He invested some money in restaurants from time to time. He would go for a promotion in a place like Amelia Island, Florida, and end up with a condominium there. I'd say to him, 'Why are you getting involved with that stuff? You're going there for a promotion, they're paying you a fee to be there and you end up buying a $90,000 condominium.' And the market then was so bad; this was the mid-eighties. He had a condominium there, he had one in Jacksonville, he had one at Hunter's Run near Palm Beach." Part of Bobby's problem, explained Johnson, was that he simply hated to say no.

Bobby's older brother John told Bobby's son Bill that when it came to business matters, Bobby "had a propensity to fuck things up."

Not surprisingly, throughout his life Bobby needed someone to act as a best friend and manager, someone willing to keep him company, look after him, keep him organized, and, most of all, someone he could trust, someone without an agenda of his or her own. When Bobby was younger, his brother John filled this role. Later, his wife Kay filled the part.

Bobby was accompanied much of the time by Lornie Kuhle. Over the years, Kuhle became Bobby's best friend, protégé, and partner in crime. In many ways, Kuhle was closer to Bobby than his own children. Kindred spirits, Kuhle loved to gamble and compete. Easygoing and humorous, he also had the time, desire, and resources to be with Bobby, and unlike Bobby's children, he had no other expectations. Over the years, Kuhle became an all-purpose personal secretary, road manager, and errand boy. "He's like a son to me," Bobby said. "And one of my best disciples."

Though Bobby was a loner, a man who insisted on living life on his own terms, he also "had a real need for companionship," recalled longtime friend Nancy Bailey. "He just hated to be alone.

Just dreaded the idea of it." For a man who spent most of his life on the road, it was people such as these who kept Bobby grounded.

While travelling around the country, Bobby continued to hustle at various events. He kept an address book organized alphabetically, not by name, but by city, and in it he listed his various contacts for golf, poker, backgammon, and tennis. Beside each name, he scribbled notes indicating the person's game of choice and particular vulnerability. Many of them were regular losers, patsies who simply enjoyed playing with Bobby and didn't mind being hustled. Bobby called it his "celebrity tax." After a victim wrote out his check, Bobby might wave it around as though he had captured the enemy's battle flag, saying, "This guy paid his annual dues again—tennis and backgammon—I get him every time."

These were players "who existed to lose," recalled Bobby's friend Doug Dean. "But what else are you gonna do? It was more fun complaining about losing to him than not to play with him at all."

Bobby was not above being hustled himself. "I just lost recently to a guy in Monte Carlo," Bobby confessed in 1978. "A guy was playing tennis, and I was looking at him and somebody says, 'You think you can beat that little guy?'

"I says, 'Yeah.' He says, 'You give him two games?' I says, 'Yeah." He says, 'We'll bet you on it. How much?' I says, 'Whatever you want, $1,000, $2,000.' Pretty soon, we had a $10,000 bet."

It turned out the player, Arvan Nehmati, was an ex-Davis Cup player for Iran, and had been put up by another Iranian, a gambler named Maurice El Ganion, to play Bobby. "I played the first game and I knew we had been hustled out of $10,000... He could have given *me* three games," sighed Bobby afterwards. "I've been hustled. Shows you can't win them all."

At the Los Angeles Tennis Club, recalled Dean, there was always a commotion when Bobby showed up. "I think he had been banned for a while because they didn't want him coming around playing for money. They talked about him like he was a bad boy, but they said it with a twinkle in their eye because they enjoyed talking about him. But they couldn't control him. He would like to come around and get into money matches, play cards with those guys in the card room or backgammon and they'd go all night long."

Though still an active club, the place where Bobby learned the game and grew to be a champion was changing. By the mid-Seventies, the L.A. Tennis Club was no longer a tennis hub for current and future champions. Open tennis had changed the face of the game. Aspiring players no longer needed a place like the L.A. Tennis Club, a place where they could learn the game by practicing against each other and against top players. Big money meant players could now afford private coaching wherever they happened to live. Top players had become like rock stars, traveling with private entourages that included managers, coaches, conditioning experts, nutritionists, friends, and groupies.

The tournaments, too, were moving away from the small, private clubs that had hosted them for decades—first to downtown arenas and resorts willing to build large grandstands to accommodate the growing number of fans, then to stadiums built specifically for tennis. In 1974, the L.A. Tennis Club hosted its last Pacific Southwest Championships. In 1978, the U.S. Open moved from the cozy confines of the West Side Tennis Club to a stadium complex built at Flushing Meadows, site of the 1939 World's Fair.

As much as Bobby loved playing the part of high-rolling hustler, he was actually a compulsive freeloader, mooching lodgings, meals, drinks, and anything else he could manage. For his appearances, he made sure that as a condition of his participation, deluxe hotel rooms, meals, first-class transportation, and greens fees were all "comped." Instead of having his client send him the plane tickets, he would have them send him cash, then fly coach and bunk on a friend's couch (or more likely, have the friend bunk on the couch while Bobby took the bed).

One time, recalled Bobby's lawyer Robert Johnson, Bobby called and said, "Let's go to Florida and set a record for the most rounds of golf without paying. We'll shoot for 30 days, and we'll only play for free. Free cart. Free balls. Free greens fees."

"That's great," Johnson replied. "Let's do it."

For 60 days, until they ran out of golf courses in southern Florida to play, Bobby would call up or walk into the clubhouse, announce his presence, and proceed to take over. After all, he was a celebrity, and he figured he deserved to be treated as such. "It was perfect," Johnson said.

As time went on, the offers grew fewer and the crowds smaller, but Bobby continued undeterred. Bobby rationalized it this way: "If I can't work for $10,000, I'll work for $5,000. If I can't work for $5,000, I'll work for $2,500." After several years, it got to the point where Bobby's calculus boiled down to, "If I can't get paid, I'll see if I can get a golf game."

By the end of the 1970s, the demand for Bobby's exhibitions declined, but Bobby found renewed joy in the game itself. He returned to the national seniors tennis circuit, becoming the top-ranked player in the country in his age group for nearly a decade. In 1979, he was the first to win a singles "Grand Slam" in the Men's 60 division, with national championships on all four surfaces: hard court, grass, clay, and indoor. He repeated the feat in 1983. Over the years, only Gardnar Mulloy, who had been playing continuously from the 1930s to the beginning of the new millennium, had more national championships than Bobby for a male player.

"In those years after the match, basically his life was one escapade after another of senior tennis, exhibitions, appearances, backgammon," said Kuhle. For Bobby, life was good.

Remarried on Valentine's Day, 1991, Priscilla and Bobby pose for a photo with their best man, Jasper, Priscilla's poodle.

23

"We can get through this."

1974-1991

Having landed solidly on his feet after his humiliating loss to Billie Jean King, Bobby liked to say "the best thing that ever happened to me was my second divorce; it set me free." In truth, he never really stopped loving his second wife, Priscilla. Despite the bitterness, the drinking, the arguing, and his dalliances both during and after their marriage, Bobby still had feelings for her, and he believed no one understood him quite as well as she did. As with his first wife, Kay, Bobby remained friendly with Priscilla, not for the sake of their children but because he genuinely cared for her. He saw no reason for ill will. The marriage simply didn't work out. If anyone was to blame, he said, it was him. "I was anything but the ideal husband and father," he admitted. So it was likely a solace to him when Priscilla remarried in 1973. Maybe now, he figured, she could have the life she wanted and deserved.

At a cocktail party, Priscilla had met Warren Hearne, a retired executive with Trans World Airlines. Tall and handsome, with blue eyes and white hair, it was, according to Priscilla's daughter Dorothy, "love at first sight." Hearne was friendly, outgoing, and an outdoorsman. He was, in Priscilla's words, "a man's man." During World War II, while in his teens, Hearne was in the U.S. Army Air Forces, assigned to a B-24 squadron stationed in North Africa. He flew aboard the planes on daring low-level attacks on the oil fields at Ploesti, Romania in 1943, a mission so dangerous that nearly a third of the 177 planes involved failed to return. Of the 1,765 men who flew the mission, 446 were killed or missing in action, and more than 100 were wounded.

After the war, Hearne went to work for TWA, where he settled into an upper-middle management job from which the company pensioned him early, leaving him financially independent but bitter toward the airline.

"In short, my mom had married another self-made man who was self-determined and adventuresome," said son John Riggs. "She sometimes commented that the boring men never interested her, and the ones who were interesting were not healthy for her."

At first, Priscilla's children were happy for their mother, and optimistic that she might finally put her life together.

Having sold the mansion at Plandome, Priscilla and Hearne moved into a two-story condominium in nearby Manhasset. The two were devoted to each other. "He was a sweetheart," Dorothy said. "I just loved him. Everyone just loved him. He was a gentleman, and very good to my grandmother [Dorothy Wheelan], who was in her nineties." The two were very much in love. They did things together, and were companions in a way that Bobby and Priscilla had not been—fishing together, taking long drives, and going on picnics. Hearne enjoyed growing roses in the backyard, and he passed this passion on to Priscilla. "I never saw my mother grow a thing in her life," Dorothy said, "but when she met Warren she fell in love with it, too. They took great pride in growing roses together in the backyard." Hearne was also a devoted family man. "He was there if you needed him," Dorothy said. "Very loyal."

After several years together on Long Island, the couple moved to Florida. For Priscilla, there was no longer any reason to remain in New York. Her children were grown, and in 1972, with American Photograph's business flagging, the family sold the company to a group of investors. Suburban malls were replacing downtown department stores, and independent photographers had begun siphoning away business. Also, said Mike Crimi, who ran American Photograph for years, "those were the years of the war and the anti-establishment movement and you couldn't get kids into stores to get their picture taken. So we sold it."

Moving to Boca Raton, Hearne and Priscilla bought a house on the Intracoastal Waterway, beside the plush Royal Palm Yacht and Country Club. They enjoyed themselves, entertained, and were active in the Boca Raton Congregational Church, where Hearne became a deacon.

Yes, all might have worked out happily except for one problem: like Priscilla, Hearne was an alcoholic. However bad things had been with Bobby, Priscilla had at least maintained a semblance of normalcy. With Hearne, things spiraled out of control.

"There were lots of scenes, lots of screaming, blackouts, threats of violence… police calls," John remembered. "I visited them where they were living in Boca Raton once and the place was a mess: empty vodka bottles, no glass in the picture frames, the furniture had been slashed, as had the car (inside and out), and the doors to the bedrooms had dents in the wood. It was awful."

While attending graduate school at Yale, John got a call one night. "It was Warren. He was whispering. And I asked him, 'Why are you whispering?' And he said, 'You've got to help me.' He had locked himself in a bedroom, and said my mom had a knife and was going to kill him. Then my mom got on the other line and said, 'Don't believe anything Mr. Grimm has to say.' Mr. Grimm was a taunt she used to tease him about his German heritage. She'd say, 'You can't believe any of his fairy tales.' Here I am on the phone, listening to two drunks scream at each other and I'm asking them, 'What do you expect me to do?'

"I finally asked my mother, 'Are you telling me this so if you do kill him I can testify at your trial that it was premeditated and they will put you in the electric chair?' And she said to me, 'That's so smart. That's exactly what I want.' What they were doing was playing me off one another and my role as confidant had put me in this position."

Trying to get a grip on their lives, Priscilla and Hearne decided jointly to get help and enter rehab. This was Priscilla's first treatment of any kind. For a while it seemed like it might work, that she and Hearne might have the life together that they really wanted. But it was short-lived. They both started drinking again and would struggle for years to get their lives on track.

Years of heavy smoking and drinking had left Hearne in poor health, and in December 1984, he died, leaving Priscilla to fend for herself. Three or four times she checked herself into the famous Menninger Clinic in Topeka, Kansas. The standard session was 30 days, but she committed herself for double or triple sessions. Each time she emerged fresh and full of hope that she had finally conquered her demons. But each time she relapsed, leaving her family more distant and cynical. Her son John stopped counting her trips to rehab at 20.

"I went through years of therapy dealing with this, and I just had to realize there was nothing I could do," John said. "I finally had to back out. I realized that alcoholism is a degenerative disease and that I couldn't be responsible. There wasn't anything I could do. I had to live my own life."

In 1975, when best friend Lornie Kuhle was working as a hitting partner and assistant to Jimmy Connors, Bobby was briefly on his own. At an exhibition in Montreal, he found himself on a hotel elevator with an attractive, young woman.

"Canadian girls have such pretty smiles," said Bobby boyishly. She turned to him and said that was a very nice compliment but that she was American.

"Where from?" he asked.

When she told him Los Angeles he struck up a conversation. Soon they discovered they had three or four mutual friends, including Bobby's first coach, Dr. Esther Bartosh. He asked her to join him for dinner but she already had plans that evening, saying maybe later that week. They exchanged numbers.

The next day, she got a call from Bobby in her hotel room. He sounded panicked. The exhibition was in a couple of days and the sponsors hadn't sold any of the advance boxes. The place would be empty, and not only would he be embarrassed but it could jeopardize future appearances. Could she, he begged, please help him work the phones to try and sell some tickets?

So began a six-year period for Nancy Bailey as Bobby's business manager, friend, and companion. For Bailey, life with Bobby was an adventure. Charming and funny, with an infectious zest for life, he was Peter Pan and Dennis the Menace rolled into one. For that, she was willing to cope with all of Bobby's quirks and idiosyncrasies: his incredible stinginess, his occasional dark moods, his insensitivity and a general obliviousness to the way he impacted those around him.

During his time with Bailey, Bobby had plenty of girlfriends. In Bailey, as with his brother John Riggs and with Lornie Kuhle, he found someone willing to act as his confidant and leading foil. Still, since Bailey didn't gamble or play tennis, Bobby spent many hours teaching her how to play backgammon so that the two would have something to do together during the many hours they were alone on the road, she recalled.

"Maybe it was a generational thing, but a lot of Bobby's guy friends just didn't understand how I could be anything other than a 'girlfriend'—not a friend, not a companion," Bailey said. "Whenever I walked with him through a casino all dressed up," she recalled, "I always felt like people just automatically took me for a prostitute or paid escort or a groupie of some kind. And they treated me that way, like I didn't really exist. But Bobby really liked women, and I think that's why he always got attached to very smart, headstrong women. He respected them. I think he always wanted and may have even envisioned himself staying married to one person his whole life, but it just didn't work. He had to live life his way. He always said, 'I just want one thing: My way. That's all I want.' "

Around the time of the Margaret Court and Billie Jean King matches, Bobby and Priscilla's third-oldest child, James Riggs, started having problems of his own. An outgoing boy who enjoyed sports and loved to laugh, Jim was always Bobby's favorite. As a child he was dyslexic. "He wasn't dumb," said Jim's brother, John, "but this was before they understood dyslexia, so he was labeled stupid and tracked into slower classes." In adolescence he started taking drugs, progressing from alcohol and marijuana to harder stuff, including hallucinogens. After Jim was caught with marijuana and suspended from school in the winter of 1970, Bobby asked Lornie Kuhle to take the 17-year-old youth around with him on the pro tennis circuit. "For about three months," Kuhle said, "I was having him run and play tennis, stuff like that, just to get him out of that environment." It did little good.

Once Jim returned home, his drug use intensified. He also developed other mental problems. Around his twentieth birthday, John recalled, "my mom and I checked him into the Institute of Living in Hartford [a psychiatric hospital in Connecticut]. She and I were his legal guardians at the time." He was diagnosed as schizophrenic. After Jim's release, Bobby offered to have him move out to California to live with him, once again thinking that if Jim followed his dad around, the golf, the tennis, the fresh air and activity might help him overcome his problems.

"Dad was always making promises to my siblings that he could never quite carry out," John said. To Jim, "he might have said, 'Come to California, we'll be together, you can play tennis and golf at La Costa,' and generally painting a lovely picture. But the whole scene in the early seventies out there was so unstructured and weird that, if anything, it made him worse."

Despite good intentions, Bobby had no understanding of Jim's problems, and no real idea of what to do. "Bobby worried constantly about Jimmy," recalled Don Rhodes, who met Bobby in 1973 when he was a teenager living next door to Bobby's Park Newport townhouse. Rhodes befriended the former tennis star and later became a member of his entourage. "He talked to me about the problems Jimmy was going through, but I don't think he knew what to do. I think he was lost, and at that point it was easier for him to turn to other people, like me."

This was going on during Bobby's preparations for the Margaret Court and Billie Jean King matches. He really had no time to devote to Jim. So he enlisted the help of Rhodes. "He wanted someone he could trust to sort of monitor Jimmy and befriend him," Rhodes said. Bobby asked him, "Don, you're young, you must have been into drugs and you know how to deal with this stuff… Don, fix him for me."

Roughly the same age as Jim, Rhodes simply kept Jim company. "Jimmy saw that I wasn't into drugs so he never involved me in it. I mean, he smoked pot once in a while and drank a lot of booze, but I never saw him get into heavy drugs." Over time, the two became close friends, Rhodes said.

Not long after the Billie Jean King match, Jim, then 20 years old, returned east, where he lived for a time with his mother and Hearne before getting his own apartment.

His drug use continued. Several times Jim checked into the drug rehab unit of North Shore Hospital where, after a short period of detox and a health check, he allowed himself to be transferred to the psychiatric ward. This pattern worried his psychiatrist and family. In 1975, Jim's psychiatrist, thinking the young man's mental problems really could not be addressed until his drug use was brought under control, made an unorthodox and ill-fated decision. He decided to place 22-year-old Jim in a unit with some hard-core drug users as a way of shocking him. The theory was that perhaps if Jim saw their depravity he would be frightened into giving up drugs altogether. "I think the counselor told my mother it was a 'calculated risk,' " recalled John. "But she didn't say anything, despite whatever fears she might have had."

The plan backfired. Instead, the outgoing Jim made friends with his new roommates, who taught him about a new drug he hadn't tried: heroin. After Jim's release, according to John, he moved into an apartment in Port Washington on Long Island, where he became a heroin user.

In early April 1976, "I remember Jimmy calling me one night," Rhodes said. "He called me, crying and upset. I believe he had hepatitis a few times that year and he told me nobody understood him; that he just didn't think he was going to be around [much longer]. I just said, 'Jimmy, you got to figure a way to get off this stuff. Come out here. I'll spend time with you. We'll work together.' And he started yelling at me. He called me because, unlike his parents, he thought I wouldn't try to lecture him, and he ended up hanging up on me."

The next day, April 10, while visiting his in-laws in Manhasset, Long Island, John got a telephone call from the Nassau County

Police Department. Jim had been found dead in his bed from an apparent drug overdose. With Priscilla in the hospital recovering from surgery, John had to go to the county morgue to identify his 22-year-old brother's body and collect his personal effects.

Bobby was in Los Angeles at a trade show at the Los Angeles Convention Center. Accompanied by Bailey, he was scheduled to make three appearances a day during the week, doing a tennis exhibition on a court set up outside the convention center and entertaining the crowd with his usual banter. He and Bailey were at the hotel playing backgammon while waiting for his final appearance of the day when the phone rang. Nancy picked it up. John delivered the news of Jim's death. Stunned, Nancy turned her head so Bobby couldn't see her reaction. She needed time to compose herself. Should she wait until after his final appearance to tell him? But it was too late. Bobby could tell something was up.

"What's wrong?" he asked. "What's all that about?"

After hearing the news Bobby took a deep breath and thought for a moment. "Don't say anything more," he said. "There's nothing we can do about it now. Let's get through this last show and then we'll take care of it."

Nancy pleaded with him. "But Bobby, we can get you out of this."

"No, no," he said, determined to fulfill his obligation. "We can get through this."

So they went to the show. Along the way a couple of people who had heard the news on the TV or radio came up and offered their condolences.

On court, Bobby looked lost and confused. He wandered aimlessly about. Instead of his usual energetic repartee, he hesitated and mumbled disjointedly. The crowd, none of whom were aware of the circumstances, grew restless. "He's drunk," someone said loudly. Bobby stumbled through the routine, at one point stopping, standing speechless, twisting his finger through his hair. "This is unbelievable!" another audience member complained. As soon as she could, Bailey whisked Bobby off the court and the two went to the airport.

John made all arrangements and conducted the funeral service, his first ever. It was a small service, family only, no friends. At the service, John recalled, "I remember standing there with my father, after the graveside committal service with my father resting his head on my chest, sobbing uncontrollably and telling me he didn't understand why this had happened."

Years later, Rhodes would wonder if there was anything he could have said or done the night Jim called him. "I've always felt guilty, and I know I shouldn't, but I always carried it with me… That was always tough. Did I say the right thing? Could I have done something differently? I don't know."

Bobby, too, may have wondered what he might have done differently. As much as he loved his children, he simply didn't know how to be a father to them. It was easier for him to deal with strangers and acquaintances. His family often despaired at the circle of deadbeats, hangers-on, and misfits that seemed to revolve around Bobby—the "inner circle of lost souls," as Kuhle described them. For whatever reason, Bobby had a soft spot for people down on their luck, offering total strangers money, time, advice, or a place to stay. His family could never understand how he could be so generous to others yet so stingy with them. Perhaps, his daughter Dorothy reasoned, Bobby felt he could expect something in return from these people. He could get them to do chores or errands, or perhaps nothing more than to hang out and give him the adulation his ego craved.

It also never made sense to family members that Bobby, though sensitive and easily hurt, could be so coarse as a father: soliciting prostitutes for his 14-year-old son, hitting on his daughter's girlfriends, involving them in his betting schemes, or simply neglecting them.

For example, in the spring of 1984, Bobby was scheduled to play in the Britannia Cup against Sweden, a Davis Cup-style series of international matches for players 65 and over. On the way over, he visited Bill in New York City.

Bobby was traveling with a girlfriend. The night before Bobby was to leave, he, along with Bill and their girlfriends, planned a night out. After dinner, Bill got the car and drove around to the front of the restaurant to pick up the others to go to the theater. Everybody piled into the car and Bill shouted, "Okay. Is everybody ready?" But with the noise, lights, and traffic, Bill didn't hear Bobby say anything. He assumed Bobby was in the car, and started to pull away. The car ran over Bobby's foot, breaking it and putting him in the hospital for three days. Of course, the trip to Austria was cancelled, and Bill felt terrible.

Don't worry, Bobby said reassuringly to Bill. "I didn't want to go to Europe, anyway."

Months later, Bill received a notice that he was being sued by Bobby for $100,000 for lost wages and damages. Disbelieving, Bill called up Bobby and asked, "What's this all about, Dad?"

"Take it easy. Take it easy," Bobby said.

At the suggestion of his attorney, Robert Johnson, Bobby agreed to sue his son as a way to make money. "It's nothing personal," Bobby explained to Bill. "It's just a way to get something from the insurance companies. They'll take care of the whole thing and come up with a settlement." Sure enough, the insurance companies worked out a deal and Bobby got a $50,000 settlement. But because Bill then had on his record that he had hit a pedestrian, he was unable to get regular insurance, forcing him to pay thousands of dollars extra in insurance premiums for several years. The situation created a rift between Bill and his father for a long time. Although they finally reconciled, it was tough, Bill said. Bobby just didn't get it. For him, it was just money, "nothing personal."

By the late 1980s, Priscilla's health problems had worsened. Living alone in Boca Raton, Florida, her alcoholism became more severe, with prolonged binges and blackout spells. On a few occasions, neighbors or housekeepers discovered her passed out.

Still, she continued to travel, visiting her children during the holidays in St. Louis, where John lived, or in San Diego, where Dorothy and Bill lived. In the spring of 1989, right around Easter, while visiting Dorothy near San Diego, she grew short of breath and disoriented.

Her daughter rushed her to Scripps Memorial Hospital in La Jolla, where she was admitted with multiple problems: alcoholism, emphysema, and depression. After several weeks of detox, counseling, and medication, her health picked up. She lost weight and her spirits lifted. Though she still sneaked an occasional cigarette to the distress of her children, she generally began to take care of herself. Once released, however, her treatment was far from over. She needed to find a place to stay to continue her recuperation.

Bobby offered to let Priscilla stay with him in his tri-level condominium overlooking the Pacific Ocean in nearby Leucadia. "When she decided to live in California again, she went hunting for a place to rent, and came to see me," said Bobby. "She went into every room and said, 'Hey, I like your place.' I said, 'All right, I'll sell it to you.' "

So he did, for $500,000. The deal made sense for Bobby. After all, he was hardly ever home. Though he'd bought the condo eight years earlier, the place looked as if he'd moved in yesterday, with stuff still in boxes, the refrigerator empty, and the walls barren of pictures or decoration. Noted a visiting writer for *World Tennis*: "The condo has an unstructured, unkempt, spontaneous look, a place where Riggs might have just finished an all-night poker game." For Bobby, who still spent most of his time on the road, the condo was simply a place to do laundry and park his belongings.

Besides, he had recently had a rather ugly break-up with a longtime girlfriend, Miriam Hartman. Bobby met Hartman, a chipper girl 30 years his junior, during the summer of 1982, not long after Nancy Bailey left Bobby to raise a family of her own. Hartman became a live-in companion to Bobby, someone to take care of his affairs, clean house, and keep him company. She had a monthly salary, and though her official title might have been "personal assistant," she was more like a geisha. Energetic and dedicated, she traveled with Bobby and took care of him, insisting that she was his wife, a pretense that Bobby permitted because, among other things, it saved her a $15,000 membership fee at his club in La Costa. When pressed about his marital status with Hartman, Bobby would only say, "I take the Fifth Amendment."

In the end, however, the difference in their personalities and outlook, not to mention their ages, was too great. When Bobby told Hartman it was over, she threatened to sue him for palimony. Bobby settled, according to attorney Johnson, by giving her a condo, a car, and $5,000.

After buying the Leucadia condo from her former husband, Priscilla moved in and got a black standard poodle named Jasper to keep her company. While continuing her treatment, she and Bobby occasionally got together.

"The three of them – Mom, Dad, and Jasper – seemed pretty happy together," son John said, even though Bobby had never had a pet, and didn't particularly like dogs. "The rough edges had worn off both of them. All the love and companionship they shared was still there, but the harsh parts of their lives that made conflict were largely gone."

One day, she called to tell him the house was bigger than she really needed. Soon after, Bobby said, "I moved back, into the guest room. And back into her life."

In September 1990, Bobby and Priscilla traveled to St. Louis for their son John's wedding. While there, John recalled, "I was driving them around in the car. With both of them riding in the backseat, I looked in the mirror and saw them holding hands and cooing to each other. It was really quite sweet. I felt like a dad driving home two sweethearts from the prom." In January, Bobby asked Priscilla to marry him. "She let him dangle several weeks or more," John said, "enjoying her power over him." Finally she said yes on one condition: "You like my dog."

Bobby agreed, and the two were married on Valentine's Day, 1991, with their son John conducting the service, John's wife, Cindy, stood in for the mother of the bride, and Jasper, the black standard poodle, served as the best man—held on a leash by Bobby's brother John.

"I remember getting a call and they wanted me to perform the service," said John, a minister. "I remember saying to myself: I've married young people. I've married old people, and I've remarried old people. But I've never remarried old people who happen to be my parents. What do I say to them?"

There was a reception after the service with roughly 50 people in attendance. After the food and the toasts, Bobby went around to each table, introducing each person there and describing what they meant to him in touching detail. When he got to Priscilla, he rested his hand on her shoulder, and in a low voice began, "What can I say? We truly love each other. We just had an intermission for 20 years… years in which we both had our ups and downs, but that's what life's all about. It's not always a bowl of cherries. [But] with our ups and downs behind us now I'm happy to say we look forward to being happy forever more."

The advantage of a second marriage, particularly to the same spouse, is that there's less chance of the union falling victim to unreasonable expectations. Priscilla knew Bobby was not going to magically change. "He continued to be that person who would go out all day long and come home when the sun came down," Dorothy said, "and my mom understood that. My mom knew that was never going to change and that would be an impossible request." Instead, she adapted.

Lornie Kuhle told the story of the day a frustrated Bobby came home from the club. He couldn't scare up a game for anything—tennis, golf, gin, not even dominoes.

"He went home and brought back his wife, Priscilla," Kuhle said. "She told him, 'I'll keep you company—I'll go around the golf course with you—but I don't want to play.'

"He said: 'That's okay, I'll play two balls: yours and mine. His and hers.'" And, just to make it interesting, he said, they'd play for $50 a hole. Okay, Priscilla agreed, perhaps smiling at the absurdity of it all. If this is what it takes to get to spend time with her husband, so be it. Of course it was a typically lucky round for Bobby. He won $750. When they got home, Priscilla wrote out the check. When the story circulated back to her children, they reacted angrily, accusing Bobby of taking advantage of their mother. Priscilla, however, was not stupid. She realized it was simply the price of keeping his company. Besides, she had all the money in the world. It meant nothing to her. What she needed was companionship.

"They really seemed happy, and I believe they thought they had some good years left with each other," John said. "I think my father thought she'd actually outlive him, and that they could make plans to travel together or whatever."

Bobby and his granddaughter Sara enjoy a moment together in 1994.

24

Nature's Cruelest Trick
1991-1995

When people asked, "Why do you color your hair?" Bobby joked, "Because I get better bets this way. I look older." In truth, aging for Bobby was a difficult process. Always a kid at heart, Bobby liked to think of himself as a sort of perpetual juvenile. "I don't believe in old and gray," he told one interviewer. It was no secret that Bobby colored his hair practically to the end. Even so, with his horned-rim glasses, boyish haircut, and perpetual smirk he always looked like an overgrown kid.

Of course, it was part of his hustle—the image of the artful, cocky underdog, the slightly naive goof, the energetic rogue, full of euphoric chatter and adolescent exaggeration, always willing to get in over his head, just for the fun of it. But he also needed it, if only to stave off the withering responsibilities of adulthood.

"A guy doesn't feel himself growing old, y'know," Bobby said. "You just look into the mirror one day and say, where did the last forty fucking years go to anyway?"

As the years caught up to him, Bobby learned that things he used to do effortlessly suddenly became impossible. He'd come off the tennis court and complain, "I go to get this ball that I've gotten 10 million times before. I know exactly what to do. I'm there. But then I'm nowhere near the ball. I cannot believe it. I just can't believe it." The effects of aging were a never-ending source of frustration. To his friend Nancy Bailey, he said, "The cruelest trick of nature was to age the body before it aged the man."

In 1993, while playing an exhibition match in the Bahamas in 90-degree heat, 74-year-old Bobby grew short of breath in the third set against a 30-year-old opponent. The aging pixie grew concerned, and he scheduled a medical exam. Afterwards, the doctor asked, "Do you want to have surgery before or after your heart attack?" Bobby didn't understand. He thought the doctor was teasing. Heart attacks were for desk-bound workaholics with weight problems, not a trim, former world-class athlete who exercised every day. What Bobby never considered was that his physical activity was perhaps the only thing that had staved off surgery years earlier. "His diet was horrible by today's standards," friend and protégé Lornie Kuhle said. "He liked knockwurst and liverwurst, high-fat, high-salt." Bobby loved to eat fatty steaks with loads of gravy, corned beef sandwiches, hot dogs, lamb, sausage, and big slabs of bacon with breakfast.

Bypass surgery was scheduled, and surgeon Leland Housman, the nationally ranked amateur tennis player who performed the procedure, negotiated part of his fee in tennis lessons. Bobby's son John recalled reaching the hospital soon before his father was wheeled into the operating room. It was winter and the NFL playoffs were under way. Bobby handed John a newspaper opened to the latest line on football games for the weekend. Bobby wrote down the name and number of his bookie, and instructed John to have Lornie Kuhle call and put in his bets. "So Lornie gets there a little later and we're all in the cardiac waiting room with all these other families," John said, "and Lornie's on the phone there placing bets for my father because that was my father's last wish before going into surgery."

It was not Bobby's first brush with mortality. Five years earlier, in the winter of 1988, Bobby had been diagnosed with prostate cancer. "He was getting up and going to the bathroom a lot in the nighttime," recalled Kuhle, who took him to a doctor. A blood test revealed the cancer.

"So now, what do you do?" Kuhle recalled asking himself. After researching the subject, Kuhle said he located a doctor at the Stanford School of Medicine, Dr. Thomas Stamey, a renowned urologist and a leader in the field of prostate cancer. Stamey recommended radiation treatment, and after six weeks, Bobby emerged smiling from the hospital, the cancer apparently stopped in its tracks. Accompanied by his girlfriend at the time, Miriam Hartman, Bobby told reporters, "We think I'm cured."

Dr. Malcolm Bagshaw, chairman of the Department of Radiation Oncology at the Stanford School of Medicine who oversaw the treatments, commended Bobby's "positive attitude" and predicted he would be back swinging a golf club and tennis racquet in no time. Among those who sent Bobby a get-well card and balloons was Billie Jean King.

Sure enough, Bobby quickly returned to hustling golf games at La Costa and playing tennis. He planned a trip to Wimbledon and began preparing to compete in the seniors tennis championships later that year. A few months later, after stepping off the court following the final of the over-70 clay court doubles championship in Arlington, Virginia, Bobby looked and sounded like the Bobby of old. Among other things, he said was looking forward to challenging professional golfer Greg Norman to a $100,000 winner-take-all match in which Norman would allow Bobby to tee off from the front tees and get one throw per hole. "Imagine, the best player in the world [Norman] against a bum," he laughed.

Bobby's ordeal, however, was far from over. When initially diagnosed, Bobby was informed that his cancer had escaped the prostate and had likely spread. This meant that despite the apparent success of the radiation treatment, there was only about a 20 percent chance that the cancer would remain in remission. In July 1989, in order to staunch the production of testosterone that feeds tumors, Bobby underwent surgery to have both his testicles removed. Statistically, the procedure would give Bobby a 50-50 chance of living another 5 to 10 years. Still, Bobby remained upbeat, even laughing at his condition. "Hey, nobody likes to lose their family jewels," he joked. "I fought it like hell, but the doctors told me it was a last resort."

Appearing on national television to tout early detection and prevention of prostate cancer, Bobby went on the *Sally Jessy Raphael Show* in 1991 and jokingly declared, "Hey, they cut off my balls! Everybody knows you can't play tennis without balls."

Despite his health problems, Bobby remained in constant motion—playing tennis, playing golf, traveling. Life, as always, was a never-ending adventure. As America's "hustler emeritus," he also managed to keep himself in the spotlight. In 1992, Bobby landed a job as a television commentator on the pay-per-view broadcast of the "Battle of the Sexes" redux, a $500,000 match between Jimmy Connors and Martina Navratilova at Caesar's Palace in Las Vegas ($300,000 for the winner, $200,000 for the loser). Unlike Bobby's match against Billie Jean King, this two-out-of-three set affair lacked drama or intrigue. For one thing, at age 40, Connors was 15 years younger than Bobby was when he played Billie Jean. Not only that, Connors was still a touring professional, making a storybook run to the semifinals at the U.S. Open the year before. To make things even, the match was handicapped. Connors was limited to a single serve to Navratilova's two, and Navratilova was allowed to hit into a wider court by Connors ceding one of the doubles alleys.

Despite the handicap, Bobby felt that a Connors victory was a lock, so much so that before the match he put down $30,000 to win $10,000 that his man wouldn't lose a set—a big bet, even by Bobby's standards. As the match progressed, Bobby's colleagues in the broadcast booth noticed that he seemed unusually quiet. At first, they assumed he had stage fright. When Navratilova drew the match even at 5-5 in the opening set, Bobby suddenly grew pale and began breathing heavily. Fearing something was wrong, Bobby's microphone was removed and a message was sent courtside to Bobby's friend Kuhle, who was told Bobby might be having a heart attack. Kuhle rushed to the booth, but by the time he got there Bobby seemed to be recovering. Connors had won the first set, 7-5. By the time Connors won the match, 7-5, 6-2, Bobby's recovery was complete. He sheepishly explained he had gotten a sudden case of nerves at the prospect of losing thirty grand. For the first time in his life, he joked, "I was a little bit tongue-tied."

Unlike the cancer treatments, Bobby's recovery from bypass surgery was slow and frustrating. Weak and exhausted, he found ordinary activity difficult. He gave up playing tennis competitively, saying, "It seems to have robbed me and my legs of quickness. I can't move at all." When invited to appear in Los Angeles for a star-studded AIDS benefit featuring singer Elton John and Billie Jean King in September 1993—an event billed as a tribute to the "Battle of the Sexes" match 20 years before and seemingly tailor-made for the attention-getting huckster—Bobby balked. "I remember I practically had to force him to go out and play," Kuhle said. "It was a big deal, [but] he just didn't care. I thought it would be a good thing for him to do." Bobby finally relented, Kuhle said, but he went under protest. "He was just getting to a state where he didn't care that much about that stuff. And maybe he wasn't feeling that good, either, [but] he liked butting heads, if he could find someone to butt heads with." Playing as doubles partners rather than adversaries, Bobby and King defeated the duo of Elton John and Martina Navratilova. Perhaps fittingly, it was Bobby's last appearance in a tennis exhibition.

Frustrated at Bobby's lack of energy and enthusiasm, Kuhle realized that if anything could lift Bobby's spirits and get him motivated it would be a big money match. So he put up $1,000 of his own cash and raised another $4,000 for Bobby to play a doubles challenge against Dorothy "Dodo" Bundy Cheney and Cortez "Corky" Murdock, the nation's top over-70 women's doubles team. As recalled by Gardnar Mulloy, whom Bobby called up in Miami to be his partner: "He had just played them with Joe Davis and they'd lost and Bobby was mad. He said they lost a lot of money, so he called me and asked me if I'd play. I said, 'Bobby, yeah, I'll play if you pay my way out there.' I was going out there anyway for the national indoors in San Francisco, but I didn't tell him that."

"You think we can beat 'em?" Bobby asked.

"Bobby, I don't know," Mulloy answered.

Recalled Mulloy: "He was pretty sick by this time. I knew he was ill, because he wasn't playing in tournaments. So anyway, I said okay."

The match was held on center court at the Los Angeles Tennis Club. A large crowd of club members, old friends, and the curious assembled to watch this mixed-sex battle of the aged, among them Bobby's old friend and rival Jack Kramer. As always, Bobby vigorously worked the crowd beforehand, rounding up bets—$50 here, $100 there. "He's foaming at the mouth, betting," recalled Mulloy. "So I tell him, 'How about quieting down and concentrating? We got a tough match to play'."

"Well, they're old ladies," Bobby said. "We can't lose."

"Bobby, you're an old man," answered Mulloy. Besides, "You're in no shape. You can't move." Even Kramer had quietly bet against Bobby.

"If they hit to me," Bobby reassured Mulloy, "I can handle it, but I can't handle anything else. You'll have to run down the lobs, you'll have to run after the drop shots… But Gar, you can do it."

For 80-year-old Mulloy, this was asking a lot, particularly against two women known for their exquisite touch and placement of the ball. In defiance of his years, Mulloy ran like a man possessed, chasing after lobs, scampering for drop shots, scurrying from side to side, forward and back. In a display of sheer determination, Mulloy played as if it was two against one, which essentially was the case, except on the rare occasion when a ball was hit directly to Bobby. Even Bobby at times could not believe what he was seeing. "I was running all around Bobby," Mulloy said, "and damned, we finally beat 'em," 7-5, 7-5.

Afterwards, Kramer went up and congratulated the exhausted Mulloy. "I don't know how you did it," Kramer told the old warhorse. Meanwhile, a smiling Bobby moved through the crowd, cheerfully collecting his winnings and basking in the embrace of his friends— for some, their last. Said Mulloy, "He went really went downhill after that."

At home, Priscilla's health, too, had declined greatly. Suffering from emphysema, overweight, and too weak to climb the stairs of their Leucadia townhouse, she lay in a hospital bed in the living room, dying. To help care for her, Bobby called upon his niece, Frances Riggs, daughter of Sanders Riggs, the eldest of Bobby's siblings. Frances, a nurse, agreed to work for Bobby and moved in.

As it turned out, she would be needed for more than just caring for Priscilla. Not long after his match with Mulloy, Bobby's health started to crumble. Cancer had spread to Bobby's bones. He was told that treatment could merely buy him some time and keep him comfortable. During much of the three years that she lived with Bobby and Priscilla, Frances said, it seemed that one or the other were in the hospital, sometimes both at the same time. In addition to Frances, Bobby's daughter Dorothy Riggs and son Bill Riggs, both of who lived nearby, also helped care for their ailing parents.

On March 19, 1995, Priscilla died. In the weeks and months leading up to her death, Bobby seemed detached. "I know he didn't want to be mean," daughter Dorothy said, "but he couldn't face it. He would go into the living room, pat her hand once a day and say hello, and that was it."

After Priscilla's death, recalled Kuhle, "Bobby was pretty stoic. I was with him when we went into the hospital when she died. He stayed in the room for an hour or two after she was already gone. He just sat there, he and his daughter."

In coming to terms with his own death, 77-year-old Bobby tried to be philosophical. He told himself he had run a good race, that he had had a good life. But like anyone faced with a terminal disease, he was also frightened. Nancy Bailey recalled Bobby calling her to say the cancer had returned and that it had metastasized. "I'm the baby [of the family] for chrissake," Bobby told Bailey. "This can't happen to the baby."

After all, his father had lived to be 84, his mother 84, his brother Sanders to 81, and his brother David to 84. "He thought that this was out of the order of things, that it wasn't fair," Bailey recalled. He figured he was entitled to a few more good years. He even had made a promise to himself to "live to at least ninety-eight or ninety-nine... I'd like to be like the late King [Gustav V] of Sweden, whom I played with and knew quite well. He played tennis until he was ninety."

Bobby felt cheated. "I asked him how he felt," recalled Bailey, "and he replied, at first really angrily."

"How in the hell do you think it feels?" Bobby said. Then, after a moment, he said, "Well, you know, it doesn't make any difference how I feel. Everything now makes no difference, whether I hurt or don't hurt, whether I feel peaceful, whether I feel angry. No matter what I feel, none of it, means anything. So, it doesn't matter how I feel. It just is."

Reconciled to his condition, Bobby approached his illness with the same passion and perseverance with which he approached tennis or golf. "It was like a challenge for him," said his physician, Dr. Lawrence Piro. "He strategized everything. Anything that came along he strategized how it would fit into the big picture, what it would mean to him and what it would be like and how it would slow him down or not slow him down." Bobby was determined to stay active as long as he could, and refused to become depressed or morose. Cancer might kill him, but it would not change him.

"We would sit down and talk in my office about his situation," Piro said. "I would tell him what I thought and how we should approach his treatment and he would ask questions. I would give him the answers and he would ask a few more questions, and at the end, every visit always ended with Bobby giving a five-minute recap of the entire conversation. He wanted to make sure he knew what was going on and to make sure he had it all right. He needed to feel he was in control and was a part of the plan."

Bailey remembered a day Bobby called up, asking that she meet him at the home of his sister, Mary Lee, in nearby Riverside, California. Assuming he wanted to have lunch with her, Bailey happily consented. When she arrived, Bobby and a minister greeted her. Mary Lee led them all into the living room and then disappeared. The atmosphere was very formal, she recalled, and a little awkward. Bobby explained that he had planned a sort of funeral rehearsal, and that he wanted them to go over what they planned to say at the service for him. Bailey and the minister didn't know how to respond.

But Bobby was serious. "He's not teary. He's not sad. He's not emotional," Bailey said. "He's very methodical and matter-of-fact. He's not doing this to play around... He's ticking off a mental list of things to do."

Turning first to the minister, Bobby said, "Okay, stand up there now. I want to hear what you're going to say." As commanded, the minister stood in the center of the room. While Bobby and Bailey sat and listened on the couch, the minister began his standard funeral service.

"Now, you're not going to use the Lord's Prayer, are you?" interrupted Bobby.

After resolving that issue, the minister began again.

"No, no, no," Bobby broke in at another point. "Don't say that." The stunned minister stood silently while his host offered him directions.

Once the minister finished, Bobby said, "Okay, now you sit down here and we're going to listen to what she's going to say. Alright Nance, you stand up there because you're going to say something."

Taken aback, Bailey replied, "I don't know if I'm going to say something or not."

"It's important that you say something," Bobby said, "and I want to know what you're gonna say."

Bailey protested. "I don't know. I don't know what I'd say. I don't know what the service is going to be like, what the circumstances will be," she said. "I don't know what I'm going to say if I do say something."

"Well, I want you to say something, and I want to hear what you might say."

So Bailey stood up in front of and did a little extemporaneous speech.

"Whoa, whoa," Bobby again interrupted. "Dear, I wish you'd say something like this…"

"I don't remember exactly the pointers he gave," Bailey recalled later. "But he was very much critiquing this and wanting to know what kinds of things somebody might say. Not because he was afraid somebody would say the wrong thing, but I think he wanted people to say things that were good about him… he wanted to be part of everything."

Bobby named his longtime friend Lornie Kuhle executor of his estate, and gave him power of attorney in decisions concerning his medical treatment. At times this created tension between Kuhle and some family members, particularly those who bore the brunt of caring for Bobby, but Bobby considered Kuhle to be like a son. Certainly no one had spent more time with him over the previous two decades, and arguably no one had been more devoted or understood Bobby as well. Nevertheless, Bobby made sure he spent time with each of his children during his final days, time he never really gave them when they were younger.

"I remember sitting down with him after my mother's funeral in March," son John Riggs recalled. "My dad talked a lot about his life. He had been attending hospice-led group meetings and he had some real peace about his life. I also remember him telling me what his mother, Agnes, told him during a visit to her in a home at the end of her life. 'Bobby,' she said, 'just remember: Life goes by in the blink of an eye.' And this was his way of telling me the same thing. What he was doing was giving me a report from the front line. He was warning me that I would be the next one to face this reality."

Insisting that he remain active, Bobby tried to get out each day—to play a round of golf, or if he felt too weak, a few holes, or if he felt even worse, to just ride along in the cart. It was important to him. He did not intend to let the disease defeat him.

But the progressive nature of his disease meant that Bobby's health continued to deteriorate. Successive surgeries included both a colostomy and a urostomy. "So now he's got two bags [in which to go to the bathroom]," Kuhle remembered. "But he's still fighting like a son-of-a-bitch, still trying to go out and play golf with these bags.

"I remember watching him play this Par 3, and he was trying to make this putt against me for a dollar. It was like a five-foot putt. He's so weak, but there he was concentrating like a son-of-a-bitch. And he sinks the putt for a dollar."

In April 1995, a month after Priscilla's death, Kuhle organized an all-star tribute for Bobby featuring all his old friends and rivals, including Jack Kramer, Pancho Gonzalez, Pancho Segura, Vic Seixas, Ted Schroeder, Gardnar Mulloy, and Gene Mako, a kind of living funeral for Bobby held at the Bobby Riggs Tennis Club near his home. During the luncheon, each of the guests stood up and gave a small speech. They talked about Bobby's place in tennis history, about his remarkable career, his consistency and touch, his powers of analysis and concentration, and his ability to outthink, if not outplay, an opponent. He had played and beat the finest players of his era, and in a phenomenal career spanning age 13 to 76 managed to remain the world's best tennis player for his age.

Said Segura: "Bobby has nerves of steel."

Bobby was boisterous and contentious as ever. At one point, recalled Vic Braden, Schroeder got up and told Bobby, "Remember when I had you cold in 1941?" Sure, Bobby replied. It was the semifinals of Forest Hills, and he won it 7-5 in the fifth. Bobby reminded Schroeder how he "hit three out balls" to give it away. The pugnacious Shroeder moved like he was going to strike Bobby, and for a brief moment it looked as if the two would come to blows, but Pancho Gonzalez got up to calm everybody down. In the end, Bobby gave a short speech and thanked everyone for coming. Gonzalez, suffering from cancer himself, died not long after the event.

Though a *Los Angeles Times* reporter at the event said Bobby looked fit enough for a round of golf, in truth he looked better than he was. Dr. Piro had given Bobby some steroids to maintain his strength.

Before the event, Kuhle commissioned a half-size sculpture modeled after a photograph of young Bobby in action during his championship days. Kuhle recalled bringing a miniature of the sculpture into the hospital where Bobby was being treated during one of his many admissions. Bobby took a quick look at the piece, Kuhle said, and proclaimed, "The grip's wrong."

"He didn't register a whole lot of emotion about it," Kuhle admitted, "but I think he did like it."

Death forced Bobby to face the unsettled issue of his spirituality. He had long abandoned the Church of Christ. Organized religion, he argued, was a sham. The Bible, he said, was nothing more than a "fairy tale." To some people, he even declared himself an atheist.

"He really thought the end was the end," Dorothy said. "That's why he thought you make the best of life while you are alive, try to live up to your potential. He didn't believe in the hereafter. He thought while you were alive, live. Go out and do your thing and do it well."

Others, however, said they saw a more spiritual side to Bobby. "My dad wasn't religious, necessarily," said his son John, "but he was spiritual. I remember one visit where he told me that he had just read the Bible straight through for the fourth time—and I have no doubt that he really did. He told me that he just didn't understand it. 'Red Seas just don't part,' he said. 'All these things just don't happen.'

"I tried to tell him that the Bible doesn't have to be literal in order to be true. But he just didn't understand. In the Church of Christ, which he grew up in, the Bible is taken literally, and many of his family still had strong ties to the church."

When asked once if he believed in God, Bobby answered, "I would say that I am confused... I believe strongly in Christianity. The doctrine is beautifully sound. I believe in the Ten Commandments. I believe in the Golden Rule. Anybody who believes in the concept of Christianity cannot help but be a better person. I really believe that if you cast your bread on the water, it comes back tenfold. I always lend a helping hand. I try to be a nice person. I always help younger people coming up without a dime. I don't cater to rich people. I was never a good politician."

John said his father wanted to believe, but refused to submit to dogma. He lived life according to his own rules, but the fact that he read the Bible and continued to be troubled by it showed that his religious upbringing stayed with him. "He may have rejected almost all of the Church of Christ's traditions and teaching," John said, "except for the one and only crucial truth: That there is a divine reality whose nature truly was grace. And so I think in that sense he had spiritual solace."

Unable to play tennis or golf, too tired even to read a book, Bobby ended up lying in bed watching sports on television. His vitality sapped and in nearly constant pain, he ate less and less, and needed oxygen to help him breathe. Everything that made his life worth living had been taken from him. He decided he'd had enough. He knew it was time.

Knowing the answer before he asked the question, Bobby had Dr. Piro detail what would happen to him if he were taken off the antibiotics. Piro told him that because of the surgeries and his weakened system, he would eventually fall victim to an infection, lapse into a coma, and die. The only question was how long it would take. In the meantime, measures could be taken to make sure he was comfortable.

Family members put out the word that now was the time to say goodbye.

Don Rhodes said he remembered calling Bobby. Frances answered the phone, and he heard her say to Bobby, "Don Rhodes is on the phone. Can he talk to you?"

Rhodes could hear Bobby's voice in the background. "And he barked out very loudly so I could hear him, 'I don't feel well, I can't talk to him. Just tell him I love him.' And coming from Bobby it was a very frightening thing to have him say that because it was not typical to have him talk of love." Determined to see Bobby, Rhodes visited Bobby the following week, and the two spent an hour or two reminiscing. "He said it had been a great run and he thanked me for what I had done for him and how much fun we had over the years. It was real tearful, a very sad time."

It was October, and Bobby was visited by three old friends: Jack Kramer, Ted Schroeder, and Philippe Chatrier, former head of the International Tennis Federation and the French Federation of Tennis, a tireless promoter of the game who had led a campaign to restore tennis to the Olympic Games. As always, recalled Schroeder, Bobby was soliciting bets on who would win the World Series, bets he likely would not be around to collect.

Billie Jean King, too, learned of Bobby's condition, and called to say she wanted to visit. A time was set up, but when it arrived, Bobby was too ill to make the appointment. Instead, a phone call was arranged. "I was sort of cradling him and holding the phone because he had been laying down," recalled Frances Riggs. "We were waiting for the call. We had a hearing-impaired phone set up."

Bobby and Billie Jean reminisced for a bit, but the more Bobby talked the weaker he became. Near the end of the conversation,

Bobby concluded by telling Billie Jean, "Well, we did it. We put women's tennis on the map."

"They had a wonderful talk," Frances Riggs said, but it was hard on Bobby. "He realized they were saying good-bye."

By the time the two hung up, Bobby was teary.

"Franny, she's a good gal," Bobby said of Billie Jean. "She's a real good gal. I got a lot of respect for her. She's the best female tennis player there was."

Finally, Frances recalled, he said, "Let me rest now, honey."

Bobby spent his final hours drifting in and out of a coma-like sleep. He was set up in a bed at his home, surrounded by family and close friends. The World Series was on television, and at times he would wake up and in a barely audible whisper ask, "What's the score?" On the morning of October 25, 1995, he died in his sleep.

To the end, however, he kept his mischievous sense of humor. Shortly before he died, during a visit by Kuhle, Bobby emerged from sleep on a Monday morning. "So I pick up the newspaper," remembered Kuhle, "and I say to him, 'Well, let's see how many [of Sunday's football] games you can pick.' So I'm going through the paper. We start. There's Boston versus Washington. I ask him who won. He says Boston by seven. I say, 'Gee, you're right. Boston by three. You're pretty close." Then Chicago against Green Bay. He says, Green Bay by eleven. 'You're right. It was Green Bay by seven.' So we continue through it. I think there's eleven games or something. So we go through the whole thing and the guy is picking games left and right like you can't believe. We get down to the last game, and it's New Orleans and Atlanta, or something. He says 'Atlanta.' And I say, no. It was New Orleans. You lost. And I said, 'I can't believe you got 10 out of 11 games.' "

Shortly, after Bobby's death, Kuhle related the story to another friend. "And I'm telling this friend of mine the story about how Bobby was able to go through all these football scores. And he says, 'Are you kidding me? I read him those results before you came in the room Monday morning.' He was putting me on."

Fathers and sons. John Wheelan Riggs holds his eight-month-old son, Andrew, at the memorial service for Bobby.

Afterword

On Monday, October 30, 1995, more than 100 people gathered at a funeral home in Encinitas, California to say a final goodbye to the man collectively remembered as athlete, competitor, champion, showman, hustler, chauvinist, huckster, smart aleck, chatterbox, blowhard, rascal, prankster, rival, lover, mentor, partner, friend, and father.

Upon a pedestal rested an urn containing Bobby's ashes. Beside it stood a large black-and-white photo of a young and handsome Bobby in his tennis whites. Those attending the service were invited to get up and share their recollections of Bobby, and among those to do so were Jack Kramer, Pancho Segura, Ted Schroeder, and Lornie Kuhle.

Everybody, it seemed, had a favorite story about Bobby. Segura remembered the early professional tours and how Bobby taught him to play poker and gin rummy. "He kept me in a state of alertness," Segura said. "He taught me how to play poker and gin rummy when we were on tour and working for $300 a week, and I had no money coming to me. He was fun."

Kramer told a story of how one Sunday afternoon in Christchurch, New Zealand, Bobby convinced Kramer, Segura, and Dinny Pails to pitch coins to see who would pay for lunch. A local constable came up, "and we almost get put in jail for gambling."

The newspapers and a local San Diego television station were there, and the next day reported how Bobby's "friends and contemporaries said goodbye with a few tears and a fair bit of laughter." Even in death Bobby was entertaining and made good copy. What they didn't report were the tributes to Bobby the athlete and champion, the memories about his ability on the court and his tenaciousness as a competitor. "He could make the ball talk," said Segura of Bobby's tennis game. "He had all the shots." Not only that, but he never gave up, fighting to the very last shot. That's why, Segura said, "I nicknamed him 'Mighty.' "

Kramer recalled how tough Bobby was to play, and how he could beat every great player of his era, including Don Budge and himself (that is, until he figured out how to beat him). "Riggs was a lot better player than anybody will ever realize," Kramer said. "People won't even mention him with Andre Agassi and Pete Sampras and those guys, but believe me, he'd have played with them."

It's an interesting debate, and on occasion, writers, editors, and other sports experts get together to list the greatest players of all time. But in tennis such an exercise is fraught with peril. Not only does it make a difference who is doing the comparing, but unlike baseball and other sports in which a mass of statistics can be used to compare players against one another, or sports in which a stopwatch or tape measure can give a concrete measure of performance, tennis is more subjective. How many titles? On what surface? Against whom? The task is made harder by the fact that the players, the game, and the equipment have changed so radically over the years as to render such comparisons meaningless—an apples versus oranges argument. Power has eclipsed artistry. Players are bigger and fitter than their predecessors. The racquets they use are more powerful, and players who play serve-and-volley tennis are considered quaint and old-fashioned. Nowadays, with players able to hit winners from anywhere on the court, the game has come to resemble Ping-Pong more than the game Bobby grew up playing.

Add to this the problem that, in an age before television, there is no collective memory of how Bobby or any other player of his era played. When *Tennis* magazine asked readers in 1999 to name the 10 greatest male players of all time, all but one played in the years since TV started airing tournaments (Roy Emerson made the list, probably because his name came up frequently in connection with Pete Sampras's closing in on his Grand Slam singles titles record.) Conspicuously absent were players such as Tilden, Budge, and Kramer.

Remember, too, that World War II cut short the careers of an entire generation of players. Who knows how many more championships Bobby, Budge, or Kramer would have won had there been no war?

And, if all this wasn't enough, before 1968, when the game went "open," tennis was split into two camps, amateur and professional. With top amateurs being lured into the professional ranks, and with professionals barred from playing in the major tournaments and excluded from the world rankings, the system left the legacies of many players in the shadows—the best example being Pancho Segura, who turned professional early, and, though he won three U.S. professional singles titles, defeating among others Jack Kramer, Frank Kovacs, and Pancho Gonzalez, is almost never recognized as one of the greats.

Despite all this, there's no doubt that Bobby, Budge, Tilden, Kramer, Gonzalez, and other players of that era should make the cut. Talent is talent, and in sports the cream inevitably rises to the top. The great players of old would make the adjustments needed to compete in today's game and realize success of their own.

In Bobby's case, Kramer once called him "by far the most underrated of all the top players," and placed him among the all-time best, alongside Budge, Ellsworth Vines, Tilden, Fred Perry, and Pancho Gonzalez. Ted Schroeder echoed the sentiment, and when asked who were the top players of his era listed, in no particular order, Budge, Bobby, Gonzalez, Kramer, and Sedgeman.

To the question of the greatest players ever, Bobby was uncharacteristically modest. When asked in 1985, he named Vines, Budge, Kramer, Gonzalez, and Rod Laver. (He placed Tilden in a category by himself, explaining that in tennis there was Tilden, and then everybody who came after him. He was a benchmark by whom all others would be compared.) As for himself, Bobby said he liked to think that from the age of 13 to 76—from the amateurs to the pros and the seniors—he was the world's best tennis player for his age. An odd but original way of looking at it—and arguably true, as Bobby played competitively throughout his life.

Bobby said he realized that he would probably never be remembered as a truly great tennis player, in part because of the way he played the game. "I didn't play up to the press or try to look good," he said. While Budge and Kramer set out to destroy every opponent love and love, Bobby enjoyed teasing his opponents, keeping them on court and prolonging the game to make the score close. "Looking back, I should have used more aggressive tactics," Bobby said shortly before his death. "I could hit the ball much harder than I did, with great control. But I was content to let the other guy do something, and I would answer it. When I arrived on the scene, I would play a second- or third-rounder and I wouldn't go out and crush him. I would beat him, 6-3, 6-4. I wouldn't look very impressive. I wouldn't use all my best shots. I would be overqualified. I didn't impress the newspaper writers or the other players. I made the mistake of not impressing the audience. I didn't beat anybody badly. That's one of the reasons I didn't go down in the history books as a great, great player... People couldn't understand when I was beating Budge."

Said Gardnar Mulloy: "I'll tell you about his game. I analyzed it for years, because I wondered how he could win this match and that match. When he was in trouble, he got out of it... Somebody asked me to put together a fantasy tournament with the sixteen greatest players of all time, and figure it out right to the finals. I had Bobby winning."

"How can you have Bobby win?" Mulloy was asked.

"Listen," Mulloy recalled answering. "Bobby was unique, he never lost a match the first time he played somebody. You play him over a series, he'll lose to greater players. But he had a way of winning, he always won a big match." Throughout his career Bobby used his powers of analysis and concentration to consistently beat bigger and better, if not younger, players.

Of course, the one big match he lost—his match against Billie Jean King—ended up defining Bobby's legacy. His reign as the world's best player—his Wimbledon triple crown, his two Forest Hills singles championships, his three professional championships, and the tours against Budge and Kramer—none of that mattered. Instead, he's remembered as the wise-guy hustler, a middle-aged buffoon. No one knew this better than Bobby.

"I will not be remembered for winning Wimbledon on my first try, but [as] the guy who lost to Billie Jean King in front of 90 million people. Which is okay with me."

Given this attitude, it's no wonder that Bobby's family has "become very protective of my father's legacy," said son John. After all, it seemed his father didn't care. "Maybe he didn't worry about it because he knew what he had done and nobody could take that away from him," John mused.

Then again, Bobby had nothing to be ashamed of. Though he knew he would never be ranked among the top players of all time, he was nevertheless great—a greatness measured not just by his athletic achievements, but by his contributions to the game and his place in tennis history. "Remember me as a guy who was a great competitor, a guy who loved the game," Bobby said. Remember him, he said, as "a player who was innovative and brought in all kinds of handicaps and motivated the women players to play him in a number of matches."

From his early days as a player, Bobby understood better than most he was in the entertainment business. It was why he relished his "bad boy" reputation, and why he never minded playing the villain. The way Bobby saw it, he felt if he couldn't get the fans to root for him, better to have them root against him. At least they'd still be watching. "He had that Hollywood 'star' mentality about such issues," said John Riggs. "He told me, point blank, 'any publicity is good publicity.' He loved hanging out with celebrities, and celebrities loved hanging out with him." As one of the game's all-time characters, Bobby was also one of the first players to trademark his personality.

For the same reason Bobby chafed at the perpetuation of the myth of the "amateur" game and the stuffed shirts who ran it. "My father had a sort of hard-scrabble, street-tough mentality," said John Riggs, "and tennis was a very elitist game for him growing up. The matches were played at these very exclusive country clubs. You had to wear all white. The men wore pants. You had to be quiet during play, [and] my father hated all that. He thought if you couldn't play unless it was quiet, you had no business being on the court, and no business being one of the world's best.

"For him, the best thing about the Billie Jean King match was that it got people who didn't necessarily know much about the game so involved," said John Riggs. "He loved the spectacle and cheering and the noise. That's what he thought tennis should be about."

Indeed, it's hard to imagine how the "Battle of the Sexes" could have succeeded without Bobby. His sense of showmanship, his flair for promotion, and his infectious glee made it more than just a novelty match or a sociopolitical statement. And while it may have been Billie Jean's match to win, Bobby made it abundantly clear it was always his show. Proof of his success can be seen in the fact the match still stands as the most-watched match in history. It made tennis fans out of people who had never held a racquet and helped inspire an interest in tennis the likes of which the sport had never seen. No one, not Budge, not Kramer, not Gonzalez, could have pulled it off as Bobby did. (In fact, Bobby's biggest problem was that he faced an opponent who understood all this at least as well as he did.)

"My father I think was very proud of what he did for the game," John Riggs said.

Bobby played for glory, he played for attention, and, yes, he played for money, but he mostly played for the sheer joy of it. In the truest sense of the word, Bobby *played* tennis, and despite his battles with the tennis establishment and the old "shamateur" system, he came closest in spirit to the root meaning of amateur. That is, someone who plays for the love of the sport. To Bobby, it was supposed to be fun. He also played golf; he played backgammon; he played gin rummy, as well as basketball, poker, table tennis, pitching pennies, marbles, paddle tennis, tossing cards into a hat… Bobby played life. Although he sometimes did so at the expense of his family and friends, he had fun—no matter what the stakes. Not only that, he spread that sense of fun to those around him. He allowed the rest of us to play with him.

One word summed up Bobby's life, said Schroeder. "Action." Wherever there was a contest, Bobby could be expected to be in the middle of it, negotiating the odds and making a deal. "He could be the most aggravating person in the world," Schroeder explained, "but when the event or the moment was over, all of a sudden you realized you had a wonderful time."

Photo Credits

Reference Notes

Foreword

iii   *"He put women on the map"*: "His Last Match Can't be Rigged," by Bob Oates, *Los Angeles Times*, April 15, 1995.

vi   *"The best thing in life is to win"*: Source unknown.

1: *A Pig Lost in the Astrodome*

5   *To prove it, Bobby once said:* "His Last Match Can't be Rigged," *Los Angeles Times*.

8   *He felt like drowning in that tub:* Interview with Larry Riggs (September 1999).

8   *"I gave her two chances—slim and none"*: "Sexes Raise Racket Again," by Jody Goldstein, *Houston Chronicle*, Sept. 25, 1992.

8   *Later, at a post-match party:* "The Intersexual Saga of Tennis," by Bud Collins, from *Rod Laver's Tennis Digest*, 1975, 1976, by Rod Laver and Bud Collins.

2: *"Strangers to the things that disturb us."*

14   *Gideon's roots trace back: More About the Riggs Family, 1590-1973*, by Clara Nichols Duggan and Helen Katherine Duggan, Benson Printing Co., Nashville, 1974, pp. 157-177, 229-237.

16   *"It was fortunate for me"*: "A Sketch of My Life," by Gideon Wright Riggs, reprinted in *More About the Riggs Family*, p. 165.

16   *The Church of Christ was:* "Restorationism and the Stone-Campbell Tradition," by David Edwin Harrell Jr. for the *Encyclopedia of the American Religious Experience*, edited by Charles H. Lippy and Peter W. Williams, Charles Scribner's Sons, New York, 1988, p. 851.

17   *Cool and low-key, Gideon:* Interviews with Frances Riggs, daughter of Sanders Riggs (July 2001), and Marian Riggs, wife of John Newton Riggs (March 2000).

17   *It was at one such Sunday sermons:* Interview with John N. Riggs, May 1999.

17   *Gideon met Michael Sanders:* "Gospel Preachers of Yesteryear," by Lloyd L. Smith, published 1983, publication unknown, provided to author by Hale Manier, a nephew of Bobby's living in College Grove, Tenn., September 1999.

19   *"I had no agreement with Brother Sanders"*: "A Sketch of My Life," p. 166.

20   *"My father was a very warm"*: *The First Time,* by Karl Fleming and Anne Taylor Fleming, 1975, Simon & Schuster, p. 242.

20   *"We were raised poor"*: Interview with Mary Lee (Riggs) Lantz, (June 1999).

20   *Agnes had little time for:* Interview with Marian Riggs.

21   *"My mother was just"*: *The First Time,* p. 239-240.

21   *Gideon occasionally returned: More About the Riggs Family,* p. 235.

21   *"I thought the country looked"*: From journal entry, August 1916, by Gideon Wright Riggs, part of personal scrapbook of his mother, Nancy Jordan Riggs, provided to author by Hale Manier.

21   *Years later, when Bobby stopped:* Interview with Hale Manier (September 1999).

3: *Tennis: Game of Kings and Sissies*

25   *"If you were in a restaurant"*: Interview with Robert "Buddy" Blatner (September 1999).

25   *"People have said to me"*: *Court Hustler,* by Bobby Riggs with George McGann, J.B. Lippincott Company, 1973, p. 46.

25   *"They handled some of the authority"*: *The First Time,* p. 241.

26   Death of Frank Riggs compiled from interviews with Kay (Fischer Riggs) Tauber (August 1999), John N. Riggs and Frances Riggs.

26   *"I guess because of Frank"*: *The First Time,* p. 240.

26   *Even a case of childhood diphtheria:* Interview with Kay Tauber.

27   *"It's all right if a better"*: *Tennis is My Racket,* by Bobby Riggs, Simon & Schuster, 1949, p. 31.

27   *"Win and you'll get"*: *Court Hustler,* p. 43.

27   *One year, his brother John:* Interview with John N. Riggs.

28   *Soon after Gideon installed: Tennis is My Racket,* p. 31.

28   *"They had Bobby box this kid"*: "Facing Life's Match Point," by Don Norcross, *San Diego Union-Tribune,* April 29, 1995.

28   *"Every once in a while"*: *Court Hustler,* p. 44.

29   *"I hardly had a pair of shoes"*: *The First Time,* p. 243.

28   *When Bobby was 11:* Interview with John N. Riggs, *Tennis is My Racket,* p. 32, and *Court Hustler,* p. 47.

29   *Bobby didn't have a racquet: Tennis is My Racket,* p. 33; and "A Racket for the Weekend Warrior," by Bobby Riggs, *Popular Mechanics,* April 1985, p. 91.

30   *"That accomplished, Bobby got down"*: *Fast Company,* by Jon Bradshaw, Random House, 1975, p. 38.

30   *The roots of the sport:* Compiled from "The Birth and Spread of Lawn Tennis," by Lance Tingay, *The Encyclopedia of Tennis,* 1974, pp. 22-24; and *Bud Collins' Tennis Encyclopedia,* 3rd ed., by Bud Collins and Zander Hollander, 1997, pp. 97-98, pp. 110-112.

33   *"I would rank Tilden alone"*: *Once a Champion,* by Stan Hart, Dodd, Mead & Co., 1984, p. 419.

33   *Jack Kramer was 13 years old: The Game,* by Jack Kramer with Frank Deford, G.P. Putnam and Sons, New York, 1979, p. 20.

34   *"It got so bad after a while"*: *Tennis is My Racket,* pp. 35.

34   *An eager student:* Bobby's introduction to the game and early days working with Esther Bartosh all described in *Tennis is My Racket,* pp. 35-49.

35   *"...took this little ragamuffin, whose mother"*: *Once a Champion,* p. 435.

36   *"The important thing is"*: *Tennis is My Racket,* p. 49.

36   *The club was founded in 1922:* Compiled from the official club history of the Los Angeles Tennis Club, 1997; *Tennis is My Racket;* and interviews with Gene Mako (May 1999) and Ted Schroeder (May 1999 and May 2000).

38   *"Just look, act and play like champions"*: Interview with Ted Schroeder.

38   *"I'm more interested in how they live"*: "The Jones Boys," *Time,* August 12, 1946, p. 46.

38   *"Budge, those are the dirtiest tennis shoes"*: *Don Budge: A Tennis Memoir,* by Don Budge and Frank Deford, Viking Press, 1969, p. 35.

39   *"Riggs is too small"*: Jones' statement and Bartosh's response both taken from *Tennis is My Racket,* p. 40.

40   *"Because we were playing for the balls"*: Interview with Ben Press (May 1999).

40   *Playing discretely for balls was one thing*: Interview with Ted Schroeder.

41   *"I was just good enough to be beaten"*: Interview with Ben Press.

41   *"He wanted to play for five dollars"*: Interview with Don Budge (June 1999).

41   *Only by waiting around long enough*: The Game, p. 166.

41   *When not at the club*: "Bobby Riggs, the Hustler," by Jeff Prugh, *Los Angeles Times,* June 12, 1972.

42   *As a ploy to help get a ride*: Compiled from *Tennis is My Racket,* pp. 41-42; and *San Francisco Chronicle,* June 25, 1932; and interview with John N. Riggs.

43   *He once won a $1,000 bet*: The Game, p. 166.

43   *Bobby asked his host*: Court Hustler, p. 51.

43   *"...took a dim view of the situation"*: Tennis is My Racket, p. 37.

44   *He remembered Gideon*: Court Hustler, p. 45.

44   *...the only time Agnes*: Compiled from "Bobby Riggs; Mother Watches Son Perform," *Los Angeles Times,* Jan. 1, 1942; and interviews with Mary Lee Lantz and Marian Riggs.

44   *Bobby would tell his wife Kay*: Interview with Kay Tauber.

45   *"I've never regretted this step"*: Court Hustler, p. 51.

4: *A Man's Game*

47   *On the soft grass*: description and quotes from *Court Hustler,* pp. 52-53.

48   *"Nobody gets to the top"*: Fast Company, p. 39.

48   *Every afternoon after school*: Tennis is My Racket, p. 65.

48   *He beat Bobby at his own game*: American Lawn Tennis, Aug. 20, 1932, p. 15.

48   *"The first lesson"*: Tennis is My Racket, p. 42.

49   *The next season*: Accounts of the California State Championships and Culver tournaments, *American Lawn Tennis,* August 5, 1933.

50   *"...the best match of the entire meeting"*: American Lawn Tennis, June 20, 1934, p. 19.

50   *Midway through the match*: Tennis is My Racket, p. 48.

51   *"...otherwise, I never would have graduated"*: Letter from Bobby to daughter of former classmate, Fred Renker, 1993.

51   *... the lone bright spot*: Interview with Bert Brown (November 1999).

51   *Perhaps he felt he didn't need*: The Game, p. 23.

52   *"...the sort of tennis"*: American Lawn Tennis, Aug. 20, 1935, p. 28.

52   *"I'm sure you'd enjoy"*: Tennis is My Racket, p. 50.

53   *Budge did pretty much as he pleased*: Match description and quote from *American Lawn Tennis,* Nov. 20, 1935, p. 10.

53   *Bobby told Perry Jones he intended*: Tennis is My Racket, p. 54.

54   Liberty *magazine labeled Bobby*: Fast Company, p. 39; and "My Side of the Story," by Robert L. Riggs, *Liberty* magazine, Feb. 7, 1942.

54   *With Bartosh's help, the two*: "All the World's a Stage," by Curry Kirkpatrick, *Sports Illustrated,* July 30, 1973, p. 54.

54   *To most club members*: Description of Jack Del Valle by Bobby in *Tennis is My Racket,* pp. 53-57, *Court Hustler,* p. 55, and interview with Jack Kramer.

56   *"Everybody was saying how good he was"*: Interview with Gardnar Mulloy (August 1999).

57   *"Even the most skeptical":* American Lawn Tennis, July 5, 1936, p. 12.

57   *"...a thoroughly rotten arrangement":* The Game, p. 63.

58   *At one tournament:* Court Hustler, p. 57.

58   *"the farther a tournament was":* The Game, p. 68.

59   *"The officials and a handful":* The Game, p. 67.

60   *Despite the disadvantage:* American Lawn Tennis, July 20, 1936, p. 15.

60   *"Riggs may become even better":* American Lawn Tennis, July 5, 1936, p. 18.

61   *"I never miss":* American Lawn Tennis, July 5, 1936, p. 18.

61   *On the changeovers:* Bobby's on-court appearance and behavior described in "Five Year Plan," by Charles Moran, Collier's, May 28, 1938, p. 22.

61   *"I remember I played him once":* Interview with John Nogrady (March 2000).

62   *"The power of Budge's game":* American Lawn Tennis, September 5, 1936, p. 12.

62   *At a crap game at Rye in 1936:* Tennis is My Racket, pp. 60-61.

63   *Bobby took the opportunity:* "Five Year Plan," Collier's.

64   *"It was my first experience":* Fast Company, p. 40.

64   *"Such return of service":* American Lawn Tennis, September 20, 1936, p. 11.

64   *Mulloy was in charge of running:* Once a Champion, p. 52.

64   *"The weather's wonderful":* Tennis is My Racket, p. 59.

65   *"We called it Cardboard College":* Once a Champion, p. 52.

65   *"The football players":* Interview with Gardnar Mulloy.

65   *Bobby took comic books to class:* Fast Company, p. 40.

65   *Bobby then found himself:* The Will to Win, by Gardnar Mulloy, A.S. Barnes & Co., 1960, p. 33.

66   *"It's a bum school":* Tennis is My Racket, p. 62.

5: *Playing By Their Rules*

69   *"Maybe we underestimated you":* Tennis is My Racket, p. 64.

71   *Each afternoon, the two would meet:* Courting Danger, by Alice Marble with Dale Leatherman, 1991, St. Martin's Press, p. 148; and "Riggs Scores With Pen," by Alice Marble, American Lawn Tennis, June 1949, p. 28.

71   *"...the most lovable player":* Once a Champion, p. 212.

71   *To help Bobby with the commute between:* Tennis is My Racket, p. 65.

72   *Bobby worked hard at his game:* Tennis is My Racket , p. 67.

72   *The Mid-Winter Championships:* American Lawn Tennis, Jan. 20, 1937, p. 10.

72   *Jones agreed that Bobby:* Tennis is My Racket, p. 67.

72   *...a group of well-wishers:* Tennis is My Racket, p. 71.

73   *About 10 days before Bobby:* Tennis is My Racket, pp. 72-74.

74   *John and Bobby developed a system:* Interviews with Bob Falkenburg (October 1999), Ben Press, and Bert Brown.

74   *"If Bobby had any drawback":* The Game, p. 165.

75   *"Against someone whom he could":* Don Budge: A Tennis Memoir, p. 85.

75   *One oft-repeated story:* "Mrs. King Versus Mr. Riggs," by Herbert Warren Wind, reprinted from The New Yorker in Game, Set, And Match: The Tennis Boom of the 1960's and '70's, 1979.

75   *He later explained:* Interview with Doug Dean (June 1999).

75   *"Being in the lead against Riggs":* American Lawn Tennis, Aug. 5, 1940, p. 4.

76   *Despite occasional indulgences for himself:* Interview with Lornie Kuhle (May 1999, October 2000, December 2001) and The First Time, p. 249.

76   *Thrift went to the core:* Court Hustler, p. 187.

76   *Bobby once claimed:* "His Last Match Can't Be Rigged," Los Angeles Times.

76   *"Ninety-five percent of the matches":* Court Hustler, p. 187.

77   *As Bobby rose to be the top seed:* The Game, p. 144.

77   *"All I needed was a facial massage":* Court Hustler, p. 158.

77   *Soon tournament directors flooded:* Tennis is My Racket, pp. 75-77; and *Court Hustler*, pp. 56-57.

78   *Budge remained too strong:* American Lawn Tennis, Sept. 5, 1937, p. 14.

78   *"The one ambition that I have":* "Bobby Riggs—Who is the Boy?" *Newport* [R.I.] *Herald*, August 24, 1937.

78   *When he looked at the draw:* Match description and quotes from "Five Year Plan," by Charles Moran, *Collier's* magazine, May 28, 1938, p. 22.

79   *"He plays just like God":* Unidentified spectator's comment quoted in *American Lawn Tennis,* Sept, 20, 1937, p. 59.

80   *Before a packed gallery:* Don Budge: A Tennis Memoir, pp. 3-20.

80   *Against von Cramm at Forest Hills:* Tennis is My Racket, p. 81 and *American Lawn Tennis*, Sept. 20, 1937, p. 15.

80   *"Oh," sang the German:* "Five Year Plan," *Collier's.*

81   *In the semifinals of the Pacific Coast:* Match description and quote from *American Lawn Tennis,* Oct. 20, 1937, p. 10.

81   *"I didn't want to be a hog":* Tennis is My Racket, p. 82.

81   *Bobby's fortunes:* The amount given by Lynch varies in Bobby's two memoirs. In *Tennis is My Racket,* he cites $50 per week. In *Court Hustler,* he cites $200 per week. Given Bobby's tendency toward exaggeration, the author chose the former.

82   *Icely came up with a deal:* Tennis is My Racket, pp. 82-84; *Court Hustler,* pp. 57-58; and *The Game,* p. 69.

83   *After a month, Bobby made plans:* Court Hustler, p. 58.

83   *During the early rounds at the Sugar Bowl:* Interview with Gardnar Mulloy.

84   *"You had to watch him":* Interview with Bob Falkenburg.

84   *For example, Mulloy recalled:* Interview with Gardnar Mulloy.

85   *Knowing that he was under scrutiny:* Tennis is My Racket, pp. 85-86.

85   *Bobby lost but one match:* American Lawn Tennis, Jan. 20, 1938, p. 4.

85   *"He had disappeared":* Tennis is My Racket, pp. 85-86.

86   *On his way out of the USLTA's offices:* Recollections of Ed Baker, former executive secretary of the USLTA, on his first meeting with Riggs, as quoted by Robert Minton in *An Illustrated History of Forest Hills,* 1975, J.B. Lippincott & Co., p. 151.

6: *"Who's going to feed the Fire Dragon today?"*

90   *"Who's going to feed":* Don Budge: A Tennis Memoir, p. 85.

90   *"He was so powerful":* Tennis is My Racket, p. 164.

90   *Budge later explained:* Don Budge: A Tennis Memoir, p. 85.

91   *"Believe me, as sure as":* Don Budge: A Tennis Memoir, p. 126.

91   *"I can assure you":* Don Budge: A Tennis Memoir, p. 129.

91   *With a $50,000 guarantee dangled:* Don Budge: A Tennis Memoir, p. 127.

91   *To the rest of the world:* The term Grand Slam was coined in 1933 by *New York Times* reporter John Kieran, a bridge player, in advance of Australian Jack Crawford's attempt to win at Forest Hills: "If Crawford wins, it would be something like scoring a grand slam on the courts, double and vulnerable." (Courtesy of Bud Collins).

92   *...he told only his doubles partner:* Don Budge: A Tennis Memoir, p. 104.

93   *"...heartening to Americans":* American Lawn Tennis, Aug. 20, 1938, p. 23.

93   *"Riggs, you'll have to fight":* Unattributed quote in *Tennis is My Racket,* p. 88.

93   *"...served, drove and volleyed":* American Lawn Tennis, Aug. 20, 1938, p. 10.

94   *"He had the most beautiful":* Interview with George Gondolman (March 2000).

94   *"...make the ball talk":* Interview with Pancho Segura (September 1999 and December 2000).

95   *"I used to get a diabolical pleasure"*: "Against All Odds," by Samantha Stevenson, *World Tennis*, March 1990, p. 34.

95   *"...rubbed a lot of people"*: The Game, p. 159.

95   *"...well-deserved rest"*: American Lawn Tennis, Aug. 20, 1938, p. 34.

95   *USLTA's "Eight-Weeks Rule"*: As explained in *American Lawn Tennis* column by Stephen W. Merrihew, Oct. 20, 1938, p 34.

95   *"...to keep outsiders"*: The Game, p. 69.

95   *"...about as important"*: Tennis is My Racket, p. 89.

96   *"the visitors, from captain"*: American Lawn Tennis, Sept. 5, 1938, p. 4.

97   *But Bobby suddenly was AWOL*: Don Budge's recollection from, "Bobby Riggs, Brash Impresario Of Tennis World, Is Dead at 77," by Robin Finn, *New York Times*, Oct. 27, 1995.

97   *"I feel reasonably sure"*: Tennis is My Racket, p. 89.

97   *"impressive wins"*: American Lawn Tennis, Sept. 20, 1938, p. 4.

98   *"I had decided before the match that he was a lot better at running"*: Interview with Gil Hunt (June 2002).

98   *"Everything he hit"*: "Psych Out" column, by Bobby Riggs, *World Tennis*, September 1981, p. 37.

98   *"...it was doubtful"*: descriptions by American Lawn Tennis, Sept. 20, 1938, p. 4.

99   *"Here, truly, is one of the great competitors"*: "Budge's Grand Slam," by Allison Danzig, first printed in the *New York Times* the day after the match and reprinted in *The Fireside Book of Tennis*, edited by Danzig and Peter Schwed, 1972, Simon & Schuster, p. 664.

99   *"...the good he could do"*: American Lawn Tennis, Nov.. 20, 1938, p. 4.

100   *But on this warm July afternoon*: Interview with Kay Tauber.

101   *"When it first happened"*: recollections of Robbie Wilson of the scene at the Colorado State Open at the Denver Country Club in "Playing to Win: The Denver Country Club's Championship Tradition," *Colorado Heritage*, Summer 2001.

101   *Having grown up around older brothers*: Bobby recollections and quotes from *The First Time*, p. 246.

102   *"...he was never content"*: The Game, p. 163.

102   *The ploy nearly got Bobby*: Tennis is My Racket, p. 75.

102   *"...if the girl"*: The Game, p. 163.

102   *"...were always strictly incidental"*: The First Time, p. 239.

102   *Kay, however, "attracted me"*: Tennis is My Racket, p. 89.

102   *She would watch as Bobby*: Interview with Kay Tauber.

7: *"I felt I had really arrived."*

105   *"Time is a strange phenomenon"*: "Will the real Bobby Riggs please stand up," by Beth Hightower, *The Sacramento Union*, July 21, 1974.

105   *When his editors at the* New York Times: Anecdote from *Big Bill Tilden*, by Frank Deford, Simon & Schuster, 1975, p. 23.

106   *"Tennis is not the same"*: Harold Parrott column, *Brooklyn Daily Eagle*, July 3, 1940.

106   *"Don't laugh, I did"*: Tennis is My Racket, p. 91.

107   *"...finally had to cave in"*: The First Time, p. 247.

107   *"Don't worry," Bobby assured her*: Interview with Kay Tauber.

107   *On May 24, Bobby sailed*: Description of voyage and accommodations in France taken from *Tennis is My Racket*, p. 93.

108   *"a bad patch of racquet trouble"*: Court Hustler, p. 63.

109   *"He was lazy and unenterprising"*: American Lawn Tennis, July 20, 1939, p. 10.

109   *...never played better in his life*: New York Times, June 18, 1939.

109   *Bobby admitted that perhaps*: Court Hustler, p. 63.

110 *"Thank you, Gottfried": London Daily Mirror,* June 26, 1939.

110 *"Ten-racket Riggs wins one game":* Headline cited in *American Lawn Tennis,* July 5, 1939, p.8.

110 *"I was not too keen to win": Court Hustler,* p. 63.

110 *As for von Cramm: The Romance of Wimbledon,* by John Olliff, Hutchinson Press, 1949, pp. 114-116.

110 *Returning to Germany: Don Budge: A Tennis Memoir,* p. 9.

111 *The court's immaculately maintained lawn: Wimbledon: A Celebration,* by John McPhee, Viking Press, 1972, pp. 105-109.

111 *Before the start of the tournament:* "The Sport Surprise," by Bill Stern, *Sport* magazine, June 1950, p. 60.

113 *He roared through the first set:* Compiled from "Nonchalance on the Court," by Clifford Webb, *London Daily Herald,* July 8, 1939; *Tennis is My Racket,* p. 96; and *American Lawn Tennis,* July 20, 1939.

114 *"Much of the tennis was academically perfect":* "Nonchalance on the Court," *London Daily Herald.*

114 *"The unfathomable Riggs": London Daily Mirror,* July 8, 1939.

114 *"...colossal Wimbledon walk-out":* "Nonchalance on the Court," *London Daily Herald.*

115 *"He began to wonder if he had done":* "The Sport Surprise," *Sport* magazine.

115 *"So I wound up": Tennis is My Racket,* p. 96.

115 *In his 1973 autobiography: Court Hustler,* pp. 64-65.

116 *"I was at the bookmaker's shop": Court Hustler,* p. 66.

116 *Bobby's first wife, Kay:* Interview with Kay Tauber.

116 *"I don't think he bet":* "His racket was hustling," by Bud Collins, *Boston Globe,* Oct. 29, 1995.

116 *Even Bobby's brother, John:* Interview with William Riggs (May 2000 and October 2000).

116 *Bobby "backed himself heavily": The Romance of Wimbledon,* p. 121.

116 *"...everything depended on our winning": Courting Danger* pp. 149-150.

117 *"...tennis writers were calling his game": American Lawn Tennis,* July 20, 1939, p. 4.

117 *Merrihew, called Bobby's victory: American Lawn Tennis,* July 5, 1939, p. 4.

117 *"...play more aggressively, hit harder": American Lawn Tennis,* July 20, 1939, p. 26.

117 *A writer for* the Los Angeles Times: As cited in *American Lawn Tennis,* April 20, 1940, p. 32.

117 *"I always have been for him": American Lawn Tennis,* May 20, 1940, p. 34.

118 *In the quarterfinals at Rye:* "Psych Out," by Bobby Riggs, *World Tennis,* Dec. 1981, p. 76; and interview with Ted Schroeder.

119 *One official complained: American Lawn Tennis,* August 20, 1939, p. 34.

119 *"When the entire court was shown, the figures": American Lawn Tennis,* Aug. 20, 1939, p. 20.

120 *"Riggs was deadly serious": American Lawn Tennis,* Sept. 20, 1939, p. 32.

121 *"He was definitely a better player":* Bromwich's recollections of the match as told to the *Sidney Morning Herald,* and recounted in *American Lawn Tennis,* Jan. 20, 1940, p. 16.

121 *"Look here, this tie isn't over yet": The Story of the Davis Cup,* Alan Trengove, 1985, Stanley Paul & Co., p. 140.

121 *"...came out flat...I wasn't loose": Once a Champion,* p. 419.

121 *A frustrated Bobby struggled: The Story of the Davis Cup,* p. 141.

121 *Bobby resorted to the only sure thing: Tennis is My Racket,* p. 99.

122 *Bobby's game responded splendidly: American Lawn Tennis,* Sept. 20, 1939, p. 4.

122 *"I had a good year":* Interview with Welby Van Horn, May 1999.

123 *"...probably the last big national tournament": New York Times,* Sept. 18, 1939.

123 *"the second coming of Don Budge": American Lawn Tennis,* Feb. 20, 1938, p. 8.

123 *Bobby and Kay married in Chicago: American Lawn Tennis,* Dec. 20, 1939, p. 15.

124 *"...quite an introduction to married life": Court Hustler,* p. 67.

8: *"Never did a champion lose his crown more gracefully."*

127   *In fact, Wingfield's biggest innovation:* "The Origins of Lawn Tennis," by the Rt. Hon. The Lord Aberdare, *The Encyclopedia of Tennis,* Viking Press, 1974, p 14.

128   *Bobby, in addition to watching his diet: Tennis is My Racket,* p. 245.

128   *To follow her husband's progress: Tennis is My Racket,* p. 103.

128   *Jack Kramer said he sometimes insisted:* Interview with Jack Kramer.

128   *Gardnar Mulloy, Prusoff's doubles partner:* Interview with Gardnar Mulloy.

129   *Don Budge, on the other hand: Don Budge: A Tennis Memoir,* p. 85.

130   *"Bobby, I shouldn't be beating you": Tennis is My Racket,* p. 103.

130   *"I don't know, Riggs, it looks bad": Tennis is My Racket,* p. 103.

131   *Gardnar Mulloy recalled one tournament: The Will to Win,* p 28.

131   *Bobby and Kay traveled around:* Interview with Kay Tauber.

131   *Also beginning to make a name for himself:* "Tennis Dizzy Dean," by Harold Parrott, *Saturday Evening Post,* April 5, 1941, p. 26.

132   *...his best shot was his backhand: The Game,* p. 51.

132   *In the San Francisco City Championships:* San Francisco and Glen Cove incidents from "Tennis Dizzy Dean," *Saturday Evening Post.*

132   *"First of all, he's 35 or 40 minutes late":* Interview with Gene Mako.

134   *"When Kovacs forgot his horseplay":* "Tennis Dizzy Dean," *Saturday Evening Post.*

134   *"To keep the pretty girls away":* "Tennis Dizzy Dean," *Saturday Evening Post.*

134   *On a blistering hot afternoon: Tennis is My Racket,* p. 104.

135   *But when the chair arrived:* "Tennis Dizzy Dean," *Saturday Evening Post.*

135   *In an attempt to throw Kovacs off his game:* Match description taken from *American Lawn Tennis,* Aug. 5, 1940, p. 4, and "Tennis Dizzy Dean," *Saturday Evening Post.*

136   *"Any dub could have made":* "Tennis Dizzy Dean," *Saturday Evening Post.*

137   *At first, an infuriated Van Horn:* Interviews Jack Kramer and Welby Van Horn (May 1999).

137   *"He figured that I was still pretty unknown": The Game,* p. 144.

137   *Jack Harris, promoter of the pro tour: Court Hustler,* p. 67.

138   *"My dear boy, your deplorable clowning":* Quotes and match description from "Tennis Dizzy Dean," *Saturday Evening Post.*

139   *Joe Hunt played Bobby in the semifinal:* It was to be one of Bobby's last matches with Hunt, who died in a mysterious plane crash during a military training exercise off Daytona Beach, Fla., on Feb. 2, 1944.

139   *Bobby had come down with a chest cold:* Interviews Kay Tauber, Jack Kramer, and "Riggs Dethroned by Don McNeill," by Allison Danzig, *New York Times,* Sept. 7, 1940, and reprinted in *The Fireside Book of Tennis,* p. 674.

139   *"...a two-fisted dead-end kid":* United Press International, Sept. 7, 1941.

140   *Minus his usual cheerful demeanor:* Match description from *Tennis is My Racket,* p. 107, *American Lawn Tennis,* Sept. 20, 1940, p. 4, and "Riggs Dethroned by Don McNeill," *New York Times.*

141   *McNeill slammed Bobby's next serve: Once a Champion,* p. 92.

142   *"Never did a champion": American Lawn Tennis,* Sept. 20, 1940, p. 16.

142   *"When Riggs walked off the court":* Associated Press, Sept. 7, 1940, and cited by Bobby in *Tennis is My Racket,* p. 108.

9: *Of Nerve and Endurance*

145   *"It seemed as though": Tennis is My Racket,* p. 108, and interviews with Kay Tauber, Jack Kramer and Ted Schroeder.

145   *"For anger, the best he could do": The Game,* p. 164.

146 *He had trouble sleeping:* As told by Kay to columnist Harold Parrott in his "Both Sides" column for the *Brooklyn Daily Eagle*, Sept. 6, 1941.

146 *Kay quickly brought Bobby back: Tennis is My Racket*, p. 109.

146 *Perry Jones forked over an until-then unheard of:* "What Price Amateurs?" *Time*, April 1, 1946, p. 65.

146 *After over three hours of play: American Lawn Tennis*, Oct. 20, 1940, p. 4.

147 *For her part, Kay completely embraced: Tennis is My Racket*, p. 109; and interview with Kay Tauber.

148 *Gardnar Mulloy recalled a match: The Will to Win*, p. 29.

148 *In Miami, Kovacs and Bobby: American Lawn Tennis*, Mar. 20, 1941, p. 4.

149 *The one-upmanship between the two players: The Will to Win*, pp. 29-30.

150 *In an attempt to reduce the painful glare: American Lawn Tennis*, Mar. 20, 1941, p. 4.

150 *On pure tennis ability: Tennis is My Racket*, p. 112.

150 *The association's watchdogs began: Tennis is My Racket*, p. 111.

152 *"The play of Riggs": American Lawn Tennis*, Aug. 5, 1941, p. 16.

152 *For Kay, there was another benefit:* Interview with Kay Tauber.

153 *One aspect of Bobby's life:* "I've given up gambling," Bobby told columnist Harold Parrott of the *Brooklyn Daily Eagle*, Aug. 1, 1940. "Dice and cards, with big money involved, use up your nervous energy. Now I've all the energy I need when I get in a bad spot, and I can really concentrate and bear down more."

153 *To win in high-stakes gambling:* Interviews with Kay Tauber, Jack Kramer and Ted Schroeder.

155 *"Does the wind bother you, Bobby?":* Harold Parrott column, *Brooklyn Daily Eagle*, Sept. 8, 1941.

155 *After settling down:* Match description taken from *American Lawn Tennis*, Sept. 20, 1941, p. 4, and "The Tennis Courts: No, It Isn't the Breeze," by D.E.L., *The New Yorker*, September 13, 1941, p. 48.

155 *Bobby knew if Kovacs went to the locker room: Tennis is My Racket*, p. 118.

156 *"I swear I've been playing":* Associated Press, Sept. 8, 1941.

158 *"Congratulations, Don":* "Money Men," *Time*, July 22, 1946, pp. 48-49.

158 *"You're probably wondering": Tennis is My Racket*, p. 126.

158 *"He left me in the hospital":* Interview with Kay Tauber.

10: *A Wonderful War*

161 *"Hey, Chief, how's chances":* Barracks scene, exchange with Irv Kupcinet and meeting with Vice President Henry Wallace from *Tennis is My Racket*, pp. 128-131.

162 *Seizing an opportunity:* Recollection of Dr. Homer Peabody Jr. from "For tennis-craving physician, playing Bobby Riggs is a net gain," by R.H. Growald, *San Diego Union-Tribune*, Oct. 3, 1992.

163 *To Bobby's surprise: American Lawn Tennis*, July 1944, p. 9.

164 *To help him get through it: Tennis is My Racket*, p. 132.

164 *"...tired of the Navy...": Tennis is My Racket*, p. 132.

164 *At the stadium, he ran into Bill Stern: Tennis is My Racket*, p. 132. (Stern was later to pen the story of Bobby's attempted parlay at Wimbledon in 1939.)

165 *Bobby joined a group of other famous athletes:* Interview with Robert "Buddy" Blattner (July 1999).

167 *The rough asphalt courts:* Details of wartime tennis taken from *American Lawn Tennis*, "Riggs Promotes Pacific Tennis," July 1, 1944, p. 6.

170 *"And don't you know it":* In his books, Bobby claims the Navy allowed him to use $1,000 of his gambling winnings to purchase a secondhand Cadillac. Following interviews with Blattner and Tauber, the author decided to use this account for several reasons. First, both Blattner and Tauber say the car was a

Packard. Also, given Bobby's tight-fistedness, it would be implausible for him to purchase a luxury sedan—even a secondhand one—for such a relatively short stay, particularly given the availability of free transportation via the military. It's also difficult to believe Bobby would admit to his superiors fleecing his fellow sailors while on the Navy's time.

170 *By now, Kay had moved to California:* Interview with Kay Tauber.
171 *"…scouting trips to find a movie":* Tennis is My Racket, p. 138.
171 *Bobby once mentioned an incident: Fast Company,* p. 45, and "Portrait of a Beautiful Hustler," by Herbert Gold, *New York Times Sunday Magazine,* Aug. 5, 1973, p. 44.
172 *"The only time Admiral Hoover":* Tennis is My Racket, p. 139.
174 *Budge's forehand was not a natural stroke: Tennis is My Racket,* p. 163.
174 *"I said to myself that the difference":* Once a Champion, p. 427.
174 *While in Officer Candidate School: Don Budge: A Tennis Memoir,* p. 144.
176 *In the first match:* Match descriptions from *Tennis is My Racket,* p. 140, pp.164-167; *Court Hustler,* pp. 73-74; *Don Budge, A Tennis Memoir,* pp. 144-145; and *American Lawn Tennis,* October 1945, p. 55.

11: *The Quest for the $100,000 Plum*

181 *…tennis limped along:* Compiled from *Bud Collins' Tennis Encyclopedia* and *American Lawn Tennis.*
182 *"Where've you been, Riggs?":* Tennis is My Racket, p. 141.
182 *Tilden suggested staging: Tennis is My Racket,* p. 182.
183 *The final pitted Budge against Bobby:* Match description from *Tennis is My Racket,* pp. 144-146; and *Fast Company,* p. 45.
183 *"I'm sorry that it happened this way":* "Riggs New Champ, Collects $5,000 Bet," *Los Angeles Herald Examiner,* Dec. 10, 1945.
184 *But few were ready for a new champion: Fast Company,* pp. 45-47; and *Tennis is My Racket,* pp. 146-147.
185 *"When ever Riggs changed sides":* "You Can Bet That Riggs Came Away a Big Winner." Letter by Frank Chamberlain to *Los Angeles Times,* April 22, 1995.
185 *"Once more Riggs proved himself":* From Tilden's "Passing Shots" column; and *American Lawn Tennis,* March 1946, p. 30.
188 *Tilden "never made passes at fellow players": Court Hustler,* p. 155.
188 *"Pro tennis owes a tremendous debt":* Tennis is My Racket, p. 191.
188 *"Tell Riggs to ease up on Budge":* Unidentified quote from, "Is the Riggs-Kramer Tour on the Level?" *American Lawn Tennis,* March 1948, p. 33.
189 *Bobby agreed to extend the tour:* Figures from *American Lawn Tennis,* May 1946, p. 10.
190 *Years later, recalling that year: Don Budge: A Tennis Memoir,* p. 145.
190 *The "Clown Prince" had since become: Tennis is My Racket,* pp. 177-179.
191 *"Look, kid. I know you're gonna":* Interview with Jack Kramer.
191 *The result, wrote Bobby: Tennis is My Racket,* pp. 12-14.
192 *"A year ago I told everyone present":* "Riggs Retains Rule," *American Lawn Tennis,* July 1947.

12: *Duel of the Decade*

195 *An almost mild 29 degrees:* "The Big Snow," *Time,* Jan. 5, 1948, p. 15.
196 *"No one will go out to see": American Lawn Tennis,* February 1948, p. 6.
196 *"…the most widely discussed topic":* "What Will Happen When Kramer Opposes Riggs?" by Allison Danzig, *American Lawn Tennis,* November 1947, p. 14.

196 *As they clambered over snowbanks: The Game*, p. 156.

196 *John Frankenheimer, a young college student:* Interview with John Frankenheimer (March 2000).

197 *"...the greatest tribute to an indoor athletic event in the history of sport":* Jimmy Powers column, *New York Daily News,* as cited in *The Game,* p. 157.

197 *Clifton Roche, an automotive engineer:* Compiled from, *The Game,* pp. 27-28, pp. 35-38; "Advantage Kramer," *Time,* Sept. 1, 1947, p. 46; and interviews with Jack Kramer and Ted Schroeder.

198 *"Eight out of ten points": Tennis is My Racket,* p. 235.

199 *In practice matches leading up:* "Bobby's Pre-match Scouting Produces Big Dividends," by Mercer Beasely, *American Lawn Tennis,* February 1948, p. 10.

200 *By the time play started: Court Hustler,* p. 78.

200 *"I made up my mind": Fast Company,* p. 48.

200 *"...it seemed that each one": American Lawn Tennis,* February 1948, p. 6.

201 *"But that's no alibi":* "Villain's Victory," *Time,* January 5, 1948, p. 47.

201 *Bobby demanded a meeting: The Game,* p. 158.

202 *"It was backbreaking work":* Interview with Bert Brown.

203 *In Little Rock: The Game,* pp. 190-197.

203 *"At each stop": The Game,* p. 61.

204 *...received just $300 per week apiece: The Game,* p. 193.

204 *"Bobby stole my money":* "The Circus Circuit," *Los Angeles Times,* July 24, 1997.

204 *When it came to cards: The Game,* p. 196.

204 *"After the matches": The Game,* p. 195.

205 *"...the best shot in the game": The Game,* p. 45.

206 *"The football players took him over":* Interview with Gardnar Mulloy.

206 *"The fans would come out": The Game,* p. 187.

207 *"His strategy was to smother me": The Game,* p. 161.

208 *"I hated it and fell apart": Fast Company,* p. 48.

208 *"...just poured it on harder and harder": Tennis is My Racket,* pp. 23-25.

208 *"More than half the audience":* "Trouper Troubles," *Newsweek,* March 29, 1948, p. 77.

209 *Years later, he remembered that shot:* "Against All Odds," *World Tennis.*

13: *The End of the Road*

213 *"They wanted to see him": Tennis is My Racket,* p. 157.

214 *"Being number two":* Interview with Bobby Riggs, April 1995 (courtesy of Doug Dean).

214 *"An older and more subdued":* "Kramer Absent, Riggs Reigns Once Again," *American Lawn Tennis,* July 15, 1949.

214 *"I was fatigued":* Interview with Bobby Riggs, April 1995 (courtesy of Doug Dean).

215 *"I could still make deals":* "Chips, chops, drops and lobs," by Gwilyn S. Brown, *Sports Illustrated,* Jan. 18, 1971, p. 60.

216 *"Ted, you've got to be kidding":* Interview with Ted Schroeder.

217 *"I was over the hill": Once a Champion,* p. 145.

217 *"The only reason I went to Wimbledon":* Interview with Ted Schroeder.

218 *"I kept telling him":* Kramer's quote and subsequent exchanges with Bobby and Ted Schroeder from *The Game,* pp. 176-177.

218 *At the time, Kramer believed:* When asked in 2000, Schroeder said he told Kramer that he "would play no competitive tennis through to Labor Day weekend," and insisted Kramer misunderstood his meaning. In *The Game,* Kramer wrote, "...whatever he thought he said, I know damn well that both Riggs and I were under the impression that he had taken himself out of the Davis Cup and Forest Hills" (p. 176).

219 *"Now, I guess everybody"*: The Game, p. 180.

219 *As a promoter, Bobby was a natural*: The Game, p. 192; and interview with Jack Kramer.

220 *The bigger problem*: The Game, pp. 199-201.

222 *...somewhere in Texas*: Interviews with Pancho Segura and John Wheelan Riggs (May 1999 and June 2000).

222 *Gonzalez, however, seemed washed up*: Gonzalez returned to professional tennis three years later, and for the next decade dominated the game, living up to his early potential and earning him a place in history as one of the game's very best.

223 *Her name was Judy*: The Game, p. 163; and interview with Jack Kramer.

223 *"Bobby was always looking"*: Interview with Gloria Kramer (May 1999).

224 *"Look out girls, here's Bobby"*: Melbourne Herald, Sept. 27, 1948.

224 *"Let's face it"*: The Game, p. 196.

224 *Kay knew there were other women*: Interview with Kay Tauber.

224 *As for Bobby, he too*: The First Time, p. 239, p. 247.

224 *"I don't think he had any roots"*: Interview with Jack Kramer.

224 *As for women, they were just*: The First Time, p. 247.

224 *"I thought if I said"*: Interview with Kay Tauber.

225 *By the end of July 1950*: "Mrs. Riggs Awarded $700 Month Alimony," Los Angeles Times, July 22, 1950.

225 *"He used to try and find people"*: Interview with Jack Kramer.

225 *Hearing of the match*: The Game, pp. 148-149; and interviews with Gardnar Mulloy and Pancho Segura. Mulloy insisted the match was not fixed. "If it was fixed. I didn't fix it," he said in 1999. "I was killing myself out there." Segura said he never told Mulloy he planned to lose, but did it as a favor to help raise money for Mulloy's Wimbledon trip.

230 *"Kid, we got a problem"*: The Game, p. 95.

230 *Bobby tried everything*: "How Bobby Runs and Talks, Talks, Talks," Time, Sept. 10, 1973, p. 54.

230 *"Unfortunately, after all the publicity"*: The Game, p. 94.

230 *Frustrated, Kramer decided*: The Game, p. 212.

231 *On top of everything else*: "Bouncing Around" column, American Lawn Tennis, November 1950, p. 20; and interviews with Kay Tauber, Jack Kramer, and Bob Feller (September 1999).

14: *"Give me a millionaire every time."*

233 *"How long has this been going on?"*: Court Hustler, p. 87.

234 *For example, in 2000*: Results from Zandi Group poll published in USA Today, Jan 30, 1998, p. 1.

235 *"You'd be amazed"*: Fast Company, p. 49.

235 *"The second worst thing in the world"*: Court Hustler, p. 88.

235 *"I just out-competed them"*: Fast Company, p. 54.

236 *Tagging along with good players*: Compiled from Court Hustler, pp. 87-113; Fast Company, pp. 53-57; and "Larceny on the Links," Life, March 26, 1956.

236 *"I could not afford the cut in pay"*: "Larceny on the Links," Life, March 26, 1956.

236 *"It was like an open-air poolroom"*: Fast Company, p. 54.

237 *"Look at that guy"*: Court Hustler, p. 90.

238 *Trevino himself grew up*: Fast Company, p. 231.

238 *"...nice people who just love"*: "Larceny on the Links," Life.

238 *"The Fat Man always gave you"*: Fast Company, p. 55.

238 *"I learned all the angles"*: Fast Company, p. 54.

238 *"I always rise to the occasion"*: Fast Company, p. 49.

239 *"I was always pretty good about figuring":* Court Hustler, p. 94.

239 *"I've played Riggs and beat him":* "Larceny on the Links," *Life.*

239 *By offering big odds or a big handicap:* Court Hustler, p. 43.

239 *"He had an obsession with winning":* Interview with Larry Riggs.

241 *Bobby, who lived nearby:* "Larceny on the Links," *Life*, and *Court Hustler*, p. 92.

241 *"These guys would try to distract me":* Court Hustler, p. 95.

242 *"Tell you what I'm gonna do":* "Larceny on the Links," *Life.*

242 *Once, in the early 1950s:* Interview with Welby Van Horn.

242 *With a sixth sense for money:* Fast Company, pp. 55-56, and "Riggs Plays for Fun and Action," by Bud Collins, *Boston Globe*, July 13, 1982.

243 *"...you'd practically think he was doing you a favor":* Interview with Steve Levy (August 2000).

244 *At Bayshore Country Club in Miami one day:* Interview with David Hackworth Riggs (May 1999).

244 *"Do you know Bobby Riggs?":* Interview with Vic Braden (October 2000).

244 *The blast was so powerful:* "Palm Springs Pioneer Killed in 'Professional' Explosion," Palm Springs *Desert Sun*, Oct. 19, 1977; and "Police Probe Mob Crime Link in Ryan Death," Palm Springs *Desert Sun*, Oct. 20, 1977.

245 *"I think it's time":* Interview with Lornie Kuhle.

245 *"People misunderstand the mentality":* "All the World's a Stage," *Sports Illustrated.*

245 *"Let me tell ya":* Fast Company, p. 56.

245 *"He'd rather hustle a bum":* Interview with Ted Schroeder.

246 *For example, one longtime friend:* Interview with Bob Barker (May 2000).

15: *"There's no winning here."*

249 *"...instant chemistry, love at first sight,"* "All the World's a Stage," *Sports Illustrated.*

252 *"My father-in-law":* Interview with Mike Crimi (September 2000).

252 *"Priscilla was very protective":* Interview with Larry Riggs.

253 *"I came into the company":* "All the World's a Stage," *Sports Illustrated.*

253 *"He just wasn't R.B.'s type":* Interview with Mike Crimi.

254 *"I never had any initiative":* "All the World's a Stage," *Sports Illustrated.*

254 *"One day, he had gone":* Fast Company, p. 50.

254 *"We put Bob in charge of several things":* Interview with Mike Crimi.

254 *"...there was always this undercurrent":* "All the World's a Stage," *Sports Illustrated.*

255 *"I was not the kind":* Court Hustler, p. 184.

255 *"One of the regular memories":* Interview with John W. Riggs.

255 *"I tried to help my wife":* The First Time, p. 250.

256 *"It seemed more like":* Interview with Dorothy Riggs (September 1999).

256 *"I remember my dad telling me":* Interview with William Riggs.

256 *"When we played our dad in tennis":* Interview with John W. Riggs.

257 *Larry recalled the same $100 bet:* Interview with Larry Riggs.

257 *"He used to tell my mom":* Interview with John W. Riggs.

258 *"Larry's always been rebellious":* "All the World's a Stage," *Sports Illustrated.*

258 *"I came to realize that my dad":* Interview with John W. Riggs.

258 *"He could say no and make you feel better":* Interview with Doug Dean.

258 *In 1973 Larry was working as a stockbroker:* Interview with Larry Riggs.

260 *"They say some men mature":* The First Time, pp. 249-250.

260 *"My mother decided":* Interview with William Riggs.

260 *Bill thought Bobby was teasing him:* Interview with Dorothy Riggs.

261 *"I have someone here":* Interview with William Riggs.

262 *"I guess I always thought the wife":* The First Time, p. 251.

262 *As it was, she didn't play sports:* Court Hustler, p. 184.

263 *"By the time I was in junior high school":* Interview with John W. Riggs.

264 *"She couldn't stand it":* Interview with Larry Riggs.

265 *When the gang got to town:* Interviews with Jack and Gloria Kramer.

265 *"She had a real knack":* Interview with John W. Riggs.

266 *"I was terrified growing up":* Interview with Dorothy Riggs.

267 *"We talked about this":* Interview with Dorothy Riggs.

267 *"He didn't dwell on it":* Interview with Doug Dean.

267 *"I never thought of my wife's money":* "All the World's a Stage," *Sports Illustrated;* and "Portrait of a Beautiful Hustler," *New York Times Sunday Magazine*, p. 12.

267 *"He was so fucking tight":* Interview with William Riggs.

268 *"I'm still wearing":* Tennis is My Racket, p. 97.

268 *"Here, I got you a present":* Interview with William Riggs.

268 *"That's where I belong":* "Riggs Sets Sight on King Rematch for Million Each," *Miami Herald*, November 9, 1975.

16: *The Greatest Salesman of All Time*

271 *"You've got to stay in action":* Fast Company, p. 54.

271 *"It was nothing":* Interview with Joe Fishbach (April 2000).

272 *"I had him flicking cards":* "How Bobby Runs and Talks, Talks, Talks," *Time;* and interview with John W. Riggs.

272 *"He had more fun":* Interview with John Nogrady.

272 *"...the greatest salesman":* Interview with Tony Vincent (May 2000).

272 *Friend and former champion Bob Falkenburg:* Interview with Bob Falkenburg.

273 *After collecting the debt:* Interviews with Bob Lutz (February 2003) and Lornie Kuhle.

273 *"Bobby would run it into the ground":* Interview with Doug Dean.

274 *"He never paid you when he lost":* Interview with John Nogrady.

274 *"I think Bobby's forte in betting":* Interview with Joe Fishbach.

274 *"...hardly touched a racquet":* Court Hustler, p. 86.

274 *"...argumentative gang of brokers":* Court Hustler, p. 123.

275 *"...they would be laying out bets":* Interview with John Nogrady.

275 *In Ashe's case, recalled one regular:* Interview with Phil Kasden, former player at Lafayette College (February 2002).

275 *"I played him 25 times":* Interview with Gene Scott (November 2000).

276 *"He was a very warm person":* Interview with George Gondolman.

276 *"There wasn't much of a clubhouse":* Interview with Renée Richards (August 2000).

277 *In the late 1960s:* Interview with Tony Vincent.

278 *"Look, I don't want to just play":* Interview with Bob Barker.

279 *"I had tried everything":* The Game, pp. 257-258.

280 *"There was a sense that being Bobby Riggs":* Interview with Gene Scott.

280 *"...the younger game in slow motion":* "Chips, chops, drops and lobs," *Sports Illustrated.*

280 *"What we lack in speed":* Court Hustler, p. 149.

280 *"...can achieve high excitement":* "Chips, chops, drops and lobs," *Sports Illustrated.*

281 *A linesman at one of Bobby's matches:* Court Hustler, p. 148.

281 *"I look at Riggs":* "Riggs Gains Senior Semis," *San Diego Union*, Sunday, Dec. 2, 1972.

281 *"Letting me back into tennis":* Court Hustler, p. 141, pp. 147-148.

282 *"...talk you out of the game":* "Chips, chops, drops and lobs," *Sports Illustrated.*

282 *"...people get up and go get a hot dog":* The Game, p. 80.

282 *"I knew we were playing far better tennis":* Court Hustler, p. 12.

283 *"I'm going to write this book":* Interview with George McGann (June 2000).

284 *"I'm willing to put my money":* "Chips, chops, drops and lobs," *Sports Illustrated.*

17: *Hype of the Century*

287 *"Oh, hi. Hi honey":* Interview with Larry Riggs.

288 *"I could live with the absences":* Interview with John W. Riggs.

288 *"I felt lost": The First Time,* p. 248.

289 *"You know, I tried":* Interview with John W. Riggs.

289 *"He would sit with his brother Dave":* "All the World's a Stage," *Sports Illustrated.*

290 *He decided to live the lifestyle:* Bobby's presentation to the Boston Ad Club, Feb. 1, 1974.

290 *Kramer told Bobby: Court Hustler,* p. 14.

290 *So he hopped over a little fence:* Billie Jean King and Bobby differ on this meeting. Bobby places it in the dining room at Wimbledon 1970, where Billie Jean King was recovering from knee surgery. Billie Jean King puts it at 1971, on the practice court at Forest Hills. However, Billie Jean didn't undergo surgery until two weeks after Wimbledon in 1970. Besides this was more than six months before the *Sports Illustrated* article appeared. Because of this, the author chose to follow Billie Jean King's scenario.

291 *"Why don't we play a fun match": Court Hustler,* p. 13.

291 *"You've got to play":* Billie Jean, by Billie Jean King with Kim Chapin, Harper & Row, 1974, p. 166.

291 *"I'd like to see you revive that": Court Hustler,* p. 15.

291 *Watt kicked in another $5,000:* As an added incentive for Bobby, Watt gave him a custom-built house alongside the development's golf course. For Watt, it was more than a fair deal. That, in addition to the $30,000 he ended up spending to promote Riggs-Court bought him an estimated $5 million in resulting press and television coverage, and helped make the development a huge success, according to Charles and Nancy Lemenager, authors of *Off the main road : San Vicente & Barona, a history of those who shaped events in the Rancho Cañada de San Vicente y Mesa del Padre Barona,* Eagle Peak Pub. Co., 1983.

291 *"Bobby Riggs, that old campaigner": Court Hustler,* p. 16.

292 *"I'd love to play her every day of the week and twice on Sunday":* "Bobby Runs, and Talks, Talks, Talks," *Time.*

292 *"We didn't need him":* "Bobby Runs, and Talks, Talks, Talks," *Time.*

292 *"She might make more noise": Court on Court,* by Margaret Court and George McGann, Dodd, Mead & Co., 1975, pg. 164, and interviews with George McGann, (June 2002) and Gladys Heldman (February 2002).

293 *"Once I admired Billie Jean a lot": Court on Court,* p. 167.

293 *"Someone won 6-0, but I don't": Tinling: Sixty Years in Tennis,* by Ted Tinling, Sedgewick & Jackson, London, 1983.

293 *Similarly, in 1936, 15-year-old Jack Kramer: The Game,* pp. 90-91

293 *"...a kind of breather for me...": Court on Court,* p. 167.

293 *At a tournament in Detroit: Billie Jean,* with Kim Chapin, p. 167; and "I just had to win," by Billie Jean King, *Tennis,* August 1998.

294 *"We didn't even think about television": Court Hustler,* pp. 15-16.

294 *"Heck, I haven't had any attention for twenty-five years": Fast Company,* p. 36.

295 *"...been so perturbed": Fast Company,* p. 32.

295 *"Look at those legs":* Unidentified quote from *Wimbledon—A Celebration,* p. 52.

295 *"I've never said we deserve ":* "Mother's Day Ms. Match," by Curry Kirkpatrick, *Sports Illustrated,* May 21, 1973, p. 34.

296 *"Why should we have to justify ourselves":* "Mother's Day Ms. Match," *Sports Illustrated.*

296 *Before going on court, Bobby:* "All the World's a Stage," *Sports Illustrated;* and interview with Lornie Kuhle.

297 *"He has a Ph.D.":* Videotaped remarks by Bobby at his wedding reception Feb. 14, 1991 (courtesy John W. Riggs).

297 *"Gosh, I won't last a set"*: Fast Company, p. 42.

298 *He sent Bobby home*: Compiled from "Bobby Runs, and Talks, Talks, Talks," *Time*; *Fast Company*, pp. 42-43; and interviews William Riggs and Don Rhodes (November 2000).

298 *"Sure, I think it stinks"*: Fast Company, p. 59.

299 *"It was as though the manic flood"*: Fast Company, p. 34.

299 *"She has a better serve"*: Associated Press, May 4, 1973.

300 *"...what was what is known in the trade"*: Fast Company, p. 34.

300 *"I play like a woman"*: Fast Company, p. 52.

300 *"...like an account executive"*: Fast Company, p. 33.

301 *"...reciting the grim list of his deficiencies"*: Fast Company, p. 33.

301 *"Hey, how do I look?"*: Fast Company, p. 35.

302 *"You don't say?"*: Fast Company, pp. 34-35.

302 *"The only way Riggs could lose"*: "Riggs vs. Margaret Court: A Mismatch?" by Charles Friedman, *Sunday New York Times*, March 4, 1973.

303 *"Do you think that blood-pushing fag?"*: Fast Company, p. 51.

303 *Bobby's regimen of pills*: Bobby never admitted to using amphetamines, and Lornie Kuhle, his closest friend and personal assistant, steadfastly denies Bobby ever used them. Bobby's sons, however, William and John W., both remember their father using them, and even recall the type and dosage of pills. Based on their recollections, and information from further interviews, the author decided it was likely Bobby used the drug to enhance his athletic performance.

303 *"If this keeps up"*: Fast Company, p. 51.

303 *While Court banged away at groundstrokes*: Fast Company, p. 61.

304 *To himself, Bobby secretly gloated*: Court Hustler, p. 28.

304 *"Lots of women have passed me"*: Fast Company, pp. 62-63.

305 *"Can't you do anything about the loudmouth?"*: Fast Company, p. 61.

306 *"I dreamed about the match"*: Fast Company, p. 64.

306 *Later, Bobby called up his friend*: Court Hustler, p 34.

306 *For Margaret, the morning's portents*: Court on Court, p. 169.

306 *"Are you going to win, Bobby?"*: Fast Company, p. 66.

307 *At precisely one o'clock*: Match description compiled from *Court Hustler*, pp. 37-39; *Fast Company*, pp. 67-73; *Court on Court*, pp. 169-171; and "All the World's a Stage," *Sports Illustrated*.

310 *"I didn't expect so many soft shots"*: "Riggs Routs Mrs. Court in Challenge Match, 6-2, 6-1," *Washington Post*, May 14, 1973.

310 *Incredulous, Bobby wondered*: Court Hustler, p. 40.

311 *"I guess it proves"*: Associated Press, May, 14, 1973.

311 *"Oh heck, it was nothing"*: Fast Company, p. 78.

18: *Both Separate and Unequal*

313 *Billie Jean King didn't watch*: Billie Jean, by Billie Jean King with Kim Chapin, p. 164.

314 *For example, in 1969*: "Sport is Unfair to Women," by Bill Gilbert and Nancy Williamson, *Sports Illustrated*, May 28, 1973, p. 88.

317 *"...about this little punk"*: Billie Jean, by Billie Jean King and Kim Chapin, p. 165.

317 *"She helped me a lot"*: Billie Jean, by Billie Jean King and Kim Chapin, p. 36.

318 *During her run at Forest Hills*: Billie Jean, by Billie Jean King and Kim Chapin, p. 76.

319 *"From a show-biz standpoint"*: Billie Jean, by Billie Jean King and Kim Chapin, p. 101.

319 *"In the long run"*: The Game, p. 100.

319 *"...it was just good business": The Game,* p. 79.
320 *"...long and loud discussion": Billie Jean,* by Billie Jean King and Kim Chapin, p. 103.
320 *With the help of Joseph Cullman:* Compiled from *Bud Collins' Tennis Encyclopedia, Billie Jean,* by Billie Jean King with Kim Chapin, pp. 104-105; and interview with Gladys Heldman (February 2002).
321 *"You know Congress":* "Women in Sports," Part one of a seven-part series, by Jeff Schultz and Mike Fish, *Atlanta Journal and Constitution,* September 20, 1998.
321 *"Before I kept out of it":* "Billie Jean Wants to Play Riggs," *Providence Journal,* May 15, 1973.

19: *The Merchants of Tennis*

323 *"When it came on": Court Hustler,* p. 175.
324 *...earning it a whopping:* Hollywood Reporter figures cited in *Court Hustler,* p. 36.
324 *"I didn't know Bobby":* Interview with Jerry Perenchio (November 1999).
324 *"Why not? After all":* "Riggs on Va. Slims Circuit? It's a matter of Dress," Associated Press, May 17, 1973.
325 *"Can't get through to the little bastard": Fast Company,* p. 190.
325 *"It's like being reincarnated":* "Riggs Enjoys the Spotlight as Promoters come Callin'," Associated Press, May 20, 1973.
325 *"Imagine that":* "Riggs Enjoys the Spotlight as Promoters come Callin'," Associated Press.
326 *"Everybody was after him":* Interview with Jerry Perenchio.
326 *"Sure, I got taken in the first match":* "All the World's a Stage," *Sports Illustrated.*
327 *His stone-faced support: Billie Jean,* by Billie Jean King with Frank Deford, Viking Press, New York, 1982, pp. 33-34.
328 *"C'mon, Bob, let's go see":* Interview with Bob Falkenburg.
328 *"The Ali-Frazier fight": Court Hustler,* p 174.
328 *"Of course, we pretty much scripted":* Interview with Jerry Perenchio.
329 *"We've got five hundred dollars to bet against you": Court Hustler,* p. 175.
330 *"That moment was a stroke of genius":* Interview with Jerry Perenchio.
330 *"The key to promotion":* "Can a Tennis Match Make $2 Million?" *Business Week,* Sept. 1, 1973, p. 22.
330 *"...we put the site up for auction":* Interview with Jerry Perenchio.
331 *"I think we can sell one million racquets":* "Can a Tennis Match Make $2 Million?" *Business Week.*
331 *"I love women":* "All the World's a Stage," *Sports Illustrated.*
332 *"The last time I went five sets":* "Is Super-Confident Riggs Really that Confident?"Associated Press, Aug. 28, 1973.
332 *"...she tap-danced across his chest in spiked heels:"* as quoted in "How Bobby Runs and Talks, Talks, Talks," *Time.*
333 *"Gosh, you'd better go":* "Billie Jean Outhustles the Hustler," by Joanne Lannin, *Portland* [Me.] *Press Herald,* Sept. 20, 1998.
334 *"It's the Grand Wizard of the KKK":* Interview with William Riggs.
334 *"...disdain for effeminate men...":* "Portrait of a Beautiful Hustler," *New York Times Sunday Magazine,* and "All the World's a Stage," *Sports Illustrated.*
334 *"...a Ford, a Chrysler, a Bristol-Meyers...":* "Portrait of a Beautiful Hustler," *New York Times Sunday Magazine.*
335 *"...it'll be hot-and-cold running women":* "How Bobby Runs and Talks, Talks, Talks," *Time.*
335 *"She had no interest in getting involved":* Interview with Jerry Perenchio.
335 *Bloomingdale's department store: Court Hustler,* p. 178.
337 *"It's true Bobby has a compulstion":* Associated Press, April 28, 1973.

337 *For much of the summer, Bobby stayed:* Steve Powers offer and subsequent anecdote about missing $1,800 from "Bobby Runs, and Talks, Talks, Talks," *Time.*

338 *"...just one huge party after another":* This and subsequent quote from interview with Larry Riggs.

338 *"Bobby didn't practice":* Interview with Lornie Kuhle.

338 *"I gave her everything that she wanted":* "Bobby Riggs bears all," by Bill Becker, *The Yell,* Mar. 20, 1974.

338 *"You know, I didn't think I could lose":* "The Happy Hustler," *Modesto Bee,* May 28, 1975.

339 *"I realized the one thing Bobby wanted":* Billie Jean, by Billie Jean King with Kim Chapin, p. 170.

339 *"Most people said I could not win":* "Legacy of the 'Battle'; 25 years ago, King-Riggs changed us": by Jody Goldstein, *Houston Chronicle,* Sept. 20, 1998.

339 *"I said to myself":* "Billie Jean Outhustles the Hustler," *Portland* [Me.] *Press Herald.*

340 *"She's trying to get sympathy":* Associated Press, Sept. 14, 1973.

340 *Working with resident pro Pete Collins:* Practice regimen and encounter with Margaret Court from *Billie Jean,* by Billie Jean King with Kim Chapin, p. 168.

341 *Twice she threatened to pull out of the match:* "I just had to win," by Billie Jean King, *Tennis,* August 1998.

341 *Billie Jean also told Roone Arledge: Billie Jean,* by Billie Jean King with Kim Chapin, p. 176.

342 *"I feel wonderful":* A Long Way, Baby, by Grace Lichtenstein, William Morrow & Co., New York, 1974, p. 26.

343 *"...his touring medicine show":* "There She is, Ms. America," by Curry Kirkpatrick, *Sports Illustrated,* Oct. 1, 1973, p. 30.

343 *...he moved to San Diego:* "Bobby Runs, and Talks, Talks, Talks," *Time.*

344 *His publisher, J.B. Lippincott:* Interview with George McGann.

344 *While accompanying his father: Famous Tennis Players,* by Trent Frayne, 1977, Dodd, Mead & Co., New York, p. 85.

345 *With reporters in tow:* "Bobby Riggs: A bag of tricks and braggadocio," by Elizabeth Bennett, *Houston Post,* Sept. 17, 1973.

345 *At one stop:* This and subsequent anecdotes from the *Houston Post,* Sept. 15, 1973, and Sept. 20, 1973.

346 *"I'm taking so many pills I must have a glass stomach":* "There She is, Ms. America," *Sports Illustrated.*

346 *"She's a damn good player":* Houston Post, Sept. 20, 1973.

347 *"I'm disturbed over that part of it":* Houston Post, Sept. 15, 1973.

347 *"Billie Jean's banking that I'm not in shape":* "There She is, Ms. America," *Sports Illustrated.*

347 *"It doesn't matter":* "All the World's a Stage," *Sports Illustrated.*

347 *"He thinks this is such a lock":* "There She is, Ms. America," *Sports Illustrated;* and *Houston Post,* Sept. 15, 1973.

347 *The day before the match:* Interview with George McGann.

347 *John had been beside himself for weeks:* Interview with David H. Riggs.

348 *"Don't take him too seriously":* "Portrait of a Beautiful Hustler," *New York Times Sunday Magazine* .

348 *Later that night, Bobby had another visitor:* Interview with Gardnar Mulloy.

20: *The Unthinkable Happens*

352 *Earlier in the day, Billie Jean went: Billie Jean,* by Billie Jean King with Kim Chapin, p. 180.

352 *If Bobby was nervous:* Interview with Gardnar Mulloy.

353 *"I was gonna give this to Billie Jean King":* A Long Way, Baby, p. 30.

353 *Gene Scott, called in to replace:* Interview with Gene Scott.

353 *"...his tennis elbow was horrible":* Interview with Lornie Kuhle.

353 *"It was like Bobby finally realized":* "How King Rained on Riggs' Parade," *Time,* Oct. 1, 1973, p. 110.

353 *"He said this was the most important match of his life":* Interview with William Riggs.

354 *"It's the fight crowd. It's ancient Rome":* A Long Way, Baby, p. 233.

355 *"...their chest heaving":* A Long Way, Baby, p. 233.

355 *"How's it going?":* "There She is, Ms. America," *Sports Illustrated.*

355 *"I want him to shut up":* A Long Way, Baby, p. 233.

356 *At a meeting the previous day:* Compiled from interviews with Don Rhodes (May 2001), Lornie Kuhle and former Nabisco executive Edward J. "Ned" Bjornson (June 2001).

357 *"He's putting me on, right?":* Billie Jean, by Billie Jean King with Kim Chapin, p. 182.

357 *Bobby, meanwhile, instructed Kuhle:* Interview with Lornie Kuhle; *A Long Way, Baby,* p. 234.

357 *"He was hyperventilating and really nervous":* "Billie Jean Outhustles the Hustler," *Portland* [Me.] *Press Herald.*

357 *"All I ever feared was the unknown":* Billie Jean, by Billie Jean King with Frank Deford, p. 15, p. 139.

358 *"As soon as I saw Billie Jean play":* Portrait in Motion, by Arthur Ashe with Frank Deford, Houghton Mifflin Co.; 1975, p. 90.

358 *"Up to that point":* Billie Jean, by Billie Jean King with Kim Chapin, p. 183.

359 *"She walked right up to the service line":* "Against All Odds," *World Tennis.*

359 *"Looks like Bobby bet on Billie Jean":* Unidentified quote from interview with Jack Kramer.

360 *"...the nerveless wonder, the man with all the angles":* A Long Way, Baby, p. 235.

360 *Arthur Ashe turned and called: Portrait in Motion,* p. 90.

360 *"Come on, Dad, wake up":* "How King Rained on Riggs' Parade," *Time.*

360 *Turning to the one thing:* Interview with Billie Jean King.

361 *"I figured I needed the extra incentive to lift my game": Court Hustler,* by Bobby Riggs with George McGann, second edition, Signet, 1974.

361 *...tongue-in-cheek invitations:* Compiled from *A Long Way, Baby,* p. 235; and ABC television broadcast, Sept. 20, 1973.

361 *"Come on, Billie Jean, start acting feminine":* Unidentified quote from "The Hustler Outhustled," by Pete Axthelm, *Newsweek,* Oct. 1, 1973, p. 63.

362 *"But as you kept watching his performance":* Interview with Gene Scott.

362 *"I pressed on the gas and I found out":* "Bobby Riggs, a constant 55, can't keep hands off women," by Sandy Banisky, *The* [Baltimore] *Sun,* Dec. 5, 1974.

363 *Though much of the match would remain a fog:* Interview with Billie Jean King.

363 *Finally, she thought:* Associated Press, September 21, 1973.

363 *"...all I remember is the celebration was not as gala":* Interview with Gene Scott.

363 *At a post-match press conference:* compiled from Associated Press, September 21, 1973, and "How King Rained on Riggs Parade," *Time,* p 110.

21: *Tennis, Everyone*

367 *"A lot of men—especially around our age": The Game,* p. 87.

367 *"He really let the game down":* Interview with Don Budge.

367 *"I was looking at the match on TV":* Int with Gene Mako.

368 *"The opinion of most of us":* Archives of the International Tennis Hall of Fame.

369 *"Against Billie Jean, he definitely threw it":* Interview with Joe Fishbach.

370 *"There are no secrets":* "I Was Quick. I Was Agile. I Had the Heart," *New York Times,* August 27, 1995.

370 *Not only that, but to silence:* Interview with Dr. Edward Gelb (July 2001).

370 *"I passed the test. I proved":* "Against All Odds," *World Tennis.*

370 *"But some guys were mad":* "Riggs Sees Double," By Ira Berkow, *New York Times,* July 27, 1982.

371 *"Bobby hated losing a bet":* Interview with Lornie Kuhle.

371 *To longtime friend Jack Kramer:* The Game, p. 87.

371 *She said she wished Casals:* Interview with Billie Jean King.

372 *"You wouldn't believe the number of people":* Billie Jean, by Billie Jean King with Kim Chapin, pp. 160-61.

373 *In 1960, the number of tennis players:* Figures attributed to *Tennis Industry,* a monthly trade journal, and to A.C. Nielsen Company, and cited in *Game, Set, and Match—The Tennis Boom of the 1960s and 70s,* by Herbert Warren Wind.

373 *Similarly, in 1960, there were fewer:* Figures from "Indoor Tennis, Chicago Style," by Jill Niemoth, *World Tennis,* May 1973, p. 34; and *Game, Set, and Match—The Tennis Boom of the 1960s and 70s.*

373 *Demand for equipment and court time:* "Now Everybody has the Bug," *Sports Illustrated,* Nov. 11, 1974, p. 95.

373 *And even with an average of:* Game, Set, and Match—The Tennis Boom of the 1960s and 70s.

373 *A typical example was Denver:* "Now Everybody has the Bug," *Sports Illustrated,* p. 95.

373 *In 1971, of the total time allotted:* "Now Everybody has the Bug," *Sports Illustrated,* p. 95.

374 *Dispelling the notion tennis was the domain:* "Tennis Everyone," *Forbes* magazine, Aug. 1, 1976, p. 25.

374 *The single largest group drawn to tennis:* "Sex & Tennis," *Time,* Sept. 6, 1976, p. 34.

374 *Between 1975 and 1976:* "Sex & Tennis," *Time,* Sept. 6, 1976.

375 *"I was a tennis pro":* Interview with Jason Morton (July 1999).

375 *"...he helped pave the way":* Interview with Doug Dean.

375 *"That was the biggest thing to happen":* "Catching" column, by Rita Calvano, *San Diego Tribune,* March 18, 1985.

375 *"They owe me a piece":* "Tennis Star Bobby Riggs Dies; Won Wimbledon, Lost to King," by Bart Barnes, *Washington Post,* October 27, 1995.

22: *The Happy Hustler*

377 *"Where are all your friends, Bobby?":* Interview with Gardnar Mulloy.

377 *"I'm very disappointed in Billie Jean":* "Riggs Still The Hustler," by Tim Horgan, *Cleveland Plain Dealer,* May 21, 1982.

378 *"That was Bobby's wishful thinking":* Interview with Jerry Perenchio.

378 *"After she beat me, we offered":* "Crusty Riggs still the living hustle," *San Diego Union-Tribune,* July 31, 1991.

379 *Bobby "went into a depression":* Interview with Lornie Kuhle.

379 *"Where is this sonuvabitch?":* Interview with Doug Dean.

380 *"Bobby Riggs, there's no way":* "Bobby Riggs bears all," *The Yell.*

380 *"Liberace showed up in rhinestone-studded hot pants":* Interview with Lornie Kuhle.

381 *"It didn't do him any good":* Interview with Edward J. Bjornson.

382 *"I should have killed":* "Evel Knievel: The World According to the American Daredevil," by Don Gilbert, printed online at www.evel1.com, March 6, 2002.

383 *"You had two positives that are clashing":* Interview with Don Rhodes.

384 *"Evel Knievel bets Bobby Riggs":* Collection of Riggs estate.

385 *Bobby was driving from his home:* Interviews with Lornie Kuhle and Robert Johnson (December 2001).

385 *"People were always giving him the finger":* Interview with Kay Tauber.

385 *"I almost failed it":* "Court Jester Riggs 'Hustles' to Idaho," by Charles Seldin, *Salt Lake Tribune,* Sept. 7, 1974.

386 *"The gas attendants thought I was a daredevil":* "Tennis or show biz, it's a Rigged racket," *Honolulu Advertiser,* Sept. 16, 1975.

386 *"I ache all over":* "Riggs Tries for Wager of Knievel," *El Cajon Daily Californian,* Sept. 7, 1974.

387 *"Oh, my god!:* Interview with Lornie Kuhle.

388 *"Come on, you mean for $3 million":* "King refuses to bow to Riggs' pressure," Associated Press, June 29, 1983.

389 *"Basically, Riggs amounted to a 67-year-old ball-and-chain":* "Battle Venal," by James Kaplan, *Vogue,* Dec. 1985, p. 152.

389 *"Who's that down there playing?":* Interviews with Renée Richards and Nancy Bailey (September 1999).

391 *She was about the only top female player: Billie Jean,* by Billie Jean King with Frank Deford, p. 137.

391 *"This has been the most difficult year":* "King-Mulloy team trounces Richards-Riggs," *The* [Baltimore] *Sun,* May 11, 1977.

392 *Billie Jean agreed to play on the condition:* Interview with Gardnar Mulloy.

392 *Bobby was named one of the country's:* Man Watchers Inc. poll printed in *Los Angeles Herald-Examiner,* Jan. 14, 1975.

392 *"I play 40 to 50 of these exhibitions":* "Riggs: Just another hustle," by Kerry Eggers, [Portland] *Oregon Journal,* April 28, 1978.

393 *"I make $300,000 a year, I guess":* "He'll hustle for $10,000 or 10 bucks" by Erik Lacitis, *Seattle Times,* Aug. 24, 1978.

393 *"The worst partner I ever had":* "Riggs: Just another hustle," [Portland] *Oregon Journal.*

393 *"Do I expect people to remember that I won":* "The Happy Hustler" by Pam King, *Los Angeles Herald Examiner,* Aug. 12, 1981.

394 *"Bobby was a high-maintenance client":* Interview with Robert Johnson.

394 *Bobby "had a propensity to fuck things up":* Interview with William Riggs.

394 *"He's like a son to me":* Videotaped remarks by Bobby at his wedding reception Feb. 14, 1991 (courtesy John W. Riggs).

394 *"...had a real need for companionship":* Interview with Nancy Bailey.

395 *"This guy paid his annual dues again":* "Riggs hustles his way into Longwood," by Bud Collins, *Boston Globe,* July 17, 1982.

395 *"But what else are you gonna do?":* Interview with Doug Dean.

395 *"I just lost recently to a guy in Monte Carlo":* Compiled from interview with Robert Johnson; "Chatter" section, *People,* Sept. 4, 1978; and "He'll hustle for $10,000 or 10 bucks" by Erik Lacitis, *Seattle Times,* Aug. 24, 1978.

397 *"If I can't work for $10,000":* Interview with Nancy Bailey.

397 *"In those years after the match":* Interview with Lornie Kuhle.

23: *"We can get through this."* ·

399 *"...the best thing that ever happened...":* "Bobby Riggs, a constant 55, can't keep hands off women," *The* [Baltimore] *Sun.*

399 *"I was anything but the ideal husband and father": Court Hustler,* p. 184.

399 *At a cocktail party, Priscilla had met:* Interview with Dorothy Riggs.

400 *"In short, my mom had married":* Interview with John W. Riggs.

400 *"...those were the years of the war":* Interview with Mike Crimi.

402 *"Canadian girls have such pretty smiles":* Interview with Nancy Bailey.

403 *"For about three months":* Interview with Lornie Kuhle.

404 *"Bobby worried constantly about Jimmy":* Interview with Don Rhodes.

407 *After dinner, Bill got the car:* Interviews with William Riggs and Robert Johnson.

409 *"When she decided to live in California again":* "His Last Match Can't Be Rigged," *Los Angeles Times.*

409 *"The condo has an unstructured":* "Against All Odds," *World Tennis.*

409 *"I take the Fifth Amendment":* Once a Champion, p. 424.

410 *"I moved back, into the guest room":* Bobby's quote taken from "His Last Match Can't Be Rigged," *Los Angeles Times.*

410 *"What can I say? ":* Videotaped remarks by Bobby at his wedding reception Feb. 14, 1991 (courtesy John W. Riggs).

24: *Nature's Cruelest Trick*

413 *"Why do you color your hair?":* Interview with Lornie Kuhle.

413 *"I don't believe in old and gray":* "Against All Odds," *World Tennis.*

413 *"A guy doesn't feel himself growing old":* Fast Company, p. 51.

413 *"I go to get this ball":* Interview with Nancy Bailey.

414 *"Do you want to have surgery":* Interview with John W. Riggs.

414 *"His diet was horrible by today's standards":* Interview with Lornie Kuhle.

415 *"We think I'm cured":* Associated Press, May 13, 1988.

415 *"Imagine, the best player in the world":* "At 70, Riggs Subdued, but Still a Hustler," by Steven Goff, *Washington Post*, Sept. 27, 1988.

415 *This meant that despite:* Figures taken from "Prostate Cancer: Who Should Be Treated?" by Dr. Tom Stamey, Chairman of the Department of Urology at Stanford University School of Medicine, April 1994.

415 "Hey, nobody likes to lose their family jewels": "Crusty Riggs still the living hustle," *San Diego Union-Tribune.*

416 *In 1992, Bobby landed a job:* Interview with Lornie Kuhle.

416 *"I was a little bit tongue-tied":* "His Last Match Can't Be Rigged," *Los Angeles Times.*

417 *"It seems to have robbed me":* "His Last Match Can't Be Rigged," *Los Angeles Times.*

417 *"He had just played them":* Interview with Gardnar Mulloy.

419 *"I'd like to be like the late King of Sweden":* Court Hustler, p. 186. Bobby met the late monarch during a tour of Europe with Don Budge, Pancho Gonzalez and Jack Kramer in 1947. Said Bobby in a 1979 interview: "He was 89 at the time, but insisted on playing some doubles with us... and the old guy did pretty good." ("Tennis' Riggs here hustling," by Bucky Walter, *San Francisco Examiner*, Aug. 22, 1979.)

420 *"It was like a challenge for him":* Interview with Dr. Lawrence Piro (September 2001).

423 *"Bobby has nerves of steel":* "His Last Match Can't Be Rigged," *Los Angeles Times.*

424 *"I would say that I'm confused":* Once a Champion, p. 429.

425 *"Don Rhodes is on the phone...":* Interview with Don Rhodes.

425 *It was October, and Bobby was visited:* Interviews with Jack Kramer and Ted Schroeder.

425 *"I was sort of cradling him":* Interview with Frances Riggs.

426 *"What's the score?":* Interview with Nancy Bailey.

Afterword

429   *"He kept me in a state of alertness":* Associated Press, Oct. 31, 1995.

430   *When* Tennis *magazine asked readers:* "The 20 Greatest Players of the 20th Century," *Tennis* magazine, December 1999/January 2000.

431   *"...by far the most underrated of all the top players":* The Game, pp. 44-45.

431   *Ted Schroeder echoed the sentiment:* Once a Champion, p. 290.

431   *Bobby was uncharacteristically modest:* Once a Champion, p. 419.

432   *Bobby said he liked to think:* "His Last Match Can't Be Rigged," *Los Angeles Times.*

433   *"I didn't play up to the press":* "Against All Odds," *World Tennis,* and "I was quick. I was agile. I had heart," *New York Times.*

433   *"I'll tell you about his game":* Interview with Gardnar Mulloy.

433   *"I will not be remembered for winning":* Interview with Bobby Riggs, April 1995 (courtesy of Doug Dean).

433   *"...become very protective of my father's legacy":* Interview with John W. Riggs.

435   *"He could be the most aggravating":* Associated Press, Oct. 31, 1995.-

Acknowledgements

L   ong before I got involved in this project, there were the stories. The stories swapped in clubhouses, across card tables or traded courtside. They were tales told with a wry smile and a fondness reserved for a mischievous, slightly naughty boy. How the puckish Bobby hustled some unsuspecting dupe; how Bobby talked his way out of another tight spot; or how Bobby once again got in way over his head, just for the fun of it. After enough time, the stories took on a life of their own, becoming, as Bobby liked to call it, the "Riggs Mythology."

In 1999, I read a letter in *Tennis* magazine from Bobby's son, John Wheelan Riggs, in which he lamented that his father's skill as a tennis player and legacy as a champion had been lost, and that "what the general population knows is what the media generally presents: the wise-guy hustler." Like most people my age, I remember watching the "Battle of the Sexes" on television, but my memory of Riggs ended there. Taking John's letter as an invitation, I began this book.

Almost without exception everyone contacted—Bobby's family, his friends and former rivals, acquaintances, and merely those interested in tennis and its history—welcomed the project and gave generously of their time and resources. Though the list is far too long to mention all those who helped, I must single out those without whose assistance this book would have been impossible.

First and foremost is Bobby's family. These include his siblings, the late John Riggs and the late Mary Lee Lantz; his children Larry, John, Bill and Dorothy (Bobby Jr. regretfully, but politely, declined to be interviewed); his former wife, the late Kay Tauber; his niece, Frances Riggs; and nephew, Dave Riggs. I must thank them all, not only for their time, but for the unflinching honesty of their recollections.

Much of the research could not have been accomplished without the help of Lornie Kuhle, Bobby's longtime friend, protégé and executor of his estate. Thanks, too, to Nancy Bailey, another longtime companion of Bobby's. Although he was in the public eye since the age of 13, and though he was generally straightforward and honest in his dealings with the press, much of what we know about Bobby was shaped by the media's portrayal. In contrast, these people offered a clear and unvarnished look at the man—a Bobby who few others knew.

Similar gratitude must be extended to Bobby's friends and rivals over the years. After all, this book is largely their story, with memories that in many cases stretch back to a time when Bobby and they were all just kids. Despite the passing of many years, these experiences remained as fresh as if they had happened yesterday. If the Bobby Riggs portrayed in this book manages to coincide with the one they remember, they have themselves to thank. Those among this group include: Ted Schroeder, Gardnar Mulloy, Pancho Segura, Sidney Wood, Bob Falkenburg, Robert "Buddy" Blattner, Renée Richards, attorney Robert Johnson, Bert Brown, the late Don Budge, Gene Mako, Tony Vincent, Gladys Heldman, Joe Fishbach, George Gondolman, John Nogrady, Doug Dean, Bob Barker, Don Rhodes, Dr. Lawrence Piro, Ned Bjornsen, Jerry Perenchio, Jack Dreyfus, the late George McGann, and of course, Billie Jean King.

I extend special thanks to Jack Kramer, who in addition to his willingness to answer yet another annoying phone call, provided a gold mine of detail in his 1979 book *The Game*, written with Frank Deford.

Similar gratitude must be extended to the International Tennis Hall of Fame, and in particular archivist Mark S. Young for his patience and assistance in guiding me through the center's collection.

It would have been easy to fill a book, and perhaps several books, with humorous, interesting and outrageous anecdotes about Bobby. However, the point of the book was to get beyond the stories, beyond the mythology, to the man. To this end, I must thank the many people who helped guide my research, critique the drafts, offer criticism and advise me at each juncture of the project. First, I must thank my brother Charley, whose encouragement, advice and firm determination that I not take the easy way out cannot be repaid. Similarly, my editor and former co-worker, Mike Kuckowski, is to be commended for spending what little spare time he had into making my uneven prose readable. Others whose criticism and assistance were invaluable include Bud Collins, whose indispensable *Tennis Encyclopedia* never left the side of my desk; Frank Deford, Gene Scott, Gladys Heldman, Edward T. Chase, Tom Huntington, James Campbell and Janet Reynolds

Special gratitude goes out to my mother, Janet LeCompte, without whose inspiration and assistance this project likely never would have started, much less finished.

Writing a book, I have learned, is a lot like building a house: There may be one architect, but there are many subcontractors. As such, I must thank those people whose services turned a concept into reality, greatly streamlined my work and made the finished product worthy of its subject, in particular editor Karl Monger and designer Stacey Davis for her elegant work.

Tom LeCompte
February 2003

Index